TOWARD A
NEW SOCIOLOGY

THE DORSEY SERIES IN SOCIOLOGY

Editor ROBIN M. WILLIAMS, Jr. *Cornell University*

Toward a
new sociology

CHARLES H. ANDERSON

 Revised Edition • 1974

THE DORSEY PRESS Homewood, Illinois 60430
Irwin-Dorsey International London, England WC2H 9NJ
Irwin-Dorsey Limited Georgetown, Ontario L7G 4B3

© THE DORSEY PRESS, 1971, 1974

All rights reserved. No part of this publication may be
reproduced, stored in a retrieval system, or transmitted,
in any form or by any means, electronic, mechanical,
photocopying, recording, or otherwise, without the prior
written permission of the publisher.

Revised Edition

First Printing, April 1974

ISBN 0-256-01538-4
Library of Congress Catalog Card No. 74–75092

Printed in the United States of America

To
C. Wendell King
and
John F. Manfredi

Introduction

This second edition is a continuation of my efforts at communicating a new introductory orientation to the study of society. The warm reception of the first edition by so many teachers and students was encouraging to to say the least. Naturally, I hope the second edition will add to the themes that were favorably received in the first edition, and improve upon those aspects which received criticism the first time around.

A relatively large amount of new materials has been introduced, and sections of old material which seemed to carry the reader from central themes have been deleted. A background chapter has been added at the outset in order to aid the reader in placing the book in broader sociological context. The two concept-oriented chapters (now 2 and 3) have been rather extensively rewritten and reorganized in an effort to give them a better articulation with subsequent materials. Chapter 4 on Marxian sociology has been entirely rewritten with the aim of conveying a more informative overview of this theoretical approach.

Chapters 5, 6, and 7 have received considerable reworking and updating intended to present the reader with a more integrated understanding of issues in class, inequality, and opportunity. Chapter 7 has been retitled to indicate a new emphasis upon the relationship between education and inequality. The chapter on poverty has benefited from more recent statistics reported by the 1970 census and other governmental sources. Chapter 9 has also been reinforced with recent statistical data and coverage of current political and economic events, which shed light on the power structure. The topic of technology has been transfered from Chapter 10 to Chapter 9, leaving Chapter 10 to deal entirely with changing conditions of work. The emphases in the chapter on ethnic groups has been changed to some extent, with a shift to more discussion of ethnicity and less of religion. Religion is considered in terms of its social consequences rather than the religiousness of Americans.

The chapter on blacks has not been significantly altered except for the incorporation of new facts and a new section on the ghetto as a colony. Chapter 13 takes up the issue of population and utilizes recent Census Bureau and United Nations data on fertility and growth patterns. The section on sexual inequality and the position of women has been expanded to include a broader spectrum of concerns. Chapter 14 on the Third World has received major revision work. Some instructors may wish to use the first part of this chapter in conjunction with Chapter 9; that is, as a continuation of the discussion of the power structure in terms of its foreign involvements. The brief final chapter offers a general synthesis and presents several points on ethical considerations in sociological research activity.

Karl Marx and C. Wright Mills continue to be the central theoretical figures of the book. The classic works of Thorstein Veblen have now also made an impression at several critical junctures. Max Weber's sociological insights remain influential. The several contemporary theorists whose ideas were employed in the first edition have been complimented by the addition of several others as well.

I would like to thank Jeffry Gibson, Martin Sheffer, and James Otis Smith for their many helpful criticisms and suggestions of earlier drafts of the revision.

March 1974   CHARLES ANDERSON

Contents

sistence. Inequality and social problems. Comparative inequality. *Soviet type systems. China.*

1

Sociological perspectives

ORIENTING STATEMENTS

To enter into a sociological study of society requires a certain kind of courage. Society is an enormously variegated and complex object to investigate, and those willing to take on the task must have active, energetic minds capable of putting seemingly infinite numbers of observations and events together into something approaching a meaningful whole. Sociology demands of its practitioners a willingness to probe social life across the full spectrum of human behavior, to examine the smallest details and yet see inclusive patterns. To think and work in such a manner requires intellectual openness and agility or the sociologist must face the certain prospect of being overwhelmed by the breadth and depth of social phenomena.

The sociologist needs more than scholarly courage and mental agility; such things are only the preliminary requirements. The most essential of such additional needs involves that of a theoretical perspective. Social reality, especially contemporary social reality, is so diverse and eventful that even the most active and energetic sociological worker must approach society with a set of predefined guidelines to help direct observation and channel investigation. A theoretical perspective or a set of orienting statements provides such guidelines to assist in the organization and interpretation of social events, observations, and facts. A guiding perspective (sometimes referred to as assumptions[1]) is an indispensable working instrument in the important sense that it allows one to initiate

---

[1] See Alvin Gouldner, *The Coming Crisis in Western Sociology* (New York: Basic Books, Inc., 1970). Gouldner refers to the overall guiding and orienting premises of a given sociological study or theory as "domain assumptions." George Homans used the term "orienting statements" in discussing essentially the same problems; see *The Nature of Social Science* (New York: Harbinger Books, 1967).

an integrated, systematic line of study, directing and conserving research effort from start to finish (and we must start and temporarily end *somewhere*). A sociologist's orienting statements do just that; they tell where to start looking in the mass of events that make up a society. One's guiding orientation also influences to an important degree what is seen and how interpretation is made.

It would be convenient if all sociologist's theoretical perspectives were identical or nearly so. But such is not the case. Perspectives are widely divergent and conflicting, not owing simply to the fact that sociologists study so many different things, but to the more troublesome fact that they frequently disagree as to appropriate perspectives pertaining to the same general object of study. A highly developed science is characterized by widely shared common perspectives or guiding assumptions among all or most members of that particular scientific or research community. This is so owing to the fact that their theoretical perspectives have led to a substantial understanding of how their subject matter behaves; prediction and explanation are thus possible within rather narrow limits. Unworkable and invalid perspectives can be eliminated quickly if they fail to lead to greater understanding.

The situation within sociology, and the social sciences in general, is otherwise. There exist several "schools" of thought each with more or less diverse and conflicting orienting statements. Members or adherents of one theoretical perspective find themselves daily promoting or defending their position against those who would assert another. While sociologists may make great efforts at being objective and systematic in their investigations and research studies, the splitting up and relative lack of agreement within sociology suggests the scientific frailty of all theoretical perspectives. None yet seem powerful enough to command the faith of sociologists whoever and wherever they might be. Thus, if there is a scientific sociology in existence today, its worth or validity goes unrecognized by other large segments of the field.

This is not to say that theoretical chaos reigns in the social sciences or even in sociology. A limited number of perspectives exist (though more can and no doubt will be developed), and such constitutes the content of a course in sociological theory. Nor is it to say that there is no range of better and worse explanations and understandings of social life and human behavior that follow from these different orienting positions—though it *would* be difficult to establish such a range of theory strengths. The nature of society makes it from difficult to impossible to conduct rigorous experimental research within sociology, and hence, to validate firmly or invalidate research propositions bearing upon one's theoretical perspective. However, observations, evidence, and facts about society can be gathered, which lend greater or lesser amounts of credibility to a theoretical perspective. In this book has been marshalled a great many such observations and facts that both negate and support given sociological points of view.

The study at hand, like any study, has its own theoretical perspective. Although our perspective here is not a completely unified one or tied directly to any single existing perspective, it is strongly influenced by the Marxist approach and theory. More generally, the book draws upon critical sociology such as is found in the work of Thorstein Veblen and C. Wright Mills. While the sociological perspective developed here will be clarified only by a complete study of the entire book, certain of the central guiding assumptions might advantageously be stated at the outset (the reader is also referred to the final summary chapter). The correctness of this perspective, to the extent that evidence can be directed to it, rests ultimately upon the events which transpire in the "laboratory" of historical time, though much has already been recorded in its support.

The perspective of the work before us may be phrased as follows:

1. Individuals as members of groups, small and large, give definition to the form and content of society and history, and as architects of society and history, individuals in groups are capable of changing the structure of society and the course of history. The extent to which people are able to accomplish such changes depends partially upon their grasp and understanding of actual social and historical events and processes, at least to the degree in which such events and processes influence their own lives.

2. The social forms or patterns created by individual and group action in the struggle to come to terms with the social and physical environments assume varying degrees of permanency and place extensive conditions and restraints upon human thought and behavior. Also, once established, these dominant social patterns or relations are widely held to be "natural" and as an inevitable reality to which people must adjust. The naturalness of the existing order is asserted most strongly by groups gaining materially the most from it, though acceptance of the natural view is often widespread. While established thought and behavior patterns are partially and gradually altered over time, a given combination of social and historical conditions permit or force fundamental breaks with the past and the development of a new order.

3. Individuals are by their very nature *social* beings who can fulfill the creative potential of the species only through mutual and cooperative endeavor. The struggle for material survival has characterized most people for most of history. Within the present historical period or epoch, capitalism, there has developed through technology and science the basis or potential for greatly expanded freedom for all people in both the material and social sense. The heightened awareness of this fact by growing numbers of people has and will increasingly lead to critical thought and action, and the search for, experimentation with, and development of new ways of living and relating. The failure of achieving constructive change would result in increased threats to human survival, not to mention security and enjoyment.

4. Society can to a large, but never to a complete, degree be objectively studied and understood. The prevailing modes of social relations can be understood theoretically through the formulation of concepts and hypotheses, systematic observation and research, and reasoning and logical analysis. Such activity can help uncover the central social regularities and tendencies that restrain or govern a large portion of human behavior and social relations within any given historical period. Unlike physical

laws, which are largely universal, ahistorical, and subject to control but never to purposive alteration, social "laws" or tendencies are largely specific to societies within given historical periods and, under suitable material conditions, are subject to conscious alteration and purposive change. The social regularities or tendencies we are subject to today are those of capitalism and capitalist development.

5. The central fact of capitalist-type society, the first worldwide or universal system in human history, is that a small property owning or property controlling elite stratum holds power over the development and application of productive social wealth and resources. If a person is to remain a member of this capitalist class, he or she has no long-range alternative but to strive constantly for the accumulation of financial profit. If such action to maximize gain is not taken, other propertied persons will expand at the cost of the less active. The drive toward acquisition of expanding wealth concentrates production in fewer hands and directs production toward profit rather than human need.

6. Power, defined as the control over the flow of social and material resources, is preserved at base through the fragmentation and extreme division of human labor resulting in a production hierarchy over which stands the propertied stratum. The elimination of this concentrated and hierarchical power, and its decentralization to the producers and consumers themselves, is a prerequisite to the construction of social relations conducive to the fullest development of human creative and productive capacities. It is also a necessary prerequisite to ecological viability and ultimately survival.

Before launching upon the full development of our own sociological perspective and analyses, we would do well to make an overview of certain other past and present orienting perspectives and modes of social thought.

PERSPECTIVES FROM THE PAST

The "father" of modern sociology, Frenchman August Comte (1798–1857), pronounced an emphatic doctrine of social conservatism. Even while eulogizing the scientific perspective, Comte reacted strongly against the 18th century's Enlightenment with its emphasis upon rationality, progress, and humanism. As the social upheavals accompanying industrialization and liberal democracy swept aside the old feudal social order, Comte responded to the triumphant middle-class (bourgeois) individualism and liberalism with the reassertion of the medieval values of hierarchy and order, community and tradition. As Nisbet pointed out, Comte admired the Middle Ages and sought to reinstate the social structure of medieval society—under the rule of paternalistic and omniscient sociologist priests![2] Social order as exemplified in the traditions of feudalism was sacred to Comte, and he would provide it with even greater per-

[2] Robert A. Nisbet, *The Sociological Tradition* (New York: Basic Books, Inc., 1966), p. 15. See also, Raymond Aron's discussion of Comte as well as Durkheim and Weber in *Main Currents in Sociological Thought* (London: Penguin Books, 1967).

manency and integration through the wisdom of a new scientific as opposed to religious and metaphysical, social theory. But Comte's sociology was not at all based on fact; rather, it was a value-laden attempt to provide tradition and a rigid social order with a theoretical justification. Unfortunately for Comte's personal aspirations, his thinking was not attuned to the interests of the rising capitalist class or bourgeoisie, which saw the need, not for the stifling rigidity of medievalism but for the freedom from lord, state, and church to pursue its own untrammeled individualism.

Comte's mistake was not that of propounding order and integration imposed upon a stratified or hierarchical society by dominant groups from above. His real mistake was that of identifying with the *wrong kind* of order, the order of the past instead of the emerging order of the 19th century, the order of industrial capitalism. Compare Comte's unsuccessful search for acceptance and recognition (he ended up with a roomful of disciples and imagining himself a prophet) with the Englishman Herbert Spencer's (1820–1903) adulatory reception among America's financial and industrial tycoons. Spencer's laissez faire doctrines justified the new order, an order he saw as based upon the evolutionary doctrine of the survival of the fittest and one which changed by gradual increments rather than revolutionary overturns. Spencer inveighed against the idea that the state should be used to intervene in "natural" social processes in an effort to improve the lot of people. Progress will be achieved by allowing nature to follow her own evolutionary course, precisely what leading citizens wanted to hear. As the regulatory and interventionist activities of the state increased, owing both to popular political pressures and the recognition of the need for such by a segment of the capitalist class, Spencer's doctrines of 19th century liberalism became the tenets of 20th century conservatism.

Two of the central figures of sociology in the early twentieth century were the Frenchman Emile Durkheim (1858–1917), and the German Max Weber (1864–1920), and their works continue to be major influences today. Although both men sought to moderate the negative social impact of the laissez faire industrial order and to maintain the rights and dignity of the individual through political action, neither sought or thought it possible to replace the main outlines of contemporary society. Durkheim's perspective emphasized the importance of social integration and adjustment to the demands of existing social forces. The social division of labor was, at least in Durkheim's early views, an important positive integrating force, creating interdependence and holding the individual within the bounds of society. Durkheim drew attention to the restraining force of "social facts" or regularities of thought and action which existed over and above the individual and channeled the individual's behavior. A similar notion is incorporated into our own theoretical perspective, though we avoid elevating social forces to an autonomous level above the reality of the social individual as Durkheim tended to do. Durkheim posited an essential antagonism between the individual and society, and stressed the importance of pervasive belief and behavioral codes in holding human pretentions in check. His concept of "anomie"

referred to a situation of social disintegration or separation from a socially binding tie to the division of labor and related integrating moral
and belief systems.[3]

Within Durkheim's sociology there exists a strong tendency to natur-
alize the existing social order and then to seek means, such as the division of collective tasks and a moral system (religious or secular), to
bind and adjust the individual to that order. The order of the period
happens to be capitalism. Thus, as John Horton pointed out, Durkheim's
"society instead of being a scientific humanism becomes a special theoretical justification for the operation of capitalism as a natural system
appearing external and transcendant to individual men."[4] Durkheim
failed to incorporate constructive conflict and purposive change into his
theoretical notions. He breathed no life into human history; he failed to
see the possibility that the very social facts he urged sociologists to study
were dividing society against itself and preventing the creation of an
integrated, stable, and morally responsible community, which he himself
sought. Durkheim never allowed for either the need nor the possibility
of individuals together overturning and reconstituting the social reality
or facts that at any given time govern their lives. His scientific sociology
precluded the attainment of his social vision.

Weber, too, tended to give a theoretical inevitability if not endorse-
ment to the system at hand, reserving his chief criticisms for the traditional and conservative remnants of aristocratic Germany. In contrast
to many radical German contemporaries, Weber considered modern industrial society to be rationally organized, especially in terms of its central form—bureaucracy. As Gerth and Mills have written, "For Weber
. . . modern capitalism is not 'irrational'; indeed, its institutions appear
to him as the very embodiment of rationality. As a type of bureaucracy,
the large corporation is rivaled only by the state bureaucracy in promoting rational efficiency, continuity of operation, speed, precision, and
calculation of results."[5] Weber considered bureaucracy to be a necessary
and inevitable form for the organization of modern social life.

Though he attacked bureaucratic rigidity and narrowness, Weber was
pessimistic about the possibility of escaping from bureaucratic hierarchies and he projected an ever expanding bureaucratization and,
hence, centralization of power and authority. This perspective has been
included within our own, but without the notion of necessity and inev-

---

[3] See John Horton, "The Dehumanization of Anomie and Alienation," *British Journal of Sociology*, 15 (December 1964), pp. 283–300; and Horton,
"Order and Conflict Theories of Social Problems as Competing Ideologies,"
American Journal of Sociology, 71 (May 1966), pp. 701–13). Durkheim's
formulation of anomie may be found in his *Suicide*, a study that also illus-
trates the notion of a "social fact."

[4] John Horton, "The Fetishism of Sociology," in J. David Colfax and Jack
L. Roach, eds., *Radical Sociology* (New York: Basic Books, Inc., 1971), pp.
171–93.

[5] Hans Gerth and C. Wright Mills, eds., *From Max Weber: Essays in Sociology* (New York: Oxford University Press, 1958), p. 49. This volume contains the central sociological ideas developed and argued by Weber.

itability attached to it. Like Durkheim, Weber conducted extensive studies on the role of religion in society, attributing to Protestantism a prominent historical role in the rise of capitalism. Unlike Durkheim, Weber made valuable contributions to the study of power and social class.

What all of these founding fathers of sociology lacked, or consciously opposed, was even the slightest hint of a revolutionary perspective in their theoretical orientations. There is a certain lifeless, even hopeless, impression established quite apart from their studied efforts in detachment and objectivity. Real living people never seem to have the opportunity to act independently and against the external forces that shape the condition of their existence.

Early American sociology also took shape in response to developments within industrial society of the late 19th century and early 20th century. Spencerians such as William Graham Sumner (1840–1910) were opposed by interventionists such as Frank Lester Ward (1841–1913). But as the Schwendingers have argued, it was the advocates of state regulation of economic life, such as Ward, who were to set the tone of American sociology: "The dominant characteristics of sociology as a discipline emerged in the United States as a reformist liberal response to developments in monopoly capitalism and modern imperialism."[6]

Although sharply criticizing the laissez faire doctrines of Spencer and Sumner as leading to internal conflict and instability, the reformers of early American sociology accepted the main outline of their society. For example, Albion Small (1858–1926) wrote that "no devices are in sight to which we can pin our faith as feasible and comprehensive substitutes for capitalism."[7] Franklin Giddings (1858–1931), holder of the chair of sociology at Columbia University and an early president of the American Sociological Society, held that imperialism helped "the spirit of liberty to grow." In a related vein, early researchers offered "proof" of the genetic superiority of Old Americans and Northern European immigrants over the waves of latecomers from Southern and Eastern Europe, precisely the kind of data the nativists could put to good use in their restrictionist arguments.[8] As Alvin Gouldner observed, "A sociology with a nonpartisan self-image can become institutionalized when the elites of a society are confident that its social scientists are, in fact, *not* neutral."[9]

Despite the strong supportive and adjustment oriented status of early academic sociology, critics and opponents were in evidence. Very much in evidence were the sharp and incisive criticisms of Thorstein Veblen (1857–1929). Veblen inveighed strongly against the central economic and social relations of the society, and we shall have occasion to draw

---

[6] Julia and Herman Schwendinger, "Sociologists of the Chair and the Natural Law Tradition," *The Insurgent Sociologist,* 3 (Winter 1973), p. 4.

[7] See Dusky Lee Smith, "Sociology and the Rise of Corporate Capitalism," *Science and Society,* 29 (Fall 1965), pp. 401–18.

[8] Anthony Oberschall, ed., *The Establishment of Empirical Sociology* (New York: Harper & Row, Publishers, 1972), especially Oberschall's "The Institutionalization of American Sociology," pp. 187–251.

[9] *The Coming Crisis in Western Sociology,* p. 470.

from Veblen's works in our own discussions. Veblen set the style and even the framework for a variety of later social critics, including Vance Packard, C. Wright Mills, and J.K. Galbraith.

In another vein, social psychology received a strong impetus from early 20th century American thinkers such as C.H. Cooley (1864–1929) and G.H. Mead (1863–1931). Focusing on the elements of human behavior and interpersonal relationships, Cooley and Mead laid the groundwork for many basic sociological concepts—certain of which we shall encounter in Chapters 2 and 3. Suffice it to point out here that these early social psychologists presented an open and flexible concept of the individual and society, quite in contrast to their European contemporary—Sigmund Freud.

The Freudian orientation

While many contemporary critics draw from Freud's insights into the repressive nature of society, we shall here emphasize another side of his thought. As is well known, Freud's theories of personality provided the original framework for psychoanalysis and much of clinical psychology in general. Despite the fact that certain aspects of Freud have had enormous appeal to critics of contemporary society, we shall draw attention to Freudianism's essential conservatism.[10]

Freud appeals to many social critics owing to his views on the antagonism between the individual and society and society's repressive qualities. But to Freud the repressive nature of modern society does not consist of its vast imbalances of property ownership, power, and privilege. The core of the problem is not even with capitalist society at all, but rather with the relationship between the biological individual and *society* per se—*any* civilized society. All social forms of civilization have been constructed upon the renunciation and the repression of instinctual gratifications. In Freud's words, "This 'cultural privation' dominates the whole field of social relations between human beings; we know already that it is the cause of antagonism against which all civilization has to fight."[11]

Freud wouldn't commit himself one way or another regarding the foundation of capitalism: "I cannot enquire into whether the abolition of private property is advantageous and expedient."[12] How convenient for the capitalist class! In his preoccupation with instinctual psychology, Freud ignores the political and economic grounds of social inequality. Thus, according to Freud, there is really no point in struggling to eliminate inequality, since "nature began the injustice by the highly unequal way in which she endows individuals physically and mentally, for which

---

[10] Isaac Deutscher, *Marxism In Our Time* (Berkeley: Ramparts Press, 1971), pp. 232–38.

[11] Sigmund Freud, *Civilization and Its Discontents* (New York: Doubleday & Company, Inc., 1958), p. 43.

[12] Ibid., p. 63.

there is no help."[13] Freud pleads ignorance on the issue of private property and hopelessness on that of social inequality.

Given Freud's assumptions regarding the nature of man, it is understandable that he refused to critically examine the political and economic structure of his own society (Freud never even bothered to take a serious look at Marxist theory, or so it would appear from his simplistic statements on "communism.") To Freud, people are aggressive, hostile, and uncooperative by nature. The individual is at war with his social surroundings and "intelligence" is nothing more than a mediator between instinctual urges and social reality. As Calvin S. Hall observes about Freud, "He did not have a very high opinion of the bulk of mankind,"[14] not to mention that of women. Sexual urges and a love of aggression are the underlying motive forces of the individual, and society throws up blocks against their realization. Liberation and freedom are sought through psychology and personal manipulation of the mind–society antagonism, not through revolutionary action aimed at restructuring the objective material basis of the society. Again, what good news for the entrenched dominant groups of the society! They are left alone to pursue freely their own aggrandizement of wealth, power, and pleasure. Almost equally happy might be the oppressed, for the struggle now is merely conducted by and within the individual (or together with his or her psychiatrist or clinician) and not against an entire and powerful social class of property owners and controllers backed up by the military and police.

Freud's view of man ruled out the possibility of a cooperative and egalitarian society. Whereas Weber based his opposition to socialism on the sociological grounds that it would merely augment the trend toward bureaucratization, Freud was ". . . able to recognize that psychologically it [communism or socialism] is founded on an untenable illusion. By abolishing private property one deprives the human love of aggression of one of its instruments, a strong one undoubtedly, but assuredly not the strongest."[15]

Upon what grounds did Freud build his assumptions and theories? Hall tells us that, "The room in which he treated his patients became his laboratory, the couch his only piece of equipment, and the ramblings of his patients his scientific data."[16] Or from Roszak, "Myth, religion, dreams, visions: such were the dark waters Freud fished to find his conception of human nature."[17] Asch states that Freud's "conclusions about social life were based on observation of impairments and disorders in psychological development, not on observation of social processes in fac-

---

[13] Ibid.

[14] *A Primer of Freudian Psychology* (New York: Mentor Books, 1955), p. 20.

[15] *Civilization and Its Discontents*, p. 63.

[16] *A Primer of Freudian Psychology*, p. 15.

[17] Theodore Roszak, *The Making of a Counter Culture* (New York: Doubleday and Company, Inc., 1969), pp. 91–92.

tory, office, political party, or even the home."[18] Surely an understanding of the central dynamics of human behavior and of society require a vastly broader observational base than that of Freudianism.

CURRENT PERSPECTIVES

C. Wright Mills identified two characteristic trends within modern sociology as "grand theory" and "abstract empiricism."[19] By grand theory Mills referred to the extensive development of all-inclusive general concepts, which lack clear social referents and application. Conversely, by abstract empiricism he referred to the accumulation of fragments of information having no integrating theoretical relevance, as well as the cultivation of statistical and mathematical methods as ends in themselves.

Much general concept analysis has been conducted under the rubric of "functionalism." Functionalism traces its sociological roots to classic theorists such as Spencer and Durkheim and to contemporary theorists such as Talcott Parsons and Robert Merton. As a general theory of society, functionalism is essentially based on an organic analogy that compares the workings of society to those of biological and evolutionary phenomena.[20] Differences between sociological and biological phenomena are recognized, but the theoretical core of functionalism assumes that society-like organisms have a natural or self-perpetuating "equilibrium," which must be maintained within given limits or perish.[21] An aspect of the society that interferes with the attainment of equilibrium is "dysfunctional" and an aspect that promotes equilibrium is "functional." Conflicts and disruptions may be considered functional, however, *if* they lead to a new equilibrium and adjustment within the system. The social system changes, but chiefly by gradual evolutionary increments in a manner similar to biological growth.[22] Like biological evolution, social forms are seen to evolve from the simple to the complex.

At first glance, such a sociological perspective seems to hold substantial appeal, demonstrated by the enormous amount of functionalist literature in sociology. However, functionalists have had great difficulty in tieing down their ideas to concrete research hypotheses and predictive propositions. The problem lies in an inability to arrive at a testable definition of equilibrium and measurable criteria of function and dysfunction (neither of which poses any serious problem in the study of animal organisms). The almost unavoidable result is to take explicitly or im-

---

[18] Solomon Asch, *Social Psychology* (Englewood Cliffs, N.J.: Prentice-Hall, Inc., 1952), p. 17.

[19] See *The Sociological Imagination* (New York: Oxford University Press, 1959), pp. 25–75.

[20] Don Martindale, *The Nature and Types of Sociological Theory* (Boston: Houghton-Mifflin Company, 1960), pp. 441–500.

[21] See Carl Hempel, "The Logic of Functional Analysis," in Llewellyn Gross, ed., *Symposium on Sociological Theory* (New York: Harper & Row, Publishers, 1959).

[22] Kenneth E. Bock, "Evolution, Function, and Change," *American Sociological Review,* 28 (April 1963), pp. 229–37.

plicitly the status quo as one's equilibrium and to define functions and dysfunctions in terms of movements toward and away from the status quo. This is usually categorically denied by functionalists, but the denial does not change things in this regard.

The political link between the functionalist perspective and the social status quo is fairly evident. There is a strong logical, if not personal, tendency to take the existing system as a given and invest it with a natural, necessary reality of its own. Gouldner states the issue as follows:

> Clearly the trouble with Functionalism is that it is committed to the present society, with all its dilemmas, contradictions, tension, and indeed, with all its immorality. The trouble with Functionalism is, in a way, that it is not really committed to social order in general, but only to preserving *its* own social order. It is committed to making things work despite wars, inequities, scarcity, and degrading work, rather than finding a way out.[23]

As Alfred McClung Lee puts it, "Thus the usual sociology course or text [frequently functionalist in assumptions] all too often *automatically* rationalizes *what is* and devotes little attention to the problems facing the individual, . . . to what society *can become,* and to how to help change society."[24]

The second tendency in sociology criticized by Mills involves the atheoretical compilation of data and facts. However much we need accurate descriptive and factual information, sociology must strive to integrate its empirical data into meaningful social theory. The tendency toward abstract empiricism that Mills noted has in some respects been greatly elaborated. More recently, one focus of research methods has shifted away from the accumulation of facts intended to reflect or capture the nature of social relations between people and groups toward pure mathematics and logical constructs, regardless of whether the operations have any concrete social references or not. In Albert Szymanski's words, "Concern with mathematical questions is increasingly replacing concern for social relations."[25] Such pseudo-science has the effect of distracting from the production of factually grounded critical theory.

Among the reasons-to-be for the atheoretical accumulation of information is its possible use to dominant elites on the economic, political, and military fronts. Gouldner directs our attention to the fact that "Established industrial societies have a need for social scientists, who can help maintain and operate them smoothly; who can be trusted conscientiously to conserve the established machinery and keep it running. . . ."[26] Economists come to mind first in this connection, but other social sciences also come into consideration. Social information can be used as an important asset in predicting, regulating, and manipulating

---

[23] *The Coming Crisis in Western Sociology,* p. 281.

[24] *Toward Humanist Sociology* (Englewood Cliffs, N.J.: Prentice-Hall, Inc., 1972), p. 38.

[25] Al Szymanski, "Marxism and Science," *The Insurgent Sociologist,* 3 (Spring 1973), p. 25.

[26] *The Coming Crisis in Western Sociology,* p. 332.

human behavior if it can help answer such questions as What are the optimal conditions for worker effort without producing a revolt? Under what conditions can one most likely expect an urban riot to occur? How can housewives be enticed to spend more for less? What are the most effective approaches to peasant "pacification"?

Yet, the utility and validity of much contracted research data has been highly questioned.[27] Indeed, much research for hire turns out to be totally useless.[28] In the case of the U.S. Army's ill-fated Project Camelot, a confidential social science research study aimed at deciphering counter-insurgency strategy and political information on underdeveloped, revolution-prone countries, the outcome was ignominious exposure and the discrediting of all parties involved.[29] However, the proliferation and accumulated costs of counterinsurgency research since 1960 suggest at least their perceived value to the status quo.[30] Nor have expenditures for domestic "pacification" research and social control shown any signs of abatement.

Regardless of whether the subject matter involves religion or war, the "scientific" value-free, ethical neutrality claim of investigators is almost always assumed. Information on worker attitudes and behavior concerns "reality" not the interests of management; the atmosphere of the ghetto is studied in the interests of science not the police network or government; and psychological conditioning is researched out of disinterested curiosity not for the advertising industry. But in truth, writes T.R. Young, "We need not protect the fraudulent image of the scientist as value-free and uninvolved in creating the conditions of repression where on every hand scientists are the paid mercenaries of a managed society."[31]

This is *not* to imply that all social science research, however valid and reliable it might be, is conducted with the intention of providing useful data and information to agencies of power and social control. In fact, a very small proportion of total research done, in the broadest sense of the term, is contract research performed in the interests of dominant elites. In terms of sums of money spent, however, the proportion of research conducted with obvious implications for the understanding and control of the powerless by the powerful increases greatly. Few public agencies, foundations, or corporations are financing social science research simply out of a devotion to knowledge for its own sake, let alone for critical pur-

---

[27] For a critique of abstract empiricism's methods, see Derek L. Phillips, *Abandoning Method: Sociological Studies of Methodology* (San Francisco: Jossey-Bass Inc., Publishers, 1973); at a more general level, Peter Park, *Sociology, Tomorrow: An Evaluation of Sociological Theories in Terms of Science* (New York: Pegasus, 1969).

[28] For a discussion as to the effectiveness of contract social research, see Harold Orlans, *On Contracting for Knowledge: Values and Limitations of Social Science Research* (San Francisco: Jossey-Bass Inc., Publishers, 1973).

[29] See Irving Louis Horowitz, *The Rise and Fall of Project Camelot* (Cambridge, Mass.: M.I.T. Press, 1967).

[30] Michael T. Klare, *War without End* (New York: Vintage Books, 1972), pp. 88–141, provides a detailed account of social research having counterinsurgency goals.

[31] "The Politics of Sociology," *The American Sociologist*, 6 (November 1971), p. 278.

poses.[32] Even knowledge for its own sake is suspect within the higher circles of power, for the truth may clash with their interests.

While the big contracted research projects are frequently oriented toward purposes of social control, the innumerable small and independent studies are typically performed out of individual interest. The subject matter itself may have only the most tangential political implications, though an increasing amount of such small-scale individual study *is* politically germane. Not only is it often politically germane, an increasing number of factual studies are undertaken for specifically critical purposes.[33] We might be reminded that such classic social critics as Marx, Veblen, and Mills were themselves active fact finders and information gatherers, though they never lost sight of larger theoretical purposes. There are no simple shortcuts to social understanding. Given a theoretical framework, factual information helps systematize and interpret the individual's practical experiences of such things as powerlessness, inequality, poverty, unemployment, taxation, war, racism, and sexism. It helps point toward the underlying causes of such experiences, links the common interests of people oppressed in different ways, and helps raise the level of social awareness. (We shall return to questions of ethics in social research in the concluding chapter.)

Popular sociology

At this point, a brief comment might be made on the role of popular sociology as exemplified in books such as Charles Reich's *The Greening of America* and Alvin Toffler's *Future Shock*. (The work of Robert Ardrey as discussed in the next section may also be included here.) No type of book can, of course, be criticized merely because it's popular. If academic sociologists are unable to communicate successfully outside their own field, this is what deserves criticism. Many academics have, in fact, written widely read books. We could go as far back as Thorstein Veblen's *The Theory of the Leisure Class*. Modern social science may cite C. Wright Mills's *White Collar* and *The Power Elite*, and J.K. Galbraith's *The Affluent Society* and *The New Industrial State*. Non-academics who draw extensively upon academic literature and research such as Vance Packard and Ferdinand Lundberg have also been able to open up to broad audiences. What is more, such works may contain substantial amounts of social criticism.

However, with some exceptions, most popular works ask very little of the reader politically speaking. Past books such as David Reisman's *The Lonely Crowd* and William H. Whyte's *The Organization Man,* as

---

[32] For an analysis of a prestigious social science funding agency, see Jay Schulman, Carol Brown, and Roger Kahn, "Report on the Russell Sage Foundation," *The Insurgent Sociologist*, 2 (Summer 1972), pp. 2–34.

[33] For example, see journals such as *Socialist Revolution, Radical America, The Insurgent Sociologist,* and *Berkeley Journal of Sociology* for research with radical orientations, and *Social Policy* and *Society(Trans-action)* for liberal research criticism. A selection of *Society's* pieces may be found in Gary T. Marx, *Muckraking Sociology: Research as Social Criticism* (New Brunswick: N.J.: Transaction Books, 1972).

well as Reich's and Toffler's, present the common themes that modern industrial society isn't the best of all possible worlds but not much can really be done about it, or even should be done. The authors attempt to provide an accounting of what's wrong, why people may be disoriented or anxious, and seek to clarify the complexities of the system. They tend to convey mild, essentially apolitical criticism, which make few if any demands upon the individual for active and purposeful social change. Reich tells his readers not only to take it easy politically speaking but also that things are actually getting better all the time. We are moving out of an era of exploitation and into an era of peace and freedom, joy and community. The "greening" process, according to Reich, is most marked among youth, and as the latter enter into the larger society— the corporations, law, the state, or whatever—the new consciousness will transform the harshness of the past into the emancipation of the future. The control over the nation's production resources and means of violence evidently need not be dislodged. Such threats will be transformed by the new consciousness of liberation. But alas, if only the road to liberation were so easily traveled, all would indeed be "green."

This is not to say that works such as these are always lacking in sociological insight; for example, those of Reisman and Whyte made some lasting contributions to sociological dialogue. The difficulty is that such books fail to come to grips with the central dynamics of advanced capitalist society, and hence draw either tangential or unrealistic conclusions about society or about social change. A related difficulty is that in coming to grips with the central dynamics of advanced capitalism, authors risk becoming *un*popular, though they are certainly by no means assured of such a fate—as "popular" writers from Marx to Marcuse attest.

Genetic Freudianism

"All is aggression, writes Robert Ardrey (*The Social Contract*). "It is coded in our genes."[34] Ardrey, and before him Konrad Lorenz (*On Aggression*), accomplish similar political ends through their conclusions based on a "biological" review of human life as Freud accomplished in psychological terms. Quite accordingly, Ardrey looks upon Freud as one of the century's scientific geniuses, while branding Marx as naive. (Ardrey asserts that the modern scientist might best walk out the back door and vanish.) Like Freud, the genetic Freudians assume "equality"—equality of what is never really specified—is a natural impossibility, and inequality is the first "law of social materials." The second "law of vertebrate life" is "equality of opportunity." Competition in the process of working out aggression develops the species in accordance with the natural laws of selection. Social systems, regardless of type, cannot change individuals, and individuals cannot change themselves.

No noteworthy differences exist between human and other animal life (proven by such facts as elephants covering human corpses with

---

[34] *The Social Contract* (New York: Delta Books, 1970), p. 258 and elsewhere throughout the text. Illustrations are from *The Social Contract*, though other Ardrey books are available.

grass, testifying to their perception of death). Thus, the U.S. intervention in Vietnam was doomed to failure from the start, not owing to conscious Vietnamese determination to free themselves from foreign economic and political control and build a cooperative society, but rather due to their animal drives of territoriality, which biologically forced them to fight. One wonders what happened to the territoriality drives of Saigon's black marketeers, the Vietnamese bourgeoisie, the military brass, etc. Perhaps their territorial drives lapsed momentarily while they had the chance to enrich and empower themselves at the expense of U.S. taxpayers and fellow Vietnamese.

According to Ardrey, a just society is one that is disorderly enough to provide "equality of opportunity" and orderly enough to protect people sufficiently to allow aggression to develop. Competition, presumably foot races as well as business, "not only brings to maturity, for worse or better, the genetic fortune of our origins, but through endless sortings evaluates unequals in terms of environmental demand." (There is only one "environment," since cultural environment doesn't count.) "The evolution of men, like the evolution of meadowlarks, is based on the recognition and adequate sorting of unequals. Injustice occurs when competition is aborted." Owing to the fact that men are irrational, it is apparently to most of our good fortunes ". . . that the superior endowments of the few become the survival guarantee for the many."[35] Thus, we must evidently conclude, if the above theses are taken as our guides, that the "environment" has objectively sorted out billionaires such as H.L. Hunt and Howard Hughes for their genetic superiority to guarantee the survival of the rest of us. Like the tycoons of the 19th century who enjoyed Herbert Spencer's ideas, these men must find the theories of Ardrey very comforting.

As for the bizarre animal stories, which seek to demonstrate how much like humans animals are, or vice versa, they may prove to be anything from enlightening to amusing. It is extremely simple to draw parallels between human and other animal behavior. However, it is quite another thing to offer logical and empirical explanations of historical events on such a basis. The welter of animal species with all of their exceedingly diverse genetic and instinctive adaptations to their various environments offer a sufficient variety of external similarities to human behavior to "explain" almost anything. The same kind of explanations may be had from astrology; but instead of the future being written in the stars, it is written in the genes. Ardrey envisages new breakthroughs in understanding human behavior once the behavioral enigmas of such academically neglected creatures as elephants, bears, lions, and wolves are cracked.

Our criticism of genetic Freudianism is not that humans are not the product of animal evolution or that humans never exhibit animal behavior. Marx himself took pains to point out that much factory labor reduced human life to pure animal functions. Without in any way demeaning other creatures, we may argue that sociologists must look at

---

[35] Ibid., pp. 40–41, 87.

social, political, and economic processes for a more complete accounting of the human condition—and for means to make that condition more distinctly human. Like Freud, the genetic Freudians fail to examine the historically specific social systems within which people have always lived and that have led them to think and act in such markedly divergent ways. Other forms of societies will most certainly follow the one we know today, and the theorists of the future will also have to look farther than the biological individual for sociological explanation and understanding.

The critical perspective

The foregoing overview of sociological perspectives is not intended to be anything but a broad orienting statement to assist the reader in placing the book at hand within what, at least from the author's point of view, constitutes certain noteworthy tendencies in the analysis of society. The project at hand has been undertaken with the assumption that sociological analysis must take its responsibilities seriously. Contemporary sociology has a responsibility to keep the critical social lens prepared by past masters such as Marx, Weber, Veblen, and Mills in polished focus.

The perspective and working methods of such a critical sociology cannot, of course, be completely understood by a reading of this book. However, it should constitute a beginning to such an understanding. In summary terms (see also Chapter 15), a responsible sociology has foremost the dual task of developing a critique of all forms of social oppression and of all forms of social science that serve to support such oppression.[36] These are the most direct and immediate tasks. A further goal of a socially responsible sociology is to assist in the development of alternative social forms that uphold human dignity and provide the conditions for the positive cultivation of human mental and physical abilities. These are imposing tasks. They are not, however, insurmountable ones.

The critical perspective as here conceived and the central assumptions of which were stated at the outset is most closely related to the classical Marxist analysis. A fuller clarification of this critical Marxist perspective must be obtained from further examination of the study at hand. What can be further pointed out here is that while the approach and analysis used in the present study share a number of common positions with what is called "critical theory,"[37] such theory departs in several important ways from the theoretical posture of this study.[38] Most

[36] J.W. Freiberg, "Sociology and the Ruling Class," *The Insurgent Sociologist,* III (Summer 1973), pp. 48–55; and Herbert Gamberg and James Stolzman, "Toward a Sociology of Oppression," unpublished paper, Dalhousie University, Halifax, Nova Scotia.

[37] Also known as the Frankfurt School, critical theory's central figure today is Jürgen Habermas, whose best known books are *Toward a Rational Society* (Boston: Beacon Press, 1970) and *Knowledge and Human Interests* (Boston: Beacon Press, 1971). Herbert Marcuse's writings also grew out of the Frankfurt School tradition.

[38] See Martin Jay, "Some Recent Developments in Critical Theory," *Berkeley Journal of Sociology,* XVIII (1973–74), pp. 27–44.

essentially, critical theory too often lacks the crucially necessary perspective of a class-divided society founded upon the material and social means of production, a point of view whose utility will become abundantly clear. There are certain methodological and philosophical differences that cannot concern us here other than to say that Marxist analysis holds a much more positivistic or logical-empirical outlook than does critical theory, which tends to deny such an approach.

Yet, one may fully appreciate critical theory's rejection of the sort of deadening scientism in sociology, which considers the social analyst as a passive recorder of a causally closed system of social relationships largely amenable to the methods of the natural sciences. Further, our perspective shares with critical theory a concern over the elevation of technology and science to ends in themselves rather than being employed as means toward the broadest possible social and individual development. Finally, it is precisely the matter of social and individual development where Marxist and critical theory are in major accord. Both seek to cultivate an understanding of what the *potential* of a society is and what that society *ought* to be given its level of social and material resources. Both turn upon the tension between actuality and potentiality and seek to liberate human thought and action for the pursuit of potentiality.[39]

The critical perspective is itself a participant in the developmental processes of social life. Its own progress depends very much upon the nature of the changes of the social milieu within which it works, while through such work it brings the strength of knowledge and ideas to bear upon that same milieu.

---

[39] Frances Hearn, "The Implications of Critical Theory for Critical Sociology," *Berkeley Journal of Sociology*, XVIII (1973–74), pp. 127–58.

2

Society and culture

SOCIETY AS SOCIAL RELATIONS

In stating our guiding assumptions, we stressed the idea that individuals create social forms within which to conduct their activities and that these social forms then acquire a certain momentum of their own in the subsequent regulation of individual behavior. Thus, as Durkheim was to emphasize (perhaps overemphasize from the standpoint of modern sociology), society as a system of social relations assumes a relatively independent status with regard to the individual actor who finds himself or herself born, raised, and living within pre-established networks of interpersonal relations. For example, a businessman *must* orient his behavior to the acquisition of profits, and all the rest which is thereby entailed, or go bankrupt and drop out of the system of business relationships. He then under the most ordinary circumstances steps into another network of activities to sustain himself and his family, say that of becoming a worker who *must* sell his labor capacity to an employer—again with all the rest which this entails. He may even decide to drop out of conventional society entirely and become a beatnik of some sort; still, he will find himself stepping into an existing pattern of social relations.

The contention that society possesses regulatory powers over the individual in no way implies that the individual is socially powerless. Not only can the individual move from one set of relations to another (though very real limits or alternatives exist here), individuals in relationship to one another can bring about changes in their social forms or networks. The crux of the matter is that social reality inheres neither in the individual person nor in society apart from individuals. As Cooley early noted, and Mead fully developed, the individual and society are essentially "twin-born"; a constant production and reproduction between individuals and society takes place.

In the construction of his theoretical perspective, Marx also indicated that the locus of human life or social reality is neither the individual or society taken separately, but is found within the web of relations formed between individuals. Marx warned us against locating social reality in the individual by saying that ". . . the human essence is no abstraction inherent in each single individual. In its reality it is the ensemble of social relations." "Society does not consist of individuals; it expresses the sum of connections and relationships in which individuals find themselves."[1] Note that Marx uses the phrase "relationships in which individuals *find themselves.*" That is, social reality is not created anew each time people come together to do something. Whereas the locus of human life does revolve around the countless relations between individuals, most of these relations have become established and relatively fixed and are variously refered to by sociologists as "structures," "institutions," or "organizations." Individuals find themselves in a given period of history, a given society, a given economy, and a given family system. Conversely, Marx argued that "What is to be avoided above all is the re-establishing of 'Society' as an abstraction *vis-à-vis* the individual."[2] And as for society, so for history, "*history* does *nothing*, it 'possesses *no* immense wealth,' it 'wages *no* battles.' It is *man*, real living man, that does all that, that possesses and fights; 'history' is not a person apart, using man as a means for *its own* particular aims; history is *nothing but* the activity of man pursuing his aims. . . ."[3] Yet, just as man is creature as well as creator of society, so has history set its own limitations on human purpose and action. In a well-known passage, Marx declared, "Men make their own history, but they do not make it just as they please; they do not make it under circumstances chosen by themselves, but under circumstances directly encountered, given, and transmitted from the past."[4]

When *are* the prevailing social relations of a given society amenable to purposive change-oriented human action? At what point can the circumstances of the past be altered? Marx contends that:

> No social order ever perishes before all the productive forces for which there is room in it have developed; and new, higher relations of production never appear before the material conditions of their existence have matured in the womb of the old society itself. Therefore mankind always sets itself only such tasks as it can solve; since, looking at the matter more closely, it will always be found that the task itself arises only when the material conditions for its solution already exist or are at least in the process of formation.[5]

[1] *Theses on Feuerbach*, in Karl Marx and Frederick Engels, *Selected Works*, Vol. 1 (Moscow: Progress Publishers, 1969), p. 14; and Karl Marx, *The Grundrisse*, ed. and trans. by David McLellan (New York: Harper & Row, Publishers, 1971), p. 77.

[2] *Essential Writings of Karl Marx*, David Caute, ed. (New York: Collier Books, 1967), p. 41.

[3] Ibid., p. 50.

[4] *The Eighteenth Brumaire of Louis Bonaparte*, in *Selected Works*, Vol. 1, p. 398.

[5] Preface to *A Contribution to the Critique of Political Economy*, in *Selected Works*, Vol. 1, p. 504.

The argument developed in this book asserts that the material conditions for the creation of a new system of social relations are, in fact, present and have been for some time. The persistent and mounting difficulties of making the present system run is testimony enough to this fact.

Levels of focus

The perspective on social reality which we have been developing does not preclude focusing upon different *levels* of that reality. A psychologist may choose to concentrate upon the individual without neglecting to take into consideration the relevance of the individual's social environment.[6] A social psychologist may choose to concentrate upon small groups of individuals, again without losing sight of the group's social and historical context.[7] A sociologist may choose to concentrate upon more abstract phenomena such as classes, large organizations, religious or ethnic groups, and society as a whole without failing to recognize that underneath these larger formations of people there are thinking, feeling, and acting individuals.[8]

A crucial but difficult task of sociological work is to remain flexible enough to move back and forth between these levels of concentration so as to fill out one's higher level social concepts with specific "grass roots" events and to illuminate such specific happenings with the general wisdom of a broad social theory. Mills appropriately labels such flexibility as the sociological imagination, and there are no better examples than Mills's own works, the most important of which we shall encounter on several occasions in the text. Gerth and Mills point out how the sociological imagination may be exercised by a social psychologist such as Mead, whose theories "enable us to link the private and the public, the innermost acts of the individual with the widest kinds of social-historical phenomena."[9]

POWER RELATIONS

A crucial concept or form of social relationship which the sociological imagination must confront squarely is that of power. The notion of power is central throughout this study. Power inheres in the social relations which regulate or control the flow of material and human resources in a society.[10] Thus, power may be measured by the degree

---

[6] For example, see Erich Fromm, *Revolution of Hope* (New York: Harper & Row Publishers, 1968).

[7] For example, see Solomon Asch, *Social Psychology* (Englewood Cliffs, N.J.: Prentice-Hall, Inc., 1952).

[8] See Charles K. Warriner, *The Emergence of Society* (Homewood, Ill.: The Dorsey Press, 1969); and Thomas P. Wilson, "Conceptions of Interaction and Forms of Sociological Explanation," *American Sociological Review*, 35 (August 1970), p. 698.

[9] Hans Gerth and C. Wright Mills, *Character and Social Structure* (New York: Harbinger Books, 1964, originally published 1953), p. xvi.

[10] See Frank Parkin, *Class Inequality and Political Order* (New York: Praeger Publishers, 1971), pp. 46–47.

to which a person or group controls the application and distribution of a society's (or the world's) resources. Powerful people and groups are able to command a disproportionate amount of resources and hence acquire a disproportionate amount of rewards, whereas powerless people tend to be excluded from control of and substantial involvement in the utilization of resources and distribution of rewards.

In the broadest sense, power consists in the ownership and control of the means of material production and the capacity to acquire the wealth produced thereby. The latter assures the reception of the greatest social privileges and rewards the society has to offer. These social rewards are also a form of power, for they are, in turn, capable of perpetuating, transmitting, and augmenting the control and acquisition of the material product. The proper education and social affiliations, to mention two kinds of social benefits, may assist or support entrance into a power relationship (though is by no means necessary to power or a guarantee of power).

In treating power as control and acquisition of material and human resources, we are departing from a frequent usage, which views power as something independent from such control and appropriation. The view of power as something that exists separately from the flow of material resources is attributed by some to Weber's theories. However, as Parkin pointed out, Weber himself equated power with the control and distribution of material and social rewards by stating that they are "phenomena of the distribution of power within a community."[11] What Weber *did* single out as a separate dimension of analysis is the *political party*. The political question to be raised is thus the extent to which a mass party can alter the control and flow of resources and rewards that now favor the powerful capitalist class.

Bureaucracy as power

The concept of bureaucracy is introduced here inasmuch as it is a form of social relation that greatly augments power. Weber carefully delineated the nature of modern bureaucracy.[12] Bureaucracy, he observed, strives to maximize efficiency through hierarchical authority relations and the application of calculable rules by trained experts, while exacting complete loyalty from men and reducing them to utterly dependent and depersonalized cogs in a machine. When carried through to its logical completeness, a bureaucratized society *is* the brave new world. Weber pointed out that bureaucracy displaces democratic self-government by small homogeneous units and inevitably accompanies a *mass society* in which the governed are systematically leveled to standardized cases, facilitating objectivity, impersonality, and efficiency in dealing with diverse types of people. "The most decisive thing here," writes Weber, "is the *leveling of the governed* in opposition to the ruling

---

[11] Ibid.

[12] *From Max Weber: Essays in Sociology,* Hans Gerth and C. Wright Mills, eds. (New York: Oxford University Press, 1958), pp. 196–244. Quotations are all from pp. 226–29.

and bureaucratically articulated group, which in its turn may occupy a quite autocratic position, both in fact and in form."

What is of most interest to us here, however, is Weber's discussion of bureaucracy as a *form of power*. To Weber, bureaucracy is a "power instrument of the first order." Why this is so should be quite evident when we consider the extent and the manner in which human, technical, and capital resources are organized under a single operating apparatus. Moreover, Weber observes that "Where bureaucratization of administration has been completely carried through, a form of power relation is established that is practically unshatterable." Any impetus toward change from within the bureaucracy is extremely unlikely, for the professional bureaucrat is chained to his activity by his entire material and ideal existence: "In the great majority of cases, he is only a single cog in an ever-moving mechanism which prescribes to him an essentially fixed route of march." Nor is change induced from the outside very likely either. In what must today be seen as one of the most ominous lines in the literature of sociology, at least for groups dedicated to change, Weber writes, "The ruled, for their part, cannot dispense with or replace the bureaucratic apparatus of authority once it exists. More and more," Weber continues, "the material fate of the masses depends upon the steady and correct functioning of the increasingly bureaucratic organizations of private capitalism. The idea of eliminating these organizations becomes more and more utopian." If neither bureaucratic functionaries nor persons outside but under the sphere of influence of bureaucracy can direct the organization's movement, who can? A contemporary political scientist, Andrew Hacker, argues (perhaps in the hope of a self-defeating prophecy!) that *people* as such are *all* cogs in bureaucratic machines; people only make decisions on behalf of machines and the principles of bureaucratic growth.[13] But such sort of mechanical determinism must be rejected.

Weber's theory of bureaucracy is stated more openly. While being an unshatterable power instrument of the first order, bureaucracy is in itself neutral. In Gabriel Kolko's words, "The function of bureaucracy is to serve constituted power."[14] Bureaucracy is a *tool* or an *instrument* of power. It may be made to serve whatever interests control it. As Weber points out, bureaucratic institutions are easily made to work for anybody who knows how to gain control over them. The way the power of a bureaucracy is used is determined "only from the very top." Weber concludes, "The consequences of bureaucracy depend therefore upon the direction which powers using the apparatus give to it." The answers to these implicit questions of power have been alluded to previously and are developed fully in Chapter 9. Suffice it to note here that the most important bureaucracies serve the interests of those who own and control the means of production.

---

[13] Andrew Hacker, ed., *The Corporation Take-Over* (New York: Doubleday & Company, Inc., 1965), p. 10.

[14] Gabriel Kolko, *The Roots of American Foreign Policy* (Boston: Beacon Press, 1969), p. 13.

CULTURE AND SOCIETY

We turn now to a consideration of a number of additional basic sociological concepts, which the students of society should be acquainted with before undertaking an examination of the substantive areas of the discipline. It is not as if the other chapters of the text could not be understood without such an acquaintance. However, by familiarizing oneself with a number of basic terms and how sociologists tend to use them, the student is able to get a better "feel" for things social and sociological. A familiarity with basic concepts helps to avoid larger misunderstandings and provides some common ground from which to approach the several concrete areas of study.

Society has been conceived of as an ensemble of social relations among individuals. If one were to trace through the objective actions of all persons within a given country vis-à-vis one another, one would come up with a very complex web of inter-personal conduct. It would be possible with the aid of a computer to diagram or chart the patterns of social interaction between members of a society, a pointless task to be sure. The sociologist is only interested in certain aspects or segments of inter-personal relations such as those found within economic, political, or family life.

In refering to the economy, the state, or the family, we may remind ourselves again that these are general concepts that gather in or subsume an enormous number of concrete inter-personal actions. They are generalizations that save us talking about an overwhelming number of particular cases. Yet, the particular cases or events are ultimately what must be of interest and observed, and from which the general concept is derived in the first place.

Now, the human events of the world involve by definition something more than mere objective inter-personal relations. These events also involve culture. Culture may be conceived of as a type of code book for members of a society, since it consists of the sum of a society's meanings, expectations, and understandings. Culture may be viewed as a way of life the members of a society develop in their attempts to maximize *adaptation* to their social and material environments. It is the instrument and medium through which the inter-personal relations of society are conducted, and it provides the channels through which the course of social relations runs. When Marx refers to history as encountered, given, and transmitted from the past, he may have used the word culture had he been an anthropologist. For culture is a set of meanings, expectations, and understanding in which people find themselves as they strive from birth to become participating members of society; culture is encountered, given, and transmitted from one generation to the next. It is immediately encountered and transmitted through language, both spoken and written. Language or communication is the conduit through which cultural meanings and expectations are transmitted, and thus lies at the center of human culture.

The capacity to communicate and convey cultural meanings sets humans apart from other animal species, many of which have through instinctual responses various forms of "societies." But closed and lacking in culture, an animal society is forever organized the same; very often the survival of the species depends upon a rigid invariance of relations within the society. A given culture does, in fact, tend to seem natural and necessary to human survival; it carries with it the authority of tradition and the momentum of habit. However, the culture in which society is embedded may be poorly suited to the material conditions man has or could produce for himself. These material conditions could call for a reconstruction of our way of life, of the cultural codes through which we order our social life. Contrary to the animal species, which for survival demand invariance in their relations to one another, human society often demands change if it is to progress—indeed, if it is to avoid retrogression and even survive.

The potential and capacity to accomplish purposive change also hinges upon ability to utilize a *flexible* communication medium, to employ symbols (in contrast to the animal world's use of natural signs). Human culture is by definition symbolic; all meanings, expectations, and understandings, whether these concern material or psychological phenomena, are couched in symbolic communication and learned through symbolic interaction with others. Humans are equipped with an openended communication system, made up of symbols subject to diverse application, negation, and novel production. The open-ended nature of symbolic communication also leads to much confusion and misunderstanding, but this disadvantage is far outweighed by the adaptive flexibility it permits its human users. The number of painful mistakes avoided by thinking (symbolizing) things out in advance and choosing among alternative courses of action is a powerful weapon in the arsenal of human survival. This is not to overlook the equally possible perversion enabled through symbolic capacity.

The late Hugh Dalziel Duncan drew our attention to the manner in which society's ruling elites employ symbols to create the images they require to legitimate and justify their power and position. Duncan observes that symbols convey the images that lead us on and that are used to uphold prestige, order, control, and courses of action. He further points to the highly developed and powerful nature of modern mass communications and argues that "The great social revolution of the 20th century has been in communication, the means whereby those in power create and control the images, or names, that will legitimize their power."[15] Mills adds that it is a grave mistake to assume that the images of reality conveyed by the powerful must prevail lest society come apart, or to fail to distinguish between such symbolic attempts at legitimizing authority and the actual rule of specific people.[16] We may see that behind the images of patriotism stand the profits of the big weapons makers, behind the myths of freedom is the Central Intelligence Agency,

---

[15] H.D. Duncan, *Symbols in Society* (New York: Oxford University Press, 1968), p. 33.

[16] C.W. Mills, *The Sociological Imagination* (New York: Oxford University Press, 1959), pp. 37–39.

and behind the symbol of private individual enterprise the international corporate conglomerate.

People have been busy tearing down the image wall and getting at those persons hiding behind it mysteriously and secretly conducting their business. Doubt and skepticism have become widespread concerning both images conveyed and the people who convey them. Such attitudes may be found not just toward the state but towards elites and authority in every sphere of culture and society. This undermining process is a prerequisite to the building of social democracy. The reaction of dominant elites must be to rely less upon symbolic and image manipulation in areas of mass communication and more upon the threat, coercion, and applied force to support their rule.[17]

Real and ideal culture

Here we might draw a useful distinction between the cultural meanings and expectations held up as the ideal or publically esteemed ones and the actual culture exhibited in people's behavior. This is a particularly useful distinction in the analysis of change, or in an era of especially rapid change.

Culture, being a way of life the members of a society develop in their attempts to maximize adaptation to their social and material environments, we might expect to change as these external environments change, or as resources available to the people involved decrease or increase. Charles Valentine, Lee Rainwater, and others have described, for example, the cultures of much of the low-income population as evincing significant discrepancies between real and ideal components.[18] The poor tend to accept as ideal the cultural expectations of the affluent regarding family stability, regular employment, and social participation, but owing to a shortage of material resources must compromise such ideals in actual behavior. Such non-conventional behavior as desertion, sporadic employment, and social withdrawal may suggest that those involved lack a culture; what they lack is conventional culture in these senses, but have developed other cultural modes of adaptation to their circumstances. In a related illustration, cultural ideals in the United States have traditionally emphasized the country's classlessness, a society of equal opportunity and rising and falling individuals within a gigantic "middle class." The reality of a highly class stratified society of grossly unequal opportunities has been slow to surface.

In practice, there may or may not be a gap between real and ideal culture. Typically, however, a gap exists to various degrees. Further, what most people perceive as ideal may not be so perceived by a minority of people, either out of faulty perception or conscious rejection of the ideal cultural standards. (The latter case shall be discussed in the next

---

[17] See H.L. Nieburg, *Political Violence* (New York: St. Martin's Press, 1969).

[18] Charles A. Valentine, *Culture and Poverty* (Chicago: University of Chicago Press, 1968); and Lee Rainwater, *Behind Ghetto Walls* (Chicago: Aldine Publishing Company, 1970).

section.) The point to be made here is that it is the movement of real culture, the concrete behavior and meanings in use that really matter, both for society and the sociologist. To focus on the way "things are supposed to be" either as defined by tradition or by specific interests may be to confuse myth with reality. Although established ideals may at some times and places "pull" actual practices toward them, the more typical case is that actual practices draw further away from established ideals until the gap is too great to uphold any longer the old ideas, which are then replaced by current practices. Easiest to illustrate here are areas of sexual behavior such as the use of contraceptives and abortion. Or, given the dissatisfying nature of much routine industrial and office work, it is not surprising to find that the "work ethic" has lost much of its force as interests shift toward off-the-job leisure-time pursuits—at least for those with adequate resources.

The shift of behavioral or actual culture away from previous standards may produce moderate to severe strains within both the individual and society. The ideal or public standard may be deeply ingrained in a person's conscience, and behavioral violations may evoke guilt and frustration. Socially, many important cultural standards are written in the law, which then clashes with growing numbers of violators. The notion of private property is held high, but in an era of affluence millions of needy and not-so-needy people help themselves to merchandise, especially in the large and impersonal businesses. (Mayor Daley's now famous pronouncement to Chicago police to shoot looters epitomizes the value placed upon private property, even above that of human life.)

Cultural efficacy

Clashes between ideal and real behavior patterns aside, the large majority of people in all societies tend to take their own culture or way of life as a "standard of normalcy" by which other cultures are judged. This tendency toward ethnocentrism, of investing special or superior qualities to one's own culture, is understandable enough. The problem is whether or not such assumptions ever have merit. Are there any empirical criteria for the measurement of how well a culture meets human ends and needs compared to any other culture? Which religion best meets man's spiritual needs and values? What family form best satisfies human sexual and emotional needs? What economic system results in the greatest good for the greatest number? What type of political order provides people with the utmost freedom and responsibility?

Certain aspects of culture, specifically aspects of productive and technological capacity, can be empirically evaluated in terms of their effectiveness, provided certain assumptions are made. Assuming that life is valuable, penicillin is superior to bleeding as a cure. Assuming food is valuable, tractors are superior to oxen. So far so good, for almost everyone on earth would agree with the assumptions on life and food. But can we assume that such things as transportation can be measured in terms of some scale of absolute value? What type of superiority does a society enjoy that can send a man to the moon or from New York to

London at 600 miles an hour?[19] What type of superiority does a society enjoy that has a registered gasoline-driven vehicle for every two of its citizens? In the later instance, "superiority" means that the society slaughters 50,000 of its people every year and injures millions, chokes on deadly carbon monoxide fumes, and blights its living spaces with freeways—among numerous other things. Further illustrations as to the dubious value of much technology seem unnecessary.[20]

Clearly, for Westerners to attribute special qualities to monogamous marriages over polygynous forms often encountered elsewhere in the world is empirically untenable. In the area of sexual codes, the superiority of premarital chastity has been significantly undermined in the direction of "primitive" culture's more permissive standards. And it is hardly provable that Christianity will achieve one paradise more readily than Buddhism.

Our previous argument has been that culture is an adaptation to a society's objective social and material circumstances. Thus, rather than compare the relative efficacy of cultures to one another, the more plausible task is to compare a given society's degree of success in bringing its available and potential resources up to maximum adaptation with its external environment. Given the available resources, has the society applied them in such a way as to compliment human capacities and provide the conditions for their maximum development? Have means and ends been put together in a rational way as they affect most people? Do all aspirations and interests, aims and goals have equal opportunities to express themselves given the level of development and resource availability? These are the kinds of questions that must be raised in assessing a culture's efficacy.

SUBCULTURE AND COUNTERCULTURE

By subculture we shall here mean nothing more than patterned variations upon the dominant cultural themes of the larger society. For example, the U.S. and many other contemporary societies contain groups of people coming originally from different religious, racial, or national origin backgrounds. Frequently, these differing background experiences and identifications carry with them distinctive cultural meanings, expectations, and understandings that set adherents or members more or less apart from other people in the society.[21] While a number of overarching cultural orientations tend to link these various "ethnic" groups together, each may tend to "stick together" socially owing to cultural

---

[19] For the kind of answer an American Indian might give, see William Eastlake, "Whitey's on the Moon Now," *The Nation*, September 15, 1969, pp. 238–39.

[20] For a critical analysis of the role of technology in modern society, see Jacques Ellul, *The Technological Society* (New York: Random House, Inc., 1967); and Eugene S. Schwartz, *Overskill: The Decline of Technology in Modern Civilization* (Chicago: Quadrangle Books, Inc., 1971).

[21] Milton M. Gordon, *Assimilation in American Life* (New York: Oxford University Press, 1964).

familiarity and identification within the group. Such has been the case with the various waves of national origin groups or immigrants to the U.S., often reinforced by their being members of different religious faiths or minority racial groups.[22] Beginning with the reduction of language differences and continuing through other cultural traits and inter-group mixing, American ethnic groups have in various degrees been "melted" down to more closely approximate the dominant Anglo-American cultural mold. In the process, the various ethnic groups have added to and modified the dominant culture, but never altering its original Anglo cast.

Recently there has been much discussion of ethnic "pluralism" and the importance of contemporary ethnic subcultures in the U.S.[23] There can be no denying the important part played by being Old American, Irish, Italian, Jewish, or especially black, Chicano, or Indian in American society. However, a crucial aspect of ethnic subculture is too often neglected, namely, how their material economic and political interests objectively converge and how ruling groups have used ethnic differences to distract, divide, and weaken the opposition. The chief subcultural variations are not *between* ethnic groups at all. Rather, the chief variations are *within* them; that is, between the propertied-rich and the propertyless worker regardless of religion, race, or national origin. Black millionaires multiply at the same time the numbers of black poor are expanding, and for a clearly common reason. We shall return to these questions in subsequent discussions of ethnic groups and economic classes.

The critical perspective is often more concerned with countercultures than subcultures, for by definition, subcultures are simply variations upon dominant cultural themes and are not agents of major change. A counterculture, as the term has been used in the defining literature,[24] goes beyond the scope of the dominant culture and posits a qualitatively new alternative. It is in conscious rebellion against established codes and standards, and it rejects both the ideal and real culture of mainstream society. Opposition meanings and symbols are employed in language, appearance, morality, diet, art, group life, production, and so on. It is in rebellion against prevailing assumptions regarding ownership, competition, material reward, individual success, authority hierarchies, technological sterility, environmental destruction, occupational specialization, professional credentials, and more.

A genuine counterculture is, then, a revolutionary culture. A culture that idealized social property, cooperation, voluntary labor, equality, humane application of technology, harmony with environment, the dismantling of wage labor and fragmented work, and the elimination of credentials would constitute a radically new way of life. Clearly, all that

---

[22] See the Ethnic Groups in American Life (Prentice-Hall, Inc.) series of books, which deal extensively with the issue of ethnic subcultures in the U.S.

[23] For example, the numerous works of Andrew M. Greeley; and Michael Novak, *The Rise of the Unmeltable Ethnics* (New York: Macmillan & Company, Inc., 1972).

[24] See Theodore Roszak, *The Making of a Counter Culture* (New York: Doubleday & Company, Inc., 1969).

2. Society and culture   29

passes for counterculture in the U.S. is obviously *not* radical or revolutionary. For example, Bennett Berger lists such counterculture themes as living for the moment, sex as liberation, childlike innocence, consciousness expansion induced by drugs, and transciency, which have nothing to do with revolution; indeed, indulgence and dissipation are perennial allies of the status quo, for they siphon off its oppression into senseless oblivion. On the other hand, the themes of community and free stores, self-expression in arts and crafts, and sexual equality overlap with constructive change.[25]

Both Berger and Kingsley Widmer point out that bohemianism and style rebellions are long established historical phenomena.[26] Widmer makes the observation that undercultures stressing conflicting life styles have cropped up periodically since the days of classic Greece. Widmer is sharply critical of such theses as that of Charles Reich in *The Greening of America* which attribute virtually revolutionary status to the contemporary counterculture as found among many of the nation's youth. But neither is he willing to dismiss it as mere fad and fashion. Rather, Widmer suggests that the historical appearances of undercultures and style rebellions serve to revitalize the dominant or main culture, which tends to ossify and sterilize itself under the weight of tradition and respectability. The outcome may be neither inconsequential nor revolutionary, but a moderate selective change of mainstream culture through the absorption of certain underculture elements. Widmer also draws our attention to the manner in which ". . . outcast styles become 'in' fashions very rapidly. The counter-culture gets plagarized for the entertainment and solace of the empty, and commercialized for the profit and dominance of the controlling." If there is any radical content, it is watered-down and denatured in the process of absorption. John Anson Warner clarifies this point in noting that "The system has demonstrated that it is capable of draining the meaning out of many forms of symbolic protest and gutting counter culture life styles of their radical content in order to absorb them into the normal youth culture norms of organization society (and even that can seep upwards into middle age.)"[27]

It may sometimes be difficult to distinguish between life style rebellion for its own sake or as substitute "middle class" culture on the one hand and genuine *counter*cultural behavior on the other. There are no quick indicators. For example, whereas unkept appearance may be thought to be a sure symbol of "radicalism" by many older adults, such "hippie" fashions have filtered into the core of reactionary mentality. Many current countercultural practices are simply acceptable substitutes for unacceptable parental hang-ups; for example, religious substitutes prolifer-

---

[25] "Hippie Morality—More Old than New," *Transaction,* 5 (December 1967), pp. 19–22.

[26] "The Rebellious Culture: Reflections on its Functions in American Society," in Charles H. Anderson, ed., *Sociological Essays and Research,* 2d ed. (Homewood, Ill.: The Dorsey Press, 1974).

[27] "Alienated Post New Left Youth: Secular Marxism and Religious Mysticism," paper delivered at the 1972 Annual Meeting of the Canadian Sociology and Anthropology Association, Montreal, 1972, p. 10.

ate in every direction: transcendental meditation, astrology, Zen, and Jesus Freakism offer true believers the same solace and explanations as the established church, perhaps even more. Vans are more functional than station wagons, and grass is less dangerous than martinis; getting married and going to the barber are bothersome and expensive nuisances; rock is easier to turn on to than the symphony. To the extent that such preferences distinguish the counterculture, it is, of course, no counterculture at all but a youth *sub*culture—of which there has always been in some form or another. Affluence and technology have given today's youth subculture a very different environment within which to develop; the alternatives are greater and the duration of involvement exceed what has gone before. The generation gap is more perceived than real, and on most fronts the gap never existed or is rapidly closing. The essential divisions within the society are not those involving age; the essential divisions involve power and property, to which age may only be very roughly correlated. Youth like any other age category may be found in the rearguard as well as the vanguard of change. We shall discuss the subject of student radicalism in Chapter 6.

The concepts of society and culture are the broadest or most general found in sociology. We turn in the following chapter to a discussion of several lower level concepts that concern the various parts or components of society and culture, such as institution, role, norm, social interaction, self, and group. These are among the conceptual building blocks of the total social structure.

3

Society and the individual

SOCIAL INSTITUTIONS

The concept of "institution" is used frequently in the social sciences. It is of the same variety as that of society and culture in that it is a general term standing for numerous specific instances of human behavior. However, an institution is a more limited configuration than the society within which it is embedded. It is possible to analytically "carve up" a society into various institutional components. Briefly stated, institutions are special clusters of interpersonal expectations and definitions that channel behavior so as to meet some human physical, psychological, or social need or value such as sex and reproduction, protection, health, learning, consumption, recreation, and faith. Thus, we may speak of the family, educational, economic, and religious institutions. We may refer to specific formalized organizations such as Harvard, AT&T, or the First Presbyterian Church as institutions, but in strict terms these are organizations or "voluntary associations" standing within a larger institutional framework. Even the individual family is formally organized in the sense of marriage licenses, birth certificates, legal responsibilities, divorce, etc. Like culture, an institution has its ideal and real aspects, and a formal organization has both its blueprints and the way things actually transpire. Like culture, an institution can be changed.

Institutions of a society interrelate, or rather people within them do. Working mothers utilizing child care facilities provided by government represents interrelation between family and state institutions; corporation executives talking with generals about the merits of a missile system represent interrelation between economic and military institutions. It is easy to see that institutions may influence one another; changes in one may produce change in another. We will fully develop the thesis that economic institutions—and this includes the participation of the state in the economy—are usually (though not always) decisive, and other

31

institutions must ultimately adjust to economic forces. The family, the school, the church, the hospital, even the state itself must conduct themselves within the environment and context set by the dominant economic institutions. Even the largest business organizations themselves are subject to the regularities of capitalist development. This does not in any way diminish the importance of studying the family, the university, the church, the hospital, the military, or any other institutional area. Such studies must be done for a complete understanding of capitalist society. But what is suggested is that in each of these cases the researcher should always be alert to the manner in which these institutional areas of social life are entangled with that of the interests of those who own and control the means of material production.

ROLES

If institutions are clusters of interpersonal expectations and definitions —routine arrangements for behaving socially in meeting a general need or value—the specific units within the institution to which the various expectations and definitions refer are roles.[1] Roles are thus smaller bundles of interpersonal definitions, rights, and responsibilities, which taken in total make up the institution. Roles may be conceived of in terms of three types or manifestations: the ideal or normative role as specified by the general culture, the perceived role or the way in which the individual interprets general cultural definitions and expections, and the actual role as performed by the individual role incumbents. Role perceptions may be erroneous or confused, and as with ideal and real culture, actual role behavior may be inconsistent with the ideal role definition.

Roles are reciprocal in that every role assumes the existence of another role or group of roles. Thus, in the educational institution the role of teacher has no meaning without that of student, in the family father without son or daughter, in the military officer without enlisted man. The process of socialization refers to the learning and acquisition of such institutional roles. As part of the cultural given, roles exist prior to their present incumbents and continue to survive after the individual departs.

Yet, roles require individuals to act them out; only individuals in relationships with others can create, perform, change, and abolish roles. The force of tradition is to perpetuate and transmit roles fundamentally unchanged from generation to generation; the force of change is to transform old roles and institute new ones in their place. Roles tend to be stacked hierarchically so that persons occupying roles "at the top" of institutions or organizations enjoy greater privilege, freedom, control, prestige, and reward; these roles hold greater power for their incumbents.

---

[1] For an original discussion of the role concept see Ralph Linton, *The Cultural Background of Personality* (New York: Appleton-Century, 1945). See also Everett K. Wilson, *Sociology: Rules, Roles, and Relationships* (Homewood, Ill.: The Dorsey Press, 1966), especially Chapter 6; and George J. McCall and J.L. Simmons, *Identities and Interactions* (New York: The Free Press, 1966).

As one works down the hierarchy of roles within an organization, these role traits reverse themselves until the powerless and narrow routines at the bottom are reached. Although larger economic forces set limits within which even the most powerful role incumbents in the most powerful organizations or bureaucracies must act, Mills points out the enormous differences in the scope and impact of action available to persons sitting at the apex of corporate and state power compared to the masses under them both inside and outside of their organizations.[2]

Roles need not always be conceived of as units of an institution or organization. General social roles of considerable importance, which shall be dealt with in Chapter 13, are sex roles, which prescribe the meanings and expectations attached to being male or female in a given society. We shall note how the actual performance of sex roles is in many quarters being subjected to change. Some observers argue that sex roles are largely biologically rooted, resulting in distinctly male and distinctly female behavior, which then has been set up as cultural ideals. However, the range of observed differences between sex roles in various societies, and even within societies, would suggest that cultural expectations are far more influential than biological dispositions. Even if genetic propensities were present, which rendered men, say, practical and women emotional, these propensities must still receive cultural definition appropriate to the needs of a given society. The women's liberation movement may as well give up now if sex roles are genetically determined. But we know that men *can* cook and tend children and that women *can* run a business and use tools; men can be gentle and sympathetic and women can be violent and hard-hearted.

In a racially mixed society, particularly in one ordered hierarchically by color, much behavior has been culturally prescribed regarding appropriate roles and in interracial contact. Typically, the lighter one's skin the more deference is expected and the darker the skin the more deference is to be displayed. Like sex roles, race roles are slowly being overturned in many areas of the world. Age also tends to carry with it special prerogatives and expectations; the child, the youth, the adult, and the aged find a number of rights and responsibilities set out for them by cultural definition.

The individual steps in and out of various roles throughout life; more than one role is usually assumed at any given point in time. The transition from one to another may be traumatic, as from active work into retirement is for many, or it may be eagerly anticipated, as from childhood to youth. Roles may conflict and compete with one another, as many careers do with being a father or a mother, or as being a devout religious believer may with being a military participant. Role inconsistencies and contradictions may go unrecognized, they may be rationalized away, or they may be recognized and struggled with. Some contradictions may be resolved by abandoning one of the roles. Role contradictions may be re-

---

[2] C. Wright Mills, *The Power Elite* (New York: Oxford University Press, 1956), p. 25.

solved by leaving a big gap between the ideal expectations and the real performances, as when the adherent of a pacifist religion participates in a war of aggression, or when expectations of brotherhood and equality are sacrificed for hatred and prejudice.

Among the most blatant role contradictions in American life is what Gunnar Myrdal called "an American dilemma."[3] The dilemma to which Myrdal refers is that which Americans suffer from embracing Christian-democratic definitions and expectations while also holding to a number of unChristian and undemocratic valuations defining relations between blacks and whites. Frank Westie has given Myrdal's thesis an empirical test in a sample of Indianapolis persons in an attempt to ascertain the actual extent of contradicting valuations, the awareness of inconsistency when present, and how it tends to be resolved.[4] Westie found that virtually all of his respondents agreed with *general*-level statements concerning equality of opportunity, helping one another in time of need, and brotherhood among men. However, when queried on *specific* statements, such as if willing to have a Negro supervisor at work (equality of opportunity), only 60 percent agreed; if willing to take a Negro into the home at night if the Negro's home had burned (helping one another), only 64 percent agreed; and if willing to invite Negroes to a dinner party in the home (brotherhood), only 29 percent agreed. In short, the dilemma of which Myrdal speaks is indeed factual for many persons, but certainly not for all.

But how many of Westie's respondents who gave inconsistent responses recognized their inconsistency? Forty-two percent *admitted* either voluntarily (60 percent of these) or under probing (40 percent) that they responded inconsistently; 43 percent recognized the "apparent" inconsistency but *denied* their responses were inconsistent; and 16 percent *did not recognize* any inconsistency, even under probing. (It is noteworthy that many of the respondents who responded consistently to the paired statements, and an overall majority did, volunteered explanations for their *consistency*.) Persons who were inconsistent and admitted it, or claimed their inconsistency was only "apparent," either invoked justifications and qualifications or simply accepted their inconsistency at face value. Significantly, most of the adjustments and qualifications were made at the level of the *specific* statement on Negroes rather than on the *general* level, leaving the abstract Christian-democratic ideology intact.

NORMS

Beneath the institution, even beneath the role, lies the norm. A norm is a rule or instruction. Norms are general, sometimes specific, cultural indications of what people *should* or *ought* to do under certain circumstances (as distinct from the statistically normal or what people, in fact, do). Like all other aspects of culture, norms arise from the social inter-

---

[3] Gunnar Myrdal, with Richard Sterner and Arnold Rose, *An American Dilemma* (New York: Harper, 1944).

[4] Frank R. Westie, "The American Dilemma: An Empirical Test," *American Sociological Review*, 30 (August 1965), pp. 527–38.

action process.[5] When grouped together in an organized pattern to guide a person's actions in a specific sphere of life, norms constitute a role. When in the form of roles, then, norms are reciprocal, inasmuch as they state appropriate modes of conduct *between* people. For example, fathers should love and support their children; soldiers should kill the enemy; and a person should not drive so as to endanger others.

Some norms carry relatively little importance and are lightly held and weakly sanctioned. Sumner called such norms *folk-ways*.[6] Others are of a more serious nature, invested with considerable emotion, and severely sanctioned; they are considered essential to the life of the group. Norms of this type Sumner called *mores*. A man walking down a big city street on a summer day without a shirt on may raise eyebrows and evoke comments, but if he takes his pants and shorts off he will probably bring out a paddy wagon. The man would have moved from a violation of folkways governing appearance or dress to a violation of sex codes. In addition to sex codes, norms governing property and physical safety are held in utmost sanctity, the former of these are sometimes given even more importance than the latter. Folkways and mores for a continuum from the relatively nonessential to the essential, from topless to rape, from petty theft to grand larceny, and from shoving to murder.

Norms may be traditional in origin or enacted in law. Violation of norms may be informally sanctioned within family, friends, and public (reprimand, gossip, ostracism) or formally sanctioned by an organization (demotion, suspension, firing) or the state (fine, imprisonment, death). The severity of the sanction is supposedly commensurate with the importance of the norm, but inconsistencies abound. For example, what possible rationale is there for sending a person to jail for four years for smoking a physically relatively harmless weed, while imposing a suspended 60-day sentence and $50 fine on a drunken driver endangering the lives of many persons? Or, what sense is there in setting a mere $50,000 fine on an industry that has polluted the priceless waters of a Great Lake?

Traditional norms considered essential to the existence of a society become laws backed by formal enforcement. Sumner argued that law must conform to traditional practice and that men cannot legislate mores. The opposing view is that law can be applied in some instances as an independent force of change if authoritative, illustrated by appropriate models, and consistently enforced.[7] In areas of personal morality such as sex, alcohol, and drugs, the law has proven singularly unsuccessful, if not exacerbating. By contrast, in many areas of interpersonal relations, or social morality, law has proven to be a very effective tool of social

---

[5] For an original treatment on the links between norms, personality, and the interaction process, see Muzafer Sherif, *The Psychology of Social Norms* (New York: Harper Torchbooks, 1969, originally published 1936).

[6] William Graham Sumner, *Folkways* (Boston: Ginn & Company, Publishers, 1907).

[7] William M. Evan, "Law as an Instrument of Social Change," in Alvin Gouldner and S.M. Miller, eds., *Applied Sociology* (New York: The Free Press, 1965), pp. 285–93.

change. Laws governing marriage and family relations in places such as China and the Middle East are substantially altering traditional kinship mores. In the United States, civil rights laws have had a marked impact on race relations, despite the fact that neither government authority, models, or enforcement have been employed with much conviction. Given the U.S. Supreme Court's liberal decision on abortion law, we are likely to see a broad shift within the population toward a majority acceptance of abortion; this is not to overlook the important social pressures brought to bear on the Court by an activist minority made up largely of women.

However, the most sacred mores of our society are those surrounding private property. While including property at the personal level, a level which socialist society also recognizes as legitimate, the realm of production property is that which is the essential core of capitalist survival. Any violation of laws in this area of private ownership of the means of production does indeed threaten the system's survival. Social ownership is permissible only where the production of goods and services may not be profitable (such as a faltering passenger rail system) or must by its nature be publically organized (such as the military). In the case of the latter, public organization is still employed as a device for private profit such as among the arms industries. The most highly paid lawyers concern themselves with the regulations governing corporate property, and many high ranking politicians including the influential Secretary of State John Foster Dulles in years past and Richard Nixon today were in private life concerned with corporate law. An attack on the mores of private ownership, no matter how large and socially essential the firm, is considered heretical. The entire structure of the state is designed to preserve the integrity of private ownership and control of the means of production; if government is law, the chief concern of law is private property. The "overthrow of the state" is of life and death concern to economic elites not because they are dedicated to democracy or government by the people, but because the state is their first and only line of defense to preserve their power and privilege against the people. Since the 1930s, the state has not only proven to be the legal guarantor of corporate property, it has been its economic lifeblood and savior.

Obedience and dissent

Why are norms obeyed? Obviously, people do not mechanically "internalize" norms and conform to them simply because norms are norms, much as they pull their hands away from fire because it is hot. Behaviorists tell us people conform to norms because they fear punishment and seek reward. Thus, we are led to believe that there is nothing inherently good or bad, right or wrong, about any given interpersonal act or role per se that would in itself lead an individual to perform or not to perform it. The same act or role may be considered right or wrong depending upon how the person has been "conditioned" (in the manner of electrodes on a rat) through punishment and reward. We would all probably agree that a reward-and-punishment schedule produces desire and fear and can exact considerable conformity as a result (in Orwell's *1984* enough electricity made Winston see five fingers on Thought Policeman O'Brien's hand when the latter held up only four).[8] But as Asch has astutely queried, how do reward and punishment produce the experience of should or obligation, of right and wrong?[9] How is a person conditioned to exercise responsibility, concern, honesty, interest, and other human virtues? Do all cultures possess some universal system of conditioning that the behaviorists haven't yet discovered?

Asch argues that men are externally oriented and are concerned with acting in a way relevant to the needs of others. He contends that we sense a certain requiredness or demand in most important interpersonal situations. Thus, very similar ethical principles are applied in all cultures, however great might be the differences in the perception and definition of the situation. For example, cultural differences exist as to the scope and limits of a person's responsibility, concern, honesty, and interest, frequently ending at the boundaries of one's own "tribe." Yet, world religions and humanism supersede tribal boundaries, and all share common ethical imperatives, doubtfully arrived at by "conditioning." "Define a situation as real as it is real in its consequences." Such were the classic words of W.I. Thomas. And Asch has ingeniously demonstrated the powerful influence of group definitions on members.[10] The critical question thus becomes; Who defines the situation? Obviously not the rat. The rat is within rather narrow limits forced to be what the experimenter wants him to be.

Yet, as elites here and elsewhere are finding out, the bureaucratic-behaviorist world view (i.e., the view that humans have an infinite capacity to endure conditioning to forced alternatives) can run up against what Asch would call the inherent requiredness of a situation. For example, take the situation of black America: A woman felt she *was required not* to give up her seat to a white man on a Montgomery, Alabama, bus. Several college students in North Carolina felt that a white lunch counter *should be required* to serve them food. An Air Force veteran felt that the state supported University of Mississippi *ought to be required* to let him enroll as a student. Poverty workers felt that basic economic changes *are required* to eliminate deprivation amid abundance. Over 150,000 blacks rebelled violently during 1964–68 against what they thought were *unrequired* injustices of their situation. The thousands of young men who defied their conditioning to conform blindly to the state's "patriotic" call to military duty since the mid-60s decided they *should not be required* to participate in an immoral war in Southeast Asia. As both blacks and war resisters have learned, to defy the behaviorists "laws" of learning can be very painful. Yet, both persisted in their struggles.

Quite predictably, people with vested interests in the bureaucratic-behaviorist world view, whatever the situation, are responding by labeling those who oppose them as "deviants." Opposition culture does in fact

---

[8] George Orwell, *1984* (New York: Signet Books, 1961), p. 13.

[9] Solomon Asch, *Social Psychology* (Englewood Cliffs, N.J.: Prentice-Hall, Inc., 1952), p. 372.

[10] Ibid., Chapter 16.

deviate from many existing economic and bureaucratic institutions designed to serve the powerful and control the powerless. But as Horowitz and Liebowitz have cogently argued, those who have engaged in protest activities and civil disobedience *are not* deviants in terms of the requirements of democracy.[11] Organized welfare recipients, student activists, black militants, wildcat strikers, and many youth gangs, argue Horowitz and Liebowitz, are not deranged or criminal groups but rather are challenging the legitimacy of oppressive political and social institutions.

Empirical data tend to support the view that people often perceive moral requirements in a social situation if they have achieved a direct familiarity with a particular situation. For example, whites who have regular contact with blacks and are socially informed, that is, whites who do not relate to blacks entirely in terms of externally imposed stereotypes, are much more likely to trace the causes of riots to social injustices and to stress social reform than are racially uninformed and unexposed whites, who trace causes to outside agitators and stress punitive solutions.[12] Though it often fails, liberal education should help emancipate a person from the restrictions of tradition and help him to see the human requirements of a situation. Thus, Olsen reports that persons with postgraduate education were twice as likely to consider such types of "deviance" as boycotts, strikes, and mass demonstrations as legitimate means of attaining fair treatment in jobs and housing as persons who had only attended college, while those with college experience were twice as likely to approve of these strategies as those with only high school education.[13] Finally, Spaeth reports that persons with college education and persons under 25 years old were about twice as likely to be sympathetic with student militancy as less educated and older persons.[14] These studies together suggest that people who come into direct contact with human problems and have achieved a degree of personal freedom from the restraints of stereotyping and conditioning are much less likely to interpret protest actions and civil disobedience as deviant behavior, but rather as legitimate requirements of an unjust situation.

Types of deviance

That there is considerable deviance from group norms, justifiable or unjustifiable, is evident to all. For example, by 1971, reported crimes against persons were up to 393 per 100,000 inhabitants from 160 in 1960, while crimes against property had risen to 2,514 per 100,000 in-

---

[11] Irving Louis Horowitz and Martin Liebowitz, "Social Deviance and Political Marginality: Toward a Redefinition of the Relations between Sociology and Politics," *Social Problems*, 15 (Winter 1968), pp. 280–96.

[12] Vincent Jeffries and H. Edward Ransford, "Interracial Social Contact and Middle-Class White Reactions to the Watts Riot," *Social Problems,* 16 (Winter 1968), pp. 312–29.

[13] Marvin E. Olsen, "Perceived Legitimacy of Social Protest Actions," *Social Problems,* 15 (Winter 1968), pp. 297–310.

[14] Joe L. Spaeth, "Public Reactions to College Student Protests," *Sociology of Education,* 42 (Spring 1969).

habitants from 967.[15] In 1970, government spent over $8.6 billion for police protection, correction, and courts compared with $4.6 billion in 1965 and $3.3 billion in 1960. Police expenditures of $5.1 billion in 1970 were alone one-half billion dollars more than all combined costs in 1965! That crime is a major problem in America today no one will deny, especially not low-income residents of the inner city. What far fewer people will admit is that the causes of much personal deviance cannot be traced to a deterioration of individual American citizens but rather to an irresponsible use of power. And this is not alluding mainly to the kind of organized greed that motivates large corporations to bedazzle the public, including the have-nots, with advertising for consumer products, while at the same time creating conditions for many that make it difficult or impossible for them to legally earn the money to buy them. Such stimulants to crime are obvious enough.

What is a less obvious but perhaps more important source of criminal behavior is the model set by the powerful themselves. People learn through a process of identification and imitation. The powerful themselves are among the nation's most habitual criminals. Ferdinand Lundberg reminds us that from 1945 to 1965 the Federal Trade Commission issued almost 4,000 cease-and-desist orders for legal violations by businesses for false advertising, false endorsements, removing or concealing law-required markings, false invoicing, mislabeling, deceptive pricing, obtaining information by subterfuge, and a number of other legally defined crimes.[16] In 1914, the Clayton Act prohibited interlocking directorships in corporations, yet this and two subsequent reinforcing statutes are violated with impunity. Fully 60 percent of America's leading corporations have had at least four court convictions for violating government acts and rulings. For example, General Electric Corporation and Westinghouse Electric Corporation were charged and found guilty of conspiracy to fix prices, rig bids, divide markets in secret cartels on electrical equipment, and other related criminal activities. The sentence? Twenty-four General Electric and Westinghouse officials were given *suspended* jail sentences and fined a few thousand dollars.[17] A company vice president was given 30 days, the usual police-court sentence for disorderly conduct. (All costs were ruled tax deductible by the Internal Revenue Service as a "business expense.") Elsewhere in high places, including state and federal governments, the violation of civil rights legislation has been openly flaunted. Beyond that, the American government by its actions in Vietnam has violated world agreements as written in the Charter of the United Nations and the Geneva Accords. More recently, and in many ways the most archetypical of modern day elite crimes, we have witnessed the exposures, indictments, and convictions surrounding the Committee to Re-elect the President's 1972 involvement in the sabotage of the Democratic Party and related acts of political espi-

---

[15] *The American Almanac* (New York: Grosset & Dunlap, Inc., 1973), p. 193.

[16] Ferdinand Lundberg, *The Rich and the Super Rich* (New York: Ballantine Books, 1969), p. 137.

[17] Ibid., p. 142.

onage and attempted cover-ups involving a series of high administration officials. Newly enacted campaign laws governing financial contributions were violated with impunity by top Committee fund raisers and corporate executives.

Little wonder, then, that the call for law and order often rings hollow to those who have witnessed so much lawbreaking on high. Obviously, much of the harping on law and order is concerned not so much with legal justice and democratic order as it is with the enforcement and protection of old hierarchies of privilege and power.

ANOMIE

The term "anomie" was used by Durkheim to refer to the separation or cutting-off of individuals from mutually binding organizational and moral norms. Durkheim argued that the members of urban industrial society had been torn from the community-binding and socially cohesive norms of traditional agrarian society ("mechanical solidarity") and thrown into a highly fluid and mobile urban society.[18] The result has been the threat and existence of social discontinuity and normlessness, of anomie. Moreover, industrial man has been pulled away from the stabilizing influence of deep and regular participation in close-knit groups and thrown back upon personal psychological resources for survival. Durkheim contended that the result of this has been the creation of many egoistic persons lacking the necessary social support for self-control and continuity. Both anomie and egoism, thought Durkheim, were sources of suicide.[19] Durkheim's general theory held that industrial society's complex organization and division of social labor were necessary adhesives to bring people into a community of interdependence and to combat anomie and egoism.[20] (Durkheim also stressed that such "organic solidarity" itself rested upon common values and must be backed up by the force of moral norms.)

Marx's thesis on integration is almost the precise opposite of Durkheim's interpretation. Marx held that the division of labor itself is the condition which *cuts people off* from both their own individuality and harmonious relations with the rest of the society; the division of labor *creates* anomie and egoism rather than these being the result of inadequate integration of people within the division of labor. Marx used the concept of *alienation* to refer to the isolating effect of the division of labor upon the individual and his social relations.

In the anomic condition (we shall employ Durkheim's terminology, since the scholars to be discussed below have done so, even though holding to the Marxist interpretation of anomie and alienation), norms governing behavior are weak and ambiguous. Because of the anxieties and

---

[18] Emile Durkheim, *The Division of Labor in Society*, trans. George Simpson (New York: The Free Press, 1964).

[19] Emile Durkheim, *Suicide* (New York: The Free Press, 1951).

[20] See A.R. Mawson, "Durkheim and Social Pathology," *British Journal of Sociology*, 21 (September 1970), pp. 298–311.

insecurities created by the weakness of integrating norms, the anomic person may react in an extreme manner. Anomic individuals, Fromm has suggested, lose a stable center to themselves and may seek order in life under the guidance and support of an all-powerful dictator or government.[21] Fromm applied the thesis to Hitler's Germany, but parallels may also be drawn with some segments of other societies today.[22] Fromm's thesis finds empirical support in the research of McClosky and Schaar, who discovered that persons high in anomie tended toward authoritarianism, chauvinism, rigidity, aggression, and inflexibility.[23] By contrast, persons with flexible intellectual orientation and political awareness tended to score low in anomie. What the anomic person may lack is a self-governing control system. In this sense the anomic person is similar to an unprogrammed robot. But like the robot, the anomic person is a prime candidate for *external* control and "programming."

Social critics such as Fromm, Aldous Huxley, and C. Wright Mills have expressed serious concern over trends toward totally planned and completely rationalized societies in which human beings have been reduced to automatons and cheerful robots. And none of these three men consider a totalitarianism based on terror and coercion as the prime threat, and certainly not as the most effective variety, of totalitarianism. The brand of totalitarianism these men fear is one based on manipulation and social engineering; citizens become *cheerful* robots and love their servitude. In Mills's words, "We know that men can be turned by coercion into robots. We did not know before our own times that they could cheerfully and willingly turn themselves into robots."[24] Thus, Fromm declares that the problem is no longer whether men can build robots acting like men but whether men can be prevented from becoming robots.[25]

Huxley surmises that a really efficient totalitarian state would be one in which all-powerful political bosses and managers control a population of slaves who do not have to be coerced, because they love their servitude.[26] How is it possible to impose successfully a totalitarian system of control upon a society? First, economic security must be assured. Huxley then cites the mass media as a foremost tool of propaganda and brainwashing. Although the mass media are also indispensable to the

---

[21] Erich Fromm, *Escape from Freedom* (New York: Holt, Rinehart, & Winston, Inc., 1941); see also by Fromm, *The Sane Society* (New York: Fawcett Books, 1967).

[22] William L. Shirer, "The *Hubris* of a President," *The Nation*, January 22, 1973, p. 107.

[23] Herbert McClosky and John H. Schaar, "Psychological Dimensions of Anomie," *American Sociological Review*, 30 (February 1965), pp. 14–40. See the theoretical analysis of anomie and related concepts as they pertain to contemporary political life in Charles Hampden-Turner, *Radical Man* (Cambridge, Mass.: Schenkman Publishing Company, 1970).

[24] C. Wright Mills, *Power, Politics, and People*, ed. Irving Louis Horowitz (New York: Oxford University Press, 1967), p. 155.

[25] Erich Fromm, *The Revolution of Hope* (New York: Harper & Row, Publishers, 1968), p. 43.

[26] Aldous Huxley, *Brave New World* (New York: Bantam Books, 1955); also *Brave New World Revisited* (New York: Harper and Row, Publishers, 1965).

survival of modern democracy, they are mainly used for nonstop and irrelevant distractions equivalent to the feelies, orgy-porgy, and centrifugal bumblepuppy of a *Brave New World*. Even politics is reduced to mindless entertainment and sideshow. Also indispensable to complete social control would be widely used and physiologically harmless narcotics, like *Brave New World*'s Soma. Even now, about half of the American population, young and old, depends upon some form of drug for regular relief from the monotony of work and life (or perhaps to add some joy to work and life). Huxley suggests further that sexual freedom as well as drugs would help compensate for the loss of political and economic freedom. Finally, scientists would be required to refine a science of human differences, so each person could be properly placed, and develop a system of genetics designed to standardize the human product to facilitate the task of managers. This is sheer fantasy for any foreseeable future, but corporations and governments are today using social science more than ever before in their efforts at control.[27] In the place of collective self-control, the Fromms and Huxleys argue, we are faced with the specter of monolithic bureaucratic control by managers and their technical staffs, whose operations cannot afford curiosity, spontaneity, questioning, or dissent among the ruled.

The research of psychologist Stanley Milgram offers some empirical support to the thinking of men like Mills, Fromm, and Huxley.[28] Milgram instructed his subjects to administer punishment (supposedly but not really an electric shock) to a person in a contrived learning experiment every time the "learner" erred. (Perhaps Milgram was testing to see how many of Orwell's O'Briens there are in American society.) Fully 62 percent of the subjects obeyed the experimenter's commands, to the point of administering the top shock level (450 volts) to the erring learner. Milgram observed several other relationships in his study, such as a decline in obedience when the experimenter gave commands in absentia or when the learner was in direct physical presence and contact with the subject (bombing from 30,000 feet presents less of a problem of conscience than direct rifle fire). But suffice it to say here that many of Milgram's subjects performed admirably as automatons, despite frequent *verbal* protests, in a carefully controlled experimental situation that there is no reason for us to believe was not taken for real by the subjects. Certain of Milgram's critics contend his entire study is invalid, inasmuch as his subjects knew it was only a laboratory experiment. The conduct of the experiment itself raises serious ethical questions about the proper role of social research.

Provided our managers and experts do not lead us on in interminable wars or into nuclear holocaust, why not let them establish social, politi-

---

[27] On social science and human freedom, see Floyd Matson, *The Broken Image* (New York: Doubleday & Company, Inc., 1966).

[28] Stanley Milgram, "Some Conditions of Obedience and Disobedience to Authority," *International Journal of Psychiatry*, 6 (October 1968), pp. 259–80.

cal, and economic norms and exercise more or less complete control? If we are all comfortable and secure, what's wrong with a *Walden Two* type of society?[29] The democratic argument against such a bureaucratically managed system would be that viable social, political, and economic norms emerge from the free play of interacting individuals who experiment with, conjecture, question, and debate the myriad of alternative life styles available to man and allow for a great diversity of livelihood within a society. Collective achievement is gained through individual and group effort, not through the dictates and paternalism of experts. Perhaps experts are available to design bridges and sewer systems, but thus far no group of managers and experts can design the good society or even a component part of it. Indeed, decision-making elites have displayed their human frailty in governing the life of society by being perilously close to destroying us all and visiting irreparable damage on our environment.

The image of the cheerful robot must not be exaggerated. The fact that the nation is spending well over $5 billion on police alone should suggest that there are large numbers of people who are not cheerful and are not robots. Workers, minorities, students, housewives, the poor, and other groups have exhibited substantial amounts of activism and militance—to the point that many politicians have made "law and order" their abiding campaign theme. (This is not to overlook the rights of the individual to personal freedoms and safety and the need for collectively-designated authority to promote and protect these rights.) We should also note in this connection that such a campaign theme has proven itself far from being a very successful one.

SOCIAL INTERACTION

We have examined thus far in this chapter the cultural components of society, whether as seen as in their ideal or actual behavioral manifestations. For the remainder of the chapter we shall consider aspects of the social process itself, including social interaction, the self, primary groups, and reference groups.

The term "interaction" may have many referents—such as the interaction of chickens in a barnyard, pool balls on a gameroom table, or protons in an atom. Our concern, obviously, is with human or social interaction. "Social" may be used with reference to some animal behavior if thought of in the most general sense, but most sociologists would prefer to limit the use of social interaction to people: only humans have the capacity to intelligently take one another into account, to symbolically project themselves into the minds of others, and to mentally reconstruct a situation from the standpoint of another. (By the same token, only humans can study themselves.) In the language of George H. Mead, who gave seminal treatment to the concept of social interaction, people have

---

[29] For an experimental psychologist's conception of the planned society, see B.F. Skinner, *Walden Two* (New York: Macmillan Company, 1962).

the capacity to "take the role of the other."[30] Mead stressed man's natural capacity for empathy, that is, the mental faculty to "get into" the psychological processes of others, both present and not present, and anticipate their possible actions and responses vis-à-vis one's own action and response.[31]

The ability to recreate in one's own mind that which is happening in another's mind is a prerequisite to the acquisition of symbolic communication and verbal meanings. Indeed, human interaction *is* symbolic interaction, for interaction is meaningful or intelligent only when the participants share a common universe or community of symbols, words, or names. Symbols and their meanings provide the content and the coloration, the flesh and blood, of an originally amorphous empathic capacity and relatively vacuous interaction. Symbols tell us what to expect as we meet another and inform us as to the meaning of the encounter for ourselves and our future. As noted below, empathy or role-taking capacity is thus a prerequisite to the emergence of the self-conceiving individual. To achieve the feelings and idea of a conscious self, we must first see ourselves through the eyes of others. Charles Horton Cooley conveyed this notion well through the metaphor of "the looking glass self."[32] The particular *kind* of self-image we have, be it good or bad, worthy or unworthy, is ascertained through our interpretations of the meaning of the various symbols used with reference to us in our various social situations. We shall have more to learn concerning the self, presently.

Also incorporated into the process of role-taking and social interaction is what W.I. Thomas called "the definition of the situation." Each participant attempts to identify socially and to place the other so that interaction may proceed as effectively and intelligently as possible. Socially defining clues and information may be derived from the physical setting itself, the personal appearance of the other, direct verbal exchange, and indirect expressions.[33] The greater is the ability and accuracy in taking the role of the other and defining the situation, the less is the probability for misunderstanding or mistakes.

Finally, we may observe that the interaction process involves not only imaginatively taking the role of the other in the attempt to anticipate and respond to the actions of the other, but also anticipating and responding to our own actions. We ask ourselves, how will the other

[30] George H. Mead, *Mind, Self, and Society* (Chicago: University of Chicago Press, 1934); for an analysis of Mead's thought, see Paul E. Pfeutz, *Self, Society, Existence* (New York: Harper Torchbooks, 1961). For a collection of research papers related to Mead's theories, see Jerome G. Manis and Bernard N. Meltzer, *Symbolic Interaction*, 2d ed. (Boston: Allyn & Bacon, Inc., 1972). On symbolic interaction theory, see also Arnold M. Rose, ed. *Human Behavior and Social Processes* (Boston: Houghton Mifflin Company, 1962).

[31] We might note, however, that recent research on chimpanzees indicates that we may have to be increasingly cautious about limiting assumptions regarding empathic capacity to humans.

[32] Charles Horton Cooley, *Human Nature and the Social Order* (New York: The Free Press, 1956).

[33] See the writings of Erving Goffman, especially *The Presentation of Self in Everyday Life* (New York: Doubleday & Company, Inc., 1959).

respond to my actions and what might be the consequences of my action for my own future alternatives? One of the recurrent questions appearing in the text has to do with the range of alternative actions available to individuals and how the actions of others tend to either enhance or delimit that range. Persons who are able to control definitions of social situations are also able to exercise greater alternatives in their own actions, while possibly narrowing the scope of actions for others. While many social situations are relatively mundane and unimportant, the ability to control the definitions of certain other social situations have far-reaching impact and importance, especially in the milieu of national economic and political life. Three U.S. presidents for ten years rather successfully controlled the public's definition of what Vietnam was about, while they and two presidents before them helped establish the definitions that led to the Cold War and arms race (see Chapter 9).

THE SELF

As both Cooley and Mead stressed, the self-conceiving, self-knowing individual arises through the process of social interaction, particularly within the family and friendship groups. The social process is something of a midwife to the biological individual, nurturing it into a self-conceiving person and a practicing member of society.[34] Thus, we are not born with a self; it is not that easy. We must struggle to achieve a self and struggle even harder to achieve a favorable self-concept. Central to the acquisition of self is the phenomenon of role-taking, the interaction process whereby one person projects himself into the mind of another. The significance of role-taking to the emergence of self lies in the necessity for transcendence in the acquisition of self. As noted previously, only by taking the attitude of another or momentarily being another are we able to get a view of ourselves; hence, we have Cooley's notion of the looking-glass self. Symbols provide the medium through which we come to define the kind of self we shall have, that is, whether we think of ourselves as competent or incompetent, beautiful or ugly, black or white, Protestant or Catholic, and so on.

Thus, the development of self-definition awaits the acquisition of language. A linguistic facility sufficient to the development of self-definition is not acquired until around one and a half to two years of age, though an amorphous sense of self occurs earlier and a differentiation between body and environment much earlier. But these early forms of self-experience are not clearly articulated in the individual's mind, and he cannot enjoy specific compliments, or suffer lasting humiliation, or contemplate personal success or failure. Only with a more complete grasp of meanings and a refinement of role-taking abilities can we see ourselves in such light. Obviously, small children are not themselves required to speak to

---

[34] For a summary discussion of theory and research on the self, see Leonard S. Cottrell, Jr., "Interpersonal Interaction and the Development of the Self," in David A. Goslin, ed., *Handbook of Socialization Theory and Research* (Chicago: Rand McNally and Company, 1969), pp. 543–70.

achieve the beginnings of a self; they "understand" the praises and ad-monitions, directions and orders of parents before beginning to sound out their own rudimentary versions of the words they hear.

In addition to the maturation process of infancy, Mead suggests that a child passes through two broad stages in the development of self.[35] First, the child passes through the *play* stage, in which he takes the role of one other person at a time. Here, self-image is not well organized or stable, as the child moves from one specific act of role-taking to another in disparate fashion. Not only does the child try to take the role of people he is with or imagines himself to be with, he actually attempts to play the role of father, mother, cowboy, nurse, teacher, and with increasing trepidation, soldier and policeman. A favorite form of play is to exchange roles with a peer, and often clothes as well for an added dimension of reality. By serially taking and playing roles of significant others, the child is able to get a better outside view of himself and thus contribute to the organization of self. Later, about the time he enters school, the child enters the *game* stage, in which the much more complex task of simul-taneously taking the roles of several other persons is encountered. Games involving second and third parties are important in the developmental process, for they require that the child try to anticipate the moves of others and fit them into his own plans. Every additional player places greater demands upon role-taking. Clearly, this complex form of role-taking is a prerequisite to participation in larger cooperative enterprises within society.

Out of the game stage Mead conceptualizes the idea of the *generalized other*. By the generalized other Mead refers to a person's synthesized view of what his group or society has defined as normal and is expecting of him. The generalized other is to the individual the objectification of his group's definitions and expectations, the embodiment of a system of social rules or norms. Thus, it stands that the contents of the generalized other may differ from one person or group to the next, depending on the extent of value and normative consensus in a society. It also stands that the generalized other is subject to modification and change through in-novations in the substratum of interaction as it generates new definitions and expectations. The generalized other may be likened to cultural norms in their ideal forms, which are subject to change when and if actual behavior shifts to new grounds. For example, the generalized other has for many people become less and less proscriptive of abortions; with legal authority behind abortion, the proscription is likely to weaken further.

Aspects of self-concept

Self-concept represents the more cognitive aspect of self, the sym-bolically articulated or defined side of personal existence. Self-concept informs the more fundamental range of emotional feelings that reside

---

[35] See Mead's *Mind, Self, and Society* for a full understanding of his theories of the genesis of consciousness, perception, intelligence, and self. On the ac-quisition of values see Jean Piaget, *The Moral Judgment of the Child* (Glencoe: The Free Press, 1948).

at the core of the self as to its more specific traits and qualities. The behavior of men is importantly influenced by their self-concepts, and their behavior importantly conditions the definitions they give to themselves. And, the social milieus within which people must live and work greatly shape both behavior and self-concept.

Self-conception is derived from *our perceptions* of how others view us, not the *actual* views of others. The congruence between our perceptions and the actual response of others depends on our own role-taking accuracy. If the congruence is low, interaction may be impaired and our participation in groups difficult and frustrating; this, in turn, may lead to ostracism or withdrawal or the crystallization of any of a number of defense mechanisms for the self.

Self-concept is at first loosely organized and subject to sharp fluctuations. As self-concept develops, it becomes more stable and immune to isolated instances of challenge and contradiction. The child adds and subtracts, and raises and lowers, aspects of self-concept on short notice and with considerable regularity. By contrast, the mature self tends to sift and sort from among current appraisals that tend to harmonize with self-concept. An adult tends to select the evaluations of only significant others and a circle of associates felt to be competent judges of his or her behavior. However, social functioning may be seriously impaired if the self is completely impervious to critical messages and unable to undergo realistic modification. Lyndon Johnson as president was, despite his desire to be everybody's president, a tragic illustration of how shutting off the critical world led to difficulties and downfall. At the other extreme, the person who is unable to do any screening of evaluations and reacts to every negative challenge and contradiction of self-concept is very likely to experience acute anxieties and self-deprecation. The widespread use of T(training)-groups to help people to develop accurate perceptions of others and self may have salutary results for some participants, but the T-group experience may have very harmful consequences for people with fragile self-conceptions or weak ego structures.[36] Furthermore, T-groups are unlikely to have any effect whatsoever on the psychopathic personality adept at charm and manipulation but unable to develop an emotional relationship. The pseudo friendly atmosphere of the T-group is merely apt to convince the psychopath of the impossibility of warmth in interpersonal relations.

Just as a badly deprecated self-concept or one out of touch with actual responses of others impairs social relations, so does a favorable self-concept or a self-concept congruent with the evaluations of others enhance interpersonal adjustment. To take just one example, Litman discovered that a large majority of hospital patients with a favorable self-concept were responding very positively to physical rehabilitation, whereas those with a poor self-image were failing to respond well.[37] Various studies of occupational achievement have also attested to the

---

[36] Michael Argyle, *The Psychology of Interpersonal Behavior* (Baltimore: Penguin Books, Inc., 1967).

[37] Theodore J. Litman, "Self-Conception and Physical Rehabilitation," in Rose, *Human Behavior and Social Processes*, p. 561.

importance of self-image in terms of both success and failure. Though self-concept is obviously itself conditioned by these kinds of successes and failures, it has a powerful independent influence in itself.

Certain aspects of self-concept are socially predefined or "built in" to social positions and then claimed or taken over when the person enters these roles. For example, the marine must be a man, tough, brave, and an efficient killer. The housewife, traditionally speaking, is expected to be a dutiful servant, long-suffering, emotional, eager for motherhood, and unfailing in love. A judge epitomizes honesty, sobriety, and wisdom. Thus we inherit, if only in broad outline, some features of self-concept through the roles we enter.

An interesting question in this regard has to do with whether people choose to enter positions and play roles that tend to be compatible with self-image as it has been formed through childhood and adolescence or if the positions taken up as an adult shape the self. Clearly there is inter-action between the traits a person brings to a position and the expecta-tions and experiences built into the position. It would seem evident that a person's self-image as formed in family and peer-group experiences tends to steer him toward certain positions and situations later in life. Nevertheless, people are often radically transformed by the expectations and experiences of the positions and situations they come or intend to occupy. A person who has lacked college aspirations for self, and seem-ingly the ability, may blossom into a bright student once the opportunity and expectations are directly before him. People apparently lacking in leadership qualities may rise to the challenges if placed in a position of responsibility.

Although a person tends to develop an overall self-concept incorporat-ing several aspects of the self, he often assigns more importance to whatever aspect of self he feels to be the strongest or most highly evalu-ated by others. As Mead pointed out, each person has as many partial self-concepts as he or she has roles in society. Top professionals and successful businessmen tend to weigh heavily their occupational identi-ties, though an increasing number may be almost equally concerned with their golf scores. Parents of 10 children would probably expand the father-mother aspect of self-concept, though not in population-conscious countries such as Japan, where they would be considered insanely irre-sponsible. Student athletes may emphasize their sports prowess while minimizing their scholastic performance, though high school athletes are often excellent students. However, close friends usually do not factor out each separate role for special evaluation or attention. Rather, they size up one another, and thus themselves, as total persons.

Rather surprisingly for a modern society, research suggests that the self-concepts of the majority of American adults are neither very numer-ous nor widely diversified. Mulford and Salisbury reported that in a sam-ple of 1200 Iowa adults an average of only four self-identities were given in an open-ended question asking for a listing of personal identities.[38]

---

[38] Harold A. Mulford and Winfield W. Salisbury, "Self-Conceptions in a Gen-eral Population," in Jerome G. Manis and Bernard N. Meltzer, eds., *Symbolic Interaction* (Boston: Allyn and Bacon, Inc., 1967), pp. 268–78.

Men tended to give occupational, family, sex-role, and religious references; women tended to do the same, occupation excluded. Among those with children at home, family references rose sharply.

Crises in identity

The people studied by Mulford and Salisbury represent the "middle Americans," the established and stable rank-and-file citizen. Herbert Gans conducted an extensive study of both a metropolitan suburb and an urban neighborhood and also learned that the inhabitants were largely content with such routine identities as those involving family, job, peer group, and ethnic or religious group.[39] Thus, the majority of the population would not seem to be involved in any identity crises. However, Orrin Klapp argues that there are a sufficient number of people who are dissatisfied or confused about their personal identities to warrant sociological concern.[40] Klapp notes such symptoms as oversensitivity, excessive self-concern, a feeling of worthlessness and being unappreciated, or a desire to be something or somebody else. Among the roots of the crises in identity Klapp perceives the breaking up of old traditions, minority rejection, much mobility, occupational dissatisfaction, boredom, and empty affluence. Attempts to fill the identity void tend to take the form of collective pursuits such as cultism, hero worship, fanatical crusading, pseudo-religious groups, style masquerades, etc.

Klapp would seem to be directing our attention to what we discussed in the previous chapter as a fail counterculture; that is, a superficially rebellious subculture in all likelihood lacking in any real force of change. This "style rebellion" is most conspicuous among the nation's youth and young adults. Its roots, as Klapp specifies, are those of alienation, of the severing of the individual from productive relations with himself and with others. The symptoms mirror this separation insofar as they concern preoccupation with the self; insofar as they are collective pursuits, the solutions attempted reflect the search for alternative forms of social involvement.

Asch cogently clarified the foregoing points in the following manner: ". . . accentuation of the self is often a response not to powerful ego-centered tendencies but to the thwarting and defeat of the need to be a part of one's group, to know that one is respected and liked, to feel that one is playing a part in the lives of others and that there are issues larger than oneself that unite one with others."[41] Asch goes on to say that "The individual has an imperious need to care for things outside himself, to be of significance to them, and for them to be significant to him. These are among the most powerful needs; in their behalf men are willing to put forth the utmost effort." If social institutions will not accommodate these propensities and contradict man's character, writes Asch, men turn

---

[39] Herbert J. Gans, *The Levittowners* (New York: Pantheon Books, Inc., 1967); and *The Urban Villagers* (New York: The Free Press, 1965).

[40] Orrin Klapp, *Collective Search for Identity* (New York: Holt, Rinehart & Winston, Inc., 1969).

[41] Asch, *Social Psychology*, p. 320.

the same potentialities towards the self: "Self-centeredness is the revenge that the ego exacts under these conditions."[42]

It should be added here that the identity-seekers analyzed by Klapp and Asch are certainly not in a majority even among youth. The majority of youth are essentially traditional and oriented toward the adult world of family and work. At the other end of the self-society spectrum from the identity-seekers is a category of political and social radicals with exceedingly stable and integrated self-concepts. Research suggests that the radical individual possesses an open, sensitive, adaptive, and constructive personality base.[43]

PRIMARY GROUPS

The concept of primary group, as developed by Cooley, has proven to be very useful.[44] A primary group is composed of one or more primary relationships, relationships in which participants meet on an intimate face-to-face basis and involve their entire personalities rather than segmentalized parts. Virtually no topic is too private and no interest too broad for exclusion in primary interaction and groups. Most important, members of a primary group tend to deal with one another as ends, and valuable as such, asking no more from one another than mere presence and immediacy. Such a relationship stands in sharp relief against much bureaucratic relations, in which participants are viewed as a means to an end and as objects of control. The essential values of a primary group are undemanding concern and spontaneity; that of bureaucracy, unquestioning obedience to a rationalized system of rules. Yet, primary groups may themselves exert strong coercion on members, while bureaucracy may at its best protect individuals from arbitrary and capricious treatment.

Who participates in primary groups? If we are to grow and develop as complete human beings, we all must be a member of a primary group. Some persons spend more time within primary groups than others, but at some point in their life, and usually at all times, everyone has primary-group experience. By "primary," Cooley meant the primary group is the first group an individual enters, first as a member of a family and then as a member of a play group. And throughout life, the primary group(s) continues to be primary in that it is usually the most important group(s) in a person's life. Most of our early learning experiences occur within the primary group. The family is still the basic socializing agent. Our close peers (friends of the same sex and age) in primary groups also mediate crucial experiences and information, both early and throughout life. In industrial society, mass media and schools, for example, may compete with and always interact with primary groups as agencies of social learning.

Thus, the primary group serves modern man as an important if not the most important medium of communication, distilling and interpret-

---

[42] Ibid., p. 321.

[43] Hampden-Turner, *Radical Man.*

[44] Charles Horton Cooley, *Social Organization* (New York: Schocken Books, Inc., 1962), especially Chapter 3.

ing information as it passes through society. Formal organizations and associations perform a similar mediating function with regard to communication, but primary groups within these formal structures tend to give final treatment to communications.[45] Most people arrive at their values, beliefs, and opinions—whether they be religious, economic, or political—mainly through the filter and conduit of primary interaction. Even the potent mass media of television and press are typically interpreted through the communication prisms of labyrinthine primary groups. The informal debate and conversation of primary groups, either within the framework of formal organizations and associations or independently of them, tends to be a bulwark against manipulation (the control of attitudes and behavior unbeknownst to the person himself) by dominant powers in society—though the primary group may serve as a vehicle of control by such dominant social interests as well.

The primary group is the main context not only for the development of the self but for self-realization throughout life. Within the primary group we are best able to express those outgoing qualities that are most distinctly human—cooperation, compassion, interest, and responsibility. (Yet we may recognize that primary groups, especially families, may become boiling cauldrons of hate, though one might argue that much of such rancor is due to isolating pressures originating outside the family or group itself, as for example chronic money shortages among the poor.) Moreover, in the primary group, verbal duels through humorous anecdote, wisecrack, and even insult may be used as acceptable vehicles for individual esteem and recognition.[46] Not only working-class ethnics, white juvenile gang members, and black street-corner men find the primary group crucial to individuality and self-realization; so does most everyone else in modern society.

Primary relations obviously require far more time to develop than do those of the impersonal variety. While we engage in countless passing such "secondary" contacts and join many different organizations throughout our lifetime, we can expect to cultivate fully only a specific number of intimate ties. Nor would most urban people prefer all of their social contacts to be primary ones. Impersonal interaction is an important means of preserving personal privacy; and such more formal and distant relations are absolutely necessary if urban man is to obtain the ends he might seek within primary group life. Yet people today need the give-and-take of the emotional support generated in primary interaction as much as did traditional man in tribal society and perhaps cherishes such intimacy even more. (Some intrepid social researcher might try to ascertain whether the quality of primary-group life is better within our society's youthful communes than it is within a suburban neighborhood.)

---

[45] On the importance of primary groups to communications within a trade union see S.M. Lipset, Martin A. Trow, and James S. Coleman, *Union Democracy* (New York: Doubleday & Company, Inc., 1963).

[46] See Gans, *The Urban Villagers*, Chapter 4; Elliot Liebow, *Tally's Corner* (Boston: Little, Brown and Company, 1967); John Horton, "Time and Cool People," *Trans-action*, 4 (April 1967), pp. 5–12; or Walter B. Miller, "White Gangs," *Trans-action*, 6 (September 1969), pp. 11–26.

Empirical studies

Research confirms the extraordinary importance of primary ties for personal happiness and positive feelings. Derek Phillips found that persons with close friends were considerably more likely to hold positive feelings about life and be very happy than those without close personal ties (happy people, of course, tend to be liked and sought out).[47] Moreover, the correlation between primary social participation and positive feelings held true at all socioeconomic levels studied. However, persons of higher class standings reported greater positive feelings than did those of lower position at similar levels of social participation, suggesting that we cannot live "on love alone." For example, 57 percent of the most socially active (including organizational activity and neighbors known, as well as close friends) respondents of high social status reported high positive feelings, compared to only 36 percent of those with high participation but low status. Likewise, with respect to a question on happiness, Phillips discovered, for example, that only six percent of the low-status respondents with low social participation said they were "very happy," compared with 42 percent of low-status persons with high participation; but again, class standing was important, as 57 percent of high-status and high-participation persons were "very happy." What Phillips's research seems to indicate is that low socioeconomic position can be cushioned by meaningful primary contacts, but such contacts cannot fully compensate for economic insecurity. A final but interesting sidelight of Phillips' research was that the differences between persons with medium and high social involvement were relatively insignificant for positive feelings and happiness. Evidently, the number of primary contacts is not nearly so important as the fact of simply having some minimum amount of primary contact.

Primary contacts have also been found to be critical for morale in the process of adjusting to older age. Lowenthal and Haven reported that the happiest and mentally healthiest older people in their study were those involved in a close personal relationship.[48] Somewhat similar to the Phillips study, the overall number of social contacts was not so important to morale as the existence of at least one stable intimate relationship, for the loss of a single primary tie had a considerably more deleterious effect on morale than a reduction of interaction per se. Moreover, the loss of responsibilities and the consequent decrease in overall social interaction among these elderly respondents were softened if close personal ties were maintained.

Until fairly recently, sociologists believed that the modern city fragments and destroys primary group life.[49] A large body of evidence now

---

[47] Derek L. Phillips, "Social Class, Social Participation, and Happiness," *Sociological Quarterly,* 10 (Winter 1969), pp. 3–21. Positive or negative feelings were measured by questions asking whether respondents felt things were going their way, were interested in something, bored, depressed, etc.

[48] Marjorie Fiske Lowenthal and Clayton Haven, "Interaction and Adaptation: Intimacy as a Critical Variable," *American Sociological Review,* 33 (February 1968), pp. 20–30.

[49] For example, see Louis Wirth, "Urbanism as a Way of Life," *American Journal of Sociology,* 44 (1938), pp. 1–24.

contradicts the thesis that primary groups are vestiges of traditional society.[50] As suggested, primary types of involvement today may be recognized as more important than in traditional society. In the latter type of society, almost all relationships were of the primary variety; for this reason traditional society has been variously termed as primary, or folk, or communal. These names all convey the idea of a more or less homogeneous people and value system that knew few, and accepted fewer, strangers. Family and village relationships tended to be all-inclusive; life itself would have seemed inconceivable without them. In an impersonal urban society, men may cherish primary relationships all the more precisely because life *is* conceivable without them, a dreadful conception to most.

The type and frequency of primary contacts varies substantially within the population. A study by Aida Tomeh indicated that in a metropolitan community younger people (21–34) reported greater primary contact than persons over 50, and persons of higher socioeconomic status more than those of lower.[51] However, at given status levels, single persons were as active in informal group life as married persons, females as much as males, and blacks as much as whites. Overall, *relatives* were found to be the most regular source of primary interaction (61 percent reported informal contact with relatives often), followed by nonrelative friends (46 percent often), neighbors (39 percent often), and co-workers (23 percent often). Interestingly, respondents who indicated high contact for one of these sources were also likely to be high on all of the others, whereas an absence of ties in one area similarly meant a paucity in the others.

Why are neighbors and co-workers less often the source of friendship than relatives and other friends? For some people, the former types of contacts are, in fact, the most important. Work associates, for example, are the most frequent friends among people whose work is their central life interest (professors are good examples).[52] But for the majority of people, work as such does not contain sufficient intrinsic value to bind co-workers together in some shared interest, though there are indications that the insecurity and hardships of much industrial labor may be drawing workers together in plant-based friendship groups much more than past data suggest. Most neighborhoods are composed of persons brought together in the same area by economic and status criteria rather than any specific commonality that might serve as a bond for primary groups, though we may cite voluntary and involuntary enclosure of certain ethnic groups that stimulates the formation of numerous neighborhood primary groups.

All urban societies are not identical to ours in the types of outlets for

---

[50] For example, see Eugene Litwak and Ivan Szelenyi, "Primary Group Structures and Their Functions: Kin, Neighbors, and Friends," *American Sociological Review*, 34 (August 1969), pp. 465–81.

[51] Aida K. Tomeh, "Informal Participation in a Metropolitan Community," *Sociological Quarterly*, 8 (Winter 1967), pp. 85–102.

[52] Charles H. Anderson and John D. Murray, eds., *The Professors: Work and Life Styles among Academicians* (Cambridge, Mass.: Schenkman Publishing Company, 1971).

primary-group ties. For example, Vogel has observed that in Japan white-collar company workers rely mainly on co-workers for primary ties.[53] The Japanese salaried man spends many hours a week in after-work-relaxation in bar or restaurant with work associates (and girls). However, in the Japanese case, the workplace has very marked importance, as the salaried man is usually entirely dependent on his company for lifetime security and remains forever loyal to the same company and group of associates.

REFERENCE GROUPS

Of closely related interest to an understanding of self-identity and primary group is the notion of reference group. The reference-group concept has proven to be of considerable value in the analyses of various kinds of behavior having to do with, for example, educational, political, economic, and ethnic life.[54] The reference group differs from the primary or formal group in that it is not necessarily identical with the group in which a person is actually participating. We may be only psychological or identificational "members" of a reference group without being involved in any direct interaction. Literally, a person refers himself to the group for various purposes. For example, the son of an unskilled laborer participating in a terminal high school peer group may nevertheless identify with higher status students having college aspirations. By attempting to pattern his thinking and behavior after a college-bound reference group, the working-class student may enhance his college prospects. We might call a reference group used in this way a *normative* reference group, for it serves as a model for behaviorial norms.

In addition to setting guides and models for action and values, a reference group may also serve as a point of *comparison* for judging whether or not a person's own situation is fair or equitable.[55] A good illustration of a comparative reference group might be that of a black college graduate who may compare himself in occupational and income equity with other Americans having similar educational credentials. When he discovers that not only is his occupational and income status considerably below that of the average for white college graduates, but it is closer to that of a white high school dropout, he naturally would consider his own situation unjust. That he is better off than most black Africans is of no comfort to him, inasmuch as black Africans are not his economic reference group.

Closely related to the reference group as equity or comparative group is the idea of relative deprivation. Relative deprivation is precisely what

[53] Ezra F. Vogel, *Japan's New Middle Class* (Berkeley: University of California Press, 1967), p. 104.

[54] For a discussion of the reference-group concept, see Robert K. Merton, *Social Theory and Social Structure* (New York: The Free Press, 1957), Chapters 8 and 9.

[55] For a typology of reference groups, see Theodore D. Kemper, "Reference Groups, Socialization, and Achievement," *American Sociological Review*, 33 (February, 1968), pp. 31–45.

black college graduates (and all racial minorities at every level of education) experience as they size up their equity in American society. Furthermore, the income gap between white and black is greater at the top end of the educational ladder than at the bottom, leading to feelings of possibly greater relative deprivation among better educated blacks than among those with lesser education. Observe that in a society espousing equalitarian values, the use of comparative reference groups are likely to stimulate conflict. However, in a society that holds as ideal natural hierarchy, not only are equity comparisons unlikely to evoke discontent but such comparisons are rarely even made.

Another form a reference group might take is that of legitimator group. Although used by adults, a legitimator group is used most frequently by children and adolescents attempting to justify most any kind of action on the basis that "everybody is doing it." Thus: "The federal government often uses violence and force in pursuit of its ends so why shouldn't we?" The legitimator group is a type of normative reference group used in a transitory or expedient fashion.

Among the most important normative reference groups for the American people have been their respective ethnic and religious groups. Most of us have looked for guidance in conduct to the value systems of ethnic and religious traditions. These traditions have been a source of pride as well as conflict. To many persons, these traditions no longer seem adequate or viable as sources or normative reference, but to the majority they continue as guides for individual conduct and to bind people together.

Competing with and often replacing ethnic and religious reference groups are occupational ones. Teachers, doctors, managers, and many other professional and business people look mainly to their respective occupational communities for behavioral codes and values. Most members of the work force use occupational groups as comparative reference groups in evaluating their income and benefits. In some countries, social classes have served as important normative reference groups, but in the United States only the upper class has enough definition and cohesion to act as a reference group to its members. The educated ranks of professional and business people also seem to constitute something of a normative reference group for themselves and others. More often than not, however, this affluent category of Americans serves as a comparative or equity reference group for the rest of the population and is consequently the source of considerable feelings of relative deprivation.

Yet another possible important normative reference group is the government, as embodied in executive, legislative, and judicial branches, "possible" because government can discredit itself as a source of norms. Despite serious recent drops in prestige and respect, the American system of government retains the confidence and esteem of a large segment of the population. As a normative reference group, the government thus maintains considerable power. For example, a person's thinking on racial issues concerned with housing and education can be substantially shaped by what the government says is right, *if* the government itself acts as though what it says is true. However, confusion and cynicism reigns when politicians publically contradict, as for campaign purposes in 1972, Supreme Court decisions and fail to fully support Congressional civil rights legislation.

Finally (though usually among the first in life), sex reference groups are of foremost importance. We learn early from same-sex parents, peers, and television how we ought to behave as masculine or feminine individuals. For the masculine female, but especially the feminine male, the normative reference group may evoke gross feelings of failure or inadequacy. Indeed, it appears it is often easier to switch reference groups. Aside from the use of such normative codes, females frequently compare themselves with other women as such in evaluating their personal equity or well-being. However, an increasing number of females are wisely comparing themselves with men!

We are now ready to direct our attention to a discussion of the Marxist theoretical perspective. Our initial assumptions merge with this perspective and the preceding conceptual discussions may be utilized in conjunction with it. Marxist theory itself has a conceptual framework, which should add greatly to anyone's understanding of society, and is basic to a solid grasp of how this book approaches social analysis and understanding.

4

Classes in industrial society: Marxian sociology

THE MARXIAN FRAMEWORK

The social theories of Karl Marx (1818–83) provide the student of industrial society with valuable conceptual and intellectual tools for comparison, analysis, and interpretation. As used in sociology, the Marxist perspective is not a political program or strict ideology. Rather, it is a set of general orienting statements and working tools with which to study social phenomena. Beyond this, Marxist theory contains a great many research propositions holding various degrees of validity. Marxism draws upon other perspectives and theories just as non-Marxists may gain insights from Marxism. Marxist sociology sets forth an interpretive framework within which the social analyst can organize his or her thinking about developments and changes within industrial society.

The validity of any sociological perspective rests ultimately upon its utility to the user in understanding the surrounding social world. Many sociologists today would agree with David Horowitz that the Marxian approach is the only one that "is capable of analyzing capitalism as an historically specific, class-determined social formation."[1] Many would also agree with J. David Colfax's view that "A Marxist class-analysis of contemporary society holds the greatest promise for the transformation of sociological and social consciousness over the next decade."[2] One need not agree with these views to find value in the Marxian approach. A theoretical perspective is of value if it informs its users where to begin the search for knowldege and understanding, leads them through a bewildering array of facts, and ultimately makes sense out of the often seem-

[1] "Marxism and Its Place in Economic Science," *Berkeley Journal of Sociology*, XVI (1971–72), p. 57.

[2] "Varieties and Prospects of 'Radical Scholarship' in Sociology," in J. David Colfax and Jack Roach, eds., *Radical Sociology* (New York: Basic Books, Inc., 1971), p. 84.

ingly senseless events of the world. In sociological terms, a valid perspective should, for example, be capable of explaining to its users why there are millions of unemployed persons in a society that has so much to do, why there are poverty-stricken people in a land of millionaires, and why lives and resources are squandered in distant jungles.

To develop a powerful explanatory perspective one must work as close to factual and historical events as possible; accuracy and objectivity are ideals of scholarship. Marx's ideals and commitments, however, went further than scholarship. As Mills pointed out regarding Marx's intellectual position, "The work of Marx taken as a whole is a savage, sustained indictment of one alleged injustice: that the profit, the comfort, the luxury of one man is paid for by the loss, the misery, the denial of another."[3] Thus, "Marxism is at once an intellectual and a moral criticism," wrote Mills. "In its documents, in its very conceptions, the two *are* often difficult to separate, but it *is* political philosophy *and* at the same time it is definitely social science."[4] Although Marx referred to his work as scientific, we should not neglect the fact that he also espoused ideals, which to most people are clearly utopian: voluntary and associated labor, the elimination of occupational specialization and the narrow division of labor, the withering away of the state bureaucratic apparatus, the liberation of the individual, and the development of a classless society. This is not to say that such conceptions are fictions; Marx's analysis of capitalist society led him to argue the potential reality of true communism. A transitional socialist society was to Marx even more of an immediate, direct possibility.

Misconceptions and distortions of Marx abound. Confusing Soviet ideological pronouncements with Soviet realities, many people view Marxism as identical with a highly bureaucratized, state-planned society. While the Soviet Union is not capitalist, neither is it Marxist or socialist; it is a highly bureaucratic, state-planned society without a private market mechanism *and* without voluntary and associated labor working within democratically organized collectives. Marx would abolish the bureaucratic hierarchy, since "Freedom consists in converting the state from an organ superimposed upon society into one completely subordinate to it."[5] The "dictatorship of the proletariat" is not regarded as centralized rule by one man or a small circle of men; rather, it refers to the political and economic power of the workers as a self-governing assemblage of soviets and collectives.

A second illustrative misconception might be mentioned, and that is the notion of Marxist "materialism." Marx was a materialist in the soci-

---

[3] C. Wright Mills, *The Marxists* (New York: Dell Publishing Company, 1963), p. 33. Marx and his family themselves lived on the brink of poverty, surviving on bread and potatoes for weeks at a time. Three of his six children died largely as a result of the conditions in which they lived. For a concise bibliographical statement of Marx, see E. Stepanova, *Karl Marx: A Short Biography* (Moscow: Progress Publishers, 1968); also, Isaiah Berlin, *Karl Marx: His Life and Environment* (New York: Oxford University Press, 1968).

[4] Mills, *The Marxists*, p. 102.

[5] *Critique of the Gotha Programme*, Marx and Engels, *Selected Works*, Vol. 3 (Moscow: Progress Publishers, 1970), p. 25.

ological sense of postulating that the manner in which people relate to one another in the process of producing their material means of life support shapes human consciousness and culture in the broadest sense. Hence, given capitalist relations of production we should expect to see decisive influences of its needs and assumptions in shaping the state and politics, law, social classes, ethics, and even philosophy, music, literature, art, and personal morals. Marx recognized that conflicting viewpoints could arise, and they must if there is to be change; but the material relations of production channel the general drift of culture and society. This is a very different kind of materialism than that frequently assumed to be Marxist; i.e., that of subjugating people to forced production and standardizing everyone to a flat personal and consumption level. As Erich Fromm wrote, "This popular picture of Marx's 'materialism—his anti-spiritual tendency, his wish for uniformity and subordination—is utterly false. Marx's aim was that of the spiritual emancipation of man, of his liberation from the chains of economic determination, of restituting him in his human wholeness, of enabling him to find unity and harmony with his fellow man and with nature."[6]

Marx was very critical of the type of uncontrolled consumption and materialism as we know it today; as he once quipped, "Too many useful things make too many useless people." Marx charged that capitalism turns people into so many commodities up for sale and chains people into a vicious cycle of work and consumption. Production of material goods should be calculated to meet human needs and assist in individual development, not as a means to financial gain or as an end in itself.

SOCIAL CLASSES

The concept of social class is central to the entirety of the Marxist perspective. The definition of a social class has a number of ingredients, but the foundation of Marxist class analysis is found in the realm of property relations. Although Marx framed many ideas regarding the social systems of pre-capitalist modes of production (slavery, feudalism, Asian), our concern is with the class system of capitalism—the existing and first world-wide mode of production. In the capitalist period of history, there exist two major social classes, the bourgeoisie and the proletariat. The bourgeoisie owns the means of production and employs land, labor, and capital in the pursuit of financial accumulation. The proletariat sells its labor power to the capitalist class to acquire the wages to purchase its means of support. Thus, the capitalist class and working class exist by definition; they are objectively present in society regardless of whether or not those who belong to them recognize the existence of classes.

The relationship to property as owners and workers is reinforced or paralleled in other spheres of society, which grow up around property relations, such as legal statutes, political ideologies and parties, social ties between members, and consciousness of class interests. Only if these

---

[6] Erich Fromm, *Marx's Concept of Man* (New York: Frederick Ungar Publishing Co., Inc., 1961), p. 3.

psychological, social, and political additions enter into the make-up of a social class is that class a completely developed class (class-for-itself). Should members of a class fail to mobilize as a collectivity around their interests, then they remain in the status of a mere class aggregate, a class-in-itself.

Marx rarely took time to specify precisely the definition of class, for his entire theory was a working clarification of the subject. However, in discussing the lack of class formation among peasants, Marx wrote:

> In so far as millions of families live under economic conditions of exis-tence that separate their mode of life, their interests and their culture from those of the other classes, and put them in hostile opposition to the latter, they form a class. Insofar as there is merely a local interconnec-tion among these small-holding peasants, and the identity of their inter-ests begets no community, no national bond, and no political organiza-tion among them, they do not form a class.[7]

Elsewhere we have, "The separate individuals form a class only insofar as they have to carry on a common battle against another class; other-wise they are on hostile terms with each other as competitors."[8] In ad-dition to the foundation of a class in its position within the means of production, then, we recognize the further requirement of social class to be an awareness of common economic interests, a separate cultural pattern, interlocking social community, conflict with an opposition class, and political mobilization. The extent of class formation depends upon the number and intensity with which these aspects are present.

The development of capitalism from an economic condition of small and competitive production units to large and monopolistic ones trans-forms the class structure in its wake. The proletariat expands as the demands of wage labor force handicraftsmen, peasants, and small traders out of their traditional roles. The capitalist class sorts itself out into ever-expanding big bourgeoisie and increasingly hard-pressed small or petit bourgeoisie, of whom growing numbers are ruthlessly forced out of business and into the wage labor market. Capitalism is a system based upon financial profit and wage labor, and all the historical forces of the period exert pressure toward a polarization of society around these two interest groups. Even modern agricultural production is di-rectly affected as fewer producers account for a larger portion of the product and more of the labor is hired out for wages.

Marx held that the proletariat played the key role in production. Its interests were evident and conflicts real. In living situation and work-ing arrangement Marx viewed the working class as ideally suited to the development of class consciousness and organization. He regarded the proletariat as representing the progressive potential of industrial society and as possessing the ability to develop and apply that potential toward the elevation of the individual and the improvement of society in the broadest physical and cultural sense. Other strata in society either

---

[7] *The Eighteenth Brumaire of Louis Bonaparte, Selected Works,* Vol. 1.

[8] *The German Ideology, Selected Works,* Vol. 1, p. 65.

espoused reactionary tendencies or lacked the potential to conduct successful revolutionary changes. Marx's support of the working class was not essentially based upon any sentimental attachment to workers but upon what he regarded as an objective socioeconomic analysis of industrial society.

The course of industrial development has markedly altered the composition of the working class. In addition to changes in the nature of much manual labor or blue-collar work, technological advance has brought about the development of a large category of primarily non-manual production personnel working as engineers, technicians, and scientists. This technological stratum has more education and skills together with a higher income than most of the traditional working class, but the technologists and scientists are for the most part hired employees who occupy a position in the means of production structurally similar to that of manual laborers. As Marx had early noted, engineers, technicians, and scientists are a "superior class of workmen" attached to the factory operative class.[9] To distinguish conceptually between these two components of the proletariat, we may refer to the more highly educated and skilled stratum as "new working class" in contrast to the traditional working class.[10] Many technical-scientific persons have themselves become propertied-rich members of the capitalist class, but the vast majority depend entirely upon modest wage or salary earnings.

Often difficult to distinguish from the material production-oriented new working class is a closely related stratum of service-oriented workers in areas such as education and medicine. Whether one prefers to use the term professionals or proletarians is not particularly significant; increasing unionization among college-educated employees suggests a growing awareness of what is essentially a new working class status. At the lower end of the non-manual or white-collar educational and income scale are what Marx refered to as commercial laborers who help organize and assist in the administrative and transactional aspects of economic activity. These "sales and clerical workers" are in many important ways similar to the blue-collar proletariat: propertyless wage and salary earners, monotonous and fragmented work tasks, relatively low income, and easy replaceability and job insecurity.

Marx singled out the *lumpenproletariat* as a special category apart from the industrial work force. The lumpenproletariat should not be confused with what Marx termed "the industrial reserve army" of unemployed proletarians. The unemployed consist of the displaced and potential members of the active, productive proletariat, whereas the lumpenproletariat is primarily an occupationally marginal assemblage of people lacking any articulation with industry. In the language of his day, Marx noted vagabonds, discharged soldiers and jailbirds, swindlers, tricksters, gamblers, beggars—"in short, the whole, indefinite, disinte-

---

[9] *Capital,* Vol. 1 (Chicago: Charles H. Kerr & Co., 1908), Chapter XV.

[10] See Stanley Aronowitz, "Does the United States Have a New Working Class?" in George Fischer, ed., *The Revival of American Socialism* (New York: Oxford University Press, 1971), pp. 188–216.

grated mass, thrown hither and thither."[11] Marx considered the lumpen-proletariat to be more dangerous than helpful to the working class insofar as the former could serve as a tool of reaction under the direction of the bourgeoisie. Like the peasantry, Marx considered the lumpen-proletariat to lack the conditions of a social class and as at best followers of a proletarian leadership and at worst reactionary.

The capitalist class or ruling class was to Marx a small, powerful, and increasingly self-conscious (class-for-itself) upper layer of society. The ruling class exercises widespread power and influence, including cultural and ideological spheres: "The ideas of the ruling class are in every epoch the ruling ideas: i.e., the class which is the ruling *material* force of society, is at the same time its ruling *intellectual* force. The class which has the means of material production at its disposal, has control at the same time over the means of mental production."[12] We shall address ourselves fully to an analysis of the ruling class in Chapter 9.

The class struggle between bourgeoisie and proletariat may rise and fall depending upon a number of other conditions, but it is this class struggle that holds the key to an understanding of what is and is not possible in the society of the immediate future. Class conflict is the chief historical dynamic, and revolution is the capstone of historical events. Thus, Marx argued that the study of society must focus upon the economic underpinnings of the class structure and upon the social and political relationships of social classes. It is necessary to take a closer look at the economic bases of social class.

THE GROWTH OF CAPITAL

Although Marx considered the bourgeoisie as reactionary in the latter stages of capitalism, his historical theory viewed the capitalist class as playing a revolutionary role as history moved out of the feudal and into the capitalist epoch. In Marx's words, "The bourgeoisie has played an extremely revolutionary role upon the stage of history. Where the bourgeoisie has risen to power, it has destroyed all feudal, patriarchal, and idyllic relationships."[13] Capitalist property relations permitted the steady accumulation of capital and the expansion of society's means of production, whereas the ruling aristocracy of feudal society perpetuated stagnation by maintaining an agrarian economy and consuming all surplus wealth. Conversely, the capitalist class had as its chief goal the accumulation of wealth. It bought and sold for financial gain, and only secondarily for personal luxury and consumption. Indeed, the concept of capital refers to the money gains made in the buying and selling process.[14]

The central question to be raised here is this: How does the capitalist accumulate capital? Does he do it by cheating other capitalists or by

[11] *The Eighteenth Brumaire of Louis Bonaparte, Selected Works,* Vol. 1, p. 442.

[12] *The German Ideology, Selected Works,* Vol. 1, p. 47.

[13] Mills, *The Marxists,* p. 48.

[14] *Capital,* Vol. 1, p. 164.

tricking his customers? Not at all, at least as far as the historical process of capital growth is concerned. If cheating and tricking were the way capitalists made money, or at least most of it, capitalism wouldn't be capitalism at all but a contest of quick deals and deception—of which there is plenty of today but which there has always been plenty of within most every mode of production or economy. Capital accumulation has a much more reliable and systematic method of operation. What, then, is the basis of capital growth?

Marx observed that a product's worth is determined by the amount of labor time (labor power) consumed in its production; i.e., the well-known labor theory of value.[15] Furthermore, a product tends to be sold, on an average basis, at its real value (the inflation of paper currency beclouds this fact). Anyone who could make gains by selling at inflated prices would always have to sell and never buy; there are short-run advantages to be had, however, and inflation does severely damage the politically powerless within a society.

If products are sold at their value, how is it possible for the capitalist class to accumulate—what makes them capitalists? Marx pointed out that there is one commodity the capitalist can purchase that yields greater value than what it cost to buy it, and that commodity is human labor power. The cost of labor is, like any other thing, the cost of its production—in this case, the cost of feeding, housing, clothing, and generally maintaining and reproducing the worker and his family (the next generation of workers). Once purchased (hired), the worker produces commodities, which upon sale not only pay for his own cost or support (necessary labor) but also enough to make his employer the capitalist a profit (surplus labor). The worker creates surplus value that is accumulated by the capitalist.

The amount of surplus value or surplus labor the capitalist is able to obtain from the worker depends to a large extent upon the *productivity* of labor power. A highly efficient and productive worker can produce more products within a shorter period of time, reducing the number of hours it takes to pay for his own wages and increasing the number of hours he is producing surplus value for the capitalist. The capitalist will thus be interested in supplying the worker with increasingly efficient machinery with which to produce, not just for his own gain but out of necessity: if he didn't so invest in improved machinery and production techniques, he would soon be hard pressed or driven out of business by other capitalists who did invest and thus could sell more for less. Marx stressed the built-in forces which pushed capitalism toward a constant revolutionizing of the means of production, and we shall consider the major stages of such development presently. Our point here is that the growth of capital stems from the appropriation of surplus value produced by the working class.

The rate of surplus value, the ratio of surplus labor (say four hours a day) to necessary labor (say four hours a day), varies depending upon several external conditions (the rate in this simple case would be 100 percent). Marx pointed out that the rate of surplus value could be

[15] See *Wages, Price and Profit, Selected Works*, Vol. 2, pp. 31–76.

raised by working the laborer *longer hours* (absolute surplus value) and by working the laborer *harder* while on the job through supervisors and speed-ups or by installing improved machinery (both forms of relative surplus value). Any combination may, of course, be utilized. A strong trade union may be successful in cutting into a part of the surplus value, whereas a weak or non-existent trade union movement results in a higher rate of surplus value (hence, the intensity with which trade unions have always been fought, especially in the developing stages of capitalism). An ample supply of labor, especially unemployed labor, is a weapon used by the capitalists against wage demands of the working class. In any case, wrote Marx, "The rate of surplus-value is an exact expression for the degree of exploitation of labour-power by capital, or of the labourer by the capitalist."[16]

Revolutionizing production

Within any given mode of production Marx distinguished two components: the forces of production and the relations of production. The forces of production include the instrumental, technical, and organization aspects of material production. Thus, machines, know-how, and work relations may be subsumed under the rubric of productive forces. Also subsumed within the forces of production is science. Marx wrote, "The *development of science*, of this ideal and at the same time practical wealth, is one aspect, on form, of the *development of human productive forces* (i.e., wealth)."[17] In brief, the productive forces encompass all the means whereby human beings build their material wealth; they are the *means* of production.

The relations of production consist of the manner in which individuals are articulated with or tied-into the productive forces. As we have previously noted, the two major positions or relationships to the productive forces are those of owner and worker. The relations of production are simply the formal property relations governing access to and utilization of society's wealth and resources.

The forces of production advance and develop throughout the capitalist epoch, but the relations of production have remained essentially unaltered. It was the property relations of the feudal period which the bourgeoisie overturned so that the forces of production could advance without the restraints of the feudal order. However, in advanced capitalism, Marx argued, the restraining factor upon the forces of production and material progress for all comes to be that very set of property relations that were once revolutionary vis-à-vis feudal society. The Marxist thesis asserts that existing relations of production should be reconstituted in harmony with the actual and especially the potential use of the forces of production. Today's property relations are no more in tune with modern technology and science than were fuedal relations con-

---

[16] *Capital*, Vol. 1, p. 241.

[17] *The Grundrisse*, trans. and ed. by David McLellan (New York: Harper & Row, 1971), p. 120.

ducive to the full utilization and progress of the productive forces available to man in the 18th and 19th centuries.

It is illuminating for us to follow Marx's analysis of the development of the capitalist mode of production through its several stages, since it gives us insight into both the historical background to the existing stage and the concept of *alienation.* The first stage of capitalist production Marx called *simple cooperation:* instead of an individual or family obtaining their own raw materials, finishing them, and marketing them for an exchange of other goods (petty commodity production), simple cooperation brought a number of producers under one roof provided by the capitalist who paid them a wage, supplied the other factors of production, and took the products to sell for profit. While the technical aspects of production did not change significantly, the relations of production were fundamentally altered. The worker still worked as a handicraftsman with traditional skills, but was deprived or alienated from the ownership of the instruments of production and the product of production. The worker has only his labor power to sell.

In the competitive drive to further increase surplus value, capitalism next worked out a division of labor within the production process that assigned a specialized task to each worker. Thus, instead of each worker converting raw materials to finished products, each worker performed one or two fragmented tasks in the process: one spun, one wove, one cut, etc. In the *manufacture* stage, then, the worker was thus not only deprived of owning the means of production and the products, but also a large portion of the manual skills previously applied. Alienation of man from individual productive skills begins. To the capitalist, however, the subdivision of tasks accelerates production and raises profit; moreover, the worker becomes semi-skilled or unskilled and is cheaper to buy and easier to replace. The worker is torn from the socially binding cooperation of a free productive group.

Up to this point capitalism developed without marked improvements within the mechanical forces of production; changes had been made in the organization of work. With the introduction of inanimate power and *machine* stage of production, capitalists were able to realize unprecedented gains in productivity and profit. However, these technological advances of the industrial revolution pushed the division of labor and task fragmentation to the point where man became a mere appendage of a machine. The machine is a tool that controls and paces the worker rather than vice versa. The process of alienation from personal skills that began in the manufacture stage was carried to completion in the machine stage. The worker had lost control of both tools and skills. Without a sense of purpose, creativity, or satisfaction, the industrial-age worker repeated psychologically and physically exhausting and degrading operations like a cog in a machine. Work had been reduced to animal functions. The drive for increased surplus value led the capitalist to maintain factory operations around the clock, if possible. Machines worked early and late, and so did the men, women, and children who tended them. (Chrysler workers have in recent periods worked 12-hour days and six- or seven-day weeks, though a recent union contract has reduced the length of such long hours.)

Being an appendage to the machine is not the end in production changes. The worker may be further reduced to a mere monitor of the machine as machine production advances toward *automated* production. However, we must remember that the capitalist does not install new or automated machinery out of technological admiration. He does so in order to maximize profit. If at some point machinery becomes more expensive than labor, it is preferable to utilize labor instead.[18] An abundance of cheap labor, wherever it might be found, is a capitalist's ideal. The rapid expansion of capitalism has resulted in recourse to both technological development and high labor availability. The role of automation shall be returned to below.

The increasing utilization of machine power increases the expendability of more and more workers. Unemployment, or the industrial reserve army, rises and falls with the cycles of economic activity, but advanced capitalism is at all times threatened with social dislocation from large scale unemployment. The wage levels of the working class tends overall toward a *relative* worsening compared to the mass of capital accumulation held by the ruling class. Credit must be extended to maintain demand. The psychological condition induced by years of repetitious labor also weighs down upon the working class.

Marx argued that the working class must revolutionize the *relations* of production if the *productive forces* are to be applied so as to release people from the cycles of wage labor and consumption to pursue self-development in both work and leisure. Marx contended that the sharp distinction between work and leisure was an artificial and destructive one and sought to integrate work and free time into a more indistinguishable whole. He argued that, although a certain amount of necessary labor will always be required, its amount can be greatly reduced in favor of both consumptive and productive leisure time. That the burden of work and the pleasure of free time should be evenly distributed he took as axiomatic. Marx's emphasis was more often upon the values of workers' control of the production process than upon the possibility of material security and equality, though he never neglected the importance of the latter.

Automation

"As soon as a machine executes, without man's help, all of the movements requisite to elaborate the raw material, needing only attendance from him, we have an automatic system of machinery, and one that is susceptible of constant improvement in its details."[19] Thus, Marx takes cognizance of what has ultimately turned out to be called automation, self-regulating machines with the capacity to operate accurately with-

---

18 *Capital*, Vol. 1, pp. 427; 429.
19 Ibid., p. 416.

out human assistance. The worker, or technician, becomes an observer or monitor of the general production process, a recorder and service agent.

Advanced machine production and automation present new considerations for the question of the labor theory of value; i.e., the value of a product is measured by the amount of labor time necessary to produce it. By the same token, the measurement of necessary labor time and hence a worker's wages are also affected. First, advanced technological production has become a completely social process with simultaneously many people involved. It is difficult to separate out any single individual's contribution. Despite the social nature of the production process, ownership and control over it remains private. Secondly, automatic machinery removes much of the human labor from the process of creating surplus value. As Marx points out, man has succeeded "for the first time in making the product of his past labour work on a large scale gratuitously, like the forces of nature."[20] As industry develops, writes Marx, "the creation of real wealth depends less on labour time and on the quantity of labour utilised than on the power of mechanical agents which are set in motion during labour time. The powerful effectiveness of these agents, in its turn, bears no relation to the immediate labour time that their production costs." "The human factor is restricted to watching and supervising the production process."[21]

What happens under automation, then, is that labor time becomes increasingly difficult to apply as a measure of the value of something, since it is no longer the principal agent in production. The entire basis of the wage system of rewards is logically undermined, owing both to the social nature of production and the difficulty of measuring value by labor time (the cost of maintaining the worker, his wages, can no longer be assessed by the labor time necessary to produce his means of subsistence since automation would affect this as well). What *does* become the measure of value under automated production if labor time has diminished in importance? Marx contends that *free* or *disposable time* becomes the measure of human value, for it is through free time the individual can pursue desired ends in life, hopefully social and creative endeavors.

The present reality, however, is that human labor still plays a predominant role in production at large. Few industrial plants can maintain profitable production, or any production at all, in the face of a strike by the workers, even plants with extensive automated machinery such as oil and chemical processing. Indeed, the capitalist class is caught in a contradiction: too much automation would lead to the elevation of free time over labor time as the basis of economic value, obviously a disaster for any class wishing or having to accumulate wealth for its very survival, while failure to keep abreast with the ubiquitous technological advances of competitors means losing out as well. A further contradiction is evident in that too much automation creates large scale unemployment

---

[20] Ibid., p. 423–24.
[21] *The Grundrisse*, pp. 141–42.

and reduces the purchasing power of the working class and the profits of capitalists as a result, whereas holding back on technical advance creates a continued dependence upon increasingly organized and demanding labor force. Automation may prove to be an extremely troublesome stage for the capitalist class, much more so than any of the preceding stages of capital growth.[22] A capitalist whose capital does not grow is destined to end up bankrupt, though credit extensions and inflation can postpone the end (which comes all the harder when it comes).

CORPORATE CAPITALISM

The transition from early to late capitalism is also a transition from an economy of small competitive units to one of large monopolistic units. Such is the necessary outcome of the expansionary and growth tendencies inherent within capitalism. Refering to mergers of units as centralization ("little fish are swallowed by the sharks and the lambs by the wolves") and internal growth as concentration, Marx anticipated the trend toward monopoly capitalism. The small owner-manager businessman becomes the big financier or board member, typically holding a relatively small share of the stocks in a company but participating in control over a financial-industrial domain that drawfs its predecessors.

Given the fact that vastly increased labor productivity today means much less labor time is required to produce a given product, the prices of things might be expected to have greatly decreased over time. However, this would be valid only under conditions of competitive selling. Today these conditions are not met. A handful of giant producers dominate in almost every industrial sector, enabling them to regulate the price level to their own advantage. Frederick Engels, Marx's close associate and collaborator, spelled out the nature of corporate or monopoly capitalism as follows:

> The producers on a large scale in a particular branch of industry in a particular country unite in a trust, a union for the purpose of regulating production. They determine the total amount to be produced, parcel it out among themselves, and thus enforce the selling price fixed beforehand. The whole of the particular industry is turned into one gigantic joint-stock company; internal competition gives place to the internal monopoly of this one company.[23]

Marx refered to corporate capitalism as being private production without the control of private property.

Competitors have not been eliminated completely. Especially problematic for the bourgeoisie of a particular country is the bourgeoisie of another country. International capitalism is at least as cutthroat and ruthless in its operations as is national capitalism. International capitalism leads to world wars of the military kind as a corollary to economic

---

[22] See Irving Zeitlin's discussion in *Marxism: A Re-examination* (Princeton, N.J.: D. Van Nostrand Company, Inc., 1967), pp. 108–15.

[23] *Socialism: Utopian and Scientific, Selected Works,* Vol. 3, pp. 143–44.

warfare, though the bourgeoisie of the developed capitalist states have since 1945 considered negotiation as the more reasonable solution to their conflicts. Violence against smaller states bent upon pursuing development outside of the world capitalist network has not, obviously, been ruled out.

Monopoly capitalism does not exclude national competition either. However, the competition is conducted largely around advertising ($20 billion a year in the United States), packaging, and sales gimmicks rather than around prices. A certain amount of competition is found among substitute products, but mergers are increasingly taking their toll on this aspect of competition. Merger and the internationalization of business operations also reduces the competitive impact of international markets.

Corporate capitalism faces a constant crisis of overproduction. Cycles of boom and recession revolve around the money demand for commodities. The maximization of profit always means that the working class will have less income to buy commodities with than the corporation is able to produce. The grossly unequal distribution of income within the society results in some people having more purchasing power than they need and a much larger group having insufficient income to meet their needs. Credit is extended by the billions of dollars, but this by definition must stop somewhere. Advertising cannot bring out the demand when the income isn't available. Built-in obsolescence and style changes help maintain demand among some segments of the population, but these options contain limits.

The major avenue to economic solvency within corporate capitalism is the intervention of the state.

The role of the state

Marx held that under normal conditions the state serves a protective function for the propertied class; the state is "nothing more than the form of organization which the bourgeois necessarily adopt for the mutual guarantee of their property and interests."[24] Under certain circumstances the state may act as a balancing mechanism between conflicting social groups, and in pre-capitalist societies the state bureaucracy could and did crush wealthy and capital-producing groups.

In mature capitalism, Marxist theory recognizes the need for the state to enter economic affairs on a large scale to assist in maintaining stability. Engels pointed out that "In any case, with trusts or without, the official representative of capitalist society—the state—will ultimately have to undertake the direction of production."[25] By direction of production is meant not only massive involvement through regulation, spending, and taxation, but also state ownership of decaying but socially essential industrial areas. This sort of state activity should not be confused

---

[24] Marx and Engels, *The German Ideology* (Moscow: Foreign Language Publishing House, 1965), p. 78.

[25] *Socialism: Utopian and Scientific*, p. 144.

with socialism; it is, rather, best termed state capitalism, since the preservation and prosperity of the capitalist class remains its chief aim and function.

Especially important is the role played by the state in maintaining a demand for industrial production on a profitable basis. Since the Second World War, military spending has been the crucial stabilizing demand factor in the United States economy. Militarization serves the further necessary function of maintaining an umbrella of power under which the international corporations can operate. The state also assists in the maintenance of those persons the corporate system doesn't need. Marx observed that the capitalist class doesn't pay for poverty, but instead "knows how to shift this burden, for the most part, from its own shoulders to those of the working class and the lower middle class."[26]

Impoverishment and subsistence

Central to Marx's economic theory is the idea that there exists an insoluable conflict of interests between labor and capital. In proportionate terms, if wages increase, surplus value decreases; if surplus value increases, wages decrease. The social conditions are typically such so that the capitalist class is able to assert its interests over those of the working class, and hence, wages decline relative to the mass of surplus value.

A proportionate decline, however, does not mean an absolute decline in the level of living. Marx never asserted that the working class would become impoverished as a whole; indeed, he expected that the part that was employed and organized would improve their material position. The stratum that could expect the worst is the unemployed and unemployable; their condition could deteriorate in an absolute fashion. Marx wrote that capitalism "overworks a part of the labouring population and keeps the other part as a reserve army, half or entirely pauperised."[27]

Despite the probability of material improvement for the working class, Marx argued that wages will always be held at or near the "subsistence level"; i.e., whatever it costs to maintain and reproduce the worker. The subsistence level is not considered to be some absolute minimum of survival; it is historically and culturally determined. In Marx's words, "Besides this mere physical element, the value of labour is in every country determined by a *traditional standard of life*. It is not mere physical life, but it is the satisfaction of certain wants springing from the social conditions in which people are placed and reared up."[28] The subsistence wage thus varies from one country and one period to the next. The subsistence wage would today be highest in countries such as the United States and Sweden and lowest in countries such as India and Bolivia. Periods of sustained high unemployment will drive down the subsistence

---

[26] Cited in Robert Pinker, *Social Theory and Social Policy* (London: Heinemann Books, Ltd., 1970), p. 36. From *Capital.*

[27] G.A. Bonner and E. Burns, eds., *Theories of Surplus Value* (London, 1957), p. 352.

[28] *Wages, Price and Profit,* pp. 71–72.

wage, whereas sustained high employment would drive it up. The strength of the working class and its trade unions falls and rises with the same pattern, bringing wage levels with it.

Revolution

The concept of revolution requires some clarification. The revolutionary idea is a central theme within Marxist political philosophy. In a sense, the concept of revolution takes as its prerequisite the entire intellectual framework of Marxism. As Tucker stressed, "Revolution was the master theme of Marx's thought, and an exposition of the Marxian revolutionary idea in complete form would be nothing other than an exposition of Marxism itself as a theoretical system."[29]

The Marxist perspective contains extensive analytical powers well beyond the revolutionary idea, but an understanding of revolution requires a prior knowledge of Marx's social science. Revolution is considered by some to be an inevitable event from the standpoint of Marx. Our view here is that Marx wrote *as if* it were inevitable in his openly ideological works; Marx was as aware of the power of self-fulfilling prophesy as anyone else. From an analytical perspective, however, revolution appears as much less inevitable in Marx. Revolution becomes an exceedingly difficult event with rather low probability of occurring within any given period of time. This is so owing to the fact that objective conditions (the economic situation) and subjective conditions (social class formation and consciousness) must be simultaneously favorable. Thus, on some occasions the economic conditions may be ripe for change, but the working class may not be subjectively prepared. Or, the class formation may be present, but the objective conditions may be unfavorable or unconducive to revolution. Moreover, it is unclear as to which point in the economic cycle, that of prosperity or of recession (or depression), may turn out to be favorable.

In terms of the general theory, the objective conditions for revolution are ripe when the relations of production are incompatible with the social development of the forces of production, a point which Marx and Engels considered to be imminent in their own time. It would seem that the chief factor is the subjective one, at least today, since the objective conditions as defined by Marxist theory are more or less present all of the time.

The population need not be completely divided or polarized to meet the conditions of revolution. What is necessary is that the majority of a well-defined working class be revolutionary and that the larger part of the population be neutral or supportive. Moreover, a revolution is an on-going event requiring an entire historical stage to fully complete, though political power itself may be transformed within a short period.

---

[29] Robert C. Tucker, "The Marxian Revolutionary Idea," in C.T. Paynton and R. Blackey, eds., *Why Revolution? Theories and Analysis* (Cambridge, Mass.: Schenkman Publishing Company, 1971), p. 215.

The socialist revolution, according to Marx, is a *transitional* stage or social order intermediary to capitalism and true communism during which the long established and deeply ingrained social institutions and cultural patterns are overcome. For example, a life-long wage laborer may find it difficult to think in terms of voluntary and freely associated, self-governing producers and consumers collectives. The institution of the hourly wage would perhaps require at least a generation to uproot and to reorganize so as to promote democratic and equalitarian work relations.

As to the location and timing of the initial revolutionary activity, Marx primarily anticipated it to happen in the more advanced capitalist countries, though he left open the possibility of revolution in a less developed country (Russia in particular) as a "signal for a proletarian revolution in the West." At the time of the Russian Revolution in 1917, Lenin adhered to the Marxist notion that a socialist revolution could not be completed within a single country and he awaited in vain for the proletarian revolutions in Europe.

MARXISM IN CRITICAL PERSPECTIVE

Weber's critique

Max Weber answered Marx's emphasis upon the material foundation of society and social class with an alternative emphasis upon the role of ideas. For example, in regard to the growth of capital, Weber stressed the importance of certain Protestant religious beliefs to the process of saving and accumulation.[30] In connection with social class criteria, Weber paid special attention to "status groups" with particular "styles of life."[31] He observed how such aspects of class as prestige, status-oriented cliques, and preferences in association and mate selection contributed to the economic and political influence of a social stratum. Social exclusiveness limited the opportunities of outsiders in access to education and other avenues of social ascent. Rather than talking of position in the relations of production as the critical economic factor, Weber analyzed economic classes in terms of "life chances." A person's life chances consist of access to goods and services offered in the marketplace, and life chances may be very positive without property ownership (a high salary may suffice). Weber also placed emphasis upon the potential of a political party to alter the positive position of a property-owning class.

Despite the apparent disagreement between the Marxian and Weberian approaches, the difference is chiefly one of emphasis rather than one of theoretical design. Weber did not dispute the fundamental importance of property ownership as the central foundation of the class

---

[30] Max Weber, *The Protestant Ethic and the Spirit of Capitalism* (New York: Charles Scribner's Sons, 1958).

[31] Max Weber, "Class, Status, and Party," in Hans Gerth and C. Wright Mills, eds., *From Max Weber* (New York: Oxford University Press, 1958).

system;[32] nor did Marx overlook the importance of the "superstructural" influences of cultural behavior and political parties. After all, the political party is the key factor in Marxist revolutionary strategy. Certain of the latter's outstanding essays dealt with these cultural and political matters.[33] Marx clearly recognized the tremendous importance of ideas in history, be they religious or revolutionary. Marx was certainly aware of the social impact of his *own ideas*. Weber saw better the later development of bureaucracy and the centralization of all aspects of social life, but Marx wrote on these phenomena as well. In the broad sense, Weber's work would not be conceivable without that of Marx, just as Marxism arose out of Hegelian world views. In specific interpretations, Weber and Marx are complementary rather than contradictory. Where Weber and Marx clearly depart is in their philosophy of historical change: Weber foresaw a unilinear expansion of bureaucratic rationality, whereas Marx foresaw historically revolutionary breaks with existing society. Weber was an incorrigible pessimist, Marx an undaunted optimist.

Centralization

If any single aspect of Marxist theory may be said to be fully confirmed, it is the proposition regarding the concentration and centralization of economic wealth and power. What was only the incipient phases of a century-long and continued trend, the economy of Marx's time has been transformed to one dominated completely by corporate giants. We shall document this fact fully in Chapter 9.

Polarization

In the objective sense, the polarization of society into a small class of large property holders and a mass of hired employees has proceeded largely in accordance with Marx's understanding. However, in the subjective sense of ideological polarization of classes, we have not witnessed any marked movement in most advanced capitalist states. There are blocks of bourgeois and working class political parties in many European countries, but the political scene is complicated by many overlapping issues. In the United States, class polarization in the subjective sense is hardly even visible in voting alignments. The persistence of a locally influential stratum of small enterprenuers and independent professionals has also given the class structure greater complexity. The growth of a stratum of surplus-consumers, neither fully capitalists nor at all proletarians, has also been increasingly visible—a development foreseen by Marx.[34] In an economy of advanced technology and affluence, a need

---

[32] Max Weber, *The Theory of Social and Economic Organization,* trans. by A.M. Henderson and Talcott Parsons (New York: Oxford University Press, 1947), pp. 424–29; and Weber, *Economy and Society,* Vol. 1, edited by Guenther Roth and Claus Wittich (New York: Bedminster Press, 1968), pp. 927–28.

[33] For example, *The Eighteenth Brumaire of Louis Bonaparte.*

[34] See Martin Nicolaus, "Proletariat and Middle Class in Marx," *Studies on the Left,* 7 (January–February, 1967), p. 24.

arises for a stratum that really does nothing but maintain demand through consumption. Whether or not an occupational position is held isn't particularly important, unless it serves as a rationalization for the distribution of surplus wealth.

Impoverishment and subsistence

The fact that we may devote an entire chapter to the examination of poverty (Chapter 8) suggests that capitalism has indeed pauperized a part of the working class. On the matter of relative impoverishment of the working class, the data presented in subsequent chapters will indicate a constant struggle of the workers to preserve their relative position. During some years the working class has clearly lost ground on the major property holders, while on other occasions modest gains have been made. However, in recent decades the unskilled and unorganized members of the working class have definitely lost ground to the bourgeoisie, as well as to the skilled and organized workers. On the question of subsistence, we will present data in Chapter 5 that suggests the working class as a whole finds itself living around the budget levels set by federal agencies as modest or low. On several occasions we shall discuss the economic pressures on working class life. There are very affluent hired workers, especially among the new working class, but also within the traditional ranks.

The state

A major reason for the lack of greater polarization and impoverishment has been the role of the state. In accordance with Marxist projections, the state has had to intervene in a large way in the economy, particularly beginning with the Depression and then on a massive scale thereafter. The liberal oriented component of the capitalist class has been foresighted enough to recognize the need for large-scale government stabilization inputs, whether it concerns regulation of business, military spending, or welfare. Considering the proportions of the tasks thrust upon it, the state has delivered rather well. The interest in the posture of the state by the ruling class may be seen in the $60 million legal and illegal contributions to Mr. Nixon's re-election campaign. While the state today is something more than the official committee of the capitalist class, there are occasions when it becomes difficult to distinguish between the two.

Class consciousness and conflict

Outside of the ruling class itself, class consciousness in the United States has failed to reach a decisive level, although there are indications of moderate and rising amounts (see Chapter 6). The European working classes have displayed considerably more collective self-interest and political awareness, but even here there does not exist the kind of class consciousness either of kind or scale required to launch a socialist revolution. However, class consciousness does exist and there are signs of increasing class politicization among many workers. White-collar workers of various kinds, especially many of those we have classified as new working class, have on occasion displayed greater class militance than the traditional workers. At both levels of the working class we have seen employees resist shut-downs and continue to operate plants themselves; this is an indisputable sign of class development.

There have been many episodes of class conflict in the 20th century. Labor battles of all sorts reflect the mutual antagonism of the classes, including those that are today institutionalized within union activity. Yet, serious and sustained class conflict has never in recent times attained a level that posed a clear threat to the status quo. The exception to this situation, if any could be cited, would be the French upheaval of 1968. The ghetto riots of the 1960s may be viewed from a class perspective, but they lacked the organizational and ideological integration that genuine class conflict displays. Much conflict in the United States is not defined in class terms even though a class factor is objectively present, as in the anti-war movement, student activism, civil rights militance, women's liberation, minority struggles, and welfare rights groups. Socially irresponsible uses of power based on corporate property underlie and are chiefly responsible for many of these conflict situations.

Revolution

No advanced capitalist society has yet experienced social revolution based upon reorganization of the economy into a democratic workers' state. The welfare states and social democracies of Europe are not socialist societies; they are capitalist societies having relatively strong labor parties and reformist liberal regimes. Real political and economic power remains with the capitalist class, still the indisputable ruling class.

However, a revolution led by the industrial working class has occurred in much the same manner Marx predicted. The relatively small Russian working class launched a socialist revolution within a society in an early stage of capital development, but was so decimated in the Civil War that followed that it could not resist the loss of its brief power to a new state bureaucracy. China represents a different case, and countries such as Cuba and North Vietnam different cases still. Some observers see a socialist revolution transpiring in China today, whereas others consider it a society of centralized coercion.[35] In any event, one must always distinguish between official ideologies and social realities. The Soviet Union has proven for history that a non-capitalist society can attain a high level of technology and economic growth, but it may not be the first country to demonstrate the workability of Marxist socialism. In its emphasis upon hierarchical authority, a system of unequal wages, individual material incentives, and heavy state regulation, the Soviet Union has reinforced the cultural values of the old society rather than experi-

---

[35] On China as a transitional socialist society, see Maria Antonietta Macciocchi, *Daily Life in Revolutionary China* (New York: Monthly Review Press, 1972).

menting with new transitional institutional forms. China has moved further in these experimental directions.

The fact that a socialist revolution has not occurred in an advanced capitalist society does not mean that one will not occur. Marxist theory views history in terms of stages encompassing several hundreds of years; industrial capitalism is a relatively young mode of production taken in historical perspective. Socialist revolution remains a possibility, and it is this possibility that has and will continue to have a powerful impact upon the world.

Alienation

No single concept in the body of Marxist thought has been researched so extensively in sociology as alienation. Alienation as defined by Marx is an objective fact of capitalist society.[36] Man is alienated from labor, self, society, and nature and will remain so as long as fragmented wage labor and compulsive materialism exists. The symptoms of alienated humanity are everywhere: absenteeism and high turnover, escapist leisure, alchoholism and drug abuse, mental illness, chronic television viewing, status anxiety and consumption, political withdrawal, environmental destruction, and much more. Given the unprecedented potential of man's material base and productivity, the existence of alienation is all the more forceful. With every increase in the Gross National Product, the alienated condition would seem to intensify; people become more and more strangers to themselves, to one another, and to their physical environment. Alienation will persist so long as we are trapped by the demands of a social system that will not allow people themselves to take charge of the productive forces and apply them in a rational manner toward essential social needs and individual development.

---

[36] Marx's conception of alienation is discussed in *Economic and Philosophic Manuscripts of 1844*. See *Karl Marx: Early Writings*, trans. and ed. T.B. Bottomore (London: Watts & Company, 1963).

5

Social inequality

FOUNDATIONS OF INEQUALITY

Among the major current controversial social and sociological debates is that which concerns the issue of social inequality. The existence of social inequality, particularly the extreme form it takes, has come under increasing attack.

The concept of social inequality itself is a broad term containing numerous and diverse aspects. A more precise usage of the term must specify which aspect(s) of social inequality one is dealing with. We may treat inequalities of property ownership, income, political power and influence, authority, educational attainment, occupational skills, personal prestige, and so on. With any of these aspects, we may concern ourselves with greater or lesser amounts possessed by individuals (or groups). The issue of social inequality thus concerns *hierarchy*. These several aspects of inequality may be assessed with varying degrees of precision; that is, individuals or groups possess greater or lesser amounts of these qualities and can thus be arranged hierarchically. (It should be noted that, with the exception of the objective aspects such as wealth, income, and education, such measurements of inequality are exceedingly difficult in terms of research.)

Sex and racial statuses, though commonly related to other factors that create inequality, may not in and of themselves be considered as hierarchical aspects of inequality. Males and females can no more intrinsically be arranged hierarchically in sociological terms than can blue-eyed and brown-eyed people. The same holds true for "racial" traits. The non-hierarchical statuses of sex and race have been culturally attached to other intrinsically hierarchical qualities such as wealth, power, and prestige. However, sexual and racial inequalities are so widespread that we tend to take them as veritable artifacts of nature.

Occupation is another aspect of inequality that is not in and of itself

77

a strong hierarchical factor, but rather is quite highly related to the hierarchical factors of property ownership, income, authority, and prestige. Although we may think of occupations in hierarchical terms as having greater or lesser amounts of skills, the occupation taken by itself has less to do with where its holder stands in a social hierarchy than do the hierarchical aspects of income, authority, educational requirements, social prestige, etc., attached to different occupational positions. No clear measure exists that can objectively place doctors above nurses simply due to their being doctors or nurses. But doctors do rank above nurses in income, education, authority, and prestige, just as men tend to be ranked above women and whites above blacks. If it were possible to separate out the hierarchical aspects from a group or society, sex, race, and occupation would to the same extent fade away as aspects of inequality.

Depending upon one's theoretical perspective, the student of social inequality (or social stratification) tends to stress certain aspects of inequality over others, even though considering as many as possible. The Marxist approach takes one's position in the relations of production as fundamental; that is, a person's relationship to the means of production and property, be it that of owner, worker, or something other, carries the most decisive impact on inequality. Although there are other inequality-creating factors that must be considered as important, a person's relationship to the means of production creates the kinds of inequalities that are most crucial and which circumscribe the nature and limits of other aspects of inequality. These other aspects of inequality tend to pale in importance when contrasted to property positions or ownership. A general hospital doctor earns a higher salary than a nurse, has four more years education, has greater authority, and more prestige, but compared to propertied-rich multi-millionaires who control the corporate drug and hospital supply monopolies, the hired doctor and nurse end up having a great deal in common. This is an objective fact, and holds true whether these hospital employees realize it or not.

To take the difference between those who own and control the major means of production and those who to live must sell their labor capacity as the fundamental grounds and the most marked aspect of inequality is not to neglect or diminish the importance of other aspects. We shall variously deal with several aspects of inequality. Our point here concerns the centrality of position in the relations of production and how this position greatly influences a person's status in almost every other regard. Significantly enough, it is not the marked differences in property ownership and control (and hence, power) a large number of people perceive on a daily basis as important. More often, many people draw comparisons between persons within the employee population concerning job level, income, education, authority, and so on. These are, indeed, often important differences; yet, what are frequently relatively small hierarchical differences may distract us from the fundamental factor of inequality in our society.

Our analysis of social inequality and social class (Chapter 6) stresses the overall weight of a person's material resources and wealth in the stratification of a society. With some exceptions, an individual's wealth and income sets decisive limits upon an entire array of other aspects of inequality, including education, occupational opportunities, power and influence, and prestige—not to mention related opportunities in health care, housing, diet and food consumption, and recreation.

The fact that societies that have abolished individual ownership of the means of production continue to display social inequality does not in any way weaken the argument regarding the centrality of material resources in creating inequality. Such societies do, in fact, contain a much narrower range of inequality than our own, and the inequalities that do exist seem to be even more of a clear consequence of differences in material reward and income than in societies organized around individual ownership of production. In at least the ideological sense, these state-planned economies aim, with varying degrees of actual determination and success, toward substantial material equality. For example, Fidel Castro argues that Cuban "policies in the coming years will move steadily toward equalization of income." "When we succeed in equalizing incomes, and establish free distribution of essential articles, we will have reached communism."[1] He adds that money will exist until the forces of production allow free distribution of nonessentials. However, as we shall discuss later in the chapter, significant inequalities persist in state-planned economies due both to persisting income ranges and the acquisition of special privileges by the political elites and managerial stratum.

The foundations of inequality and the processes that develop and sustain it vary considerably from one historical period to the next, and between different modes of production today. Our chief concern, however, is with inequality in the United States today. Before looking further at this inequality, we shall critically examine a theoretical perspective that contends that inequality is not only inevitable but necessary to the maintenance of social well-being.

IS INEQUALITY NECESSARY?

Social inequality within industrial society, as well as within the feudal period that preceded it, has been persistent and marked. The seemingly ubiquitous character of social inequality raises the question as to its inevitability and necessity. A thoroughly democratic society of voluntarily associated workers and families without a hierarchy of authority and reward *is* conceivable. Certainly it is impossible for such an equalitarian system to operate within the bounds of capitalism, since the essence of capitalism is inequality. Capitalism could not function for a day without rich and poor, owners and workers, powerful and powerless people.

The fact that an industrial society without substantial inequality has never existed can in no way be taken as proof that an equalitarian so-

---

[1] Saul Landau, "Socialist Democracy in Cuba: An Interview with Fidel Castro," *Socialist Revolution*, 1 (March–April 1970), p. 139.

ciety is socially impossible. Given the extraordinary power of the defenders of inequality, it is not surprising at all that an equalitarian system has not emerged or even been given an opportunity to exist within an advanced industrial society. The persistence of inequality has led certain sociologists to conclude that it is "functional" and necessary to the survival of society. These functionalists do not say, as they should, that inequality is necessary to the kind of society we now live in, but rather theorize in general terms. Our criticisms of the functionalist theory of inequality (and any view of the necessity of inequality) will thus be directed to the argument that inequality is a functional and necessary social phenomenon within industrial society in general. We shall even criticize the extent of inequality regarded as necessary for capitalism to maintain itself, as well as the arguments used in support of such inequality.

Although the functionalist argument is similar to the common sense view often presented in defense of social inequality, Davis and Moore state the argument in more sophisticated and precise form.[2] It runs something like this: Every society must distribute its members into the various jobs within the division of labor and induce them to perform their work competently. If all positions were equally important and required equal skill, it would then make little difference as to what individuals performed what jobs; but such is not the case. Thus, a society must offer rewards, as incentives to acquire the skill level needed to perform important jobs. The greater the skill requirements and importance of the job, the greater must be the rewards "built into" that position. In the words of Davis and Moore, "Social inequality is thus an unconsciously evolved device by which societies insure that the most important positions are conscientiously filled by the more qualified persons."

Better known recent supporters of the inequality argument are the psychological functionalists such as Richard Herrnstein and Arthur R. Jensen who make essentially similar assumptions and arguments as the sociological functionalists and attempt to back them with I.Q. data.[3] However, they are similar to the sociologists in assuming that inequality is a necessary device through which the most competent people are selected and motivated to perform the most important tasks. By showing a relationship between I.Q. and occupational placement, Herrnstein argues that the point is all but proven. He also contends that genetic competence runs in the family, competent people intermarry, and society ends up with a permanent, privileged higher stratum based upon merit.

[2] See Kingsley Davis and Wilbert E. Moore, "Some Principles of Stratification," *American Sociological Review,* 10 (April 1945), pp. 242–49. See their own and their critics' papers, especially Melvin Tumin's, as collected in Reinhard Bendix and Seymour Martin Lipset, eds., *Class, Status, and Power* (New York: The Free Press, 1966); see also the discussion and criticism by Milton M. Gordon, *Social Class in American Sociology* (Durham, N.C.: Duke University Press, 1958).

[3] See Richard Herrnstein, "IQ," *Atlantic Monthly,* September 1971, pp. 43–64; and Arthur R. Jensen, "How Much Can We Boost IQ and Scholastic Achievement?" *Harvard Educational Review,* Reprint Series No. 2, 1969, pp. 126–34.

A critique

Numerous problems are involved with the functionalist arguments on the necessity of inequality. First, the major division of inequality within our society is between the large property holders and those having little or no property. To say that this form of inequality is necessary is to say that capitalism is necessary, obviously quite untrue since there are already societies running relatively well without such a division of inequality of ownership. In a similar vein, to say that the most competent people require greater material rewards to fill the most important positions is to say that the corporate rich are the most competent people and require huge financial holdings to induce them into positions of being large stock holders, a senseless point indeed. Certainly capitalists must be competent at making profits and acquiring property, and making profits and acquiring property are important (absolutely necessary) to capitalism. However, there is no reason to assume, as functionalists tend to do, that the existing system is the only possible system. Quite aside from this, the substantial majority of the propertied-rich inherit their properties, and inheritance of wealth is entirely separate from the sifting and sorting of ability posited by the functionalists. Nor does society require I.Q. tests of inheritors.

However, the functionalist argument on inequality actually neglects to even deal with the major divisive factor of property ownership. Rather, functionalism focuses on society as a continuous hierarchy of positions with no qualitative breaks. Specifically, the inequality argument focuses upon material reward and occupational placement rather than property ownership. So let us meet the argument on these grounds.

Similar to the case of property per se, placement within the general system of material reward is dominated by family background or inheritance factors. In T.B. Bottomore's evaluation, "Indeed, it would be a more accurate description of the social class system to say that it operates, largely through the inheritance of property, to *ensure* that each individual *maintains* a certain social position, determined by his birth and *irrespective of his particular abilities*."[4] The overriding fact of our system of inequality is not a meritocratic placement of qualified people in important positions, but the transmission and inheritance of family and economic privilege from one generation to the next. There is some sifting and sorting of individuals that contributes to inequality, but it is of a different kind than that conceived by functionalism.

The sifting and sorting accomplished by the system of inequality has comparatively little directly to do with competence or personal qualifications in general, inherited intelligence, creative abilities, or even I.Q. As to the latter sacred cow, Bowles and Gintis point out that "The intense debate on the heritability of I.Q. is largely irrelevant to an understanding of poverty, wealth, and inequality of opportunity in the United

---

[4] T.B. Bottomore, *Classes in Modern Society* (New York: Vintage Books, 1968), p. 11. Italics are mine to emphasize the precisely opposite description of the dynamics of inequality from that offered by Davis and Moore.

States."[5] I.Q. lacks significant relationship to inherited intelligence or creativity, and may even be negatively related to the latter. I.Q. is a test device that reflects and certifies that an individual has more or less successfully adjusted mind and habit to the mechanical and fragmented mode of thought required by the highly specialized division of labor. In a self-fulfilling manner, I.Q. is used, in turn, to "prove" that those higher up on this reward ladder are more deserving than those beneath them. Such reproduced intelligence lacks clear relationship to broad inherited intellectual capacities. Even I.Q., tailor made to pick out the minds best adapted to a mechanical and fragmented specialization, does not display an impressively high correlation with the material reward factors of income and occupation.[6]

Chomsky offers an alternative account of the sorting out of unequal material rewards, which have nothing to do with intelligence per se: "Wealth and power tend to accrue to those who are ruthless, cunning, avaricious, self-seeking, lacking in sympathy and compassion, subservient to authority, willing to abandon principle for material gain. . . ."[7] Such an interpretation can muster as much if not more practical proof in its support than can the I.Q. account. This counter thesis holds that those who have most successfully adapted themselves to the needs of profit and property interests acquire material advantages. It argues that the system motivates, sifts, and sorts only a certain limited kind of competence and ability, while shutting out a broad spectrum of diverse capacities.

In a closely related vein, the existing system is built upon a scarcity principle, and thus we witness a variety of certifications and controls on occupational entrance. M.D.s wouldn't rank at or near the top of the occupational income ladder if some of the surplus wealth was used to freely educate all persons interested in becoming doctors and if health care were delivered to all as a free social service. As Theobald observes, ". . . it is those who are willing and able to preserve scarcity who will increase their claims on available abundance."[8] Or from Gross, the

---

[5] See Samuel Bowles and Herbert Gintis, "I.Q. in the U.S. Class Structure," *Social Policy*, November–February, 1972–73, pp. 65–96.

[6] See the extensive analysis by Christopher Jencks et al., *Inequality* (New York: Basic Books, Inc., 1972). While Jencks's analyses demonstrate the relatively weak strength of I.Q. as an explanatory factor of income, occupation, and educational inequality, and the strong impact of social and cultural factors, a correlation of .50 between I.Q. and occupation or education *is* quite high by social science standards. It is precisely this kind of correlation that Herrnstein reads as proving his case for the explanatory value of I.Q., just the opposite of Jencks. The point is, as we have stated above, that I.Q. is correlated with occupation owing to its use as a selective device and self-fulfilling rationalization of inequality. I.Q. is largely artificially (spuriously) correlated with occupational or income success, for if people having different I.Q. levels but the same class origins and levels of education are examined, I.Q. tends to disappear as an explanatory factor of economic success.

[7] Noam Chomsky, "The Fallacy of Richard Herrnstein's IQ," *Social Policy*, (May–June, 1972), p. 21.

[8] Robert Theobald, *Free Men and Free Markets* (New York: Doubleday, Inc., 1965), pp. 62–63.

$44,000 a year physician ". . . is a by-product of the doctor shortage and his ability to command a seller's market among the ill. . . ."[9]

But let us assume that somehow the most "competent" people did, in fact, enter the most important positions. What are these "most important" positions? According to the functionalist premise, we would have to conclude that the $30,000 a year accountant or lawyer working at corporate tax deductions is socially more important than the $8,000 a year lumberjack. (The Herrnstein I.Q. analysis also uses such occupations as proof, since accountants score higher on I.Q. than lumberjacks—which we might expect for reasons having nothing to do with inherited intelligence.) The examples could be multiplied, but the point is obvious enough: importance seems to be a very nebulous quality. Even to the corporate employer himself, the accountant may seem immediately more important than the lumberjack for saving large sums in taxes; but the corporation is also aware that the accountant wouldn't have anything to calculate if the lumberjacks quit working. And to society itself, the lumberjack is essential whereas the corporate tax lawyer may well be pushing a greater tax burden onto the rest of the population. Such a case would reverse the importance rating in relation to the existing reward structure. Many people perceive this frequent reversal of importance and reward. A British sample survey disclosed that blue-collar workers such as drivers and dock workers were considered more important to the nation than accountants and civil servants; yet, the latter are about twice as well off economically as the former.[10]

Further, assuming even that somehow a hierarchy of importance could be objectively established, where is the hard evidence confirming the assertion that unequal rewards must be built-into the more important positions to get them filled? Nor are we given any guidelines as to *how* unequal the rewards must be in order for society to persist and continue as viable. Must there be billionaires and paupers? idle rentiers and poverty-line workers? or only six-figure and four-figure income spreads? or something even less unequal? Put another way, how much of a re-

---

[9] Martin Gross, *The Doctors* (New York: Dell Publishing Co., Inc., 1967), p. 25. This explanation strikes some people as being too crude. Perhaps Samuelson's account is more suitable: ". . . suppose that (1) as many babies were born each year with the capacity necessary for a surgeon as with the capacity necessary for a butcher, (2) we knew how to train surgeons in no time at all, and (3) a surgeon's activities and responsibilities were not regarded as less pleasant or more taxing than those of a butcher. Then do you really think that surgeons would continue to receive higher earnings than butchers?"—Paul A. Samuelson, *Economics* (New York: McGraw-Hill Book Company, 1970), p. 557. Yes, I think so, because these factors are largely irrelevant to the observed income differences and total wealth holdings of surgeons and butchers. There are plenty of babies born with the capacity to do surgical work; once initiated a training program can turn out finished products on an annual or semiannual basis; and it is highly doubtful that a butcher has greater work satisfaction than a surgeon. Again we encounter the surgeon's infinitely greater capacity to control supply of services, compared with the butcher's.

[10] Mark Abrams, "Some Measurements of Social Stratification in Britain," in J.A. Jackson, ed., *Social Stratification* (Cambridge: Cambridge University Press, 1968), p. 139.

ward is necessary for society to bribe its members into becoming high ranking administrators and executives, physicians, scientists and professors, generals and admirals, large stock and bond holders, presidents, consultants, corporate lawyers, university deans, movie stars, and so on. At what level of material reward would such positions go wanting for lack of able candidates? Would the unemployment rate among these categories jump if a $20,000 ceiling were placed on earnings? And for positions of relative "insignificance," what is the size of the shrunken pittance society dangles before the eyes of the unqualified? Subsistence wages? Welfare? Nothing? Where do the millions of unemployed fit into this scheme? dependent mothers and children? the incapacitated? the elderly? Quite clearly, these types don't "fit" anyplace; most are, in fact, counted out.

Here we see more revealing light as to why most people do, in fact, work in a wage-labor society, and it has very little to do with hierarchically built-in rewards: they sell their labor capacity because they must in order to survive. The higher-paid strata must also sell their labor, but the incentive that brought them into the career is hardly a solid cash deal. As Chomsky surmises about the inequality theorist Herrnstein, "I doubt very much that Herrnstein would become a baker or lumberjack if he could earn more money that way."[11] The rewards of high-paying positions have a very strong *intrinsic* satisfaction or incentive to them, whereas the low-paying jobs tend to be the dullest and most dissatisfying.[12]

The intrinsic rewards and satisfactions derived from many kinds of work, particularly work that invites imagination and application of skills, may often be considered as sufficient to draw people into them. The feeling of making a social contribution should also be regarded as a potential incentive. Social altruism in conjunction with the intrinsic satisfaction that comes with knowing work has been done effectively and makes a contribution to one's own group cannot be overestimated as a source of motivation and incentive. Given material security, such social psychological incentives toward work could take over completely. We may witness these incentives even today in China and the Israeli kibbutzim, as well as among many persons in our own society. All too often today, there are no supporting outlets for the large numbers of people who have distinctly nonmaterial aspirations. Many people are forced to choose to enter a job on the material basis of incentive, for they cannot support themselves and their family in preferred work chosen voluntarily. In

---

[11] Chomsky, "The Fallacy of Richard Herrnstein's IQ," p. 20.

[12] Even the "laws" of bourgeois economics are confounded by the direct increase of income with work satisfaction. The hypothesis of "equalizing differences" asserts that "Jobs that involve dirt, nerve strain, tiresome responsibility, tedium, low social prestige, irregular employment, seasonal layoff, short working life, and much dull training all tend to be less attractive to people. To recruit workers for such occupations you must raise the pay. On the other hand, jobs that are especially pleasant or attractive find many applicants, and remuneration is bid down."—Samuelson, *Economics*, p. 555. Surely this is an extremely plausible hypothesis, but as most empirical cases of work testify, the fact does not follow.

Chapter 10 we shall examine the evidence demonstrating the increasing influence of non-economic factors upon worker productivity and job satisfaction.

If a hierarchy of importance cannot be established, could it not be argued anyway that the executive, scientist, doctor, and other top wealth earners sacrificed greatly while studying and training in preparation for their careers and thereby are due large compensations? First of all, there is a serious question as to whether all of the schooling required of many professionals is necessary from the standpoint of actual job performance. As Bowles and Gintis have argued, schooling serves more non-cognitive learning functions than it does develop cognitive and technical abilities.[13] Practical professional and occupational skills are largely learned from actual experience on the job. The long years of schooling do not sort out competence intellectually speaking, but rather attest to other factors employers and professions desire. Among these factors are personality traits such as perseverance and tact; self-presentation in speech, dress, and behavioral codes; and loyalty to the profession or amenability to hierarchy and order. Cognitive abilities and skills are plentiful, widespread, and easily developed outside of long educational routines.

Secondly, education is not necessarily a sacrifice to be compensated for, particularly so if the cost has been assumed by society or someone else in the family. Is four or eight years of additional schooling worth a compensation of $60,000 a year for the remainder of an active career? Actually, the financial loss of higher education could be retired within a few years at an income of just a few thousand dollars above the average. Moreover, one could just as well argue that the manual laborer has lost four to eight years of advanced schooling by going immediately onto the job. How shall we compensate him for a lifetime loss of earnings as an upper-white-collar manager or professional? The worker has missed the opportunity and privilege of self-development in the university, while constricting himself to a grinding and often physically hazardous job. Fidel Castro captured well what we are saying here when he said ". . . it would not be fair if the one that you sent [to study] to be an engineer earned three times more than the one who had to remain working with a tractor in the field."[14]

The general thrust of the functionalist and I.Q. arguments for the necessity of inequality are, in effect, supporting rationalizations on behalf of the existing hierarchy and system of motivations and rewards. These arguments neglect the real underpinnings of inequality, beginning with the system of property relations and following through to inheritance of privilege, the role of profit and service to capital, and the artificial preservation of scarcity and the certification system. The functional argument neglects the fundamental importance of the family and economic background, and how these social and cultural situations predispose people towards successful adaptation to the reward network.

---

[13] Bowles and Gintis, "I.Q. in the U.S. Class Structure," pp. 83–84.

[14] Landau, "Socialist Democracy in Cuba: An Interview with Fidel Castro."

The affluent family rears children who know how to think and act successfully within the network of selecting and certifying institutions, especially the schools (see Chapter 7).

Equalitarianism argues that everyone's essential needs should be met on an equal basis. The poet gets as hungry as the doctor, the dull require clothing and shelter much like the bright. Equality requires that we strive to break down the very specializations that are used to help justify inequality of reward and would establish the conditions in which the doctor would have time to read and write poetry, while the poet could learn of physiology and biology. The dull could enjoy the richest of environments to accentuate every possible talent and enjoyment, while the bright could be more broadly challenged and utilized. The equality perspective contends that everyone has important contributions to make to society, and that given maximum possible freedom from narrow economic necessity, such contributions will flow abundantly and without threat or material bribe.

However, the democratic equalitarian ideal seems distant in the face of present reality. We turn next to an examination of the material aspects of inequality in the United States.

INEQUALITY IN THE UNITED STATES

Economic inequality among persons may be viewed from several perspectives. We shall examine four: total wealth, corporate wealth, income, and savings. Easily the most critical of these is corporate wealth; corporate wealth is not only the prime source of all large money incomes and great fortunes, but far more important, the source of the power to decide what the nation's resources will ultimately be spent for, or wasted upon. Let us look first at the extent of inequality in the sphere of corporate wealth, then at wealth in general.

Wealth

Data dealing with the distribution of corporate wealth in the United States, though not in abundance and difficult to gather owing to the secrecy and subterfuge used in disguising possession of great wealth, reflects the careful study of both government and university economists.[15] The most striking fact about the distribution of corporate wealth is its almost unbelievable concentration in the hands of a miniscule percentage of the American people. The next most striking fact is that the extent of concentration has not changed much over the past decades. And a third salient point is that there has been marked continuity of corporate wealth among the same people or families.

---

[15] Research by Robert Lampman, Gabriel Kolko, the University of Michigan, and the government have been helpfully summarized and evaluated by Ferdinand Lundberg, *The Rich and the Super Rich* (New York: Bantam Books, Inc., 1968), chapter 1. Lampman's research may be found in *The Share of Top Wealth-Holders in National Wealth* (Princeton, N.J.: Princeton University Press, 1962).

The data on corporate wealth converge on the figures that about one percent of the American adult population owns about 80 percent of all publicly held corporate stock.[16] And *within* this one percent a mere five percent hold 40 percent of the total stock. Thus, one-twentieth of one percent hold two-fifths of corporate wealth. Several hundreds to a few thousand heavily propertied persons and families easily claim *controlling* ownership (5 to 10 percent or more) of the corporate world, while they and a few hundred thousand others reap the bulk of the financial dividends. In 1971 there were $1.25 trillion in private industrial and bank assets largely under the sway of the miniscule capitalist class.[17] Kolko has pointed out that estimates of concentration of stock ownership may be underestimated, as about one third of all stock is held in foundations and trusts, though ultimately controlled by top-bracket individuals.[18]

As of 1968, there were about 100,000 millionaires (153 centimillionaires) in America, or .049 percent of the population.[19] These and a couple of hundred thousand persons worth from one-half to a million dollars own the lion's share of corporate wealth. Significantly, about two thirds of the 200,000 top corporate wealth holders (1962) with a half million dollars worth of stock counted *inherited* assets.[20] Millionaires are thus nearly all made from birth or from property. In fact, a bare 4.2 percent of the income of persons taking in one million dollars or more in 1970 came from salaries and 9.5 percent for those getting one-half to one million dollars.[21] Nearly all of the income of the propertied-rich expectedly comes from property—capital gains, dividends, and interest, among other sources. Conversely, for those with incomes from $5,000 to $15,000, 91 percent is derived from wages or salaries. Such is the difference between capitalist and working classes.

With so much corporate wealth held by so few, we would obviously expect to find little such wealth in the rest of the population. Actually, 86 percent of all households in 1960 directly owned no corporate wealth at all.[22] And of the remaining portion of the population who did hold corporate stock, all but three percent held less, most much less, than $10,000 worth.

Although corporate wealth underlies economic power and control in

---

[16] Lampman, *The Share of Top Wealth-Holders in National Wealth*, p. 8. The careful investigations of C. Wright Mills revealed that 0.2 or 0.3 percent of the population hold the payoff shares of corporate wealth. *The Power Elite* (New York: Oxford University Press, 1956), p. 122.

[17] *The American Almanac* (New York: Grosset & Dunlap, 1973), pp. 445, 477.

[18] Gabriel Kolko, *Wealth and Power in America* (New York: Frederick A. Praeger, Inc., 1962), p. 51.

[19] George Kirstein, *The Rich. Are They Different?* (Boston: Houghton Mifflin Company, 1968), p. 8.

[20] Lundberg, *The Rich and the Super Rich*, p. 25.

[21] *The American Almanac*, 1973, p. 394.

[22] Lundberg, *The Rich and the Super Rich*, p. 13. Indirectly, millions of workers have been tied into the fortunes of the corporate economy through retirement pension systems.

society at large, we should also consider total wealth, or that which includes nonindustrial wealth such as insurance policies, bonds, home and business ownership, cash deposits, and, especially, real estate. On the score of total wealth, 0.5 percent of the adult population accounts for at least one-third of the nation's private-sector wealth (about one-fifth of all wealth is held by government), probably a larger proportion than the top one-half of one percent owned in the 1920s.[23] Wealth is no more evenly distributed once we move beyond this circle, for as Federal Reserve Board data from the mid-1960s reveals, the top five percent of adults held 53 percent of total wealth and the top 20 percent held 77 percent. The top one percent holds most privately held corporate bonds, nearly all privately held municipal bonds (tax exempt), two-fifths of federal bonds, and over one-third of all mortgages and notes.

With so much wealth at the top, we would naturally expect very little elsewhere. The bottom 20 percent of the population claims a meager one-half of one percent of total wealth, while the entire lower four-fifths of the population must divide up slightly over one-fifth of the wealth. A significant minority of households are worth less than $1,000 or report deficits. In 1967, the median gross total estate stood at $6,721, while the liquid portion of this accounted for only 13 percent; home equity accounted for the largest portion.

Finally, turning to liquid cash assets or savings, the top income tenth has held around three-fourths of net savings since the 1920s, while the bottom tenth has been far in the hole.[24] Indeed, the bottom half of the society fluctuates precariously near being flat broke. In 1970, 16 percent of families held zero or minus liquid cash assets, 14 percent less than $200, and 12 percent between $200 and $499. Twenty-two percent held a cash hoard between $500 and $1,999.[25] Median liquid holdings in 1970 were $800.

All told, Lundberg makes a pertinent point when he says that "It would be difficult in the 1960s [or 1970s] for a large majority of Americans to show fewer significant possessions if the country had long labored under a grasping dictatorship."[26]

Income

The overwhelming majority of the population must rely on annual salaries, hourly wages, personal fees, or insurance-transfer payments for their incomes. As a rule, only salaries and fees will permit what Americans imagine as the Good Life complete, but they far, very far, from guarantee it. Usually, even the salaried middle-range businessman must rely heavily on company expense accounts and in-kind privileges to enjoy regularly the embellishments of the truly affluent life style. Ironically, but understandably, as one moves up into the higher salary brackets of

---

[23] Ibid., p. 11.
[24] Kolko, *Wealth and Power in America*, p. 48.
[25] *The American Almanac*, 1972, p. 315.
[26] Lundberg, *The Rich and the Super Rich*, p. 1.

$25,000, $50,000, $75,000 and beyond, the income in kind via expense accounts and company privileges increases commensurately. Expensive automobiles, small jet aircraft, class restaurants, the "best" entertainment, topflight clubs, exclusive hunting and fishing resorts, and world travel are not obtainable (after family, clothing, and housing "essentials" are paid for) even on salaries that stagger the imagination of the camper-driving American. Such luxuries and privileges are "fringe" benefits that vastly augment actual income.

The best and only reliable way to make really big money is through large holdings of corporate stock, and especially through the purchase and sale of stock options, that is, the purchase of company stock at some fraction of market value and subsequent sale at inflated values. (Don't head for the nearest broker and ask him for a stock option; stock options are the prerogatives of corporate executives only. As some sage once said, "Those that have shall receive more"; perhaps even better, "Those that

Table 1
INCOME CLASSES IN THE UNITED STATES (1970)

Income	Percent of white families	Percent of nonwhite families	Percent of white unrelated individuals	Percent of nonwhite unrelated individuals
$15,000+	24%	11%	{10%	{3%
10,000–15,000	28	17		
7,000–10,000	20	18	13	9
5,000– 7,000	11	17	12	11
3,000– 5,000	9	17	18	18
Under $3,000	8	20	47	59
	100% (46.5m)	100% (5.4m)	100% (13.4m)	100% (1.9m)
Median	$10,236	$6,516	$3,283	$2,243

Source: U.S. Bureau of the Census, *Current Population Reports*, Series P-60, No. 80, "Income in 1970 of Families and Persons in the United States," U.S. Government Printing Office, Washington, D.C., 1971, Table 9, p. 23.

have shall *give* themselves more.") For example, U.S. Steel granted its executives stock options with a *face value* of $49 million in 1951, and in 1957 the stocks were worth $133 million.[27] This fantastic increase of wealth is appropriately called "capital *appreciation*" (not to be confused with dividends or interest, unlikely to make one wealthy unless already wealthy enough to own very large blocks of stock).

The median income in 1970 for white families was $10,232 and for nonwhite families, $6,516 (Table 1). In that year, eight percent of all white families and 20 percent of all nonwhite families had incomes under $3,000; conversely, 24 percent of white families and 11 percent of nonwhite (which includes Chinese and Japanese) reported incomes of over $15,000. (*All* families could average approximately $15,000 if personal

[27] Kolko, *Wealth and Power in America*, p. 42. Ex-Secretary of Defense Robert McNamara made a small fortune at Ford exercising executive stock options at one-third price.

income were equally divided, suggesting that over three-fourths of the population would gain from equalization of income and a very small minority would lose *significantly*.) Unrelated individuals, frequently senior citizens, exist at pathetically low standards. During the 1960s, the income gap between the upper income categories and the lower *increased* (relative immiseration in Marxist terms).[28] (Low-income groups must realize larger annual percentage-point increases just to maintain the previous year's absolute dollar gap between themselves and the higher income groups. Instead rates of percentage increase for higher income groups were larger.)

Is personal income in the United States moving in the long run toward a more equitable or toward a less equitable distribution within the pop-

Table 2

PERCENTAGE SHARE OF AGGREGATE INCOME IN 1947 AND 1970 RECEIVED BY EACH FIFTH OF FAMILIES AND UNRELATED INDIVIDUALS, RANKED BY INCOME, BY RACE OF HEAD OF HOUSEHOLD

Families	*White*		*Nonwhite*	
	1947	1970	1947	1970
Percent	100.0	100.0	100.0	100.0
Lowest Fifth	5.4	5.8	4.3	4.5
Second Fifth	12.1	12.3	10.3	10.4
Third Fifth	16.9	17.4	16.0	16.5
Fourth Fifth	22.7	23.4	23.7	24.5
Highest Fifth	42.8	41.1	45.7	44.0
Top 5 percent	17.7	14.2	17.1	15.4
Unrelated individuals				
Percent	100.0	100.0	100.0	100.0
Lowest Fifth	1.8	3.5	2.6	3.0
Second Fifth	5.7	8.0	7.9	7.9
Third Fifth	11.8	13.9	15.2	13.5
Fourth Fifth	21.3	24.5	25.4	24.5
Highest Fifth	59.4	50.2	48.9	51.0
Top 5 percent	34.2	20.3		19.6

Source: U.S. Bureau of the Census, *Current Population Reports*, Series P-60, No. 80, "Income in 1970 of Families and Persons in the United States," U.S. Government Printing Office, Washington, D.C., 1971, Table 14, p. 28.

ulation? Government statistics suggest there have been no noteworthy changes in income distribution since 1947. Since then, the highest fifth of white family income units has received about 42 percent of the total personal money income (this is also the money-in-kind expense account category as well), the bottom fifth, only five percent (Table 2). The median income of the bottom fifth in 1970 was $3,054 compared with the top fifth's $23,100, a gap at least $3,000 *larger* than in 1947 (despite the large increase in the number of working women in the lower income

---

[28] Herman P. Miller, "A Profile of the Blue-Collar American," in Sar A. Levitan, ed., *Blue-Collar Workers* (New York: McGraw-Hill Book Company, 1971), p. 59.

groups). Note that the imbalance among nonwhites is slightly greater than for whites. Among unrelated individuals the imbalance is severe. In terms of income tenths, the top garners 28 percent of the total, the bottom only one percent, the second lowest three percent, the third five percent, and the fourth six percent. Thus, the bottom 40 percent of the income ladder *combined* can muster only *one-half* of what the top 10 percent takes. The 80 percentile only slightly more than breaks even, further suggesting the wide impact of an income equalization policy. Income taxes have slight redistributive effect, so the distribution of disposable income would be approximately the same as before taxes.

Taxation

"When all tax payments are taken into account, there is a real question as to whether taxes have a significant effect on the equalization of income."[29] So writes Herman P. Miller, government statistician and economist. Miller's Census Bureau figures disclose that the richest five percent of the population has its 20 percent share of personal income reduced by two percentage points by federal taxes, while the rest of the population moves only one point in either direction. Whereas the federal tax is slightly progressive, state and local taxes are regressive, and so nullify what minor equalization is accomplished at the federal level. Although figures vary somewhat depending upon the sources, it is safe to say that, whether one is living in poverty or untold luxury or somewhere in between, the combined government taxes take on the average between 25 and 35 percent of reported personal earnings.[30] If *unearned* income, particularly capital gains, is included in the calculations, the rich are more likely than not to come off ahead of the poor in proportionate terms (even in absolute dollar terms there are the fabled rich who escape the income tax collector entirely). For example, persons reporting total incomes of $200,000 or more pay an effective federal rate of 30 percent, less than half the official rate schedule.[31] By contrast, workers earning less than $3,000 a year may find themselves paying an overall tax rate as high or even higher than 30 percent.

What the figures suggest, then, is that millionaires tend to pay a percentage of their income taxes which is not much different than that of an average white- or blue-collar wage worker. Indeed, millionaires pay

[29] Herman P. Miller, *Rich Man, Poor Man* (New York: Signet Books, 1968), p. 53. Lipsey and Steiner, authors of a basic economics text, have an answer to Miller's question: "If the purpose of our tax structure has been to be neutral with respect to the over-all income distribution, it has been a success. If its purpose has been to be an instrument of general redistribution from rich to poor, it has not been a success."—Richard G. Lipsey and Peter O. Steiner, *Economics* (New York: Harper and Row, 1966), p. 508.

[30] Joseph Pechman, "The Rich, the Poor, and the Taxes They Pay," *The Public Interest*, 17 (Fall 1968), pp. 21–43; Thomas Bodenheimer, "The Poverty of the State," *Monthly Review*, 24 (November 1972), pp. 7–18; and Jerry J. Jasinowski, "Mr. Nixon's Tax Mythology," *The Nation*, October 30, 1972, pp. 399–404.

[31] Jasinowski, "Mr. Nixon's Tax Mythology."

less in tax percentage than does the ordinary American, if we consider the chief sources of their wealth—capital gains. Law Professor W. David Slawson calculates that the wealthiest one percent of adults receive income of upward of $30 billion a year from capital appreciation (this does *not* include dividends), but this income produces only about $1 billion in tax—"a rate of only 3.3 percent despite the income's being received by persons most of whom are (or should be) in the 70 percent bracket."[32] Nor do inheritance taxes seem to be any more effective than income or capital gains taxes in achieving the goal of redistribution. The largest estates seldom pay more than 20 percent inheritance taxes, and frequently much less.[33] Thus, we have already noted the marked continuity of wealthy families in this century. How is it possible that some $77 billion in taxes annually dodge the tax collector? The explanation lies in the fact that the rich simply deal themselves tax advantages and loopholes through a very compliant Congress. Of great significance is the fact that a very large group of congressmen are themselves millionaires eager to preserve their fortunes for themselves and their children.

Let us examine a few of the major tax dodges used by the propertied-rich. We have already illustrated the evasive and minimizing effect of the capital gains tax—a special tax loophole designed by and for the capitalist class to protect its major source of income. Also in this connection, capital gains are passed on to inheritors untaxed, an opening costing the Treasury (the working class) several billions annually. Inheritance trusts which skip tax obligations for entire generations also help preserve family fortunes. Tax-exempt bonds re-make millionaires on an annual basis, and they never pay a cent. Perhaps most notorious is the oil depletion allowance, which allows a write-off of 20 percent (27.5 percent prior to 1970); this combined with foreign tax credits has such results as Standard Oil of N.J. paying a tax rate of 1.7 percent in 1964 and Texaco 0.8 percent; in 1971 Standard Oil of California paid 1.6 percent, Conoco 2.1 percent, and Gulf 2.3 percent. The list of loopholes is endless, but philanthropy and foundations, estate dividing, executive profit-sharing plans, expense accounts, and deferred compensation of executive remuneration might be mentioned among the more prominent.

Applying the loopholes, 43 percent of the nation's corporations paid less than five per cent income tax. These are not necessarily small operations; nine of the largest 86 industrial corporations paid no federal income taxes in 1970 yet had profits of $682 million.[34] Five firms totaled $382 million profits in 1971 and paid no federal income taxes. The major corporation average in 1969 was 27 percent, but a conservative adminis-

---

[32] W. David Slawson, "Moves to Patch the Loopholes," *The Nation*, June 16, 1969, p. 763. Unfortunately, the loopholes were not patched in 1970.

[33] Kolko, *Wealth and Power in America*, p. 32.

[34] See Joseph A. Ruskay, "Tax Reform: The Loopholes Still With Us," *The Nation*, March 22, 1971, pp. 268–71; Jasinowski, "Mr. Nixon's Tax Mythology"; and Philip M. Stern, "Oil: How It Raids the Treasury," *The Progressive*, April 1973, pp. 22–26.

tration has since been hard at work for corporate tax breaks and has been quite successful. The IT&T paid an effective rate of 5 percent in 1971. The tax breaks given to big business supposedly stimulate production, but the shortages of oil and gas should be sufficient evidence to refute such mythical thinking (Congressional investigations revealed that seven difference tax subsidies worth $23 billion a year failed to produce at all or adversely; $1.4 billion worth of oil subsidies generated only $150 million petroleum reserves). Regarding time trends and the tax burden, Perlo points out that from 1941 to 1970 labor's proportion of the federal tax load increased from 45 to 68 percent while capital's share declined from 55 to 32 percent of the total.[35]

It is doubtful that taxation could ever be an effective instrument of substantive income redistribution in a society dominated by giant corporations. The logic is simple: the propertied-rich dominate the state, the state writes the tax laws, and the tax laws thus protect the propertied-rich. Only a powerful and determined popular political party could make a significant redistributive dent in income distribution via taxation. In social democratic Sweden, for example, family heads receiving $4,000 or less in 1967 accounted for 26 percent of personal income before taxes but 51 percent after taxes, while the upper end of the income ladder had 21 percent before and only five percent after taxes.[36] In addition, there exists a tax on wealth, a measure that would raise several billions of dollars annually in the U.S. Swedish corporations pay an average 40 percent rate, considerably higher than the 27 percent rate in the U.S. Yet, inequality is quite extensive in Sweden, and it is unlikely that much more equality can be achieved through further changes in the tax structure. In a planned economy such as China, taxation plays a very small role, since prices and costs are relatively fixed and the difference between them constitutes investment resources. Wages are also adjusted in relation to prices and costs, further reducing any need for taxation. If substantial equality is to be achieved, it must be done apart from taxation. Taxation is typically a device designed to shift costs and financial burdens in a manner supportive of the property-owning class. We shall examine in detail certain prominent cases of cost shifting and profit-receiving, especially that of militarization (see Chapter 9).

WORKING CLASS SUBSISTENCE

The data presented thus far suggest that, in contemporary terms, Marx's proposition concerning the *relative* decline of the working class vis-à-vis the capitalist class contains a degree of validity. The number of propertied-rich and the size of their wealth has increased incomparably more than the inflation-damaged income crawl of most of the working class. The affluence of the propertied class seems unlimited, while the

---

[35] Victor Perlo, *The Unstable Economy* (New York: International Publishers, 1973), p. 142.

[36] Martin Schnitzer, *The Economy of Sweden* (New York: Praeger Publishers, 1970), p. 129.

working class spends time bargain shopping and saving pennies wherever possible. The chief wage earner often "moonlights" on extra jobs, and the wife works part-time or however much she is able; working wives contribute between one-fourth and one-third of their total family income, thus preventing severe income shortages and even poverty in many cases. A growing percentage of the paycheck goes toward debt retirement. Whether white or blue collar, economic margins are typically very thin. As Arthur Shostak has remarked regarding manual workers, "Blue-collar prosperity is precariously supported, maintained as it is largely by heavy installment debt and steadily declining purchasing power." "Pathos and 'affluence' to the contrary," Shostak continues, "blue-collarites today in America are *not* especially well off."[37]

The working class as a whole is living near or below present-day subsistence levels. The average weekly take-home earnings of a manufacturing worker with three dependents did not improve—in constant or inflation neutralized dollar terms—from 1965 through 1971; at both times take-home pay was $102 (1967 dollars).[38] (In current dollar terms, the worker earned $97 a week in 1965 and $124 a week in 1971, but—thanks largely to sharply increased military spending—saw the purchasing power of the dollar shrink by 24 cents.) If the worker were on the job a full 52 weeks, yearly take-home constant dollar income would come to $5,304; for six years he has been on a treadmill going nowhere. Meanwhile, the major shareholders in his firm have been reaping ever larger profit harvests importantly due to a 10–25 point increase in worker productivity during the period.[39]

In this connection, Perlo reported that the increase from 1946 to 1969 in manufacturing's productivity index was 139 percent (61 to 146), whereas the real take-home pay after tax and price increases are reckoned was raised by only 41 percent for production workers in manufacturing. Given a rate of surplus value of 100 percent in 1946, the rate would stand at 175 percent in 1969. Perlo also observed that, during these years, the index of real take-home pay per unit of production decreased from 131.9 to 77.5, or by 41 percent, "that is, the worker's share in the values he produced declined by two-fifths!"[40] From such data we may readily see that price inflation has much less to do with "wage push" than with "profit pull."

The Bureau of Labor Statistics set a "lower" budget level for a family of four (1970) at $6,960;[41] in current dollars, the manufacturing worker with three dependents took-home $116 a week or $6,032 in 52 weeks. The average manufacturing worker depending on his own income is thus living well under the subsistence level as defined by the state itself. The manufacturing worker is not an exception. All full-time wage and

---

[37] Arthur Shostak, *Blue Collar Life* (New York: Random House, Inc., 1969), pp. 274–75.

[38] *The American Almanac,* 1973, p. 233.

[39] Ibid., p. 232.

[40] Perlo, *The Unstable Economy,* p. 30.

[41] *The American Almanac,* 1973, p. 350.

salary workers had weekly *gross* earnings of $130 in 1970 current dol-
lars,[42] for a 52 week income of $6,760. Clerical workers, operatives,
nonfarm laborers, service workers, and farmworkers did worse than the
average. The full-time farmworker, producer of the most basic means
of existence, earned $71 a week and $3,692 a year before taxes. Professionals, managers, salesworkers, and craftsmen did better than the
average. Males did better than the average, females worse; whites did
better than the average, blacks worse. Regardless of sex or color, or even
occupation, the individual worker taken alone finds salary or wage within
short distance of the lower budget level.

As noted at the outset of the section, the chief earner frequently must
moonlight or put other members of the family to work, especially the
spouse. Taking total family money income for 1970 and comparing it to
the government's family budget level for that year, we may calculate
that 31 percent of families had incomes beneath the lower level ($6,960),
20 percent beneath the intermediate ($10,664) but above the lower
level, 27 percent between the middle and upper ($15,511), and 22 per-
cent above the upper level.[43] Quite clearly, 51 percent of families must
be rated as "precarious," a category within which is found the large
majority of production workers. The fact that 3.3 million workers went
out on strike in 1970 with a loss of 66.4 million man-days attests to the
tooth and nail struggle in the working class to "make ends meet."

A piece of research may be cited here that bears directly on the issue
of the subsistence level and capitalism's propensity to hold workers at or
beneath it. Kahl and Goering studied a sample of urban working class
people who defined the "good life" as having the material resources to
obtain what our culture has defined as necessities such as an operable
mode of transportation, a decent home, adequate funds for food and
clothing, and enough money for a modicum of recreation.[44] With such a
"good life" placed on a 7-point scale, respondents on the average rated
themselves two points short of this good life level (the bourgeoisie would
consider such a level of living as deprived). The "squeeze" on the working class has not gone unnoticed by the critical observer.[45]

There has been some debate as to whether the lower ranks of white-
collar workers are as well off as the highest ranks of blue-collar workers,
the craftsmen or skilled workers. Skilled workers definitely stand above
semiskilled workers (operatives) in terms of income and job security.
And skilled workers far outdistance unskilled and blue-collar service
workers, who for some time have been losing ground to the rest of the
working class. Overall, the income of skilled workers has been slightly

---

[42] Ibid., p. 231.

[43] Ibid., p. 322.

[44] Joseph A. Kahl and John M. Goering, "Stable Workers, Black and White,"
Social Problems, 18 (Winter 1971), p. 315.

[45] See, for example, Dennis Duggan, "Still Forgotten: The Working Poor,"
The Nation, June 9, 1969, p. 726; Al Bilik, "The Alienated Rank and File,"
The Nation, November 17, 1969, pp. 527–30; Abraham Ribicoff, "The Alienation of the American Worker," *Saturday Review,* April 22, 1972, pp. 29–33;
and Gus Tyler, "White Worker/Blue Mood," *Dissent,* Winter 1972, 190–96.

higher than that of lower white-collar workers. However, if only full-time, male lower white-collar workers are included in the comparison (skilled workers would not tend to compare themselves to white-collar females or part-time student workers), differences between the two occupational groups are insignificant.[46] If anything, the lower white-collar worker's income is slightly higher. Furthermore, persons in white-collar jobs usually desire and often think they have relatively good opportunities for both job and income promotions and a few, in fact, are "on the way up." By contrast, blue-collar workers usually hold slim hopes for promotion, banking mainly on occasional hourly wage increases to remain abreast of inflation. Full-time male white-collar fringe benefits and job security are often better than those of even the skilled wage worker, though not always.

However, the mass of white-collar office workers are not markedly better off than the manual laborer, and increasing numbers of both categories are beginning to recognize this fact. Very often, white- and blue-collars are mixed in the same family and more often the same neighborhood. Our model considers most of them as being part of the larger working class, and white-collar workers are increasingly doing the same.

Shostak declares that the "American working class is one that fears to dare. . . ."[47] The working class—employed and unemployed, skilled and unskilled, white and black—must learn to dare or be faced with endless treadmill subsistence or the indignities of the existing welfare system. They might demand from America's unprecedented and unparalleled material base free education, from nursery to professional school; free health care, from dental fillings to death; recreational facilities and parks where they might take their children; low income housing in city, suburb, and town; the right to a respectable job; the right to a guaranteed income; and consumer price and quality protection against corporate profiteers. The working class and its allies should see that idle and underutilized capital and human beings be put to work in the interest of all members of society, that their cities be made livable, that economic waste be eliminated, and that misused and maldistributed resources be put to constructive social purposes. Finally, and in conjunction with all of the above, workers could well demand something better from their taxes than moon shots, faster jet fighters, bigger transport planes and bombers, missiles, antimissile missiles, and war. Why shouldn't an American worker (whose effective taxes are as high and country wealthier) enjoy the economic security of a Scandinavian or West German worker?

INEQUALITY AND SOCIAL PROBLEMS

So the United States has a rather marked degree of economic inequality. So what? Highly educated people contend that a more equitable dis-

---

[46] See Richard F. Hamilton, "Income, Class, and Reference Groups," *American Sociological Review,* 29 (August 1964), pp. 576–79; and "The Marginal Middle Class," *American Sociological Review,* 31 (April 1966), pp. 192–99.

[47] Shostak, *Blue-Collar Life,* p. 290.

tribution of income and wealth would solve only the poverty problem, implying that poverty sits in a corner unrelated to what might be considered other social problems and also that the poor require considerably more than a better share of the nation's wealth to set them straight. We shall deal with these questions at greater length in Chapter 8. Suffice it to point out here that the elimination of poverty and marked economic inequality would seem to deserve a higher rating than "only." With liberals viewing the problem so calmly it should not be surprising that the distribution of income has not changed during the past generation or two. While receiving a subsistence income when others are inheriting fortunes may seem like an "only" problem to the affluent, it ranks very high among the pressing problems of the working class and poor.

And is subsistence or poverty and marked inequality of condition an isolated problem? Definitely not. The maldistribution of economic means (in a society that banks more heavily on personal than social spending) has tremendous relevance for educational inequality, the ghettoization of the city, discrepancies in health and diet, crime, drugs, family dissolution and rising welfare costs, and a host of other things in the area of race relations and urban life. And at the top-heavy end of the distribution, economic inequality has steadily contributed to greater and greater concentration of social and political power. In combination, these discrepancies of wealth and power have threatened to destroy democratic sensibilities and have already impaired democratic functioning. Minimizing the importance of economic inequality strikes us as a diversion tactic of the well-to-do.[48]

COMPARATIVE INEQUALITY

How great is inequality in the United States as compared to other nations in the world? Roughly speaking, the extent of inequality in the U.S. is less than in most of the underdeveloped countries, though it is difficult to make any precise comparisons owing to the vastly different levels of industrialization. The underdeveloped countries have been extensively dominated by Europe and America (see Chapter 14). The result has been massive inequalities between a small wealthy class of pro-Western elites and a large impoverished mass. The size of the industrial working class and commercial white-collar stratum is much smaller than in the developed countries. In Latin America in the mid-1960s, Frank reported that top five percent of the population takes 33 percent of the income (compared with approximately 16 percent in the U.S.), the top 20 percent takes 63 percent of the income (compared with approximately 44 percent in the U.S.), and the bottom 20 percent only three percent (5 percent in the U.S.).[49] Forty percent of the population lives in destitution. However, in terms of total wealth, U.S. and Latin American con-

[48] Leading the way for the "new conservatives" of academia was Edward C. Banfield, *The Un-heavenly City* (Boston: Little, Brown and Company, 1970).

[49] Andre Gunder Frank, *Lumpen-Bourgeoisie and Lumpen-Development* (New York: Monthly Review Press, 1970), pp. 116–17.

centrations are similar (remembering that the U.S. propertied-rich are as a class *much* richer than their Latin American counterparts). In Brazil, 17 percent of the population holds 63 percent of wealth, in Venezuela 12 percent holds 50 percent, and in Colombia five percent holds 41 percent.[50] (In the U.S., five percent holds 53 percent of wealth, and 20 percent holds 77 percent of wealth.)

In absolute terms, of course, the entire U.S. material wealth structure is on almost a completely different plane than the Latin American, though there exists a sizeable number of poor persons in the U.S. whose material conditions are absolutely destitute. Certainly, the bottom tenth of the U.S. population is materially far better off than their Latin American counterparts. Yet, in comparative terms, this is not the issue. The issue concerns expected cultural standards at given levels of development. Within the development structure of their own societies, much of the U.S. working class and poor are not significantly better off than the Latin American working class and poor.

Compared with other developed capitalist countries the U.S. does not seem to stand out one way or another. Certainly the working classes of Northern Europe, particularly of Scandinavia and West Germany, both have higher expectations regarding material security and welfare and receive more social benefits. (In the political and industrial sense, the European working classes are also much stronger than the American counterpart.) The U.S. worker may be able to outspend his European counterpart (a rapidly changing situation, however), but disposable income is not the whole story in defining material well-being and security. The Swedish worker (and German as well), for example, enjoys health, educational, family, retirement, and unemployment benefits which the U.S. worker would envy.[51] This is so owing to the fact that Sweden's working class, or rather its political party representative the Social Democrats, has dominated the government since about 1920. At first socialist in doctrine, the Social Democrats moderated their stance to that of welfare state capitalism. The state is deeply involved in the regulation of the industrial economy, which is itself largely in private hands. As previously noted, Sweden has achieved a substantive redistribution of wealth by way of taxation and the universal provision of social services and benefits. Neither the extremes of poverty nor wealth are so visible as they are in the U.S., though the range of inequality is nevertheless substantial.

While European working-class political parties have made a greater impact on government than in the U.S., the extent of inequality is still great. The English government has instituted a number of social welfare schemes that go beyond those existing in the U.S.; yet, England's distribution of wealth is more highly concentrated than that of the U.S. One percent of the adult population holds 42 percent of all wealth (compared

---

[50] Irving Louis Horowitz, *Three Worlds of Development* (New York: Oxford University Press, 1966), pp. 199–201.

[51] See Paul Dickson, "Sweden's Quest for Equality," *The Progressive*, November 1972, pp. 23–25; Albert H. Rosenthal, *The Social Programs of Sweden* (Minneapolis: University of Minnesota Press, 1967); and Richard Tomasson, *Sweden: Prototype of Modern Society* (New York: Random House, Inc., 1970).

with about 33 percent in the U.S.) and five percent holds 75 percent of wealth (compared with 53 percent in the U.S.). However, political parties backed largely by the industrial working class have made marked gains in many European countries. In France in 1973, a left coalition polled 46.5 percent of the national vote, and were perhaps robbed of victory by a last minute government propaganda blitz that swung the center toward the regime.[52] The West German working class is strong and would probably not tolerate a marked deterioration in their condition. Italian and English workers have demonstrated considerable militance in recent years as well. Patience with economic cycles and unnecessary inequalities may be running out.

Soviet type systems

What of the state-planned "communist" economies? Have they made any definite strides toward social equality? British sociologist David Lane has marshalled considerable evidence that suggests they have, in fact, done so. Lane summarizes, "We may confidently generalize that one of the results of the Soviet pattern of nationalization and industrialization is a considerable equalization of income and living conditions.[53] For example, differences in income between technicians and engineers with higher education and skilled laborers with eight years education are not large, and not nearly so large as in capitalist countries. We pointed out in the previous section how white-collar employees are on the average economically better off than blue-collar workers in the U.S. and Great Britain; the reverse holds true in the Soviet Union and some Eastern European countries where skilled workers have on the average larger yearly incomes than office employees. For example, a 1967 report on the Leningrad labor force indicates that skilled pipe fitters and welders had an income of 120 rubles per month (8.3 years education), but qualified non-manual technologists and bookkeepers had 110 rubles per month (12.5 years education).[54] Indeed, highly qualified personnel in technical-scientific jobs with 14 years education were earning only 7 rubles per month more than the skilled craftsmen; these new working class professionals averaged only 30 rubles per month more than unskilled laborers with only 6 years schooling. Factory directors, equivalent to U.S. chief executive officers (who are often multimillionaires), had incomes only twice as large as the lowest listed job category—office workers of medium qualifications.

At every level of qualification, the production worker is better paid than the white-collar employee. Production work, especially of the skilled variety, receives higher *prestige* as well, surpassed only by the more

---

[52] Claude Bourdet, "French Elections: The 'Too-Pretty Bride,'" *The Nation*, April 9, 1973, pp. 454–56.

[53] David Lane, *The End of Inequality? Stratification under State Socialism* (Baltimore: Penguin Books, 1971), p. 75. See also Mervyn Matthews, *Class and Society in Soviet Russia* (London: The Penguin Press, 1972).

[54] Ibid., pp. 64–65; see also Murray Yanowitch, "The Soviet Income Revolution," in Celia S. Heller, *Structured Social Inequality* (New York: Macmillan Company, 1969), p. 147.

highly educated scientific and intellectual (intelligentsia) occupations. Another data source suggests that a skilled blue-collar worker with a wife working as a salesclerk and a son in a factory will have an income as large as an engineer married to a doctor with a son in a university.[55] The same worker may earn up to twice as much as a doctor, the latter being in the same income bracket as teachers, legal officials, salesmen, and bureaucrats. We have cited typical examples of income distribution in the U.S.S.R., and there are, of course, exceptions. However, the trends since the 1930s—when disparities were very large—have been toward increasing equalization (reversals are, of course, a real possibility).

Even given occasional exceptional ratios of five to one, say between a university scientist of outstanding achievement and an unskilled menial laborer, such is by comparison nothing to the income spreads found in the U.S. The top officer in IT&T receives a salary and bonus of over $800,000 a year, not to mention the income derived from the millions of dollars of stock he holds in the company.[56] And this income is rather small compared with that of the top circle of financiers. Further, the Soviet citizen has benefited from the equalizing influences of universal state services and subsidies such as in health, child care, education, and retirement. (Urban areas do benefit more than rural areas, especially the more remote places.) As the proportion of surplus value spent socially increases, so does the amount of material inequality tend to decrease.

But what of the Soviet elite? Haven't the top stratum of officialdom created a reservoir of power and wealth that sets them apart from the Soviet people much in the same way that capitalists have enriched themselves at the expense of their working class?[57] The answer is definitely no. Although Soviet society is not socialist, for it among other things remains tied to a hierarchical system of wage labor, it has no class of propertied-rich who appropriate fortunes from the social surplus and transmit them to inheritors. As Isaac Deutscher pointed out,

> Officialdom still dominates society and lords over it, yet it lacks the cohesion and unity which would make of it a separate class in the Marxist sense of the word. The bureaucrats enjoy power and some measure of prosperity, yet they cannot bequeath their prosperity and wealth to their children. They cannot accumulate capital, or invest it for the benefit of their descendants: they cannot perpetuate themselves or their kith and kin.[58]

This lack of property ownership in the social sense does not preclude the acquisition of a substantial number of personal goods and privileges in the form of a villa, auto, luxury goods, expensive vacations, and so on.

A final point on the Soviet system should be made with regard to women. Advances in the material, legal, political, and social rights of

---

[55] Pierre Sorlin, *The Soviet People and Their Society* (New York: Frederick A. Praeger, Inc., 1968), p. 233.

[56] *Forbes*, May 15, 1972, p. 205.

[57] For a critical discussion of Soviet-style elites, see Milovan Djilas, *The New Class* (New York: Frederick A. Praeger, Inc., Publishers, 1957).

[58] Isaac Deutscher, *Marxism In Our Time* (Berkeley: Ramparts Press, 1971), p. 205.

women have been marked.[59] In the public or legal sense, women are considered to be the equal of men. The same applies to Eastern Europe.[60] Women have increasingly participated in positions of economic, political, and social responsibility, while their own material support and privileges have been elevated to a par with those of men. However, men continue to predominate in the most powerful and privileged positions of government and society, and it is unclear as to whether this is a consequence of generations of female self-subordination and withdrawal or an essential aspect of the system. A further sexual inequity is the continued burden of most household and domestic chores for the female, *despite* her extensive involvement in full-time paid labor. Polish women face the same double burden; the double work-load is also widespread in China (and Cuba). There can be no real sexual equality until the total work loads are shared by both male and female.[61]

What has been said about the U.S.S.R. may be generally applied to much of the rest of Eastern Europe. Polish data indicate that the extent of pre-World War inequality to be markedly greater than today.[62] The working class has relatively improved its position vis-à-vis officials and white-collar workers, though evidently not to the same extent as have Soviet workers. In Poland, where agricultural production is dominated by independent producers who exact maximum prices from the government and food buyers, the rural population often lives considerably better than the urban working class. The Polish working class has evinced considerable discontent over food prices and wage inequality in general.

China

In contrast with Eastern European countries, which have introduced some form of the quality-creating "profit-sharing" within industries, China has launched upon a somewhat different course of development. Despite its enormous size and population, inequality in China is perhaps less than in any other nation in the world, and it is no longer an equality in poverty.[63] (The Israeli kibbutzim would be the excep-

---

[59] *Women in the Soviet Union* (Moscow: Progress Publishers, 1970); H. Kent Geiger, *The Family in Soviet Russia* (Cambridge: Harvard University Press, 1968).

[60] Krystyna Wrochno, *Women in Poland* (Warsaw: Interpress Publishers, 1969; Chicago: Imported Publications).

[61] See Janet Weitzner Salaff and Judith Merkle, "Women in Revolution: The Lessons of the Soviet Union and China," *Berkeley Journal of Sociology*, XV (1970), pp. 166–91; and Petur Gudjonsson, "Women in Castro's Cuba," *The Progressive*, August 1972, pp. 25–29.

[62] Wlodzimierz Wesolowski and Kazimierz Slomczynski, "Social Stratification in Polish Cities," in *Social Stratification*, J.A. Jackson, ed. (Cambridge: Cambridge University Press, 1968), pp. 175–211.

[63] See Maria Antoinetta Macciocchi, *Daily Life in Revolutionary China* (New York: Monthly Review Press, 1972); *China! Inside the People's Republic,* Committee of Concerned Asian Scholars (New York: Bantam Books, Inc., 1972); and E.L. Wheelwright and Bruce McFarlane, *The Chinese Road to Socialism* (New York: Monthly Review Press, 1970).

tion.[64] Wages are more equal than in the Soviet Union. Wages are determined by the workers themselves, both in factories and on agricultural communes. The decision is based on both ability to produce and upon political behavior. The outcome is by Western and even Soviet standards a quite small income range.

Helping to reduce wage disparities is the principle of workers' control. Authority hierarchies have been pruned down and operating control placed in the hands of revolutionary committees, which are instruments of the workers, farmers, students, soldiers, or whatever the case may be. In addition, occupational specialization is being attacked in an attempt to integrate manual and mental labor and to generalize abilities within these categories. Thus, it becomes more difficult to single out isolated individuals as especially important or indispensible. Scientists and doctors learn humility; laborers and peasants learn self-confidence. Prestige hierarchies orient themselves around social contribution instead of individual success and wealth. (Scientists don't publish papers or books under their personal name.)

While rural communes have a form of surplus-sharing plan within each one (and hence inequality between them), factory units do not use profit or surplus production as a wage-setting device. Work incentives are thus largely socially and culturally conditioned. Wage differentials are not great from factory to factory, nor are they very large within individual factories. Seniority plays an important role, so that an older unskilled worker may earn about as much as the young factory engineer, or even the director (increasingly indistinguishable in appearance and behavior from the rest of the plant work force). Social services are more equally distributed than in the Soviet Union, largely due to the ideological motivations of medical workers and teachers who volunteer tours of duty into the hinterlands. Food is abundant and perhaps can be obtained in greater quality and quantity at a lower price than any place in the world. Since profit-oriented production does not exist, increases in production result in steadily declining prices, an essential component of social equality. This is in itself a material incentive, for the more that is collectively produced, the more the family can purchase with their income. All students of inequality would do well to follow as closely as possible these Chinese developments.

---

[64] See Haim Barkai, "The Kibbutz as Social Institution," *Dissent,* XIX (Spring 1972), pp. 354–70. The kibbutz has instituted the principle of "from each according to abilities and to each according to need." Material inequalities are thus minimal. Labor is voluntary, and thus individual material incentives do not exist. Collective decision-making is stressed, and jobs and managerial positions are rotated.

6

Social class

PROPERTY AND SOCIAL CLASS

In our discussion of inequality in the previous chapter, we emphasized a person's position in the means of production as the most decisive aspect of inequality. Insofar as persons occupy similar positions of inequality, they may form the basis of a social class. Thus, a person's relationship to property is the foremost criterion of class placement, although as with inequality there are other related factors that must be considered. There is no problem in the identification of the main section of the capitalist class through the criterion of property position. Having a capitalist relationship to property means quite simply that one is living largely or entirely off of surplus value of the social surplus. Most typically, and in every instance of the main section of the capitalist class, this "surplus living" is accomplished through holding paper claims (usually stocks) on the means of production. Thorstein Veblen referred these claims on productive property as vested interests, "a marketable right to get something for nothing."[1] He also used the term "vested interests" to apply to the capitalist class. The money derived from property holdings he termed "free income." Substantial amounts of free or unearned income derived from property ownership is the first step in capitalist class membership.

But surely not everyone who holds a vested interest or stock is a member of the capitalist class. We must further ask to what extent does one depend upon free income for support and how much free income does one receive. Anyone holding over one million dollars in income producing property is clearly a capitalist, regardless of whether the person is a career dishwasher or a highly salaried executive. We noted in

---

[1] Thorstein Veblen, *The Vested Interests and the Common Man* (New York: The Viking Press, 1946; first published 1919).

the previous chapter that millionaires count an insignificant portion of their income as earned through salaries or wages. Taking the government's "higher budget" of about $15,000 as a guide to the minimum amount of money required to live well, we might generously say that anyone deriving more than twice that amount from unearned property income is living or could live off of free income and is a member of the capitalist class. Conversely, to derive free income in insufficient amounts to support oneself comfortably and save for future security (and $15,000 *is* required to achieve this today) is to be dependent upon wages or salaries to a greater or lesser degree. We have already observed that persons in the under $15,000 category are almost entirely dependent upon wages or salaries. In fact, persons having incomes up to $50,000 owe 80 percent of it to salaries,[2] which would leave them with $10,000 of free income. But from there things change importantly. Up to $500,-000 annual income, only 38 percent of this is salary, meaning that someone with an income of $200,000 receives $125,000 in the form of free income and someone with $500,000 receives $310,000. Up to one million dollars, free income could come to over nine-tenths of the total, while our annual millionaires and multi-millionaires could barely detect their salaries, if they draw such. (Interestingly enough, many members of the capitalist class maintain an active and official watch over their vested interests and pay themselves generously for so doing; for example, Henry Ford II "earned" $370,000 in 1971, Raymond C. Firestone $275,-000, David Rockefeller $230,000, and Amory Houghton, Jr. a modest $180,000.[3])

But say our person is not heir to a fortune in free income and holds little if any stock in corporate property. Say he is forced to hire himself out—as a $15,000 a year manager. Now, although middle and lower management positions do not create value per se in the same manner as the proletariat or goods-producing class, they do belong to the stratum of commercial laborers who *save* the capitalist class surplus value by organizing the production process more efficiently. They are actually well-paid commercial or upper-white-collar workers. They are themselves not *directly* involved in the appropriation of surplus value. Socialization of the means of production and workers' control would not significantly alter their material position, though their job description would change.

What of top management living far above the upper budget levels on salaries of well over $30,000 or $50,000? Here we enter a new realm. In the first place, anyone with an annual income of over $50,000—as we have noted above—ends up buying corporate property and building up unearned income to a point where salary progressively declines in importance. Secondly, even if every cent were spent within the year, no one with salaries this high is doing predominantly unpaid commercial labor for the owners; like the owners, top management is living to various degrees off the social surplus. Further, as Mills observes, "Top-level managers are socially and politically in tune with other large

---

[2] *The American Almanac* (New York: Grosset & Dunlap, 1973), p. 394.
[3] *Forbes*, May 15, 1972, p. 205 ff.

property holders."[4] They typically are seeking full entrance into the capitalist class, and many succeed in their aims.

The capitalist class constitutes a miniscule proportion of the population. In the previous chapter, we observed that only one percent of the adult population held most corporate stock, and that far fewer than this held the payoff shares. Only approximately two percent have had a net worth of over $200,000, one percent over $500,000, and one-half of one percent over one million dollars.[5] Only one-half of one percent of all families reported total incomes of over $50,000 in 1970.[6] Very clearly, the propertied-rich and their top hired employees comprise at the very maximum two percent of the population, while the propertied-rich as such make up less than one percent. The ultimate power of the capitalist class lies within less than 0.5 percent and very probably less than 0.2 percent of the population.

Veblen further identifies what he calls "outlying and subsidiary vested interests." He counts among these the professional military, the police, the legal apparatus, and the clergy (Veblen took sharp aim at religion, viewing it both with amusement and contempt). Veblen would also add state elites working on behalf of the big property interests. Further, an entire array of subsidiary vested interests exist, which depend largely or entirely on surplus consumption, including insurance, real estate, finance, and advertising. The subsidiary interests, argued Veblen, produce nothing in the area of material or essential social support, but rather enter as necessary components to the maintenance of the private profit system. In Veblen's words, "By sentiment and habitual outlook they belong with the kept classes, in that they are staunch defenders of the established order of law and custom which secures the great vested interests in power and insures the free income of the kept classes."[7]

While analytically considering these categories as system-supporting and system-dependent, the large majority of wage and salary employees working within these institutional systems are saving their employers money in excess of what they are paid; thus, the majority are doing some unpaid labor, such as the mass of minor functionaries working in finance, law and real estate. A structural transformation of the system could only improve their material and social position, and increasing numbers are beginning to resent the monotony, drudgery, insecurity, and depersonalizing nature of their work. Conversely, the elites—such as Clement Stone (insurance) and John Ehrlichman (real estate)—in these system-dependent areas have deep interests in the status quo, and are typically themselves involved extensively in share-holding and finan-

---

[4] C. Wright Mills, *White Collar* (New York: Oxford University Press, 1951), p. 104.

[5] Ferdinand Lundberg, *The Rich and the Super Rich* (New York: Bantam Books, 1968), p. 18.

[6] U.S. Bureau of the Census, *Current Population Reports*, Series P-60, No. 80, "Income in 1970 of Families and Persons in the United States," U.S. Government Printing Office, Washington, D.C., 1971, pp. 30–31.

[7] Veblen, *The Vested Interests and the Common Man*, pp. 163–64.

cial speculation. Such is, in fact, their business. The rank-and-file of administrative and financial personnel are lower-white-collar workers having much more in common with production workers and other corporate employees than with top management.

Old middle class

C. Wright Mills has referred to those who both own and manage their own means of production as the old middle class.[8] Occupationally

Table 3
THE U.S. CLASS STRUCTURE, 1970–71

	Total	Male	Female	Family income§
Capitalist class	0.5–2%*	†	†	$50,000 and over
Old middle class	9	10	3	10,015
Self-employed business . .	3	4	1	10,015
Self-employed professional and others	4	4	2	21,096
Farmers	2	2	‡	6,138
New working class	19	22	17	
Professional-technical . . .	12	12	14	14,135
Managerial-administrative	7	10	3	15,114
White collar	23	13	41	
Salesworkers	6	6	7	12,325
Clerical workers	17	7	34	10,471
Old working class	35	47	16	
Craftsmen and foremen .	12	20	1	11,294
Operatives	18	20	15	9,602
Laborers	5	7	‡	8,118
Farm workers	2	2	1	4,672
Service workers	12	6	22	8,562
Total and median	100%	100%	100%	11,842

* Not in labor force or distributed within old middle and new working class statistical categories. See pp. 103–5 for calculation base. Less than 0.5 of all families with total money incomes in 1970 of $50,000 or over.

† The capitalist class may be viewed in terms of families containing equal numbers of males and females.

‡ Less than one percent.

§ Median 1970 total median money income of families by occupation of full-time year-around employed head.

Sources: U.S. Bureau of the Census, *Current Population Reports*, Series P-23, No. 37, "Social and Economic Characteristics of the Population in Metropolitan and Nonmetropolitan Areas: 1970 and 1960," U.S. Government Printing Office, Washington, D.C., 1971; *The Statistical Abstract of the United States/American Almanac* (New York: Grosset & Dunlap, 1973), pp. 230–31; and U.S. Bureau of the Census, *Current Population Reports*, Series P-60, No. 80, "Income in 1970 of Families and Persons in the United States," U.S. Government Printing Office, Washington, D.C., 1971, p. 73.

speaking, the old middle class consists largely of small businessmen, self-employed professionals, and small independent farmers. The old middle class (petit bourgeoisie) has greatly diminished in *relative* size

[8] Mills, *White Collar*, pp. 3–62.

and importance as property ownership centralized into the hands of monopolists and as the ranks of hired workers expanded. The percentage of independent entrepreneurs has declined to less than three percent of the labor force, and the percentage of independent farmers is barely over two percent (see Table 3). The industrialization of agriculture has gradually driven the small farmer off the land into the urban proletariat. Agricultural production has itself been proletarianized, for 40 percent of persons employed therein are wage laborers. Owing to the fact that most of these people work on large operations that account for a large portion of the nation's agricultural production, the agricultural wage worker produces a major part of our food. Including other self-employed persons of the old middle class, the main group of which are doctors and lawyers, less than nine percent of the civilian labor force were self-employed in 1971 (7.1 million out of over 78 million).[9]

The old middle class has traditionally been politically conservative.[10] The old middle class represents an earlier stage of capitalist development and its politics reflect this fact. As the prototypes of the pre-industrial capitalist economy and the dominant figures for much of the 19th century, the old middle class has been weakened and pushed aside by the march of monopoly capital and the bureaucratic state. The political and social mentality of the old middle class still predominates in most of rural America, and state legislatures and the House of Representatives still strongly reflect the views of the old middle class.

New working class

At the same time he analyzed the old middle class, Mills distinguished the *new* middle class. By new middle class (or new working class) Mills meant the hired white-collar workers, including top professionals and managers as well as salesworkers and clerks. Without distinguishing between elites and non-elites we may note that approximately one-fifth of the labor force belongs to the new middle (new working) class— professional (12 percent) and managerial-administrative (7 percent). (See Table 3.) To this is added the clerical (17 percent) and sales workers (6 percent) or lower-white collar people, which together compose slightly less than one-fourth of the labor force. The new middle (or new working) class, in all of its components, thus constitutes between 40 and 45 percent of employed persons.

During the past century, the new middle class has grown at the expense of the old middle class. In absolute as well as relative numbers, the latter is being replaced by the former. Although the old middle class will continue to persist, its influence and proportions will in all likelihood continue to diminish. The white-collar organizations and unions will gradually displace in importance the organizational bastions of the

---

[9] *The American Almanac*, 1973, p. 230.

[10] For a discussion of the ideology of the far right, see G. William Domhoff, *The Higher Circles* (New York: Vintage Books, 1971), pp. 281–308.

old middle class as embodied in the National Association of Manufacturers, the Chamber of Commerce, the American Medical Association, and the farm groups. Already, these latter organizations are much more influential than either their economic importance or numbers would suggest.

The chief reason for the disproportionate influence of the old middle class is that the new middle class has only recently started to view itself as a separate stratum with common interests. Mills painted a very drab picture of the hired white-collar worker in the early 1950s; in his view, they were the very opposite of a self-conscious social class. Mills describes the new middle class as "estranged from community and society in a context of distrust and manipulation; alienated from work and, on the personality market, from self; expropriated of individual rationality, and politically apathetic—these are the new little people, the unwilling vanguard of modern society."[11]

For the large majority of white-collar people, however, Mills recognized that they objectively occupied a substantially proletarian or working-class status. Thus, he writes that "Mechanized and standardized work, the decline of any chance for employee to see and understand the whole operation, the loss of any chance, save for a very few, for private contact with those in authority—these form the model of the future." And "No longer free to plan his work, much less to modify the plan to which he is subordinated, the individual is to a great extent managed and manipulated in his work."[12] Add to these points of proletarian work status the proletarian status of propertylesssness and the proletarian function of doing (some) unpaid labor, we may conclude with Mills that ". . . in historical reality, the 'new middle class' is merely a peculiar sort of new proletariat, having the same basic interests."[13]

A new proletariat, or a new working class, is indeed what the new middle class of white-collar workers really are.[14] In Chapter 4 we distinguished two major components of the new working class—the goods-producing and the service-producing sectors. We also noted the overlap between these two sectors. However, the core of the new working class consists of scientists, engineers, and technicians involved in the production of use-values or products contributing to the material support of society. These are the highly trained workers to which Marx alluded.

---

[11] Mills, *White Collar,* p. xviii.

[12] Ibid., pp. 212, 226.

[13] Ibid., p. 291.

[14] See Paul Goldman, "The Organization Caste System and the New Working Class," *The Insurgent Sociologist,* 3 (Winter 1973), pp. 41–51; Bogdan Denitch, "The New Left and the New Working Class," in J. David Colfax and Jack L. Roach, eds., *Radical Sociology* (New York: Basic Books, Inc., 1971), p. 343; Stanley Aronowitz, "Does the United States Have a New Working Class?" in George Fischer, ed., *The Revival of American Socialism* (New York: Oxford University Press, 1971), pp. 188–216; David Laibman, "Technologists—Part of the Working Class," *Political Affairs,* April 1969, pp. 52–59; and Michael Harrington, "Old Working Class, New Working Class," *Dissent,* Winter 1972, pp. 146–62.

They are the engineers about which Veblen wrote.[15] The great advances in the forces of production and productivity find their source in the technological component of the new working class. The service-producing sector has a strong "professional" strain and is represented primarily in health, education, and welfare. The idea of "professionalism" and "career" is stressed by the employers and elites within the entire new working class in an effort to make employees think of themselves as (old) middle class and above collective action and working-class organization. The Ehrenreichs have pointed out how these individuating emphases are used by hospitals in an attempt to maintain hierarchy and prevent collectivization of their work force.[16]

Over one-half century ago, Veblen perceived little political threat out of the new working class, "By settled habit the technicians, the engineers, and industrial experts, are a harmless and docile sort, well fed on the whole, and somewhat placidly content with the 'full dinner-pail,' which the lieutenants of the Vested Interests habitually allow them."[17] While this evaluation of the new working class was upheld through even Mills's period, there are indications that the new educated stratum are viewing themselves less and less as individual "entrepreneurs" and more and more as trained and specialized workers. Unionization has been on the upswing; in France in 1968 the new working class played a prominent role in the near overthrow of status quo.[18] Highly educated but typically narrowly restricted in field of responsibility and decision-making, the new working class embodies as much if not more of a contradiction between human abilities and work requirements than the "old" or traditional blue-collar working class. The problem of alienation as regards the working class, new and old, will be taken up in Chapter 10.

Within the new working class, as we shall define it, are educational workers as well as production workers. Educational workers are largely teachers who produce services rather than goods, though educational institutions are very much part and parcel of the scientific and technological basis of production. The humanities and social sciences have largely educational or social ends per se, and those who teach them may consider themselves as intellectuals rather than as white-collar or professional workers.[19] Intellectuals working as hired employees have much objectively in common with the rest of the new working class and may be viewed simply as part of the service-producing sector of the new working class. We shall treat the notion of intellectuals (and students) in terms of class at the end of the chapter.

---

[15] See Veblen, *The Engineers and the Price System* (New York: Harcourt, Brace & World, Inc., 1963; first published in 1921).

[16] John and Barbara Ehrenreich, "Hospital Workers: A Case Study in the New Working Class," *Monthly Review,* January 1973, pp. 12–27.

[17] Veblen, *The Engineers and the Price System*, p. 138.

[18] See Henri Lefebvre, *The Explosion: Marxism and the French Upheaval* (New York: Monthly Review Press, 1969).

[19] Charles H. Anderson and John D. Murray, eds., *The Professors: Work and Life Styles among Academicians* (Cambridge, Mass.: Schenkman Publishing Company, 1971).

The blue-collar proletariat

The largest single stratum within contemporary society is that of the manual wage worker. Popular sociology tends to portray the blue-collar proletariat as a disappearing category, washed out by automation. As we shall note in Chapter 10, automation has had a major impact on production work. Whatever the full *potential* of automation, and this is generally what the apolitical observer considers instead of what major investors will actually do, the goods-producing blue-collar category has declined in proportionate terms by only one percentage point from 1960 to April 1972 (36 to 35 percent) and only four percentage points since 1950.[20] Over the same 22 year period the absolute number of manual production workers increased by 4.4 million, though since the end of 1965 the figure has fluctuated with a given limit.

The persistence of the blue-collar worker is even more marked than the above statistics would suggest. The large-scale entrance of women into lower-white-collar jobs since the 1940s has given the overall labor force more of a "white-collar look" than it, in fact, has if one considers *families* as units. The percentage of *male* manual workers has persisted at approximately 45 to 47 percent of the labor force since 1940 (or even 1920).[21] Furthermore, some two-fifths of married clerical and sales women have blue-collar husbands. What has occurred is that the old middle class has declined and into its place has stepped the lower-white-collar proletariat with its large compliment of female labor (two-thirds are female); and the remainder of the space has been filled by upper-white-collar employees. These shifts have taken place around a relatively stable male category of manual production workers. Advanced mechanization and automation has succeeded in stabilizing the blue-collar proletariat, while simultaneously greatly increasing the quantity of material goods they produce. Unless consumers are found in greater numbers with greater purchasing power, further advances in automation must necessarily put increased pressure on manual production jobs. Yet, the competition for jobs will hold down wages beneath the cost of automated production, at least in many sectors. Blue-collar workers are thus locked into dependence upon wages.

Service workers

To some extent, the service worker is the less skilled, less educated counterpart of the service-producing sector of the new working class. For the new working class nurse, there is a service worker nurse's aid; for the dietician, there is a cook; for the hotel manager, there is a waitress; for the social worker, there is a policeman; and for the teacher, there is a cleaning lady. In view of the subservient status of most service workers, it is not surprising to find females (two-thirds of the total) and

---

[20] *The American Almanac,* 1973, p. 230.

[21] See Albert Szymanski, "Trends in the American Working Class," *Socialist Revolution,* 2 (July–August 1972), pp. 101–22; also, Andrew Levison, "The Working-Class Majority," *The Nation,* December 13, 1971, p. 628.

minorities in disproportionate numbers (90 percent of naval officers' personal servants or orderlies are Filipinos). Whereas 13 percent of the combined labor force are service workers, 22 percent of the female labor force are service and only 6.5 percent of the male. Similarly 12 percent of whites are service workers compared with 28 percent of nonwhites.[22]

The ranks of service workers have increased substantially with the growth of the affluent society. The service worker lives entirely from surplus value. However, the service worker does not derive income from the appropriation of surplus value as does the capitalist. Rather, service consumers (of which we virtually all are in greater or lesser amounts) pay the service worker out of surplus value acquired elsewhere such as through profits or taxation, or out of earned wages. The income of the typical service worker is among the lowest found anywhere outside of agricultural labor, though a cocktail waitress in the right lounge can occasionally clear more income than a full professor.

The typical service worker, together with the unskilled laborer, does most of society's "dirty work." Their jobs are frequently monotonous and degrading and lack material security. They can be easily replaced, and usually work for small, scattered establishments and are thus difficult to organize. Yet, the service workers are among the most rapidly multiplying stratum in the work force, increasing from 6.6 million in 1950 to 11.0 in 1972. The affluent strata in general prefer dirty work done for them, much of which derives from the process of entertainment and travel, or simply easy living.

Not all or even the majority of service workers are chiefly servants of affluence. A large portion are social servants working at tasks that save other workers time and inconvenience, such as doing laundry, picking up garbage, preparing lunches, emptying hospital bed pans, or tending children. Much service work could be automated, but when low-wage help is available, we can expect little advance in automation in the service sector.

In addition to low income, replaceability, insecurity, subordination, alienation, and propertylessness, the service worker shares a further factor with the lower-white-collar worker: the service worker frequently assists in realizing much greater surplus value for the employer than he or she is paid; that is, they do unpaid labor. A $1.60 an hour waitress may turn over $200 in clear profit every day for a restaurant chain, or a domestic servant getting $8 a day may permit her employer to go out and earn $40 or $100 a day. However, many service workers catering primarily to the working public or taxpayer are actually subsidizing society through "voluntary" labor at low wages. Whatever the case, a large segment of the service workers confront an objective situation which disposes them toward a working class position. Efforts toward unionization among city employees, restaurant and hotel workers, and

---

[22] U.S. Bureau of the Census, *Current Population Reports*, Series P-23, No. 37, "Social and Economic Characteristics of the Population in Metropolitan and Nonmetropolitan Areas: 1970 and 1960," U.S. Government Printing Office, Washington, D.C., 1971, p. 60; and *The American Almanac*, 1973, pp. 230–31.

hospital attendants reflect this fact. Minority and female rights movements have given an important impetus to this process.

Insofar as the family is the basic unit of class stratification, and the head is typically male, we shall take the figures given for males in Table 3 as our guide to the proportionate class distribution. The reader, however, is free to interpret these figures in whatever might be most useful for specific purposes.

SUPPORTING CLASS CRITERIA

A social class is thus essentially and objectively defined by property relationships; i.e., the manner in which a person relates to the means of production and the value produced through these means. As directly related aspects of the property relation are such things as work alienation, economic insecurity, subordination to higher authority, and source of sustaining income. Alienation, insecurity, powerlessness, and wage labor all derive in a direct fashion from propertylessness; this configuration of objective circumstances contribute to working-class formation. Their opposites are freedom, security, power, and free income, and these things today derive from property; this configuration of objective circumstances contribute to capitalist class formation.

The objective material conditions of class are not sufficient by themselves to produce a politically active and self-conscious social class. A completely formed class requires the social and psychological actualization of the objective class conditions. As pointed out in our discussion of Marx's class model, a common cultural way of life, a social community, an awareness of mutual interests and opponents, and a collective political effort and conflict fill out a more complete social class. Thus, cultural behavior, social interaction, class consciousness, and political organization belong to the larger constellation of social class criteria. In the following sections, we take up each of these aspects of class relations in an effort to decipher the extent of class formation in the U.S.

The focus here shall be upon class or social strata distinctions within the broad underlying population. One stratum within the underlying population, the materially impoverished or poor, shall be treated separately in Chapter 8. The ruling or capitalist class shall be discussed in Chapter 9. Suffice it to note here in its regard, that the capitalist class is a quite fully developed class. As Veblen suggested, ". . . the vested interests and the kept classes, on the other hand, have reached insight and definition of what they need, want, and are entitled to."[23] Beginning with Veblen's own *The Theory of the Leisure Class*, the research on the capitalist class as a ruling *social* class is definitive.[24]

---

[23] Veblen, *The Theory of the Leisure Class* (New York: Mentor Books Edition, 1953; first published in 1899), p. 29.

[24] For example, E. Digby Baltzell, *An American Business Aristocracy* (New York: Collier Books, 1962); and G. William Domhoff, *Who Rules America?* (Englewood Cliffs, N.J.: Prentice-Hall, Inc., 1967).

Contrary to the ruling class, no stratum within the underlying population has developed significant class formation. Not even the working class has moved decisively in this direction, although segments of the working class evince definite signs of so moving. In describing the different social and psychological aspects of social class, there is no intention of conveying the idea that genuine class cleavages exist within the larger working class or underlying population. Although clear differences may be observed, say between the new and old working classes in terms of cultural behavior and group interaction, these differences are a matter of degree and are based upon a similar material foundation of powerlessness and propertylessness.

CULTURAL BEHAVIOR

The underlying population displays no *clear-cut, distinctive* cleavages in cultural behavior that could be associated with social classes. But because sharp behavioral or life-style distinctions along class lines do not exist does not mean there are not a number of central cultural tendencies within certain layers of American society. The new working class, for example, may espouse a more liberal set of values on questions of racial integration and equality, civil rights and civil liberties, and international relations than do members of the old middle and blue-collar working class.[25] The old middle and new working classes tend to be more active in community organizations, education groups, civic and political associations, and occupational societies.[26] In leisure, owing partially to education and higher incomes, these upper white-collarites more often pursue cultural or artistic edification, reading, travel, fashion, formal entertainment in the home, and sports such as golf and skiing. In brief, what we are describing as "upper middle class" cultural tendencies more or less amount to, or stem from, differences in family and personal educational backgrounds. Of course, not all college graduates fit the new working class pattern, in part due to the fact that not all college graduates have received the same kind of education or are receiving similar incomes.

Only a very small minority of white-collar people pursue what amounts to an intellectual orientation in life. For example, a very small percentage of even upper white-collar people regularly read quality newspapers, periodicals, and books.[27] Most are as susceptible to the distractions of indiscriminate television viewing, pocketbook murder and sex,

---

[25] For example, see Norval D. Glenn and Jon P. Alston, "Cultural Distances among Occupational Categories," *American Sociological Review,* 33 (June 1968), pp. 365–82.

[26] For a study of values and attitudes among college-educated women, see Theodore M. Newcomb et al., *Persistence and Change* (New York: John Wiley & Sons, Inc., 1967).

[27] Marvin Dicker, "The Intellectual as a Social Type: A Study in Role and Community," Ph.D. dissertation, University of Wisconsin, 1969; and Harold L. Wilensky, "Mass Society and Mass Culture," *American Sociological Review,* 29 (April 1964), pp. 192–93.

slick magazines, and second-rate newspapers as "the masses." Even college professors, many of whom are, in effect, paid to be intellectuals, are not always critical culture consumers.[28] The organized social life, downtown entertainment, bookshelves and paintings, fashion, travel, and modern living that seem to lend the "upper middle class" an aura of sophistication and intellectuality are to a large extent a cultural facade built of money. Any distinction that one might care to draw in American society between "urban sophisticates" and "rural populists" or between college educated and working class has a less of an intellectual base than a financial one.[29]

Some researchers have noted life-style differences between professional and business persons. Glenn and Alston discovered that on a large battery of attitudinal and behavioral questions the overall differences between professional and business respondents were about as great as the differences between lower white-collar and blue-collar workers. Professionals tend to be more liberal than business people on political, economic, and social issues.[30] Professionals also tend to exhibit a more intensive interest in work and do not make as sharp a distinction between work and leisure as do businessmen. Teachers and other social service professionals place a greater emphasis on the values of helping others and social contribution, while businessmen give higher ratings to such things as mobility prospects, making money, and competitiveness.[31] In terms of media behavior, professionals make a greater effort to cultivate serious reading, listening, and viewing habits.[32]

The new working class, especially in its service-producing component, is more likely than other stratum to seek out critical cultural ideas, and does this much more so than the old middle class with equivalent amount of money and education.[33]

Blue-collar values

The cultural break between white- and blue-collar workers has traditionally been considered of some significance. Yet, as already noted, broad-spectrum data suggest that on points having to do with such things as intergroup attitudes, family behavior, religion, political and

---

[28] See Anderson and Murray, *The Professors*, pp. 153–84.

[29] Arthur J. Vidich and Joseph Bensman, *Small Town in Mass Society* (Princeton, N.J.: Princeton University Press, 1958), Chapter 12, draw such a distinction.

[30] Glenn and Alston, "Cultural Differences among Occupational Categories."

[31] Leonard Goodwin, "The Academic World and The Business World: A Comparison of Occupational Goals," *Sociology of Education*, 42 (Spring 1969), pp. 171–87.

[32] Dicker, "The Intellectual as a Social Type"; Glenn and Alston, "Cultural Differences among Occupational Categories"; Wilensky, "Mass Society and Mass Culture."

[33] Joel E. Gerstl, "Leisure, Taste, and Occupational Milieu," in Anderson and Murray, eds., *The Professors*, pp. 153–73.

economic issues, and media behavior, lower white-collar and blue-collar differences are small. Owing in part to their similar financial resources and educational levels, lower white-collar and blue-collar workers exhibit very similar life styles. In his study of Levittown, Herbert Gans discovered more overlaps between these categories than between the lower and upper white collar.[34] The outstanding trait in both white collar and working class is their home-centeredness and strictly casual social life.[35] Informal family outings, puttering around the house, and television viewing consume the bulk of their leisure time. Interest in serious reading or the arts is negligible. Interest in sports is typically intense, and they often participate in softball, bowling, and hunting and fishing. Very often they inhabit the same neighborhoods, whether it be in the city or suburb. Both groups invest heavily, you might say their whole lives, in their family and their home. To both white-collar and blue-collar persons, work is viewed largely as a means to enjoy the casual privacy of family and home; the professional and manager tend to focus more interest on the job.

The blue-collar worker has often been singled out for his "authoritarian" points of view and values. The worker has variously been described as being physical-punishment oriented, anti-intellectual, chauvinistic, and intolerant. Some of the general portrayals of blue-collar workers tend to suggest very restricted views on youthful cultural deviations, international relations, race relations, and government welfare programs.[36] Other research suggests that working class people as a group are not any more authoritarian and intolerant than higher income strata and may even be more flexible and liberal on such things as government intervention to achieve racial progress in income and jobs.[37] Richard Hamilton has suggested that there has been a significant inflow of working class culture into white-collar life owing to the large number of white-collar workers who were born and raised in blue-collar families.[38] It thus becomes increasingly difficult to perceive any definite differences in cultural values between white- and blue-collar workers. Very careful empirical reviews and studies suggest that blue-collar workers are no more authoritarian than are educated "upper middle class"

---

[34] Herbert Gans, *The Levittowners* (New York: Pantheon Books, Inc., 1967).

[35] Bennett Berger, *Working Class Suburb* (Berkeley: University of California Press, 1967); and William M. Dobriner, *Class in Suburbia* (Englewood Cliffs, N.J.: Prentice-Hall, Inc., 1963).

[36] For example, Kenneth Lasson, *The Workers* (New York: Grossman Publishing, 1971); Robert Coles, *The Middle Americans* (Boston: Little, Brown, and Company, 1971); Patricia Cayo Sexton and Brendan Sexton, *Blue Collars and Hard Hats* (New York: Random House, Inc., 1971); and Arthur B. Shostak and William Gomberg, eds., *Blue-Collar World* (Englewood Cliffs, N.J.: Prentice-Hall, Inc., 1964), Part I.

[37] Lewis Lipsitz, "Working Class Authoritarianism: A Re-evaluaion," *American Sociological Review*, 30 (February 1965), pp. 103–9; and Richard F. Hamilton, "The Marginal Middle Class: A Reconsideration," *American Sociological Review*, 31 (April 1966), pp. 192–99.

[38] Ibid.

persons.[39] As Ransford and Jeffries argue, "There has probably been a tendency in the mass media to overstereotype the white working man as a narrow-minded intolerant bigot."[40]

The events of the 1972 presidential campaign and elections have been read by some observers as indicating working-class reaction, especially racism. Goertzel writes that "The success of Nixon in fashioning an electoral majority by capitalizing on the conservative and racist tendencies of the white working class (together with his traditional upper- and middle-class supporters) has been discouraging to anyone who looks forward to a broad socialist coalition of manual workers, intellectual workers, and minority groups."[41] The blue-collar support for Governor George Wallace in the primaries, and then the three to one Wallace-supporter vote for Nixon over Senator McGovern, tends to encourage acceptance of these views. (Recent research indicates that workers for Wallace display more authoritarian tendencies than other workers.[42]) Further, one-half of blue-collar union membership who voted went to the pro-business President over his Democratic opponent, who had a near perfect AFL-CIO approved congressional voting record.[43] If President Nixon won his landslide victory by linking Senator McGovern with political radicalism, counterculture, and minorities, as Michael Harrington suggests,[44] what else can we conclude except that a large section of the working class is indeed confused on the subject of friends and foes.

However, half of union members did vote for McGovern "radicalism" despite the cascade of anti-McGovern propaganda and the "neutrality" of AFL-CIO President George Meany; among the factory workers of the large cities, a majority of workers so voted. As an indication of political alienation, half of the larger working class didn't even bother to vote at all—a poor showing compared with the large turnouts among European workers (90 percent in the 1973 Swedish general election). Interestingly enough, polls conducted in mid-1973 suggested that Senator McGovern would be the winner if the election were held at that later

---

[39] For example, Martin Patcher, "Social Class and Dimensions of Foreign Policy Attitudes," *Social Science Quarterly,* 51 (December 1970), pp. 649–57; Richard F. Hamilton, "Class and Race in the United States," in Fischer, ed., *The Revival of American Socialism,* pp. 81–106; and H. Edward Ransford and Vincent Jeffries, "Blue-Collar Anger: Reactions to Student and Black Protest Movements," presented to American Sociological Association, Denver, 1971.

[40] Ibid.

[41] Ted Goertzel, "Class and Politics in the 1970's," *The Insurgent Sociologist,* 3 (Spring 1973), p. 44; see also Richard A. Long, "Scapegoat Victory: The President's White Mandate," *The Nation,* December 4, 1972, pp. 555–57.

[42] Harold L. Sheppard and Neal Q. Herrick, *Where Have All the Robots Gone?* (New York: The Free Press, 1972), pp. 77–93; 144–49.

[43] See Ronnie Dugger, "George McGovern: A Jeffersonian for our Time," *The Progressive,* November 1972, pp. 14–19.

[44] "Negative Landslide: The Myth That Was Real," *The Nation,* November 27, 1972, pp. 518–21.

date. Perception of political interests among workers had evidently sharpened.

Herbert Gans's notion that working-class people tend to be *person-oriented* as opposed to object-oriented is a point of some interest.[45] Person-orientation implies that the individual tends to perceive his entire social world in terms of primary-group relationships, stresses the over-riding importance of primary-group ties, and thus views people as ends rather than as means to further goals. By contrast the object-oriented person places emphasis on occupational, material, social, and other extra-personal life objectives; he is able to function effectively in bureaucratic environments that require individuals to consider one another in impersonal terms. The person-oriented individual considers object-oriented people as cold, exploitative, and ambitious; the person-oriented individual would often admittedly enjoy more material possessions, but he refuses or is unable to take an object-oriented style of life.

The person-orientation dovetails with the home-centeredness of working class people; the object-orientation similarly blends with the organizational, career, and mobility values of the higher strata. This does not imply that person-oriented people are always incapable of operating in a strange or bureaucratic setting, or that object-oriented people are unable to interact with people on a completely personal and intimate basis. Gans, for example, argues that object-orientation is the dominant mode of a transitional period in the life of a upward-bound or aspiring person who develops more of a person-orientation *after* his nonpersonal objects or goals have been achieved. One could tend to take issue with Gans on this point; an object-orientation is often nursed into young school children and continually hammered into them throughout the duration of school. Success in a career also requires an unwavering object-orientation. Is it possible that after 25 years in and out of different organizations the finished product can overcome a bureaucratic orientation in favor of person-centeredness? For some, maybe so; for others it may be more difficult.

Another view of working-class life in the modern period suggests that the blue-collar proletariat has underwent a process of *embourgeoisement*.[46] This notion contends that the working class has given up on collectivist political and social ways of life to take up the affluent life of suburbia and individual success. The very environment of the suburb was thought to transform workers into organizationally-minded conservatives. The system had purportedly won them completely over with high wages, material security, and a cornucopia of material goods. Instead of

---

[45] Herbert J. Gans, *The Urban Villagers* (New York: The Free Press, 1965); also see Jack E. Weller, *Yesterday's People* (Lexington: University of Kentucky Press, 1966).

[46] See the critical discussion of the embourgeoisement thesis as applied to the English working class in John Goldthrope, et al., *The Affluent Worker in the Class Structure* (Cambridge: Cambridge University Press, 1969); and James W. Rinehart, "Affluence and the Embourgeoisement of the Working Class: A Critical Look," *Social Problems*, 19 (Fall 1971), pp. 150–62.

the majority being proletarianized, the majority was handed over to bourgeoisie—placated and well-adjusted.

Such a conception has only the most tenuous link with reality, supported largely by post-War and cold war boom and defense spending. What truth there was has greatly evaporated with the growing problems of an imbalanced society and an unreliable economic system that is proletarianizing white-collar people instead of making paragons of rugged individualism out of the workers.[47] Culturally the blue-collar worker may appear increasingly like his white-collar counterpart, but *neither* are middle-class in the traditional sense. White- and blue-collar workers *are* being brought closer together, not as members of the bourgeoisie, but as proletarians.[48]

Life in suburbia

Still unsettled is what could be called the Mills-Gans debate, though these two scholars doubtfully ever had the opportunity to confront each other on the issue. C. Wright Mills portrayed white-collar Americans as frightened, alienated, uprooted, steeped in malaise, bored, restless, and disoriented, "the unwilling vanguard of modern society." Among white-collar people, declares Mills, there is no plan in life, no firm roots; they are without any order of belief and morally defenseless. "Here are people," Mills charges, "who have been stood up by life."[49]

In opposition to Mills, Herbert Gans has described white-collar life in very different terms.[50] Working in his customary manner, Gans took up long-term residence among his "subjects," in this case the then-new community of Levittown, New Jersey. Gans attended gatherings in homes; visited clubs, churches, civic meetings, and schools; and conducted interviews. In Gans's view, the suburbs are not filled with bored, uprooted, disoriented, and apathetic people. Rather, he found the middle classes to be largely enmeshed in myriad primary groups, frequently active in civic affairs, attuned to local and often national politics, interested in home and family, and generally integrated and contented in life. The upper middle class was more active in community and political affairs than the lower middle and working class, but most everyone was ingratiated with friends, family, and home. The discontented elements of the population tended to be bored teen-agers and couples who had left familiar neighborhoods and had not yet become socially adjusted in their new ones.

According to which aspect of the argument one focuses upon, both Mills and Gans could be upheld as correct. Mills focuses on the "big" questions: alienation from work, absence of class consciousness, lack of nationally effective political organization, low pitched intellectual and

---

[47] On the French case, see Richard Hamilton, *Affluence and the French Worker in the Fourth Republic* (Princeton: Princeton University Press, 1967).

[48] Studies such as Lasson, *The Workers,* and Coles, *The Middle Americans,* bring out the commonality shared in white- and blue-collar life.

[49] Mills, *White Collar,* pp. xviii–xi.

[50] Gans, *The Levittowners.*

cultural life, and unrealized potentiality. On all of these points Mills is largely correct, although there are significant exceptions today, which were perhaps not as conspicuous to Mills in the early 1950s. Mills demands much from people: rationality, freedom, self-realization in work and play, and craftsmanship.

By contrast, Gans feels radicals such as Mills project their own preferences for political activism and cultural liberation on people who get along quite well without such things. Gans focuses on the parochial side of life; the informal chat, the neighborly advice and borrowing, coffee parties, cocktail parties, PTA meetings, local politics, and religious organizations. All this, plus television, local newspapers, photoplay magazines, fiction books, bridge, family drives, and a trip to the country or beach may seem bleak to the outsider, but may be the good life to those involved.

In the short run, we may tend to sympathize with Gans's view. If white-collar people find life going smoothly without raising the big questions related to alienation in work, constructive use of manual and mental capacities in leisure, the direction the economy is moving, where technology is taking us, and who is making the major decisions that govern their lives, then they are entitled to be left alone in their parochialism. But in the long run, the home-centeredness and local politics of white collar are insufficient for the kinds of challenges that are threatening to overwhelm them. The next riot they witness may not be on television; the next chemical warfare mistake may kill them rather than sheep; the next person lost in imperialistic war may be one of their sons; the next rise in unemployment may include their family; and the next mistake an overworked doctor makes may be on one of their children. It is not possible for the "middle classes" to go on living in their quiet, withdrawn, uninformed, and privatized style of life. They cannot continue to trust the social managers to run things in the public interest. No picket fence, no locked doors can keep today's big issues from inevitably encroaching on their homes and families. From taxes to consumption and inflation, from automation to militarization and war, from environment to mental and physical health, events are closing in on the "unwilling vanguard of modern society." Their own children have often deserted them, perhaps because their children have a better feeling for the major trends of our times (the only times they know) and a greater awareness of how they themselves are going to have to cope with these trends.

It is often the *quality* of their parents' lives that many children are raising questions about. Despite what Gans has to say about the integration of white-collar life, we may be left with certain doubts, even in terms of the short run. What does it mean that half the population depends on some form of drug to maintain satisfactory levels of bodily and psychological functioning? Or that one in four of all marriage attempts ends in divorce? Or that old men must drive wildcats and cobras, and read *Playboy*? Or that tens of millions wither in front of television screens watching precision-trained superhumans mete out punishment to one another. Perhaps it means that many people in middle America do, in fact, find life scarcely tolerable for its demoralizing rounds of alienating work, escapist leisure, and crass materialism.

CLASS AS INTERACTION

If an objective social class is to develop into a force for change, it must within its various components coalesce to form a series of interlocking associations and primary groups within which interests and goals can be discussed, formed, and set into action. In point of fact, there is a notable extent of within-class interaction and association. Although persons at the same economic level do not always belong to one another's social groups, there is a tendency for social closure within economic strata. Laumann, for example, discovered that three-fourths of the close friendships of professionals and businessmen in a metropolitan sample were confined to others at their occupational level and nearly all the rest with other white-collar persons, while the blue-collar workers found the large majority of their closest friends among other blue-collar workers.[51] Similarly, lower white-collarites formed the largest group of friends for clerical and salespeople, though they drew many friends from other blue- and white-collar occupations as well.

The fact that manual workers associate mainly with one another does not at all imply that such interaction is infused with class overtones in any political or Marxist sense. Quite to the contrary, working-class primary-group life is not typically politicized, at least for the moment. Despite the traditional research indicating a lack of blue-collar interest in workplace associations and friends, recent activity such as "illegal" and wildcat strikes and pickets, slow-downs, minority and youth caucases, and efforts at organizing the unorganized suggest that plant-based concerns and social relationships may be assuming greater importance today. This trend receives accentuation by the fact of there being a large number of minority and young workers in industry with a natural group-making bond in common ethnic and generational experiences. The sociological groundwork for class consciousness is thus enhanced.

Just as manual workers who tend to parcel out their intimate social ties to others at their income and skill levels have not in the recent past focused on class interests, neither do most of the white-collar groups interact as anything resembling a political interest group. In his book *White Collar*, Mills delivers a very grim view of the political status of the white-collar worker. About the white-collar classes Mills argues that "whatever common interests they have do not lead to unity; whatever future they have will not be of their own making;"[52] Mills's 1951 perspective on white-collar people is largely accurate today; for the majority they remain unpoliticized, unorganized, and alienated from work.[53]

---

[51] Edward O. Laumann, *Prestige and Association in an Urban Community* (Indianapolis: Bobbs-Merrill Co., Inc., 1966), p. 64.

[52] Mills, *White Collar*, pp. ix–xviii.

[53] For example, on engineers, see Robert Perrucci and Joel E. Gerstl, *Profession without Community* (New York: Random House, Inc., 1969).

People within the various white-collar ranks do indeed belong to and participate in formal groups and voluntary associations at a fairly high level, and considerably higher than blue-collar workers.[54] But evidently few of these organizations perform a political function, direct or indirect, despite theories regarding the mediating and communicating political functions of formal groups and associations. Olsen's data (on Indianapolis), for example, disclosed that an extremely low percentage of white-collar persons (white and black respondents) were active members of a political organization, had a high partisan political involvement, or actively participated in partisan political activities. However, informal political discussions were more frequent and political news exposure fairly high. But informal political talk and passive reception of political news media, while important, far from constitutes a politicized class.

Yet many persons within certain upper white-collar groups are intensely class and work-oriented in both interest and interaction (top business executives, teachers, professional medical personnel, and social workers, to name a few),[55] organized or beginning to organize, and increasingly politicized. Indeed, it is between members of partially organized and politicized upper white-collar groups that conflict has frequently been sustained, namely service-producing professionals versus big businessmen and bureaucrats. The addition of millions of college graduates into the professions and social service occupations compared to the relatively fewer prospective openings for executives and bureaucrats may profoundly alter the balance of power at least at the upper middle levels of society. But businessmen and bureaucrats are firmly entrenched where it really counts: in the top levels of power and decision making. This top level of power can reduce the flow of funds for liberal arts education and professional jobs, though the resulting unrest may be more threatening to the ruling class than a well-funded and securely employed professional class.

CLASS CONSCIOUSNESS

Has the U.S. working class developed class consciousness—"the sense, become conscious," in Lukacs words, "of the historical role of the [working] class."[56] Aronson would answer in the negative: "For a long time it has been all too obvious that the key sectors of the American working class are integrated into the capitalist system. This is a fact: proletarian

---

[54] Marvin E. Olsen, "Social and Political Participation of Blacks," *American Sociological Review*, 35 (August 1970), p. 689–91. Data are presented for both blacks and whites at four socioeconomic levels.

[55] For example, Louis H. Orzack, "Work as a 'Central Life Interest' of Professionals," in Erwin O. Smigel, ed., *Work and Leisure* (New Haven: College and University Press, 1963), pp. 73–84; and Harold L. Wilensky and Jack Ladinsky, "From Religious Community to Occupational Group: Structural Assimilation among Professors, Lawyers, and Engineers," *American Sociological Review*, 32 (August 1967), pp. 541–61.

[56] Georg Lukács, *History and Class Consciousness* (Cambridge, Mass.: M.I.T. Press, 1971; originally published in 1922), p. 73.

class-consciousness does not exist in the United States."[57] This conclusion, at least since the 1930s, has been widely held by observers of all political persuasion, though class consciousness among a small minority of workers is often perceived as being real enough. There are changes taking place, though, and views on class consciousness among sociologists are also changing as a result.

Mills considers "the first lesson" of sociology to be the importance of class consciousness: "The first lesson of modern sociology is that the individual cannot understand his own experience or gauge his own fate without locating himself within the trends of his epoch and the life-chances of all the individuals of his social layer."[58] Mills conceives of class consciousness in a Marxist fashion: (1) a rational awareness and identification with one's own class interests; (2) an awareness of and rejection of other class interests as legitimate; and (3) an awareness of and readiness to use collective political means to the collective political end of realizing one's interests.[59] Mills cautions us that to know a person's objective class situation is not necessarily to know what kind of class consciousness he or she might possess. And he adds that "If political mentalities are not in line with objectively defined strata, that lack of correspondence is a problem to be explained; in fact, it is the grand problem of the psychology of social strata."[60]

As the following chart suggests, class consciousness may itself be conceived of in terms of degrees; and within each level various depths of perception or involvement may be deciphered. Nearly all Americans acknowledge a status hierarchy and the existence of broad class categories (class awareness); the large majority will report a class affiliation. The overwhelming number will identify with either the "middle" or "working" class.[61] The same holds true in other capitalist countries.

LEVELS OF CLASS CONSCIOUSNESS

Level	Condition	Example
None	Denies class differences	Commune, primary group
Status awareness	Perceives continuous hierarchy of statuses	Military ranking
Class awareness	Perceives discrete categories	The rich, the workers
Class affiliation	Feeling of belonging to a class	Capitalist, working class
Class consciousness	Commitment to class interest or ideology	Capitalism, socialism
Class action	Action for class interest or ideology	Wage freeze, strike

Basic source: Richard T. Morris and Raymond S. Murphy, "A Paradigm for the Study of Class Consciousness," *Sociology and Social Research*, 50 (April 1966), pp. 298–313.

---

[57] Ronald Aronson, *Studies on the Left*, 6 (September–October 1966), p. 52.

[58] Mills, *White Collar*, p. xx.

[59] Ibid., p. 235.

[60] Ibid., pp. 294–95.

[61] Robert W. Hodge and Donald J. Treiman, "Class Identification in the United States," *American Journal of Sociology*, 73 (March 1968), pp. 535–47.

Further, although there is a definite tendency for white-collar persons to think of themselves as middle class and blue-collar workers as working class, a considerable amount of overlap exists between non-manual—manual occupation and class identification.

The fact that the large majority of Americans think of themselves as vaguely middle, average, or working class is not necessarily an indication of a lack of class consciousness or confused thinking on class matters, though it may be this as well. As we have previously documented with regard to wealth and income, the large mass of people *are* much more alike one another than they are the propertied-rich (who they rarely see and hardly know exist as individuals) or the totally destitute poor (who are also rarely seen or known as persons). The vast majority of people are propertyless wage and salary workers living within varying degrees of subsistence levels without great expectation of becoming wealthy. They are the great "middle class," the underlying population, and they tend to think of themselves as such. The underlying population shares similarity of interests in job security and insecurity, inflationary squeezes, tax burdens, living costs, environment, consumer rights, war, personal safety, and many other matters. The propertied-rich are rarely beset by such problems; they generally *benefit* from them. Women, minorities, youth, and the poor each separately confront problems stemming from corporate capitalism, and should be led to identify with the overlapping interests of the rest of the underlying population.

Lenin held that "Class political consciousness can be brought to the workers *only from without;* that is, only from outside the economic struggle, from outside the sphere of relations between workers and employers."[62] The aforesaid common day to day difficulties of the working class are precisely what Lenin meant by "from without." It is when the worker sees what his plant is doing to his family's water playgrounds, or when his wife shops for groceries, or when his partner is seriously injured or killed on the job, or when he finds all of his taxes are going for military purposes, and so forth, that he begins to think in the larger terms of class as opposed to simple wage bargaining with an employer. This is the process that seems currently to be developing. As a corollary of class consciousness coming from without, Lenin stressed the role of persons already class conscious in stimulating class understanding in others, the so-called vanguard group (Lenin did not equate "vanguard" with "elites"—as his critics frequently charge). In contemporary terms, Gilbert Merk argues that the critical task for the class conscious left ". . . is to promote the consciousness of a common class situation and interests among structurally alienated groups [minorities, women, youth, and the poor], and develop the recognition of common interest between these groups and the working class."[63]

Research by sociologists that taps class consciousness as a commitment to class interest or ideology and as action on behalf of such interest

---

[62] V.I. Lenin, *What Is To Be Done?, Selected Works,* Vol. 1 (Moscow: Progress Publishers, 1971), p. 182.

[63] *Monthly Review,* 24 (September 1972), pp. 63–64.

or ideology indicates the presence of a considerable amount, and of perhaps a growing amount, of class consciousness. We should also note that class consciousness rises and falls in a cyclical fashion (not necessarily corresponding to the ups and downs of the economic cycle) rather than growing in a unilinear fashion. John Leggett's 1960 investigation of Detroit auto workers indicated that three-fifths of black workers and almost one-fourth of white workers were class conscious.[64] Leggett's data confirm the hypothesis that economic insecurity (as defined by unemployment and race) and organization (as defined by union membership) heighten class consciousness. Thus, we have class conscious percentages as follows:

White employed	20%	Black unemployed	56%
White unemployed	32	Black unemployed nonunion	27
Black employed	57	Black unemployed union	80

Black workers were about twice as likely to express class consciousness as whites. Is this the result of racial or class membership? The answer seems to be both, with class the more important of the two: only 7 percent of black respondents used racial symbols only, whereas 38 percent used class symbols only and 51 percent both race and class symbols.

A second and more recent (1970) study by Martin Scheffer of a sample of Boise, Idaho, workers revealed greater class consciousness than found by Leggett.[65] One sample component were blue-collarites with husband-wife incomes of $8,000 or more; a second sample had incomes of $3,500 or less. The "upper-blue-collar" respondents were more class conscious than the poverty groups: over one-third of the former and about one-fifth of the latter were rated class conscious on a measure similar to that used by Leggett. Class-conscious workers made the following kinds of observations on the class structure:

> Big business has this state controlled. The profits don't go to the low income or to my class of people, the working class.

> The business class gets the profits; there's no profit to be had for the workin' man. I sure don't favor it—workin' man goes broke trying to keep his family in what it needs while they is puttin' away all the profits.

> The classes are clear to me—money makes the difference. The big organizations and the money people are gettin' the profits, not the working people. I agree that we ought to divide the wealth equally.

> The workingman's lot is getting worse in most places. When they begin to realize this they will get together and demand their share.

If one-third of working-class people are thinking in these terms in a conservative mountain town of 70,000 population, we may well expect that

---

[64] John D. Leggett, "Economic Insecurity and Working Class Consciousness," *American Sociological Review*, 29 (April 1964), pp. 226–34; see also Leggett's *Class, Race, and Labor* (New York: Oxford University Press, 1968), especially Chapters 6 and 7.

[65] Martin Scheffer, "The Poor, Separate Class or Working Class: A Comparative Study," Ph.D. Dissertation, University of Utah, 1971. Quotations from pp. 84–88.

today's Detroit auto workers are considerably more class conscious than they were when Leggett studied them more than a decade ago.

The resurgence of working-class militance has received a large impetus from the younger workers. The under-30 blue-collar work force now numbers approximately one-third of the total. This is a post-War work force in birth and upbringing. Expectations are different. Experiences have been different. The young workers are more aware of the gap between potential and reality; they have received more formal education, and large numbers have received an informal education in Vietnam. The younger workers are less willing to subject themselves to factory discipline and rules (disciplinarian action against workers breaking rules rose from a few hundred in 1965 to 3,400 in 1970).[66] They are less subject to manipulation by threats of lay-off or being fired, and more willing to challenge orders and speed-ups. Rates of absenteeism are so high as to cause industry-wide concern and study. Money alone is proving to be an insufficient incentive. Too much affluence and not enough scarcity is a persistent problem for the ruling class in regard to maintaining labor discipline and subservity.

Widick draws our attention to the new mood: "Observe the picket lines of teachers, policemen, other municipal workers, auto workers, electrical employees, truck drivers anywhere in the country and the new impression is the young brashness."[67] Edelman concurs: "There is a new mood of militancy, anger, and readiness to struggle among many of today's young workers."[68] Levison argues that "This is the first generation since the Thirties to view itself realistically as workers. . . ."[69] Many have been influenced by the counterculture with new life styles and values and the unwillingness to be manipulated by threats of material scarcity and insecurity—the chief weapon of labor discipline. Events in Quebec in May 1972 demonstrate the rapidity with which working-class consciousness and action can develop, when a general strike spread across city and country and all levels of the working class.[70] The same applies to France in 1968.[71]

If class consciousness has not fully developed in the U.S. working class, why hasn't it. The ruling ideas have proven too potent. The ideology of individual success and mobility has done much to keep workers apart and focusing on their own prospects and those of their children. A high degree of occupational movement, up, down, and horizontally, has given the impression of perpetual progress, as has increasing amounts of education. Yet, more often than not, and this is being increasingly perceived, occupational movement does not significantly

[66] Andrew Levison, "The Rebellion of Blue Collar Youth," *The Progressive*, October 1972, pp. 38–42; and Sheppard and Herrick, *Where Have All The Robots Gone?*, pp. 122–43.

[67] B.J. Widick, "Labor's New Style," *The Nation*, March 22, 1971, p. 358.

[68] Judy Edelman, "Young Workers: A Force for Change," *Political Affairs*, L (November 1971), pp. 13–16.

[69] Levison, "The Rebellion of Blue Collar Youth," p. 41.

[70] See *Radical America* (September–October 1972).

[71] Lefebvre, *The Explosion*.

change things for most people, and greater amounts of education do little good when the entire system of credentials has been raised and inflated. The ruling elites have done much to keep the worker's attention directed toward "private property" in the form of his house, car, and personal possessions, telling him that if he works hard, more money will come his way to buy more new possessions (and pay off old debts). Lately, this tactic has been failing somewhat, as the recognition of outside social and collective problems protrude as insoluble even against a 50 cent an hour wage increase. Finally, the ruling elites have utilized the divisive potential of national origin, religious, and racial differences to the maximum, pitting the working class against itself and heightening racism and chauvinism.

Although many factors have influenced the retardation of working class consciousness, most if not all of these factors are variously being eroded by the experiences of daily life. Whether new working class or old, many indicators point to increasing class consciousness. An economic crises of only a fraction of that which shook the country in the 1930s would in all likelihood tremendously accelerate this tendency. Much of today's working class is simply not cut out to be soup-line participants depending on welfare payments.

Class conflict

To what extent has the class consciousness that does exist been objectified into an open class struggle in the U.S., and how much class-type conflict has there been that has taken place without having an explicit or conscious class impetus? The history of industrial America is steeped in class struggles.[72] Class-based conflicts antedate even the industrial revolution, going back to the colonial period when commercial and agricultural classes opposed one another, or when higher status ethnic groups engaged newcomers and déclassé elements. Similar class-based ethnic clashes occurred throughout the 19th and early 20th centuries: higher-status natives versus lower-status immigrants and higher-status Protestants versus lower-status Catholics. By the latter half of the 19th century, labor began to fight violent battles with big business as the workers sought to organize. Labor battles continued into the 1930s, only to resume once again shortly after the War. However, working-class militance and critical thinking probably attained peaks just prior to both World Wars. A growing socialist movement was drowned in the patriotic fervor of World War I and a growing labor movement was aborted by the emergencies and peak employment levels of World War II and its aftermath of rebuilding and cold war spending.

Over 50 years ago Veblen could write that "the business interests of

---

[72] See, for example, Norman S. Cohen, *Civil Strife in America* (Hinsdale, Ill.: The Dryden Press, Inc., 1972); J. John Palen and Karl H. Flaming, eds., *Urban America: Conflict and Change* (New York: Holt, Rinehart and Winston, Inc., 1972); and "Workers' Struggles in the 1930's," *Radical America*, 6 (November–December 1972). On Europe, see Wolfgang Abendroth, *A Short History of the European Working Class* (New York: Monthly Review Press, 1972).

these absentee owners no longer coincide in any passable degree with the material interests of the underlying population, whose livelihood is bound up with the due working of this industrial system at large and in detail."[73] Since the mid-1930s, it was not until the late 1960s that large segments of the population again began to show significant awareness that basic contradicting interests were present within contemporary society. The Vietnam War and its social and economic ramifications provided the capstone. Beginning with the civil rights movement and spreading through the ghettos and universities and out into the society at large, class conflict generated by racism, militarism, war, poverty, sexual inequality, unemployment, and other breakdowns has been sporadically growing. Alienation and cynicism regarding the effectiveness of the existing political system is widespread at all levels of the working class.[74] Class conflict may be seen in every ghetto riot and urban disorder, picket line and strike, consumer boycott, welfare demonstration, disobedience to authority, slow down, prison riot, and military desertion.

Not all proponents of change consider the working class as an historical agent of change. Murray Bookchin contends that ". . . to infect the new revolutionary movement of our time with 'workeritis' is *reactionary to the core.*"[75] I.L. Horowitz argues that "The working class has turned to the Leviathan with a vengeance. Not the liquidation of the state, but its celebration, has become of crucial importance. The working-class demands legitimacy, law, order, and a ruling class willing and capable of exercising full authority."[76] However, Isaac Deutscher contends that "Your [proponents of change] only salvation is in carrying back the idea of socialism to the working class and coming back with the working class to storm—to storm, yes, to storm—the bastions of capitalism."[77]

These views may all conceivably muster persuasive amounts of evidence on their own behalf. This is partially because the working class, especially as we have defined it in the larger sense here, is not a uniform political entity. One may find almost anything one chooses to find. Yet, it is clear that human society is constructed upon a material base, and it is only the working class that is in a position to take control of that base and operate it with social ends in mind. Who else could conceivably do so? The working class is the large majority, and social transformation must always be the work of the large majority.

INTELLECTUALS, STUDENTS AND SOCIAL CLASS

Intellectuals have traditionally occupied an ambiguous status with regard to social class. By definition, intellectuals are persons who work

---

[73] *Absentee Ownership and Business Enterprise in Recent Times* (New York: The Viking Press, 1938; first published in 1923). Available as Beacon Press paperback, 1967.

[74] See Penn Kimball, *The Disconnected* (New York: Columbia University Press, 1972).

[75] *Post Scarcity Anarchism* (Berkeley: The Ramparts Press, 1971), p. 186.

[76] *Three Worlds of Development*, Second Edition (New York: Oxford University Press, 1972), p. xvii.

[77] *Marxism In Our Time*, pp. 250–54.

with ideas, concepts, and theories. They may be found working independently as writers, scientists, artists, and musicians, but much more often they must hire themselves out to supporting organizations; the large majority are connected with colleges and universities. Intellectuals may work in solitary isolation their entire lives; or they may lead world-shaking revolutions. Mills and a number of more recent critics have inveighed strongly against the political posture of American intellectuals, charging them with complicity in the perpetuation of an irrational and inhumane social order.[78] Intellectuals have been assigned the very responsibility of constructing theoretical and ideological rationalizations for the existing order. Many have consciously or unconsciously accepted the assignment; others have rejected it.

Among the developments producing critical thought among intellectuals has been their own proletarianization within the system. Once a "free-floating" stratum of curiosity seekers and idea speculators, intellectuals have been put to work on behalf of the state and the corporation in both scientific and advisory capacities. Science and education are major industries within corporate capitalism and are crucial to its continued stability. Intellectuals are the researchers and teachers in the knowledge industry.[79] As employees in the knowledge factory, intellectuals have become part of the new working class. Like other members of the new working class, intellectuals are increasingly proletarianized and alienated in their work.[80] Both the intellectual and what he produces —students and ideas—have been reduced to commodity status. Relations between the intellectual and the means of production, the objects of production, and the administration of production are alienated relations, much as those between the worker and the forces of production he confronts.

In the non-economic aspects of class formation, the intellectual is favorably positioned to develop class consciousness—close working proximity, long years of mutual study and association, frequent contact and critical discussion, and numerous common objective interests. Intellectuals in the employ of colleges and universities do form a relatively cohesive social community.[81] Clearly, internal political divisions do exist. Intellectuals, both scientific and humanistic, occupy strategic positions within corporate capitalism and are inescapably involved in the clash of ideologies and conflicting political forces.

The majority of intellectuals may be considered to be politically liberal. Some represent conservatism. Some are radical. We might note that

---

[78] See the selections by Mills, Chomsky, Roszak, Horowitz, and Lippman in Anderson and Murray, *The Professors*, pp. 305–50; and those in Theodore Roszak, ed., *The Dissenting Academy* (New York: Random House, Inc., 1968).

[79] See Irving Louis Horowitz and William H. Friedland, *The Knowledge Factory* (Chicago: Aldine Publishing Company, 1970).

[80] Bettina Aptheker, *The Academic Rebellion in the United States* (Secaucus, N.J.: The Citadel Press, 1972). Aptheker presents an incisive Marxist analysis of the contemporary university, including a definitive discussion of the question of academic freedom.

[81] See the studies in Anderson and Murray, *The Professors*, pp. 217–87.

many of those who have contributed incisive social criticism, such as Herbert Gans, "cannot share their [radicals'] belief in the need to over-turn 'the system.' "[82] On the next page, Gans nevertheless contends he wants "immediate change that improves the condition of the deprived immediately"—a desire that would seem to require overturning rather large parts of the system.

Students

Like intellectuals, students have presented difficulty for class analysis. In the past, when they were relatively few in number, college and university students derived largely from the propertied and professional strata. Today, with almost eight million students working toward college degrees and almost one-half of persons between 18 and 21 years of age enrolled, the situation is entirely different. Students still come dispro-portionately from the higher income categories (see Chapter 7), but the numbers from lower-white-collar and blue-collar backgrounds have greatly increased in recent years. There remains a marked tendency for colleges to be ranked by the socioeconomic status of students—universities, state colleges, and junior colleges with private schools mixed through these ranks according to their entrance qualifications and prestige.

Thus, the system of higher education itself class stratifies students within it, more or less perpetuating and reinforcing the strata hierarchy existing in the larger society. But within the various institutions them-selves, and even to a certain extent between those of different status ranking, student life has an important independent homogenizing in-fluence upon participants from all levels of society. The knowledge fac-tory proletarianizes the student much like it does the faculty. Beginning in early teens and continuing into the late 20s for those who go on to graduate school, school and student life tends to generate a common culture, a social community, a student identity, and an awareness of common interests. A growing sense of alienation within the university as well as toward society at large combined with the civil rights move-ment, the war on poverty, the arms race, and most importantly the Vietnam War galvanized increasing numbers of students into political activism.[83] The movement that Mills presaged as the new left was taking

---

[82] Herbert J. Gans, *People and Plans* (New York: Basic Books, Inc., Pub-lishers, 1968), pp. xi–xii.

[83] Analysis of the new left may be found in Lyman T. Sargent, *New Left Thought* (Homewood, Ill.: The Dorsey Press, 1972); James O'Brien, "Beyond Reminiscence: The New Left in History," *Radical America,* July–August, 1972, pp. 11–46; Richard Flacks, *Youth and Social Change* (Chicago: Mark-ham Publishing Company, 1971); Ted Goertzel, "Generational Conflict and Social Change," *Youth and Society,* March 1972, pp. 327–52; and Jack New-field, *A Prophetic Minority* (New York: Signet Books, 1967. Psychologically oriented studies include Kenneth Keniston, *Young Radicals* (New York: Har-court, Brace & World, Inc., 1968); and Charles Hampden-Turner, *Radical Man* (Cambridge, Mass: Schenkman Publishing Company, 1970).

shape (in contradistinction to the "old left" of the Depression years).[84] From its inception in the early 1960s through the peak of Vietnam War and the Cambodian invasion of 1970, the student left grew steadily in numerical strength.[85] Political actions as a class increased accordingly, and much credit is due the student left for bringing the kinds of social pressures to bear upon both Johnson and Nixon to alter course in Southeast Asia; the costs in terms of social upheaval and disruption of normal profit-making activity were too great to risk.

Yet, the kinds of changes that student militants were seeking never seemed to materialize; even the war continued. The ineffectualness of student dissent throughout the 1960s turned increasing numbers of young militants from criticism to protest to resistance and finally to direct confrontation.[86] Open confrontation had subsided by 1971–72, but the indications are that the new left of the 1960s, with its anti-organizational and atheoretical orientations, is being quietly transformed into a more theoretically informed and politically matured group. A critical consciousness is perhaps in the process of being transformed into class consciousness.

The class conscious student left is not, however, a majority among students. As J.A. Warner remarks, "Most youth still are in a mode of consciousness that can be termed 'traditional' or 'organizational.'"[87] Surveys suggest that only perhaps as many as one-fifth of students are amenable to socialism, with approximately another one-third open to liberal reform.[88] One-fifth consider themselves conservatives and the remainder are "neutral." Students are to the left and liberal side more so than the general population, but not nearly to the point of setting them off as a separate political group. However, we may well expect that the younger college-educated new working class, as well as those with vocational and junior college training who enter blue-collar jobs, will be at the forefront of political criticism and activity in the future.

Yesterday's new left and student activists, and today's socialist and left-oriented students, are not likely to be re-educated to the ways of corporate capitalism. (Parenthetically, it was first noted that the student left originated in left or liberal and affluent families;[89] by the end of

---

[84] On the distinction between old and new left, see Armand L. Mauss, "The Lost Promise of Reconciliation: New Left vs. Old Left," *Journal of Social Issues*, 27 (Summer 1971), pp. 1–20.

[85] See the review of public poll data by Seymour M. Lipset, *Rebellion in the University* (Boston: Little, Brown and Company, 1971), pp. 38–79.

[86] Kingsley Widmer, "Why Dissent Turns Violent," *The Nation*, April 7, 1969, pp. 425–29; Richard Flacks and Milton Mankoff, "Revolt in Santa Barbara: Why They Burned The Bank," *The Nation*, March 23, 1970, pp. 337–40; and Jerome Skolnick, *The Politics of Protest* (New York: Ballantine Books, 1969), pp. 25–124.

[87] "Alienated Post New Left Youth: Secular Marxism and Religious Mysticism," presented to the Canadian Sociology and Anthropology Association, 1972, Montreal, p. 10.

[88] Lipset, *Rebellion in the University*, pp. 49–60.

[89] See David L. Westby and Richard G. Baungart, "Class and Politics in the

the 1960s, however, left-oriented students originated from very diverse social and income strata.[90]) Material support by way of employment poses a major problem for student radicals, for the usual fare of corporate and government jobs is either politically distasteful or, if appealing, are glutted with applicants (education, social welfare, graduate school, etc.).[91] Even "straight" organizational jobs are highly competitive and scarce. Poverty programs have been sharply cut back, and the Peace Corps has lost its image as an instrument of constructive change (a logical fate for an organization conceived by a President who also altered the emphasis of military preparedness from that of massive retaliation toward green beret-type counterrevolutionary warfare in the underdeveloped world).[92] The country has never had an unemployed or unengaged pool of highly educated surplus labor, let alone a politicized and critical thinking one; these have been the ingredients of many student revolutionary movements abroad, and continue to be a serious de-stabilizing factor almost everywhere. The authorities who oversee the organization of higher education are unlikely to recommend the kinds of changes in employment opportunity that are required.[93] Employment outlets for new needs and aspirations could be created, but this would too often conflict with the interests of big capital.

A danger is present in this situation, which is that an overwhelming sense of hopelessness will dissolve critical idealism into apathetic withdrawal. A pseudo-counterculture, with all of its spiritual and chemical opiates, awaits the de-politicized drop-out and virtually returns the person to a bourgeois culture glossed over with thinly veiled substitute trimmings. A mystical, drugged, and style-seeking subculture is an

---

Family Backgrounds of Student Political Activists," *American Sociological Review,* 31 (October 1966), pp. 690–93; Richard Flacks, "The Liberated Generation: An Exploration of the Roots of Student Protest," *Journal of Social Issues,* 23 (July 1967), pp. 52–75; and "Social and Cultural Meanings of Student Revolt," *Social Problems,* 17 (Winter 1970), pp. 341–57.

[90] See the research by Douglas Kirby, "A Counter-Culture Explanation of Student Activism," *Social Problems,* 19 (Fall 1971), pp. 203 16; and Henry C. Finney, "Political Libertarianism at Berkeley," *Journal of Social Issues,* 27 (Summer 1971), pp. 35–61. On Working-class students, see Alan Wolfe, "Working With the Working Class," *Change,* February 1972, pp. 48–53.

[91] Alan Wolfe, "The Ph.D. Glut: Hard Times on Campus," *The Nation,* May 25, 1970, pp. 623–27.

[92] See Michael T. Klare, *War Without End* (New York: Vintage Books, 1972), pp. 29–55, for a discussion of the Kennedy administration's shift in military emphasis from deterrence to counterrevolutionary warfare.

[93] A 1969 survey conducted by the Educational Testing Service of 5,000 trustees from more than 500 colleges and universities found that 60 percent of the trustees (largely white, male, middle-aged, conservative, and rich) believed that campus speakers should be screened, 40 percent that the administration should control the contents of student newspapers, 53 percent that it is reasonable to require loyalty oaths from faculty members, 64 percent that trustees and not faculty should bestow tenure, and fully 92 percent that college attendance is a privilege, not a right. See Bettina Aptheker, "Berkeley's Meddlesome Regents," *The Nation,* September 7, 1970, pp. 169–73.

adjunct to the status quo, for it leaves the external world untouched. As to one aspect of escapist culture, Keniston writes that

> Sustained engagement in an effort to change the world is rarely compatible with the kind of self-absorption and inwardness that results from intensive and regular drug use; conversely, however strongly the committed drug user may feel about the inequities of American society, his primary efforts are usually directed toward self-change, rather than changing the world around him."[94]

To this might be added Marcuse's argument that there can be ". . . no individual liberation without a political struggle on a social scale against the prevailing unfreedom."[95]

---

[94] Kenneth Keniston, "Heads and Seekers: Drugs on Campus, Counter-Cultures and American Society," *The American Scholar*, 38 (Winter 1968–69).

[95] Herbert Marcuse, "The Movement in an Era of Repression," *Berkeley Journal of Sociology*, XVI (1971–72), p. 11.

7

Education and class inequality

SOCIAL MOBILITY

Within the constellation of analytical concepts dealing with social inequality and social class is that of social mobility. In general terms, social mobility refers to the movement of an individual upward or downward in the structure of inequality. This implies that social mobility may take place on any of the hierarchical dimensions which were previously discussed in connection with inequality—i.e., property ownership, wealth, income, education, power, prestige, and so forth. The most frequently used indicator of social mobility is occupational placement and change, insofar as a person's occupation is both readily accessible information and tends to be a relatively good guide to one's location on the other factors of inequality. However, to obtain a more accurate description of individual mobility, a composite measure that incorporates as many aspects of inequality as possible (with each aspect weighted according to its importance) should be used. Occupational position in itself can only be taken as a very general and rough guide to social mobility.

Social mobility may be viewed *intra*generationally or *inter*generationally. That is, an individual may be examined for changes in position within the structure of inequality during his or her own lifetime, or an individual's position at a given point in his or her own lifetime may be examined relative to that of the individual's parents (usually father). The majority of studies dealing with social mobility focus on the latter type (intergenerational) of mobility, although there is no shortage of the intragenerational variety.

Social mobility of either kind has the effect of moving an individual from one social class or stratum to another. For example, a person's father may have been a machine operator in a factory, whereas the person himself may be an engineer. This represents movement from the traditional or blue-collar working class in one generation to the new working class in the next. Owing to the extensive technological changes that have occurred during the past 50 years, there has been substantial amounts of social mobility in every industrial society. Kahl has referred to such type of mobility as technological mobility.[1] The opportunity to move from positions of lower income, education, skill, and prestige to positions of higher requirements and reward has thus multiplied greatly as industrialization moved forward. Unskilled labor occupational categories contract, while skilled and white-collar categories expand (see Chapter 10). Such opportunities are created not as a result of there being a democratic political structure, for technological mobility is just as much a part of a dictatorship.

The idea of an "open" society in terms of social mobility refers to the extent to which an able individual from a lower status or stratum has the chance to rise to a higher status or stratum despite family background, racial or ethnic status, sex, etc. An open society is also one that allows a higher status person to fall in the class structure. A "closed" society is one that displays a very high degree of continuity of class or status position from one generation to the next so that a person's position within the structure of inequality is ascribed by birth rather than achieved by self. In the extreme case, we may speak of a *caste* system whereby formal and informal rules governing marriage, occupational choice, and group participation are socially prescribed. India represents the classic case of a caste society, though we might look to the American South for aspects of caste as well.[2] Most societies, including India, are neither open nor closed but rather partially open. While industrial society and technological change demand a socially mobile labor force, there is also an extensive amount of intergenerational transmission of privilege and inheritance of position. During a period of rapid industrialization, as has taken place in the Soviet Union, social mobility rates tend to be high over and above the limiting influence of family transmission. Later industrial society, however, does not open up new opportunities at such a high rate, and thus the influence of family transmission pushes the system toward greater closure. In any event, technological change (and administrative growth as well) is the decisive factor in determining the amount of social mobility in industrial societies.

The amount of technological progress also is decisive in determining the size of the social surplus available to a society. Labor productivity through technological advance enlarges the service sector of a society; greater productivity and wealth also enlarges the absolute size of the capitalist class. The number of fortunes have increased rapidly during the present century. Millionaires are made (and unmade) almost daily. The idea of anybody being able to make a million dollars has been a part of the traditional mythology of America. As the centimillionaire

---

[1] Joseph A. Kahl, *The American Class Structure* (New York: Rinehart & Company, Inc., 1957), pp. 251–57.

[2] John Dollard, *Caste and Class in a Southern Town* (New York: Doubleday and Company, 1957; first edition published 1937).

insurance tycoon W. Clement Stone once asserted, "Success is achieved by those who *try*," and "Act like a winner and you *are* a winner."[3] To Mr. Stone, the move from selling newspapers on a street to having a million dollars to toss into two presidential campaigns is anybody's opportunity. What Mr. Stone failed to tell us is that his fortune was taken from the social surplus created by millions of workers, all of whom "tried" but very few of whom ever became or will become "winners." And what of Mr. Stone's heirs? How hard will they have to try for their success?

The opposite side of technological advance and the social surplus is the permanent class of unskilled, unusable poor. Social mobility becomes all the more difficult and poverty becomes all the more humiliating and unbearable.

Social mobility has great ideological and practical stabilizing value within the system. The prospects of individual improvement encourages individual striving as opposed to collective action. Mobility itself conveys the feeling of "moving up" and of continual improvement from one generation to the next. It encourages patience and discourages immediate mobilization for group interests and needs. Social mobility has the effect of dissolving old ties and associations, of weakening traditional common class interests. In brief, social mobility works against class formation.

The period of rising expectations and continual feeling of moving up may be drawing to a close. Many people are recognizing that much social mobility is more illusory than real. Many young adults no longer feel they have improved upon their parent's position and life situation. Many even consider the situations of their grandparents better than their own, and return to many traditional customs and life styles as best they can. This is not the essential point, though it may be viewed as symbolic. The essential point is that additional years of education, more dollars a day, a bigger house, and a newer car may not do for a person what it has always been thought to do. A kind of economic and social inflation has been going on for some time now, and increasing numbers of people are beginning to realize this fact. The treadmill is becoming more evident than the escalator. So much of what would constitute improvements in a person's life now concern social, society-wide needs unattainable from the standpoint of the average person's actual or potential resources. Social mobility for most people increasingly demands structural changes in the society rather than moving up to the next rung on the job ladder.

For the present, however, our analysis must be limited to what exists, and the differentials in opportunities for individual improvement within the population are substantial and meaningful. Especially significant today are educational opportunities, and we shall devote the substance of the present chapter to an examination of education and the class structure.

---

[3] Lois Wille, "From Rags to Nixon: Clement Stone Feels Great," *The Nation*, March 17, 1969, p. 338.

THE OPPORTUNITY LADDER

The opportunity to improve one's social and economic circumstances is for most persons based largely upon the educational and occupational structures. Educational achievement is especially regarded by many as the primary means to a better life, and well it might. But what is not always clearly understood is the manner in which the educational system also operates so as to *reinforce* inequality rather than open up the opportunity structure. We shall devote a full discussion to this issue later in the chapter. Educational achievement puts one in a position for occupational success, which, in turn, opens the door to mobility of income and material wealth. Our concern in this chapter will thus be with the manner in which the educational system distributes its opportunities within the population.

Opportunity within the present context refers to the degree of openness or equality of access to valued things, especially education in view of its key role in social mobility. Equality of opportunity would imply that a random member of any given stratum will have the same chance or probability of ending up in, say, a salaried profession as the random member of any other given stratum. The actual inequality of opportunity may be demonstrated by figures confirming the strong tendency, especially strong at the higher and lower ends of the ladder, for sons to remain in the same broad occupational category as their fathers. In terms of hard data (national sample), over 40 percent of sons of self-employed professionals enter a profession and 30 percent some other white-collar job.[4] In sharp contrast, only about 5 percent of sons of laborers enter a profession and a mere 15 percent other white-collar jobs; the majority end up back in lower blue-collar or service jobs. The chances of sons attaining real economic security in an upper white-collar professional or business career steadily diminish as one moves down the occupational ladder. Here are the percentages of sons who made it into professional or managerial positions by the occupations of their fathers:

Professional	55%	Skilled	28%
Managerial	49	Semi-skilled	20
Sales	46	Service	21
Clerical	38	Unskilled	12

Thus, from the standpoint of the son of a laborer, opportunities for a professional or managerial career are unequal by a ratio of almost 5 to 1. Moreover, these are crude categories and do not take into account the high probability that the laborer's mobile son enters a *lower status* profession or business career than the professional's son (for example, possession of a teaching certificate as opposed to a Ph.D., and assistant manager of a small business as opposed to an executive in a large company).

Survey data from an industrial Michigan community indicates that the majority of neither blacks nor whites are taken in by the equality of

---

[4] Peter M. Blau, "The Flow of Occupational Supply and Recruitment," *American Sociological Review*, 30 (August 1965), pp. 475–90.

opportunity ideology.[5] Most respondents recognized the slim chances of a working-class son to become an executive and the equally slim chance of an executive's son ending up in a laborer's job; lower income respondents were especially pessimistic over the amount of opportunity in the U.S., not to mention equality of opportunity. Still, one-half of the total sample did agree that rich and poor had equal opportunity; the myth is evidently far from being dead.

The transmission of privilege from one generation to the next is not typical only of the United States and other Western societies;[6] a similar pattern exists in economies under state direction such as the Soviet Union and Poland.[7] In Japan, the population also tends to be mobility-oriented with an image of the open society, but there, as elsewhere, class of origin weighs heavily in an individual's life chances. The critical junctures for Japanese mobility are the several examinations which are administered at certain intervals in the education system.[8] Scores on nationwide examinations determine the length and quality of education, which in turn determine occupational placement. Despite such emphases on merit, social mobility in Japan is very much conditioned by family resources and class background.

THE IMPORTANCE OF COLLEGE

The channels of upward mobility are today largely educational channels. The ruling elites depend heavily upon the educational system to select and prepare the kinds of reliable recruits needed to administer and carry out the administrative and technical work required in production and organizational operations. The school hierarchy, from grades, to high school, college, and graduate and professional schools, is designed to accomplish the task of reproducing people to fit into the division of labor. The school system also develops and teaches the social and technical abilities required to maintain and advance the forces of production; in particular the university is an essential component to the augmentation of power and wealth through science and technology.

A century ago, a full eight years education was considered adequate to social functioning and anything beyond qualified one for higher placement. The first part of the present century witnessed the democratization of the high school diploma, but even it paved the way for social mobility. By mid-century, the high school diploma was losing ground rapidly to the encroaching boom in higher education, and it had already been deter-

---

[5] Joan Huber Rytina, William H. Form, and John Pease, "Income and Stratification Ideology: Beliefs about the American Opportunity Structure," *American Journal of Sociology*, 75 (January 1970), pp. 703–16.

[6] Phillips Cutright, "Occupational Inheritance: A Cross-National Analysis," *American Journal of Sociology*, 73 (January 1968), pp. 400–416.

[7] See data on Polish occupational inheritance in Stefan Nowak, "Changes of Social Structure in Social Consciousness," in Celia S. Heller, ed., *Structured Social Inequality* (New York: Macmillan Company, 1969), pp. 235–47.

[8] R.P. Dore, *City Life in Japan* (Berkeley: University of California Press, 1967), Chapter 12.

mined that the bachelor's degree was a safer guide to competency. Today, that same sacred bachelor's degree is losing its potency; employers look upon it in the same way they did a high school diploma in 1925 or even 1940. The aspiring person today must look forward to post-graduate study. Where the "credential inflation" will stop is anybody's guess, but the traditionally outer limits (the Ph.D.) are being approached. Ivar Berg has drawn our attention to the substantial superfluity of education and the degree inflation to the practical performance of jobs.[9] Educational performance evinces no consistent relationship to post-educational job performance and productivity.[10] Employers simply reason that someone who has earned a bachelor's or master's degree is a "better bet" than a high school grad or dropout (highly technical ones present a different situation). So students keep on plugging through the educational mazes, hoping for the opportunity to eventually prove themselves on a job.

While there may be evidence that higher education is itself not greatly relevant to the cognitive performance of most jobs and that an operating integration of education and work is far more likely to be effective and productive, we have just argued that higher education is more than ever before important to social and economic mobility. Furthermore, a college education is in all likelihood at least as hard to complete today as previously. As high school diplomas lose their power on the job market (their power in the past is reflected by the fact that 38 percent of high school graduates held skilled or white-collar jobs in 1968 compared with only 19 percent of dropouts),[11] high school graduates are more and more forced to enter college. Grade competition is often intense, especially at the leading colleges and universities, which open wider doors to favorable job placement and graduate study. We might also note that the majority of high school graduates still do not enter colleges of any kind, and far fewer eventually will graduate. In short, there remains a strong importance attached to the college degree. It is virtually a prerequisite to social mobility.

Who goes to college?

Thus, the critical questions in the study of social mobility are, Who goes to college? and Who finishes college? The first response that comes to the minds of many people is "those with enough intelligence to make it." Although intelligence has something to do with who goes to college, it is certainly not the only nor the most important factor in explaining who goes to college. Let's examine some of the influences on college aspirations and attendance.

What quite clearly seems to be the most important factor in explaining

---

[9] *Education and Jobs: The Great Training Robbery* (New York: Praeger Publishers, 1970); also Berg's "Rich Man's Qualifications for Poor Man's Jobs," *Trans-action*, 6 (March 1969), pp. 45–50.

[10] See Herbert Gintis, "Education and the Characteristics of Worker Productivity," *American Economic Review*, 61 (May 1971), pp. 266–79.

[11] U.S. Bureau of the Census, *Statistical Abstract of the United States, 1969* (Washington, D.C., 1969), p. 110.

who goes to college is a person's socioeconomic (parent's education, occupation, and income) background. The higher a person's class background, the greater the probability that the person will attend college. Even when holding constant (matching for) other apparent influences such as scores on intelligence tests and size of community of residence (the larger the community the more likely is college attendance), a person's class background continues to exert a definite influence on college attendance.[12] In point of fact, the transmission of privilege through social class is so effective that a high school graduate with a *high intelligence* score but from a *low socioeconomic* background is no more likely to attend college than one scoring *low in intelligence* but from a *high socioeconomic* background.

The data in Table 4 point out the influence of family income upon college attendance. Sixty-two percent of families with incomes of $15,-000 and over had one or more members in college in October 1970 compared with less than 20 percent for families with incomes beneath $5,000. Data presented by Bowles indicate that fully 80 percent of 1965 high school seniors who graduated did not attend college in 1967 if their

Table 4

FAMILIES WITH CHILDREN 18 TO 24 YEARS OLD, PERCENT WITH FULL-TIME COLLEGE STUDENTS IN OCTOBER 1970, BY FAMILY INCOME

	No. *college students*	*One or more* *college students*
Under $3,000	86%	14%
$3,000–$4,999	80	20
$5,000–$7,499	70	30
$7,500–$9,999	62	38
$10,000–$14,999	54	46
$15,000 and over	38	62

Source: U.S. Bureau of the Census, *Current Population Reports,* Series P-20, No. 222, "School Enrollment: October 1970," U.S. Government Printing Office, Washington, D.C., 1971, Table 13, p. 36.

family income was under $3,000 as compared with only 13 percent of those with family incomes of $15,000 and over.[13] And the probability of going to college for low socioeconomic high school students in the second from top ability quartile is less than that of high socioeconomic students in the lowest ability quartile.

Despite the strong link between family income and college attendance, Milner presents evidence that suggests that simply making financial aid available to high school graduates would not greatly increase the probability that they would enter college, except for perhaps the poverty-stricken and minorities.[14] Milner's contention is that a history of income

[12] William H. Sewell, "Community of Residence and College Plans," *American Sociological Review,* 29 (February 1964), pp. 24–38.

[13] Samuel Bowles, "Getting Nowhere: Programmed Class Stagnation," *Society,* 9 (June 1972), p. 47.

[14] Murray Milner, Jr. *The Illusion of Equality* (San Francisco: Jossey-Bass Inc., Publishers, 1972).

scarcity has shifted family traditions and aspirations away from higher education so that family culture does not cultivate college orientation. Furthermore education for the working classes is diluted by more education for higher income groups. Funding of higher education, argues Milner, could not accomplish what income redistribution in the larger society could.

Evidence is plentiful regarding the importance of parental models and encouragement in college attendance.[15] Nevertheless, given equal levels of parental encouragement (and similar intelligence scores), lower socioeconomic high school graduates are still significantly less likely to go on to college than those from higher status backgrounds. But the kind of encouragement and the ability of college-educated parents to cultivate aspirations and skills leading to higher education would differ from those parents educationally inexperienced. Family income margins may restrict the intensity of realistic encouragement. The economic crunch is readily visible in the fact that in families with two or more members between 18 and 24 years old, families with incomes of $15,000 or over account for 44 percent of families with two full-time college students compared with 22 percent for families having incomes of $10,000 or less (the reverse of what one might expect from the general distribution of family incomes).[16]

Also of importance to college plans and closely linked to the family factor are the college aspirations of a high school student's close friends.[17] If the student's friends plan to go to college, he may be influenced by their higher educational goals. In a study of California youth, Krauss discovered that among blue-collar respondents with all of their close friends planning to attend college, 81 percent themselves aspired to college, 60 percent aspired if most of their friends did, 29 percent if some of their friends did, and 10 percent if none of their friends had college plans.[18] Students from white-collar homes were also strongly influenced by their peers' college intentions, though these students were more likely than blue-collar ones to plan to go to college even if only some or none of their friends were going. That Krauss's findings reflect the operation of reference groups is substantiated by the fact that college-bound blue-collar youth were very similar to college-oriented white-collar youth in career attitudes, interest in national and international affairs, beliefs

[15] Ernest Q. Campbell and C. Norman Alexander, Jr., "Peer Influences on Adolescent Educational Aspirations and Attainments," *American Sociological Review*, 29 (August 1964), pp. 58–75; Robert L. Havighurst, *Growing Up in River City* (New York: John Wiley & Sons, Inc., 1962); and William H. Sewell and Vimal P. Shah, "Social Class, Parental Encouragement, and Educational Aspirations," *American Journal of Sociology*, 73 (March 1968), pp. 559–72.

[16] U.S. Bureau of the Census, *Current Population Reports*, Series P-20, No. 222, "School Enrollment: October 1970," U.S. Government Printing Office, Washington, D.C. 1971, Table 13, p. 35.

[17] Campbell and Alexander, "Peer Influences on Adolescent Educational Aspirations and Attainments."

[18] Irving Krauss, "Sources of Educational Aspirations among Working-Class Youth," *American Sociological Review*, 29 (December 1964), pp. 867–79.

in opportunity, and reading habits. The chief difference between the two college-oriented groups was that blue-collar youth were more liberal in attitude toward government economic programs. With reference-group influence working in the opposite direction, white-collar youth without college aspirations reported attitudes and behavior similar to noncollege blue-collar students.

Krauss's data also demonstrated family-based stimulants to college attendance and related mainly to college-oriented reference groups and models. Perhaps the most important of these college references and models, and obviously tied to parental encouragement, is a father with some college experience: among *both* white- and blue-collar students, those having a father who had attended college were almost *twice* as likely to aspire to college themselves than those whose fathers had not completed high school. Also of significance in producing college aspirations in both classes was having a mother from a white-collar background (especially for working-class youths whose mother had married "down"), college-educated siblings or close family friends, and attendance at a predominantly middle-class high school.

Virtually all of the college stimulants we have mentioned are variations on one common underlying factor: regular contact and exposure to people who themselves have had college experience or who hold a college education in high esteem, whether these persons be fathers, mothers, brothers and sisters, family friends, high school students, or close personal friends. Even community of residence directly reflects social milieus; the city presents more college models and support systems than the small town, not to mention the greater presence and availability of colleges in the city. Intelligence scores, too, are in large part determined by peer, school, and especially parental interest. Easily the most important of the college reference models, it seems to me, is that of guidance and encouragement of a college-educated parent.

The outstanding exception to the college model and reference-group factor is the first discussed, the economic factor, or the ability to pay. Irrespective of how much parental encouragement or how many peer references a high school student might have, family economics sets major limitations on what he might realistically aspire to. The transmission of privilege is easy to follow: College-educated parents are better able to provide both college models and money, and the presence of the latter justifies realistic encouragement for college aspirations in their children. In a completely free educational system, and in one that consciously provides an abundance of college models, information, and sympathetic advisers, major correctives could be made in the social inequities perpetuated through restricted opportunities for a college education.

College and occupational placement

Going to college and finishing college are two very different things indeed. Finishing college is the key to an opportunity at high occupational placement. Most significantly, the possession of a college degree helps in part to eliminate the influence of class background on occupational placement. Eckland discovered that among college *graduates*, general class background had little bearing on their level of occupational placement.[19] Eckland observed that slightly over three-fourths of high-ability college graduates (as measured by high school rank and college entrance exams) entered upper white-collar jobs regardless of class background. At other ability levels, while progressively fewer graduates entered high-status occupations, Eckland found no significant variation by class background of respondents.

Thus, some equalizing begins to work *after* a college degree is in hand. However, by the point of graduation, inequalitarian processes have drastically reduced the proportion of capable lower status persons. As we have already observed, class of origin exerts a marked influence on who *graduates:* the higher the student's class background the greater the chances that he will finish college.[20] Who graduates is also conditioned by other *class-linked* factors such as rank in high school class, college entrance scores, and occupational aspirations.[21] College students from blue-collar backgrounds, especially those at prestigious schools with low proportions of blue-collar students, have been found to experience more social isolation and feelings of self-estrangement than higher status college youths, disrupting scholastic performance and success in graduation.[22] In brief, although a completed college education tends to overcome at least in part the disadvantages of a lower status background for social mobility prospects, a considerable amount of damage to the open society has already been carried out before college graduation has taken place.

A question of related importance concerns the influence of class background on the occupational placement of college *dropouts.* Eckland's data again reveal some very disturbing things in the way of inequities in American society. Higher status college dropouts at given levels of ability do not slide down the occupational ladder nearly as easily as do lower status dropouts. While about 40 percent of Eckland's high-ability *lower status* dropouts ended up in lower status occupations, *none* of the high-ability *higher status* dropouts did so. This "cushioning" role played by higher class backgrounds may be seen as an extension of the tendency toward occupational inheritance that we previously discussed.

ACHIEVEMENT ORIENTATION

We might here comment upon the role of personal aspiration or achievement orientation in connection with social mobility. A large body of empirical literature documents the fact that people vary or differ in response to indicators designed to measure achievement orientation or

---

[19] Bruce Eckland, "Academic Ability, Higher Education, and Occupational Mobility," *American Sociological Review,* 30 (October 1965), pp. 735–46.

[20] Ibid.

[21] Eldon L. Wegner and William H. Sewell, "Selection and Context as Factors Affecting the Probability of Graduation from College," *American Journal of Sociology,* 75 (January 1970), pp. 665–79.

[22] Robert A. Ellis and W. Clayton Lane, "Social Mobility and Social Isolation: A Test of Sorokin's Dissociative Hypothesis," *American Sociological Review,* 32 (April 1967), pp. 237–52.

need for achievement.[23] Achievement orientation, in turn, tends to be directly related to social mobility. Whatever our beliefs might be regarding the distribution and role of genetic ability in a group or population (I prefer to believe, and act upon the belief, that most people are capable of attaining far more than the goals authorities often hold out as "appropriate" or "realistic" for them), it is quite evident that there are very fundamental differences among people in "motivation" or "drive." Although motivation or drive may have some genetic bases, cultural determinants would certainly far outweigh inheritance.

What *are* the cultural sources of achievement orientation? There is, in fact, considerable agreement on this question. Whatever terms might be used to describe it, the major source of achievement orientation seems to be a family milieu that emphasizes self-direction and independence in children and democratic relations between parent and children[24] (self-directing and democratic functioning should *not be equated* with permissiveness). By contrast, parental dominance and decision making produces passivity and dependence and inhibits achievement orientation.[25]

In what kinds of families does one tend to find an emphasis on autonomy and independence in children? Pearlin and Kohn have presented empirical data, from both Latin and Anglo areas of the world, that "middle-class" families more often provide an atmosphere of intellectual and behavioral autonomy for children than do working-class parents.[26] By contrast working-class parents, Pearlin and Kohn argue, tend to value conformity and obedience more than white-collar parents. Pearlin and Kohn contend that middle-class fathers' occupations cultivate in those who practice them a predisposition toward self-control, accessibility of ideas, and freedom from direct supervision. These occupationally generated values, then, are injected into the child socialization process. Working-class occupations, by contrast, are more strictly regulated by the production process, beyond the purpose and control of the worker, and almost entirely preconceived and planned (by nonmanual personnel). Some blue-collar jobs allow for greater autonomy than some white-collar jobs, but the tendency for less control and supervision in much nonmanual work is evident.

Furthermore, upper-white-collar careers now require college and graduate education, often itself a stimulus to intellectual autonomy and emphasis on personal control. Thus, families with one and especially both parents having college educations, more often than families with

---

[23] Bernard C. Rosen, H.J. Crockett, and C.Z. Nunn, eds., *Achievement in American Society* (Cambridge, Mass.: Schenkman Publishing Company, 1969).

[24] Ibid.

[25] Glen H. Elder, Jr., "Family Structure and Educational Attainment: A Cross-National Study," *American Sociological Review*, 30 (February 1965), pp. 81–96.

[26] Leonard Pearlin and Melvin Kohn, "Social Class, Occupation, and Parental Values: A Cross-National Study," *American Sociological Review*, 31 (August 1966), pp. 466–79; also see Melvin Kohn, *Class and Conformity* (Homewood, Ill.: The Dorsey Press, 1969).

lower educational backgrounds, would provide a democratic and open decision-making atmosphere for children. Moreover, owing to occupational and educational inheritance, each new generation would not only benefit from a family value system conducive to mobility aspirations but would themselves often go on to experience the same educational and occupational effects that contributed to the values of self-direction and autonomy in their parents. Through such cyclical mechanisms operate the joint influences of economics and cultural values in perpetuating privilege and social mobility patterns.

In addition to occupational and educational background of families, religious affiliation has been found to be related to value emphases on autonomy and independence in children, and hence to higher achievement orientation. White Protestants and Jews have been found to place greater stress on child autonomy and decision making than Catholics and black Protestants. However, the fact that white and black Protestants and, for instance, Irish- and French-American Catholics seem to differ in certain child-rearing values suggests that the sources of the variation in value emphases are not religious but ethnic.

By now the reader might be asking, "Achievement orientation and need of achieving *what?*" Just as a person may seek power for the sake of power, or friendship for the sake of friendship, so may he desire achievement for the sake of achievement. In the extreme case of need for achievement, every task, every event, no matter what or where, is infused with the desire to excel, to master; in the opposite extreme, no task, no event, seems to be worth effort beyond the absolute essentials or minimum. The conscious urge to compete with others tends to accompany the need for achievement, though it may not; however, the achiever is always competing with himself, pushing or striving to get the most and best of his capabilities. Yet, every case of achievement orientation must be anchored to a concrete goal, whether it be financial, occupational, educational, social, or cultural. What's more, every person who sets out to achieve some concrete goal must make an evaluation of his actual achievement prospects. The higher a person sets his goals, the greater the probability of failure and self-deprecation; the lower the goals that are set, the greater the probability of achievement and self-acceptance.

Herein lies what might well be the major source of differences in achievement orientation, and one which may largely account for the previously mentioned sources such as occupation, education, and religion or ethnicity. College-educated, middle-income whites may realistically instill and encourage, whether consciously or unconsciously, the establishment of self-direction and high goals in their children, and children may uncritically and realistically accept these aspirations and goals without serious threat of failure and self-deprecation. An unskilled high school dropout, white or nonwhite, can scarcely do the same for his children. Even if he does so (as many do), the children themselves may be in a better position to give a more realistic assessment of how high they might safely set their level of achievement. Almost invariably, groups found to be low in achievement orientation are of lower occupational, educational, and ethnic status, and it is much too facile and self-righteous simply to argue that these same people are low status *because* of their lower achievement orientation. The protection of self-concept requires that lower status persons adjust their aspirations to often abysmally low levels or even eliminate aspirations altogether. Clement Stone's motto, "Success is achieved by those who try," is to many an invitation to inevitable frustration and self-degradation.

A person may lower his levels of aspiration either because he feels *himself* inadequate or because he feels *society* is discriminatory and lacks equality of opportunity. Coping with low-achievement potential is more tolerable if society rather than self can be blamed. But until quite recently, America's working poor typically held themselves largely responsible for their plight. Thus, their self-image has been commensurately low. All of this is now changing, but in particular among the nonwhite minorities. Lower income whites are much more gradually moving toward social rather than self-criticism, but they *are* moving. Self-confidence and a desire to achieve are prerequisites to social change; these prerequisites are increasingly present in America's working and lower classes.

EDUCATION AND ECONOMIC SUCCESS

The economic value of higher education is completely documented in Table 5. The fact that the monetary value of higher education *increases* through time should especially be noticed. Between the age periods 25-34 and 45-54 the average college graduate's median income increases by nearly $6,000 compared with $3,000 for the high school graduate. A post-graduate's income increases by $7,300. Another manner of documentation is found in Table 6 where it is revealed that those families whose head in 1970 had completed four years of college or more compose approximately one-half of the top five percent of the income distribution but only 14 percent of all families. The high school graduate

Table 5

FAMILIES WITH HEAD 25 YEARS OLD AND OVER BY TOTAL MEDIAN MONEY INCOME IN 1970 FOR YEAR-ROUND FULL-TIME, BY YEARS OF SCHOOL COMPLETED AND AGE

	Total	25–34	35–44	45–54	55–64	65 or over
College						
5 years or more	$19,083	$15,211	$19,044	$22,534	$21,640	
4 years	16,356	13,538	17,340	19,179	17,213	$14,169
1 to 3 years	13,566	11,834	13,843	15,638	14,804	11,394
High school						
4 years	11,807	10,478	11,953	13,363	12,496	10,166
1 to 3 years	10,832	9,142	10,713	12,041	11,602	8,425
Elementary school						
8 years	9,772	8,047	9,740	10,366	10,240	8,266
Less than 8 years	8,424	6,994	8,087	9,023	8,761	6,902

Source: U.S. Bureau of the Census, Current Population Reports, Series P-60, No. 80 "Income in 1970 of Families and Persons in the United States," U.S. Government Printing Office, Washington, D.C., 1971, Table 28, pp. 61–63.

Table 6

FIFTHS OF FAMILIES RANKED BY SIZE OF MONEY INCOME IN 1970, BY
YEARS OF SCHOOL COMPLETED BY HEAD

	Total	Lowest fifth	Second fifth	Third fifth	Fourth fifth	Highest fifth	Top 5 percent
College							
4 years or more	13.9	3.7	6.1	10.3	17.7	31.7	49.2
1 to 3 years	11.2	5.5	8.7	11.6	14.3	16.0	15.2
High school							
4 years	32.0	19.8	32.9	38.4	38.1	30.7	22.5
1 to 3 years	16.7	18.7	19.9	18.3	15.0	11.7	6.9
Elementary school							
8 years	12.7	20.6	16.1	12.0	8.7	6.2	3.8
Less than 8 years	13.5	31.7	16.2	9.4	6.2	3.7	2.3
	100.0	100.0	100.0	100.0	100.0	100.0	100.0

Source: U.S. Bureau of the Census, Current Population Reports, Series P-60, No. 80 "Income in 1970 of Families and Persons in the Uinted States," U.S. Government Printing Office, Washington, D.C., 1971, Table 12, p. 26.

finds roughly equal distribution across income fifths, but proportionate representation in the upper fifths significantly improves with more education and declines with less. On a lifetime basis (1968 calculation base), a college degree or better returns on the average $236,000 more than a high school degree and $175,000 more than one to three years of college.[27]

Given the significant monetary value of higher education, not to mention the possibility of improved occupational responsibilities and challenges, why is it that only 17 percent of the white population 25 years old or more, seven percent of the black, and five percent of the Spanish-speaking have completed four or more years of higher education?[28] Or that for every 1,000 children who entered the fifth grade in 1962 only three-fourths completed high school and 46 percent entered college.[29] These figures are, in fact, relatively high for developed nations. But there are sharp differences within the population as suggested by the above figures for minorities. There are also sharp differences in per pupil expenditures in the public schools; New York spends almost three times as much as Alabama. White suburban students are better financed and equipped than central city students, black or white.[30] The affluent

[27] The American Almanac (New York: Grosset & Dunlap, 1973), p. 114.

[28] U.S. Bureau of the Census, Current Population Reports, Series P-23, No. 37, "Social and Economic Characteristics of the Population in Metropolitan and Nonmetropolitan Areas: 1970 and 1960," U.S. Government Printing Office, Washington, D.C., 1971, Table 11, p. 53; and Series P-20, No. 221, "Characteristics of the Population by Ethnic Origin: November, 1969," Table 13, p. 19.

[29] The American Almanac, 1973, p. 128.

[30] For a nationwide study of inequality in education, see James S. Coleman, et al., Equality of Educational Opportunity (Washington, D.C.: U.S. Government Printing Office, 1966). See, also, Jonathon Kozol, Death at an Early Age (Boston: Houghton Mifflin Company, 1967).

suburbs enjoy lower student-teacher ratios, better paid and educated teachers, more college preparatory courses, extra-curricular opportunities, and special programs. The total learning atmosphere of a white-collar suburban school stands in marked contrast to a central city working-class or minority school. The negative evaluation of city public schools by upper white-collar parents is suggested by the marked growth of private schools.

It might be argued that unequal expenditures on schools results in unequal learning performances among students, which, in turn, greatly reduces the number of students, especially blue-collar and minority, who enter college. The property tax as a means of unequal school financing has been judged unconstitutional by the courts, with the implication that imbalances in expenditures result in educational inequality.

However, a major investigation of education and inequality directed by Christopher Jencks suggests that ". . . eliminating differences between schools would do almost nothing to make adults more equal."[31] Jencks contends that expenditures on schools should be ample enough to make the school experience enjoyable and pleasant, but not to expect greater social equality outside of the schools to be the result (recall that Milner argued the same thing with regard to higher education, but made an exception for spending on minorities). The "Coleman Report" cited previously (from which Jencks derived much of his own analytic data) draws the same conclusions regarding the secondary importance of pure financial and physical features of public schools with regard to educational achievement (and thus economic success). Could it be that unequal public spending on education per se is not an important cause of social inequality in the larger society? A blue-collar worker who dropped out of high school rather than continue and go on to college and finds that on the average he is earning only a few hundred dollars less than another blue-collar worker with a couple years of college may not think that more spending on education will create more equality. Nor might the average black college graduate who sees himself earning only a few hundred dollars more than a white high school dropout.

Our own analysis in this context would suggest that economic inequality is *related* to educational achievement but not *caused* by it, and hence, can't be cured by it. Our society has its own inequality-producing mechanisms quite apart from educational institutions per se; in part educational institutions serve to legitimize and justify the system of inequality, which corporate capitalism requires for its operation.

Education and inequality

It is among the tasks of the school system, from primary to university, to make certain that people accept the legitimacy of inequality and the necessity of a hierarchical division of labor. If education is not highly related to job performance, and most occupational skills could be learned on the job, there must be other major reasons behind the expenditure

---

[31] Christopher Jencks, et al., *Inequality* (New York: Basic Books, Inc., 1972), p. 16.

of some $48 billion. Literacy itself could be achieved for much less. Education serves an enormous stabilizing function within society—economically, politically, culturally, and socially. In particular, Jencks contends that ". . . schools serve primarily as selection and certification agencies, whose job is to measure and label people, and only secondarily as socialization agencies, whose job is to change people. This implies that schools serve primarily to legitimize inequality, not to create it."[32] Illich argues further that "School has lost the power, which reigned supreme during the first half of this century, to blind its participants to the divergence between the egalitarian myth its rhetoric serves and the rationalization of a stratified society its certificates produce."[33] Bowles declares that "The educational system serves less to change the results of primary socialization in the home than to ratify them and render them in adult form."[34] The crux of the critical literature is that education serves largely to reproduce the hierarchical division of labor as already found embedded in the class strata of the society.

An important aspect of this rationalization and legitimization process is the role of the certificate or degree, a short-cut (not in terms of public cost) to the sorting out and evaluation of the labor force by owners and employers (and by the professions). The certificate or degree informs the employer or the profession of the holder's willingness to submit to discipline, authority, personal sacrifice, conforming behavior, mechanical learning, and so forth. As Carney points out, ". . . employers use certification as a convenient screening device that is highly correlated with the hierarchical rules."[35] Or from Bowles and Gintis, "Thus the perpetuation and legitimation of the hierarchical division of labor within the enterprise is an important additional objective of employers in the selection and placement of workers."[36] We might note here the destructive influence of excessive grade competition, degree requirements, and deadening bureaucracy upon the substance of learning and education per se. Baldwin reminds us that "Bureaucracy has taken over as the living educational structures have withered."[37]

The I.Q. question may also be seen within this general context. No relationship has ever been demonstrated between inherited intelligence and social achievement represented by income, occupation, or education, or between basic intelligence and class strata. As described previously, economic placement is largely determined by transmitted class, and hence, personality factors, all of which combine to produce definite

[32] Ibid., p. 135.

[33] Ivan Illich, "After Deschooling, What?" *Social Policy,* September–October 1971, p. 6.

[34] Samuel Bowles, "Unequal Education and the Reproduction of the Social Division of Labor," in Martin Carney, ed., *Schooling in a Corporate Society* (New York: David McKay Company, Inc., 1972), pp. 58–59.

[35] Ibid., p. 5.

[36] Samuel Bowles and Herbert Gintis, "I.Q. In the U.S. Class Structure," *Social Policy,* November–February 1972–73, p. 82.

[37] See Richard E. Baldwin, "Down With the Degree Structure!" *Change,* March 1973, p. 55.

advantages in educational and educational testing success. The I.Q. is among these tests, and thus turns out to be "related" (in Jencks's data .50) to such indicators of economic success as income and occupation. Bowles and Gintis have statistically demonstrated how the relationship between I.Q. and economic success can be virtually eliminated if the influence of class and education are removed.[38]

Other stabilizing functions of education aside from reinforcing a stratified society might also be observed, such as the role of high school and college in keeping the size of the labor force down. The addition of several million students into the labor market would create severe disruptions. The build-up of the community and junior college programs are paving the way toward 14 years compulsory education. Open admissions, though typically charged with democratic and liberal idealism, may also be viewed from one perspective as an effort to hold and socialize lower income persons within institutions controlled by the authorities. This is not to argue against major extensions of education per se. Quite to the contrary, the educational arts are needed more than ever, but not as part of a certifying bureaucracy. Rather, they are needed on an open and voluntary basis for people of all ages, *especially* adults who have labored for years as white- and blue-collar workers and as housewives.

Despite the predominant role of class and family background in educational and economic success, we should not ignore the *independent* influence of the schools themselves upon achievement and social inequality—especially their *potential* independent influence. Compare the differences in student opportunities and personal freedom within a ghetto high school and a prep school, between a community college and a richly endowed private college, between a teachers college and a major university. There are major material as well as social and cultural differences between such institutions; and the material advantages provide for enhanced social and cultural freedom. Schools as they are presently structured frequently add to class differences students bring to them. In connection with these differences, we might finally make some observations on the school context itself in an effort to decipher further reasons why so many students retrieve so little out of education, and hence, why so many fail to pursue it further.

THE SCHOOL CONTEXT: TRAINING VERSUS EDUCATION

A definite reason for educational attrition has to do with the rigidity and stifling atmosphere of many schools, especially working-class schools. Employers usually want trained people, not educated ones. And the entire educational spectrum, from kindergarten through graduate school, largely attests to the overwhelming ascendancy of the training emphasis. The watchwords of much public education are "stay in line" and "keep quiet"; its hallmarks discipline and obedience. Considering

---

[38] "I.Q. In the U.S. Class Structure," pp. 70–73.

the crowds of students that individual teachers and administrators often must deal with, and the often inadequate educational tools at their disposal, it is conceivable how supervision and order might become an obsession. But from years of financial pressures and infusion of the industrial work ethos into the schools, conformity and dependence have become ends in themselves. Witness the deterioration of the fresh and eager child in primary school as he grinds away on the educational treadmill through the higher grades and high school. Freshness too often turns stale and eagerness is too often stifled.

Educator John Holt compares students in the public schools with convicts in jails: "What is most shocking and horrifying about public education today is that in almost all schools the children are treated, most of the time, like convicts in a jail."[39] In a similar vein, historian Richard Hofstadter contends that the American educational system "is the only educational system in the world vital segments of which have fallen into the hands of people who joyfully and militantly proclaim their hostility to intellect and their eagerness to identify with children who show the least intellectual promise."[40] Hofstadter is not saying that teachers and administrators devote extra time to intellectually less developed students, but rather that school officials hold up as ideal models children who are most obedient and pliant.

Achievement tends to be narrowly defined in terms of scores on structured and standardized class exercises and "intelligence" tests and willingness to submit to the rigid discipline required to do well in such tests. Spontaneity and creativity are often repressed in favor of predefined notions of intelligence that emphasize rote memory. Educational psychologists stress the importance of recognizing two very distinctive mental abilities, each of which may develop independently in a given individual.[41] The first is intelligence, involving such things as memory and retention, logic and problem-solving skill, and ability to manipulate concepts. The second is creativity, involving the flow of ideas and the uniqueness of their expression. Creativity varies completely independently from intelligence; a person high in one has no better than a 50-50 chance of being high in the other. For its development, creativity requires "playful contemplation" without concern for personal success or failure and self-image. The mind with creative propensities requires openness, freedom, and room to operate, while intelligence flourishes best within narrow and predictable ranges and clearly stated objectives and goals.

Research conducted by Wallach and Kogan revealed some interesting findings concerning the performance and adjustment of children possessing varying propensities toward intelligence and creativity. The chart

---

[39] "Education for the Future," in Robert Theobald, ed., *Social Policies for America in the Seventies* (New York: Doubleday & Company, Inc., 1969), p. 185.

[40] Richard Hofstadter, *Anti-Intellectualism in American Life* (New York: Random House, Inc., 1963), p. 51.

[41] See Michael A. Wallach and Nathan Kogan, "Creativity and Intelligence in Children's Thinking," *Trans-action*, 4 (January 1967), pp. 38–43.

INTELLIGENCE AND CREATIVITY IN CHILDREN

		INTELLIGENCE	
		Higher	*Lower*
CREATIVITY	*Lower*	Strong academic Long attention span High self-image Socially outgoing Often disruptive	Weak academic Short attention span Low self-image Socially isolated Very disruptive
	Higher	Strong academic Long attention span Reserved, hesitant Socially aloof Conforming	Weak academic Short attention span Average self-image Socially outgoing Conforming

summarizes Wallach and Kogan's findings on the educational and social traits of children with given abilities of intelligence and creativity. Obviously, the most fortunate of the intelligence-creativity types are the high-highs. The least fortunate are those high in creativity and low in intelligence, for the abilities of these students clash head-on with the achievement structure as found in most schools. This category's lower propensity for memorization and manipulation of symbols puts them at an extreme disadvantage in today's highly structured, intelligence-oriented educational environment. And their consequent failure to achieve in the strict academic sense produces a negative self image. All of this is exacerbated by this category's imaginative or spontaneous— i.e., disruptive, behavior. Clearly, the high creativity–low intelligence students would be the most likely candidates for future dropouts. Only an educational system that recognizes human differences and the potential value of these differences could possibly prevent their dropping out. The arid atmosphere of schools "turns them off," or stability-minded officials "push" them out. By virtue of their dropping out, the high creativity–low intelligence students probably compose a sizable reservoir of talent in the bottom half of society, where their talents may be withering or being expressed in less than socially constructive ways.

A viable school must allow and work for the expression and development of both creativity and intelligence in the student. Especially urgent is the need for an open learning environment. Holt argues, for instance, that children learn better when they learn what they want to learn, when they want to learn it, and how they want to learn it.[42] Individual curiosity is a more effective learning force than an order. Instead of training, measuring, grading, testing, and disciplining as used in their present sense, Holt believes that learning should be largely self-initiated and self-correcting as the student moves on his own mental powers towards a constructive mastery of his environment. Teachers should raise questions, pose alternatives, offer limited guidance, and provide feedback. Not only would Holt's suggestions pave the way for a greater utilization and expression of creative minds, but they would also greatly enhance

---

[42] John Holt, *The Underachieving School* (New York: Pitman Publishing Co., 1969).

intelligence as well. But in a society where computers and automated machinery may be displacing the kinds of structured mental activity defined as intelligence, creativity takes on greater importance. As Theobald has stressed, education of today must be education for a future in an automated society where memorization will not be as important as imagination, self-discipline not as essential as ability for self-expression, and industrial work skills not as indispensable as craft and cultural skills.[43]

To emphasize greater self-expression and autonomy within education is not identical with the chaos which often prevails in "free schools." Teachers cannot escape the responsibility of presenting a challenge, offering continual guidance, and especially critically evaluating work. These activities are necessary to the development of intellectual and artistic skills and abilities. The student is perhaps the first to sense this fact, both when it is present and especially when it is absent.

Other routes to dropping out

Where finances and educational rigor mortis are not responsible for termination of a student's education, a number of other closely related reasons suggest themselves. Among the worst offenders are the tracking system, teacher apathy, and low levels of expectation set by teachers. In the tracking system, intelligence tests that discriminate against lower status groups and creative minds are used early in a student's educational career to place him or her with a group of students similar in measured intelligence. Rather than receive the compensatory instruction they need, slower or remedial tracks are given inferior education so that the gap between the tracks widens rather than narrows as education progresses. Shunting children early in their school years into groups that inevitably channel them toward or away from college is among the worst forms of anti-egalitarianism conceivable. The tracking system strongly parallels and reinforces class stratification.

Teachers' attitudes toward students and the levels of expectation they set for students are also of marked importance. Working-class and minority children are often written off in the minds of many teachers as low potential or losers. Just how important teachers' attitudes can be for student performance has been documented in a report by Rosenthal and Jacobson of a study of a predominantly Mexican-American California grade school.[44] The experiment placed at random a group of students into a "high-potential" class and the others into a control group. Although the students in the two groups were actually similar, the teachers *expected* differences in performance. In tests administered over the next two years, the academic "spurters" did just what their teachers expected them to do: perform above the average! Multiply this case many thou-

---

[43] Robert Theobald, *An Alternative Future for America* (Chicago: Swallow Press, Inc., 1968).

[44] Robert Rosenthal and Lenore F. Jacobson, *Pygmalion in the Classroom* (New York: Holt, Rinehart, & Winston, Inc., 1968), pp. 61–97.

sands of times and you have a large part of the explanation of why working-class and minority students drop out of school or fail to go on in education at several times the rates of middle-income whites. Lower status boys and girls have been convinced, through both direct and indirect means, by tactless and inept teachers, counselors and administrators that they are unworthy and unable to succeed in life. However, many of these lower status students, especially minority students, are more often rejecting such negative definitions and low expectations set by their bureaucratic superiors, often igniting sharp conflict between them.

Dropping out or termination may for some be an entirely personal decision based on evaluations of what relevance further education might have for the type of work they have cut out for themselves. Working-class youth who are inclined to enter mechanical, technological, or sales jobs may prefer not to postpone earnings and may quit school or look for work immediately after high school graduation. Many more blue- than white-collar youth enter vocational schools and apprenticeships in the building trades (if they happen to be white). Many blue-collar youth enter commercial colleges. However, their interests would possibly be better met and elaborated had they the chance to go on to study engineering or business in college. But much earlier in life lower status students are taught or absorb by osmosis that they would be incapable of achieving at the college level. The economy needs them for lower positions in the division of labor.

If ever the degree and credential system should be eliminated, actual performance become the guide to occupational placement and retention, and a secure economic standard be provided as a right of citizenship, only then can education be put in its proper perspective: a voluntary learning experience, equally accessible for all who desire to learn. More people would learn more and develop themselves more completely. And in the process, the largely artificial and narrow (both in subject and in personal product) specialization within education would begin to break down.

8

The poor

THE DISCOVERY OF POVERTY

In the 1950s social scientists focused popular attention on problems arising out of material abundance or affluence, especially those involving character, individuality, and leisure.[1] Not much noticed were the some 40 million Americans living in poverty, including men, women, and children of all ages, color, and residence. (As shall be pointed out in a subsequent section, where the poverty line is drawn varies, and with it the number of poor.) The concern of most social critics in the fifties seemed to be how to live creatively and individually in an advanced technological society. But while the affluent were grappling with problems concerning the quality of life, tens of millions of other persons were desperately struggling to feed, clothe, transport, and house themselves and their families, not to mention problems of education and health.

The poor began to be widely noticed in the early sixties partially because of such writers as Michael Harrington, Thomas Gladwin, David Caplovitz, and Lee Rainwater.[2] By the mid-sixties, popular and professional media and literature were suffused with speeches, conferences, empirical data, and witnesses to the extent of poverty in the United States. Indeed, the late but hardly great "War on Poverty" was initiated

[1] For example, David Riesman, *The Lonely Crowd* (New Haven: Yale University Press, 1950); David Potter, *People of Plenty* (Chicago: University of Chicago Press, 1954); and John Kenneth Galbraith, *The Affluent Society* (Boston: Houghton Mifflin Company, 1958).

[2] Michael Harrington, *The Other America* (Baltimore: Penguin Books, Inc., 1963); Thomas Gladwin, *Poverty, U.S.A.* (Boston: Little, Brown and Company, 1967); David Caplovitz, *The Poor Pay More* (New York: The Free Press, 1963); and Lee Rainwater, *And the Poor Get Children* (Chicago: Quadrangle Books, Inc., 1960).

154

by federal politicians and administrators, and a few skirmishes were fought here and there for a few years. While the official War on Poverty was all but over by late 1968, journalists, clergymen, students, academicians, professional organizers, social workers, and a few politicians continue to fight. Preparing themselves for a large-scale attack on poverty in the seventies, America's minority groups are mobilized for action on many fronts and are currently fighting the war on poverty without the material promised by the poverty generals of the sixties. The poverty generals, as the poor and their allies were soon to learn, were primarily warlords of another kind and had no stomach or desire to conduct a major drive against a domestic enemy such as poverty.

Despite the large stock of evidence concerning the extent and degree of poverty in America, many people, sociologists among them, deny that serious poverty exists here. For example, Pierre van den Berghe argues that "real" poverty has practically disappeared in America.[3] Aside from Indians, van den Berghe declares, poverty in the United States is largely psychological. How could it be otherwise when nearly all Americans own automobiles and television sets? The word for American-style poverty, argues van den Berghe, is "affluent" poverty. In a similar vein, government welfare statistician Mollie Orshansky argues that in many parts of the world men are preoccupied with merely staying alive, while in the United States the chief question is not whether a person will live but how he will live.[4]

What people like van den Berghe and Orshansky seem to be saying to America's poor is, "You ought to have seen what it was like back around the turn of the century in this country or what it is like right now in other parts of the world; then you would realize that your problems are really only psychological." That poverty in America must be assessed with a different set of criteria than poverty in, say Africa or India, is obvious enough. Thus, whether the American poor are actually suffering less, materially or psychologically, than the poor of other nations is in most instances a moot point. To say that, because a large percentage (far from all) of America's poor have automobiles and television sets at their disposal, poverty becomes a psychological rather than material problem is simply ludicrous. Unlike most people in the world, most Americans must have an automobile at their disposal if they are to get along at all, especially a working family. Moreover, the old-model cars that most poor families drive are frequently not paid for, while their maintenance is a continual drain on meager financial resources. (Only 44 percent of households with incomes of $3,000 or less in 1971 had a car of any kind; 67 percent of those with incomes of $25,000 or more had *two or more* cars.[5]) And in the drab and involuntary idleness of a poor family, television, too, becomes almost as essential as food itself. Like

---

[3] Pierre van den Berghe, "Poverty as Underdevelopment," *Trans-action,* 6 (July 1969), pp. 3–4; 62.

[4] Mollie Orshansky, "Consumption, Work, and Poverty," in Ben B. Seligman, ed., *Poverty as a Public Issue* (New York: The Free Press, 1965), p. 56.

[5] *The American Almanac* (New York: Grosset & Dunlap, 1973), p. 328.

autos, TVs for the poor are frequently fuzzy hand-me-downs or second-hand purchases at exorbitant interest rates.

Because personal transportation and television are so essential, cars and TVs are often purchased and maintained at the cost of medical and dental care, meat and milk, clothes, and other basic physical and material needs. Those persons who criticize the poor for even driving cars and watching television, or who take such items as an indication of material well-being, are in gross error. To argue that the poor have distorted values because they purchase automobiles and television sets is to completely miss the point of poverty; if the poor bought cars and TVs because they thought they were material luxuries rather than necessities, they would probably own late-model cars or two cars (only about 1 in 20 of low income households have two cars, both of which in these cases are probably junkers) and colored television sets (about one in ten do so). In some instances, poor people do in fact throw everything they have or ever will have into a new car or color TV, for it is perhaps their only means or chance of "being somebody" in the value system of today's middle-class America. The poor may thus be "middle class," if only vicariously. But few poor have the audacity to walk into a new-car dealer's or a color television showroom.

In brief, having to possess a car to get around and television to escape the harsh realities of life doesn't automatically relegate poverty to the realm of psychology; food, housing, clothes, medicine, and many other material necessities are in perilously short supply among the nation's poor. Physical survival *is* a day-to-day problem for millions of Americans; to these millions, the idea of relative or psychological poverty must be incomprehensible, for they are absolutely poor and are often literally painfully aware of it. This is not to imply that American poverty does not have an important psychological aspect to it. To be sure, the psychological pains of being without the bare essentials of life, when the large majority of others in your society do have the essentials and some are smothering under superfluous goods and services, is probably often greater than the physical hardships that accompany being without them. Poverty today must certainly seem more hopeless and depressing, a dead end, than it did among the immigrants at the turn of the century. But for the bulk of the poor, an equal share of the material wealth is a thought that never crosses their minds. All most desire is a chance to live securely and decently. To achieve these ends, much more than psychology will be required.[6]

LIFE IN POVERTY

Among the several contemporary accounts of life among the poor, one of the most direct and depressing is that given by Arthur Simon, a

---

[6] It would be an interesting experiment if people who think American poverty is psychological or a matter of "relative" deprivation would exchange their $25,000–plus annual incomes and material possessions with the incomes and possessions of a poor family and see how many years would elapse before the former decided poverty was not all so relative and psychological after all.

Lutheran minister serving a Lower East Side Manhattan parish.[7] Simon details the careers of several families whom he served over an extended period of time.

Perhaps not untypical of millions of urban poor, the Millers are a white family of four who through a series of financial disasters have been forced to move interminably from one dilapidated apartment to the next, trying to live near always-ephemeral jobs and to make miserably low paychecks meet rents. Starting from a stable working-class background, Mr. Miller was plagued with health problems such as varicose veins, bad feet and teeth, and a glass eye. Physical disabilities and job layoffs combined to completely undermine the Millers' financial base, forcing them into welfare, successively worse apartments, and high-interest loans. To finance the delivery of their second child, the Millers were forced to borrow $300 from a loan company that charged them $100 interest (if Mr. Miller were not poor he could have gotten the money for $30 at a commercial bank). To help pay back the loan on the baby, the Millers had their gas and electricity turned off, but their economizing backfired as their food spoiled and the cockroaches invaded. With half of Mr. Miller's $50 weekly paycheck going for rent, little money was left for the bare minimum for raising two children.

Once, while cleaning his glass eye, Mr. Miller dropped and broke it. He immediately contacted welfare about it, but welfare delays in fitting him with a new eye resulted in a socket infection, surgery, socket shrinkage, and finally replacement with a "baby eye," leaving it sunken and almost completely shut. In the course of a traumatic and disturbing family history, the Millers' girl developed severe mental aberrations and had to be institutionalized, while their boy dropped out of school for lack of money for busfare, books, and clothes. Thus, the scene is set for the transmission of class position to the next generation. But even today Simon argues, "there are socially useful jobs Mr. Miller could do to make himself and his family feel worthwhile. Instead we label him 'unemployable.' We pay him to be useless and heap upon his family an indignity which few of us would be able to bear."[8]

Simon also relates the history of poverty experienced by Wilma Smith, a black mother of six children, all the result of unwanted pregnancies. In the mid-fifties Wilma worked, earning $36 a week, but failed to tell her welfare agency the source of $25 a week. As a result, she was taken to court and required to *pay back* to welfare $30 a month, which she did for six months. When she was unable to pay the $100 a month rent for her family's two-room apartment while also paying $30 a month to welfare, the latter sum was reduced to $20. By 1965 Wilma had paid in over $1,500 but still "owed" $1,600, on which she was still paying $5 a month when Simon wrote his book. Odd jobs, taking in ironing, and small loans have helped Wilma try to make ends meet. A 25-year-old son, after completing vocational school with a good record, was unable to find a job in machine repairing or metal trades so worked as a doorman for $68 a

---

[7] Arthur Simon, *Faces of Poverty* (New York: Macmillan Company, 1968).
[8] Ibid., p. 21.

week in a middle-class housing project. Many of the young man's neighbors were drug addicts. About drugs he told Simon, "I think the employment problem has a lot to do with it. When you're high (on dope) you have no problems. People do it to get away. I know two guys who got married, started families, and were doing okay. Then they lost their jobs and were dispossessed. Pretty soon they were high."[9]

A sizable minority of the poor are elderly persons; if they live alone their poverty is usually worse, both psychologically and materially. Simon reports that one elderly lady he knew was left with $1,500 by her husband, but funeral costs and doctor bills took every cent of it. (Funerals cost the American people about $2 billion annually.) Half of her meager Social Security checks went for rent. The woman's main difficulty was getting around to procure the things she needed. Though her cash was totally inadequate for her most essential needs, like many older persons accustomed to self-sufficiency she was repulsed by the personal indignities that she felt awaited the elderly person who goes on old-age assistance. Social isolation is also devastating for the elderly: "Being alone is hard too, but I'm not crying about it. I always try to keep a sense of humor. I do the best I can. The Lord has been good to me. I just wish He would take me away. What good am I to anybody? But I have no complaint. I have everything I want—if I can only get in the [rest] home."[10]

Rural poverty is usually no prettier or tolerable than urban poverty. Any gains in fresh air or open space are usually offset by poorer employment, educational, medical, and housing opportunities. Whether it be in hills and hollows, barren plains, on the road, or in the city, poverty carries with it the same degradation and misery for those involved. The *constant daily realities* of life among the poor are concerned with getting enough to eat, holding or looking for a job, staying healthy enough to get around, keeping the children clean and dressed well enough to go to school, trying to prevent repossession of furniture, paying back high-interest loans and debts, avoiding unwanted children, and getting home safely. To tell the poor their poverty is not "real" or relative would surely be to heap further abuse on an already desperate or severely depressed situation. It certainly would not alleviate the harsh realities of their daily lives or make them more tolerant of these realities.

How many poor?

The official government figures based upon the 1970 census data report 25.5 million persons living in poverty—that is, beneath the federally defined poverty thresholds based upon family size, residence, and sex (men are awarded a higher threshold than women).[11] The 1970 threshold, for example, for an urban family of four was given at $3,968. The 25.5 million persons consisted of 5.1 million families and 5 million

---

[9] Ibid., p. 35.

[10] Ibid., p. 54.

[11] For a comprehensive statistical description of the federally defined poor, see U.S. Bureau of the Census, *Current Population Reports*, Series P-60, No. 81, "Characteristics of the Low-Income Population, 1970," U.S. Government Printing Office, Washington, D.C., 1971.

unrelated individuals, or 13 percent of the population. Another 10.2 million persons had incomes sufficiently near the threshold to be classified as near-poor, raising the number to 35.7 million or nearly one-fifth of the population.

Now, the bottom one-fifth of the (family) income distribution had a median income of $3,054 and the bottom 13 percent a mere $1,300 in 1970. Quite clearly the bottom fifth—and recalling also that this fifth has but one-half of one percent of the wealth—is living in poverty. We may also recall that the bottom 16 percent of the families had zero or minus liquid net assets in 1970 and another 14 percent reported $200 or less. If almost one-fifth of the population lives beneath the government poverty threshold, we might consider further that almost one-third lives beneath, the Bureau of Labor Statistics "lower budget" level ($6,960 for a family of four). The Welfare Rights Organization demands $6,500 as a minimum family income, suggesting also that 30 percent is closer to an accurate poverty estimation than 20 percent. The poverty category varies depending upon where the standard is set. But given consideration of both the requirements of subsistence living and the level of affluence in the upper income groups, the proportion of the population living beneath the subsistence level is substantial.

The locus of poverty

Considering the relationship that exists between a person's position in the means of production and income, we would expect the incidence of poverty to be higher among categories of the population having a more negative relationship to production; i.e., females, children, minorities, rural-farm, and unemployed. Table 7 confirms this expectation. The incidence or probability of poverty (federally defined) increases signifi-

Table 7

PERCENT OF PERSONS UNDER FEDERALLY DEFINED POVERTY
THRESHOLDS BY GIVEN CATEGORIES

Male head employed	5%	Elderly male head	7%
Male head unemployed	12	Elderly female head	33
Male head not in labor force	21	Elderly male unrelated individual	39
Female head employed	19	Elderly female unrelated individual	50
Female head unemployed	47		
Female head not in labor force	47		
White male head	6	College graduate head	2
Nonwhite male head	18	High school graduate head	6
White female head	25	8th grade head	13
Nonwhite female head	54	7th or less grade head	25
Children under 18 male head	9	Male professional	2
Children under 18 female head	53	Female professional	7
		Male laborer	12
		Female blue-collar	24
		Nonfarm	10
		Farm	19

Source: U.S. Bureau of the Census, *Current Population Reports*, Series P-60, No. 81, "Characteristics of the Low-Income Population, 1970," U.S. Government Printing Office, Washington, D.C., 1971, pp. 2–10.

cantly for persons in these categories. The combination of these factors compounds the incidence, so that persons under 18 years old in female-headed families are more likely to be poor than to be above the poverty threshold. An elderly female living alone is also as likely to be poor as not. Male-headed nonwhite families are three times as likely to be poor as white male-headed. Yet, even being an employed white male is no assurance of being above the poverty threshold, as the 5 percent of this category attest to (3.2 million male family heads were under the poverty line in 1970, over 1 million of whom worked full time all year).

The distribution of poverty by age, ethnicity, residence (many urban poor were *raised* in rural areas), and sex of family head and unrelated individuals is presented in Table 8. The expected frequencies compared with the actual frequencies also provide confirmation of poverty as a consequence of relation to the means of production. Combining children and school age persons and elderly, we see that 68 percent of the poor may be placed here; unrelated females and females heading families between the ages of 21–64 add another 13 percent for a total of 81 percent. Of the remaining 19 percent of males, a few additional percent

Table 8

DISTRIBUTION OF FEDERALLY DEFINED POVERTY BY SELECTED CATEGORIES

	Percent of poor	Percent of population	Percent of Difference
Ethnic group			
White ("Anglo")	60	84	−24
Black and Nonwhite	31	12	+19
Spanish origin	9	5	+4
	100	100	
Residence			
Metropolitan city	28	28	0
Metropolitan suburb	18	34	−16
Non-metropolitan	46	33	+13
Farm	8	5	+3
	100	100	
Age			
Under 14	34	27	+7
14–20	15	11	+4
21–64	32	52	−20
65 and Over	19	10	+9
	100	100	
Persons by sex of household head			
In male-headed families and male individuals	56	78	−22
In female-headed families and female individuals ..	44	22	+22
	100	100	

Source: U.S. Bureau of the Census, *Current Population Reports,* Series P-60, No. 81, "Characteristics of the Low-Income Population, 1970," U.S. Government Printing Office, Washington, D.C., 1971, pp. 2–10; and *The American Almanac* (New York: Grosset and Dunlap, 1973).

could be accounted for by unemployed and unemployable. The rest are employed males of labor force age. It is easy to see that "welfare" has little to do with "able-bodied men," for relatively few of the poor as defined by the government—less than one-fifth—are men of labor force age. And even among these, few qualify for welfare assistance. (The number of poverty males is probably underestimated due to the existence of many uncounted "missing" persons, few of whom could qualify for welfare either.)

How do the poor differ from the non-poor? What is responsible for poverty conditions among the poor? We have already given a general Marxist account of the roots of poverty under capitalism. But the question of the roots of poverty is too important to be left uncontested. To a discussion of the arguments surrounding poverty in the U.S. we turn next.

The roots of poverty

Explanations of poverty tend to fall within three areas: the personal, the cultural, and the economic. The personal account of poverty locates the source of poverty squarely within the individual himself; a person is poor because he is morally or personally defective and that is that. This is a frequent layman's account.[12] The cultural account is similar to the personal account in that both attribute the causes of poverty to the defective behavior of the individual himself, but differs in that, rather than tracing the defections of the poor individual to independent sources within the individual himself, the cultural account explains poverty-producing defections as originating in a lower class *way of life* and as being transmitted in the socialization process from one generation to the next. In short, it is a culture or subculture that is defective and responsible for poverty rather than random moral aberrations within specific individuals. The cultural account has been the most popular among the poverty professionals and underlies implicitly the existing poverty programs. The economic account holds that people are poor because they lack money; have unnecessarily low levels of purchasing power with the money they have; have low-paying jobs, or no jobs at all; and are broke, underconsuming, low paid, or unemployed through no moral or cultural defects of their own but due to defects in the economic structure of society.

---

[12] A nationwide opinion poll found that 34 percent of those queried believed that poverty is the result of lack of personal effort; 38 percent, the result of both lack of personal effort and circumstances; and 25 percent, circumstances only. See Lloyd A. Free and Hadley Cantril, *The Political Beliefs of Americans* (New York: Clarion Books, 1968), p. 28. Another study asked samples of whites and blacks if they agreed or disagreed with "People who are very poor are lazy people who should help themselves"; it was found that 40 percent of whites and 20 percent of blacks were in agreement.—Joseph A. Kahl and John M. Goering, "Stable Workers, Black and White," *Social Problems*, Winter 1971, pp. 306–18. Both of these sources, however, suggest that a majority of the population recognizes the importance of society in shaping poverty.

In the following discussion, we include the personal account with the cultural account, inasmuch as, for purposes of change, they are the same. Both require that allegedly defective individuals change their style of life to eliminate poverty.

THE CULTURE OF POVERTY

Among the first systematic attempts to put poverty in terms of defective culture that is transmitted intergenerationally was that by Genevieve Knupfer in an article entitled "Portrait of the Underdog."[13] The underdog, according to Knupfer, is socially withdrawn, mentally isolated, timid and naive, feels incompetent, doesn't know anything, is politically indifferent, has limited aspirations, and can't communicate very well. Anthropologist Oscar Lewis has given the most systematic treatment to the "culture-of-poverty" idea.[14] In addition to behavior traits noted by Knupfer, Lewis adds such characteristics as lack of impulse control, present-time orientation, inability to defer gratification and to plan, and fatalism and resignation. Lewis notes that the poor often are aware of conventional values and even claim some of them as their own, but on the whole do not live by them. A number of other aspects of the culture of poverty pointed out by Lewis such as pawning; use of informal credit devices; absence of savings; lack of property ownership; little use of hospitals, stores and banks; poor housing; crowding; and mother-centered families are so obviously economic rather than transmitted cultural traits that nothing more need be said of them.

Edward Banfield reiterates that "the lower class" is governed by impulse, has no sense of the future, is "radically improvident," has a weak sense of self, lacks social attachments, and is driven primarily by the bodily needs of sex and "action" (aggression).[15]

Certain alleged cultural traits of the poor reappear time and again throughout the literature on poverty: social isolation, low self-image, limited aspirations, inability to communicate, impulsiveness, existence-oriented rather than improvement-oriented, fear, resignation, fatalism, and inability to understand bureaucratic behavior are among the most commonly cited attributes of the poor.[16]

Let us briefly examine a number of these alleged culture-of-poverty traits. First of all, if all of the traits allegedly characteristic of the cul-

---

[13] Genevieve Knupfer, "Portrait of the Underdog," *Public Opinion Quarterly,* 11 (Spring 1947), pp. 103–14.

[14] Oscar Lewis, *La Vida* (New York: Random House, Inc., 1966), pp. xlii–lii.

[15] *The Unheavenly City* (Boston: Little, Brown and Company, 1970), p. 53.

[16] In addition to Knupfer, Lewis, and Banfield, see, for example, Jack E. Weller, *Yesterday's People* (Lexington: University of Kentucky Press, 1966), and Richard A. Ball, "A Poverty-Case: The Analgesic Subculture of the Southern Appalachians," *American Sociological Review,* 33 (December 1968), pp. 885–995. See also Charles A. Valentine's critical summary of the poverty literature in *Culture and Poverty* (Chicago: University of Chicago Press, 1968).

ture of poverty were actually present in some group, the group could only be, to quote Valentine, "the chronic patient population in the back ward of a state mental hospital."[17] Obviously, then, the culture-of-poverty paradigm must be considered as a caricature with regard to the American poor. Nevertheless, the caricature needs examination.

Aspirations

First, how much validity is there to the assertion that the poor lack aspiration and are fatalistic? In cases where aspirations are low or gone and fatalism and resignation are high, it would be a very realistic and appropriate frame of mind considering the life chances of the poor. By adolescence and certainly by adulthood, the poor must be keenly aware of their mobility prospects. Lowered aspiration and resignation are a way to try to avoid humiliation and to find some sort of self-acceptance in the face of precarious life chances. However, that the individual poor may resort to a depressed life style after confronting the overwhelming odds against them is far from saying low aspirations and resignation are part of an ingrained or intergenerationally transmitted character structure preventing them from economic success. In fact, the low self-image of many poor persons is low precisely because they continue to judge themselves in terms of the ideals of the larger society.

Despite the overwhelming odds against them, the fatalistic and apathetic poor are the exception rather than the rule. Most poor people strongly desire a better life and more opportunities for themselves and their children. A recent empirical study of attitudes among a California sample of Anglo, Mexican, and black poor resulted in the almost complete rejection of the culture-of-poverty caricature. For example, nearly all respondents in all three groups reported that they would take or stay in a job requiring them to leave their friends, to learn a new routine, to work harder than most, and to take on more responsibility.[18] Another piece of empirical research suggests that the majority of the poor believe that men should take risks.[19] Further research indicates that the large majority of a sample of low-income rural southerners were dissatisfied with their incomes and willing to work longer hours to augment it; only 17 percent of them said they would refuse to work in a higher paying factory job if it were available, while the youths typically aspired to white-collar jobs.[20] These rural Southerners were aware, however, of the magnitude of the obstacles to change.

An investigation of a Boise, Idaho, poverty sample by Martin Scheffer indicated ample amounts of aspiration, but also realistic assessments of

---

[17] Valentine, *Culture and Poverty*, p. 77.

[18] Lola M. Irelan, Oliver C. Moles, and Robert M. O'Shea, "Ethnicity, Poverty, and Selected Attitudes: A Test of the 'Culture of Poverty' Hypothesis," *Social Forces*, 4 (June 1969), pp. 405–13.

[19] Ephraim Harold Mizruchi, "Aspiration and Poverty," *The Sociological Quarterly*, 8 (Autumn 1967), p. 444.

[20] Lee Taylor, *Urban-Rural Problems*, (Belmont, Cal.: Dickenson Publishing Co., 1968), pp. 15–17.

limited opportunities: "Getting ahead for me is staying out of debt"; "[Getting ahead] is keeping a steady job with a livin' wage"; and "Being able to pay your bills so you can be happy and satisfied."[21] Fifty percent felt that they did not have much chance of getting ahead, and 38 percent only a fair chance (64 percent of the blue-collar *non*-poverty sample felt *they* didn't have much of a chance either!) Yet, regarding their children, the majority aspired to a college degree for them, though a majority also assessed the actual possibilities to be lower or much lower. As one put it, "I would like to see them go as far as they can—into college and get a degree. They won't get much more than I did (9 years) unless things start lookin' up." Or, "I'd like to see him get through college if he can. Might get into high school or finish it, but he may not be capable of it." The poor often read society's message regarding their "place" quite accurately. But some know well the reasons behind failure; as a poor white in Chicago put it, "A poor kid don't have the opportunity. They claim they do, but a poor kid don't have the same privileges in school a rich kid does. A poor kid don't get the same teachin' that that rich kid gets. A poor kid can ask the teacher a question, she'll ignore it."[22]

In the heart of Appalachia, a region environmentally and economically exploited by high-profit corporations, an unemployed West Virginia coal miner could hardly be called resigned to the apparent fate of his children: "This girl of mine, she's thirteen going on fourteen, and she wants to be a teacher. They talk about this all the time and while they're talking I'm hoping. Every night I pray; they've got to get out of here." In South Carolina, a poverty farmer displays similar hopes for his family: "Mostly I hope my kids do better than I'm doing. They'll have to achieve something on their own and they'll have to study for that, learn modern farming, or a trade like brickmasonry. Everyone can't do farming. But I hope they won't have to leave home. But I want them to do better than I have."[23] Aspirations to be teachers, bricklayers, and modern farmers doesn't seem like asking for much, but from the standpoint of a welfare family or a dirt farmer, it's like shooting for the moon. (Tragically, shooting for the moon is now an ill-chosen metaphor from the standpoint of the poor.)

After an in-depth study of a circle of black street-corner men, sociologist John Horton observes that the street-corner man ". . . dreams about the day when he will get himself together and move ahead to the rewards of a good job, money, and a family." Though the men desire the material amenities and security of middle-class life, Horton notes, they do not want ". . . the hypocrisy, the venality, the coldness, the being forced to do what one does not want to do."[24] The poor themselves emphatically

[21] Martin Scheffer, "The Poor, Separate Class or Working Class; A Comparative Study," Ph.D. dissertation, University of Utah, 1971.

[22] Todd Gitlin and Nanci Hollander, *Uptown: Poor Whites in Chicago* (New York: Harper & Row, Publishers, 1971), p. 203.

[23] Ben H. Bagdikian, *In the Midst of Plenty* (New York: Signet Books, 1964), pp. 53; 82.

[24] John Horton, "Time and Cool People," *Trans-action*, 4 (April 1967), pp. 5–12.

reject any insinuation that they possess or exhibit fatalistic or apathetic values or behavior. All of a sample of black poor living in a Michigan industrial community *disagreed* with the views that the poor don't work as hard and don't want to get ahead as much as others in society, as did nearly all of the white poor.[25] (In contrast, two fifths of whites with incomes over $15,000 *agreed* with these notions concerning the poor!)

In a related vein, one of the most frequently cited traits of the poor is their inability to understand bureaucratic behavior and person- as opposed to object-orientation. Among many persons in poverty, it is perhaps not so much that they are unable to understand bureaucratic behavior per se as it is their *unwillingness* or *refusal* to do so on the grounds of what it requires them to be as people. That this is the case is strongly suggested in Horton's study as well as in studies of Appalachian and white urban poor. To make allusions that somehow this unbureaucratic propensity belongs to some culture of poverty would be mighty far-fetched. No one has yet explicitly argued that people *should* be poor if they do not possess bureaucratic propensities, but such would be the next logical step.

Time orientation

Another behavioral trait often asserted to be part of poor people's culture is present or existence orientation as opposed to the future or planning orientation of mainstream society. If the social scientists who make such distinctions were more fully aware of what the demands of a life in poverty are really like, they would perhaps see that a so-called present-time or existence orientation is not a *cause* of poverty but a necessary *response* to it. If one is poor, one *must* go out and immediately spend wages or a welfare check. And it is the affluent who run up the big liquor and party bills, not the poor. The poor spend almost half of their money on food. What they do spend for hedonistic purposes would seem far more justifiable, in view of their oppressive environment, than it would for the wealthier segments of the society. And in the final analysis, to have a future orientation, there must be a future to orientate yourself towards. What future is there for today's poor? Indeed, as anthropologist Jules Henry points out, rather than moving toward some promising future, "The culture of the very poor is a *flight from death*."[26]

Concerning the supposedly hedonistic impulsive values among the poor, we might note that Rokeach discovered persons with incomes of less than $2,000 ranked pleasure and an exciting life at the very bottom of a hierarchy of a battery of values, while placing honesty, cleanliness, and family security at the very top.[27] Nor should this finding come as

[25] Joan Huber Rytina, William H. Form, and John Pease, "Income and Stratification Ideology: Beliefs about the American Opportunity Structure," *American Journal of Sociology,* 75 (January 1970), p. 712.

[26] Jules Henry, "White People's Time, Colored People's Time," *Trans-action,* 2 (March 1965), pp. 31–34.

[27] Milton Rokeach, "Value Systems in Religion," *Review of Religious Research,* 11 (Fall 1969), pp. 3–23.

much of a surprise to anyone who has given the question much thought: How much fun and excitement can a class of people have who must try to live on two or three thousand dollars a year when it takes about four times that amount just to have some of the minimum comforts of life?

Social participation

The poor are also frequently alleged to be deficient in the extent of their social participation. We have already noted (Chapter 3) that low-status people have fewer of all types of social contacts than those above them in the class structure. We have just noted one reason for this, their aversion to formal organizations and associations. But the culture-of-poverty thesis carries the argument into the core of primary-group life, as if somehow people living in poverty lack certain basic human traits that would allow them to make and maintain close friends, form neighborhood ties, and even get along with family members. Once again, poverty theorists tend to confuse the causes or sources of poverty with the consequences of trying, to use Miller and Riessman's metaphor, to make do with string where rope is needed. How much psychological energy or desire is left to cultivate friendships and family ties after years of grinding poverty? What might be the building blocks or interests that cement friendships and families together? Where are the material resources and comforts that are prerequisites to relaxation and sociability with friends and family? Elliot Liebow, in his participant study of black-street-corner society, puts the whole issue in proper perspective when he says, "Friendships are precious relationships and of special importance to one's sense of physical and emotional security," but "Conflicts of interest and a general dearth of material and inner resources eat away at the whole structure of personal relationships."[28]

Rainwater's intensive research into the black ghetto leads him to conclude that "The community structure of the lower-class Negro ghetto is weak and disorganized in its ability to provide structural support and social control over its members," but also that the ghetto resident is ". . . continually confronted with a world full of dangers—not just the physical dangers of the ghetto world, but also the interpersonal and moral dangers of this exploitative milieu."[29] Rainwater observes that people must be defensive and cautious in social relationships, for the situation is unpredictable. Social life must be stripped down due to the uncertainty of a material resource base to sustain it.

Despite the unfavorable climate for viable primary-group and family life, the poor *do* in fact involve themselves, often extensively, in groups of friends and exercise considerably ingenuity and mutual support in holding the large majority of their families together.[30] Rainwater reports

---

[28] Elliot Liebow, *Tally's Corner* (Boston: Little, Brown and Company, 1967), p. 216.

[29] Lee Rainwater, *Behind Ghetto Walls* (Chicago: Aldine Publishing Company, 1970), pp. 371; 373.

[30] Gitlin and Hollander, *Uptown;* and Scheffer, "The Poor, Separate Class or Working Class."

that his respondents averaged five to six regular close visiting associations, about one-third of which were kin. About the women, Rainwater writes that "However much their situations depart from those of ordinary, conventional American families, the women of Pruitt-Igoe are bound up in the quite ordinary role of housewife. Their daily routines have much in common with those of more fortunately situated stable working class and lower-middle class housewives across the country." Yet, they are faced with constant economic, psychological, and physical threats and dangers; for both men and women "life is both tense and depressing" and interlaced with considerable illness.[31] The crisis-permeated life of the poor thus discourages stable personal relationships, while at the same time relying heavily upon such relationships for emotional and material survival.

ADAPTING TO POVERTY

Is there, then, a culture of poverty transmitted as a way of life from one generation to the next that guarantees its holders another round of subsistence living? Obviously, there is not. Rather than a self-contained, self-sustaining culture or subculture separately marked off from mainstream culture, the poor are very much in (though not of) the larger society. The failure of poverty is painful for precisely that reason. For as Gans has pointed out, if a lower class poverty culture with its own independent aspirations and values really existed, then the people in that culture would be satisfied with that way of life.[32] Rainwater declares that the slum individual "has had a strong desire to perform successfully in terms of the norms of the larger society and has made efforts in this direction."[33] Thus, Valentine summed up his thorough study of the poverty literature as follows: ". . . lower-class life does not actually constitute a distinct subculture in the sense often used by poverty analysts, because it does not embody any design for living to which people give sufficient allegiance or emotional investment to pass it on to their children."[34]

Even people such as the late Oscar Lewis, who has more than anyone else been identified with the culture-of-poverty thesis, later clarified his position by saying that he never meant that *all* of the poor supported a self-sufficient, self-contained, poverty-promoting culture.[35] Rather, only about one fifth of the poor, explained Lewis, display what he had previously described as a poverty culture and would thus require value change in addition to jobs and income support to pull them out of poverty. Lewis even more significantly has written that "the subculture of poverty is part of the larger culture of capitalism, whose social and

---

[31] Rainwater, *Behind Ghetto Walls*, pp. 101–5; 111.

[32] Herbert J. Gans, *People and Plans* (New York: Basic Books, Inc., 1968), p. 333.

[33] Rainwater, *Behind Ghetto Walls*, p. 393.

[34] Valentine, *Culture and Poverty*, p. 113.

[35] See the culture-of-poverty debate as recorded in "Culture and Poverty," *Current Anthropology*, 10 (April–June 1969), pp. 181–202.

economic system channels wealth into the hands of a relatively small group and thereby makes for the growth of sharp class distinctions."[36] Lewis may well have gone on further to state explicitly that poverty is not largely generated *or* sustained by a poverty *culture* but by the capitalist system. Lewis *had* early stressed that the culture of poverty is *found* in capitalist societies, but then instead of going on to explain it in economic and political terms he provided a cultural accounting.

But to say that a distinctive poverty-generating culture does not exist is not to say that the poor will not remain poor or that the children of the poor will not be poor themselves. For the same economic system that made one generation of people poor will usually do the same kind of job on their children. As Mills has remarked, "The accumulation of advantages at the very top parallels the vicious cycle of poverty at the very bottom."[37] No one has better clarified the distinction between culturally transmitted poverty and poverty produced anew in each generation than Liebow in the following passage: ". . . the son goes out and independently experiences the same failures, in the same areas, and for much the same reasons as his father. What appears as a dynamic, self-sustaining cultural process is, in part at least, a relatively simple piece of social machinery which turns out, in rather mechanical fashion, independently produced look-alikes."[38]

Nor to say that low-income people share the general values and aspirations of the rest of the population is it to say that poor people are simply bankrupt members of the bourgeoisie. When a person's life chances are as bad as are those of the poor, it is by definition impossible to attain many conventional values and aspirations, no matter how highly they are regarded. Being keenly aware of the discrepancy between conventional norms and values and their own chances of achieving them, the poor would be entertaining the worst odds to judge themselves and their counterparts by national cultural standards. Though many do, in fact, form a self-image based entirely on conventional standards, the majority have had no psychological and practical alternative but to accept a number of modifications and qualifications to mainstream values. Although lower class people do not really reject dominant values, argues Rainwater, "It is simply that their whole experience of life teaches them that it is impossible to achieve a viable sense of self-esteem in terms of those values."[39] Other strategies of survival and self-acceptance must be worked out as adaptations to an oppressive economic environment. For example, though permanent marriage and biparental families may

[36] "The Culture of Poverty," in Daniel P. Moynihan, ed., *On Understanding Poverty* (New York: Basic Books, Inc., 1968), pp. 198–99.

[37] C. Wright Mills, *The Power Elite* (New York: Oxford University Press, 1956), p. 111.

[38] Liebow, *Tally's Corner*, p. 223. On the distinction between certain life styles of the poor as a cause and as a response to poverty, see Jack L. Roach and Orville R. Gursslin, "An Evaluation of the Concept 'Culture of Poverty,'" *Social Forces*, 45 (March 1967), pp. 383–92.

[39] Lee Rainwater, "The Lessons of Pruitt-Igoe," *The Public Interest*, 8 (Summer 1967), p. 123.

be the ideal, individual failures and female-centered families must frequently be accepted as economically conditioned realities of life. Or when legitimate avenues of breadwinning are not open or available to the poor, what alternatives are there but to hustle for a living?[40]

Hyman Rodman has referred to the tendency among low-income people to accept a *wider range* of values than others in society as the "value stretch."[41] By value stretch, Rodman means that ". . . the lower-class person, without abandoning the general values of the society, develops an alternative set of values. Without abandoning the values placed upon success, such as high income and high educational and occupational attainment, he stretches the values so that lesser degree [and other kinds] of success also become desirable." The value stretch, then, partially compensates for the poor's dearth of economic resources by means of which others are able to realize conventional standards of behavior. While not flouting conventional values, the poor cannot by necessity continually maintain a strong commitment to conform to them. A Swedish observer, Ulf Hannerz, has noted that mainstream norms are held up as *more valid but less attainable under the situational constraints.*[42] Hannerz's study of ghetto residents led him to conjecture about the possibility of a certain amount of subcultural distinctiveness and intergenerational transmission of ghetto-specific culture, along with mainstream culture. He points out, in particular, the sex-role behavior of street-corner males as being shared and transmitted across generations. Hannerz seems to be dealing with the value stretch rather than self-contained values, for he also notes that family security and steady employment are the ideals, however unattainable they seem to be.

The idea of the value stretch among low-income people strikes me as useful but not markedly different from the idea of there being variations on or specific manifestations of the national culture in the form of overlapping subcultures or cultural strata. And to say that there are broad cultural strata is, of course, to say nothing at all about poverty. The distinction being drawn is between ideal and behavioral culture, and the conclusion is that the ideal culture of the poor is very similar to that of the rest of the working class, even though behavior must regularly be modified to adapt to the material and social situation. Rainwater suggests that the poor have created "a range of institutions to give structure to the tasks of living a victimized life and to minimize the pain it inevitably produces."[43] And before these accommodations to material deprivation and social insecurity can be eliminated, ". . . the social and

---

[40] See the critique by Julius Lester, *Look Out, Whitey! Black Power's Gon' Get Your Mama!* (New York: Grove Press, Inc., 1969).

[41] Hyman Rodman, "The Lower-Class Value Stretch," *Social Forces*, 42 (December 1963), pp. 205–15. Also, *Lower Class Families* (New York: Oxford University Press, 1971).

[42] Ulf Hannerz, "Roots of Black Manhood," *Trans-action*, 6 (October 1969), pp. 12–21, and *Soulside* (New York: Columbia University Press, 1969).

[43] Rainwater, *Behind Ghetto Walls*, p. 6.

ecological situation to which lower class people adapt must be changed."[44] The view of many researchers, including Rainwater, Liebow, Hannerz, Valentine, Gitlin and Hollander, and Gans, is that a changed social and economic environment would produce rapid changes in low-income subculture, at least to the extent that they depart significantly with that of the working class. Scheffer's comparative research cited previously on working class and poor whites also indicates that financial resources, simply put, would wipe out most observed behavioral differences between the two groups. It supports Rainwater's contention that "A person is poor when he does not have enough money."

The interpretation one places upon poverty essentially defines what action or inaction is recommended for its elimination.[45] The culture of poverty account would dictate an individual approach designed to alter the values and behavior of the poor person. The economic approach dictates changes within the structure of the society itself. As Gans points out, "When the concept culture of poverty is applied only to the poor, the onus for change falls too much on them, when in reality the prime obstacles to the elimination of poverty lie in an economic, political, and social structure that operates to protect and increase the wealth of the already affluent."[46]

POLITICS AND POVERTY

By now the poor no longer believe or have faith in promises from high places about "new frontiers," "great societies," or "new Americas." They and most of the rest of the population can no longer be stirred by empty rhetoric and easy slogans. However sincere the intentions behind each new government "assault" on poverty, nothing of significance ever seems to materialize; only talk, blue-ribbon research committees, and bureaucracies of various sizes. Despite the deluge of speeches, the volume of literature, and the proliferation of small programs, hardly a single major change has been made in the opportunity structure of the poor or in shoring up the sagging budgets of the near-poor. They are still faced with the same job shortages and inadequate income levels that faced them a decade ago. They have heard that America has the power and resources to abolish poverty, but by now they may be quite dubious about the possibilities of that power or those resources ever being put to work. They see America's power and resources being used in other ways, like buying defective billion-dollar cargo planes, fighting little wars on a large scale, going to the Moon, and subsidizing the affluent.

The poor themselves have very little power or resources with which to act politically or economically. But their dearth of resources does not always prevent them from trying to bring about change through demo-

---

[44] Ibid., p. 402.

[45] See Rainwater, "The Problem of Lower-Class Culture and Poverty-War Strategy," in Moynihan, *On Understanding Poverty*, pp. 229–59.

[46] Herbert Gans, "Culture and Class in the Study of Poverty," in Moynihan, *On Understanding Poverty*, p. 216.

cratic processes. The first protest movement of the poor was the 1894 march on Washington by "Coxey's Army." Like so many of his modern-day counterparts, Coxey was arrested (for walking on the grass). About 75 years later, another army of poor people descended on Washington in an attempt to dramatize their desperate situation. Congressional response was an overwhelming majority vote to ban all sit-ins, camp-ins, and sleep-ins in the capital. The poor were charged by the Congress with disrupting the seat of government and destroying public property. From Coxey's Army to Resurrection City, the message to the poor from the nation's legislature is clear: Don't bother us.

For the most part, the poor *don't* bother the politicians. Kimball reports that a substantial majority of a poverty sample declared that they didn't have much energy for politics (one-half *preferred* to avoid controversy). Kimball points out that ". . . those who neither register nor vote are drawn disproportionately from the ranks of the nation's poor, from ethnic minority groups, from disadvantaged residents of our largest urban centers." The poor "have the least connection with the political structure, which is the supposed instrument of orderly change."[47] Thus, the poor appear too fragmented and disconnected from the larger society to constitute a cohesive class political force.

However, the minorities have an ethnic bond which is capable of pulling them together into a unified political force, as blacks, Mexican-Americans, and American Indians have all demonstrated. Poor whites, while much less unified, frequently evince a sharp political understanding. A poor West Virginian remarked, "They came in here, the big companies, and bled us dry. They took everything, our coal, our land, our trees, our health. We died like we were in a war, fighting for these companies, and we were lucky to get enough money to bury our kin."[48] A low-income white Chicagoan declares regarding Vietnam, "Oh, it's all a money racket, to tell you the truth about it. You ever seen a rich man in the army? Oh shore, once in a while they take one. But it's a rich man's war, and the pore people fight it. It's a pore man's fight and a big man's money. That's all there is to it."[49]

With help from their allies in the new working class, the poor are learning of political struggle, and are conducting much of it entirely on their own. Welfare rights groups, farm workers, and inner-city poor have displayed considerable amounts of un-culture of poverty behavior.[50] The United Farm Workers have for years fought against the heavy-handed tactics of the big growers and their collusive practices with the Teamsters in California, the American Indian movement has dramatized Indian demands for human justice in their actions at Wounded Knee,

[47] Penn Kimball, *The Disconnected* (New York: Columbia University Press, 1972), pp. 5; 289.

[48] Robert Coles, "Life in Appalachia—the Case of Hugh McCaslin," in Marc Pilisuk and Phyllis Pilisuk, eds., *Poor Americans: How the Poor White Live* (Chicago: Aldine Publishing Company, 1971), pp. 38–39.

[49] Gitlin and Hollander, *Uptown*, p. 39.

[50] See Robert H. Binstock and Katherine Ely, eds., *The Politics of the Powerless* (Cambridge, Mass.: Winthrop Publishers, 1971).

and the "cheap labor" at the Farah plant in El Paso have struck for better treatment and union rights. The need is to draw all segments of the working class together in a coordinated effort against the power of capital over their lives. Such coordination has throughout American history been extremely difficult to obtain.

Losing a war

What, then, about the vaunted War on Poverty? Begun in 1964 with the fanfare of ten New Deals rolled into one, the War on Poverty, under the auspices of the Office of Economic Opportunity, was launched with the sum of three quarters of a billion dollars and escalated to almost two billion dollars by 1967. The Pentagon, in the meantime, was in the process of doing some war escalating of its own that soon ran up to 30 billion dollars annually. As the money and energy poured into the destruction of a preindustrial society, the poverty generals soon saw the handwriting on the wall. Retreat was sounded before any major battles had even been fought. Back down to about $750 million in 1971, by the end of 1972 re-elected President Nixon began his assault upon social programs and soon set one of his eager young lieutenants (whose temporary appointment was subsequently declared illegal in court) to work dismantling the entire OEO operation. Since the Congress had passed upon OEO operation until 1975, the President was in violation of law, whereupon a rural development group in Missouri took the case to court and won. The President directed his man at the OEO to refrain from axing further programs.

Besides its badly insufficient funding, the War on Poverty was based on erroneous strategies. It implicitly or explicitly accepted the personal and cultural accounts of poverty rather than the economic one and geared its programs to *change people rather than to change institutions*. The only people to benefit fully economically from the War on Poverty were the highly paid bureaucrats who administered the program. Why the poor people were not placed in these jobs seems paradoxical, when it was they who all along needed employment. But the paradox vanishes when it becomes clear that powerful people look out for themselves and one another; there are literally hundreds upon hundreds of aid programs, appropriations, departments, bureaus, and offices that provide white-collar jobs and high pay for tens of thousands of middle- and upper-income people, involving relatively little trickle-down effect for the poor. The main thrust of the War on Poverty was to try to develop middle-class values and working-class skills among poor youth. But the problem all along has never been that of insufficient motivation, immoral values, or unwillingness to train for a real job. Stable and secure jobs were simply not available or open in sufficient quantities to go around, and the War on Poverty did absolutely nothing in the way of rectifying these shortages.

The War on Poverty did not even propose, let alone attempt, to make any changes in the economic system that underlies poverty and economic insecurity. As we have already pointed out, poverty is not entirely a problem of employment. Many of the poor *are* employed. Many are elderly, women, and children outside of the labor force. The Community Action Programs were to serve a larger cross section of the poor than Job Corps and Neighborhood Youth Corps, but hardly any of these CAP programs had even minimal operations in such vital areas as credit union, health, or legal services. And what was the caliber of weapons that the Volunteers in Service to America (VISTA) workers were sent out to combat poverty with? Goodwill? Poverty fighters and poor people need hard money to work with; goodwill alone can't eradicate poverty.

Like the public welfare system, which we shall examine in a moment, the War on Poverty failed because it proposed or made no changes in the economic institutions that are responsible for inequality of income, wealth, and power in the American class system. Strategies aimed at moral uplift and cultural therapy for the poor can only be expected to arouse resentment and righteous ingratitude among low-income people. They feel, and rightly so, that they are entitled to a secure and comfortable life, for they and their families have long performed the menial and strenuous labor that has been so essential to the economic success of the higher strata. The poor need an office of economic opportunity that is not a mere facade, a make-work enterprise for bureaucrats. But to have real economic change in this country, the poor must come to terms with the corporate power structure and its government allies, a political contest no odds makers would dare to take on.

THE WELFARE SYSTEM

To hear some people talk, an outsider might get the impression that American government is in the business of taking from the rich and giving to the poor. Nothing could be further from the truth. To date, government is preeminently concerned with maintaining the viability of the corporate economy. The poor have largely been left to fend for themselves. The existing welfare system is a stop-gap operation that has failed miserably in eliminating economic deprivation and insecurity, while succeeding in heaping mountains of abuse and indignities on people in need of economic assistance. The stop-gap welfare system has also succeeded in preventing mass political action and the passage of legislation that would bring about fundamental change in America's economic institutions. Through small concessions here and there, the power elite has managed to siphon off discontent in small doses before it has had a chance to build into a formidable force for social change, while at the same time reducing the recipients to the status of virtual beggars.

Two experienced critics of the welfare system, Piven and Cloward, have argued that "Expansive relief policies are designed to mute civil disorder, and restrictive ones to reinforce work norms."[51] With historical review, Piven and Cloward describe how mass unemployment eventu-

---

[51] Frances Fox Piven and Richard A. Cloward, *Regulating the Poor: The Functions of Public Welfare* (New York: Pantheon Books, 1971), p. xiii.

ally brings relief programs designed to absorb enough of the unemployed to mute social disruption, and then with the passing of the political threat, the relief system contracts and expels people into the labor market for whatever wages are available. With regard to one such period of mass unemployment and need, the depression of the 1930s in the U.S. (the survey goes back to 16th century France), Piven and Cloward point out that "The spread of destitution itself was no great force; for a considerable period of time elites remained aloof from the suffering in their midst. But then the destitute became volatile, and unrest spread throughout the country. It was only when these conditions, in turn, produced a massive electoral convulsion that government responded."[52] As radical threats subsided, New Deal programs were cut back, pushing workers out of government work and aid programs into the low wage private market. Relief is always kept well beneath wage minimums, and working-age men are usually excluded entirely. Piven and Cloward place the upswing in welfare spending since 1965, much of it ghetto directed, in the same theoretical context of mass unemployment and political volatility. In effect, welfare is used by the ruling class as a tool to control the labor force *and* to dampen political discontent.

Welfare spending

When politicians start talking about welfare spending, few are very specific in what they say. Nearly everything but that budgeted for military purposes (in the recent past two-fifths of the total budget) and space and atomic energy (quasi-military purposes) is labeled as "welfare." Lumped under welfare are such things as all social security programs (financed through regressive payroll taxes), education, civil service retirement, unemployment compensation, veterans' compensation, health, housing, and urban development. As may be seen from this listing, most of the funds spent under the rubric of welfare go to or for the benefit of middle-income people and above. In medicine, for example, thousands of physicians receive over $25,000 from the government annually on the Medicare and Medicaid programs. Many receive over $100,000.[53]

---

[52] Ibid., pp. 76–77.

[53] Robert E. Burger, "Commercializing the Aged: Medicare and Medicaid," *The Nation*, May 11, 1970, pp. 557–60. The rapid inflation of physicians' fees following passage of Medicare is common knowledge ($2.4 billion submitted in 1971). While thousands of physicians receive over $25,000 a year from medicare payments, and many over $100,000, most make an effort to remain within the letter of the law. Some don't as the 1,884 cases of Medicare fraud pending trial or under investigation in late 1972 suggest. A conviction was obtained on a former Chief of Psychiatry at Philadelphia General Hospital (39 other doctors have also been convicted) who provided "music therapy" at nursing homes. The doctor, who collected $47,000 in payments in the first six months of 1971, was accompanied by a violinist or other musician and a female assistant to the homes where the music would draw the elderly out of their rooms to listen. Urging the "patients" to clap, the doctor instructed his assistant to go around the room and obtain the medicare number of each

Only about one half of the poor receive government transfer payments of any kind, and the majority of these are not receiving public assistance but rather earned transfer payments, such as social security and veterans' compensation. Recent estimates have only about one in five persons with poverty incomes receiving direct public aid such as Old-Age Assistance and Aid to Families with Dependent Children. Many are not eligible under existing welfare statutes. Many who are eligible won't apply or fail to apply for various reasons. A 1965 New York study disclosed four prevalent explanations for the eligible not being on welfare rolls: (1) they believed that they would be found ineligible; (2) they believed that they would be given so little that it would not be worth the harassments of the application process; (3) they had had previous humiliating experiences with the welfare department; and (4) they did not know that financial assistance could be available (the largest single group in a similar Detroit study).[54] And as Piven and Cloward point out, "Many of the applicants who meet all eligibility requirements are arbitrarily turned down." Once on, it is possible to be cut off at any time without notice even when no other means of support are available.

Direct financial aid to the poor composes about five percent of total government budgets, and about 10 percent of so-called welfare expenditures. The major federal assistance programs are Old-Age Assistance ($1.9 billion total and $77 monthly average per person in 1971), Aid to Families with Dependent Children ($6.2 billion and $188 monthly average per family), and Aid to Permanently and Totally Disabled ($1.2 billion and $102 monthly average per person).[55] To put it in relative perspective, the $19 billion that state and local government spend on highways is more than twice what they spend on welfare assistance, the military-derived *interest* payment on the federal debt is six times the amount of old-age assistance, and private advertising spends three times more than is spent on families with dependent children. Public relief totally pales up against the over $80 billion spent for "defense."

Financially speaking, existing social insurance and public assistance programs are totally inadequate, in terms of both coverage and level of support. All welfare checks are poverty checks, precisely what we would expect from Piven and Cloward's analysis regarding the functions of welfare. For the elderly, Social Security payments are scarcely large enough to cover a single need such as housing. Old-Age Assistance helps keep alive about one in ten older persons. Only one-fifth of the elderly

---

person; he then sent in bills for "psychiatric treatment." When caught, the doctor offered the government agent $15,000 a year as director of a "music therapy" corporation, which would minister to additional nursing homes. The bribe failed and the doctor was fined $40,000 and placed on probation for five years (what would a blue-collar worker have been sentenced for stealing at least $47,000 from an insurance company and offering a bribe to a federal agent?). See Rose Dewold, "Medicare: The Easy Swindle," *The Nation*, November 6, 1972, pp. 429–31.

[54] Piven and Cloward, *Regulating the Poor*, pp. 150–57.

[55] *The American Almanac*, 1973, pp. 299–302.

are receiving income from private pension programs, and the main source of their income is earnings. While Medicare was supposed to help eliminate the medical costs of aging, the elderly had to cover one-fourth of the $8.4 billion in hospital (in-patient) and physician charges in 1971, the better part of which is out-of-pocket. Mr. Nixon's "economy drive" (never mind the heavy B-52 bombing raids that were on-going at the same time) against social programs was expected to sharply increase the cost of medical care for the aged in 1973. "For more and more people, middle-class as well as poor," write the Ehrenreichs, "health care is not a right, and not even a privilege—as the A.M.A. would have it— but a luxury."[56]

Aid to dependent children is also poverty-level and scarcely sufficient to cover any single major budget item. Two-fifths of female-headed families are receiving AFDC monthly payments, most of which find the father separated or divorced, dead, or absent for other reasons. Only in a minority of states has an able man recently been allowed to be present in the home of a family receiving aid, a strong inducement to separation in a family with an unemployed head.

The unemployed themselves have about a three in five chance of being covered (worse if poor) by unemployment compensation and a one in three chance of exhausting eligibility before finding another job. During the weeks covered, if such is the case, living expenses must be met on a little over one-third of ordinary wages. If a worker is disabled, as millions are each year, he or she can also expect to receive only a small fraction of the ordinary wage, and again if the person is not among the one-fourth of the labor force not covered by workman's compensation. Owing to requirements concerning length of time worked and other restrictions, only about one-half of the millions of long-term disabled workers receive public payments. Like payments to retired workers, these disability payments are poverty level (suggesting that low relief payments are due not only to the desire to push workers back into menial jobs, but also to conserve surplus value for use by the ruling class). Only a tiny fraction of the billions of dollars of income lost to disabled workers of any kind is replaced by private and public disability plans.

The majority of the population, at least according to opinion surveys, are much more liberal toward public assistance for the poor and social welfare in general than are the existing programs. On subjects of education, income maintenance, medical and dental care, employment, and housing, a large proportion of the population would institute more adequate and thorough coverage.[57] While the large majority of whites with incomes over $25,000 feel that the government has already done *too much* for the poor, only about one in four of the rest of the whites and

[56] Barbara and John Ehrenreich, *The American Health Empire: Power, Profits, and Politics* (New York: Vintage Books, 1971), p. 136.

[57] Milton Rokeach, "Religious Values and Social Compassion," *Review of Religious Research*, 11 (Fall 1969), p. 34. The data are based on a 1968 systematic random national sample of 1,400 adults; and Free and Cantril, *The Political Beliefs of Americans,* Chapter 3.

one in ten of the blacks agree with them.[58] But in housing, health, transportation, employment, welfare, education, or whatever may be the social needs, the ruling class is interested only if the needs can be translated into profit (usually via the taxpayer) or if needs must be placated to prevent social unrest. Mr. Nixon's 1969 welfare change proposals, first modified and later shelved, were geared primarily to undercut freedom of choice and to force (especially) mothers into low-wage jobs (employers often prefer women for their low-wage demands and lack of unionization). This general strategy is still in force.

THE ECONOMICS OF POVERTY

The economic account of poverty is increasingly accepted as the most tenable one. People are poor in America because they lack secure jobs and adequate money incomes relative to the prices they must pay for goods and services. People are not poor in America because they lack moral fiber or cultural integrity. They are certainly not poor as a result of economic scarcity. Poverty in America exists due to misallocation, maldistribution, and waste of resources and income, and the closely related fact of the elevation of corporate profit and growth over the elevation of human need. There can be no other rationalizations, justifications, or excuses. The political rulers and economic managers of the United States are largely responsible for this misallocation, maldistribution, and waste, for it is their decisions that govern how the country uses and invests or *fails to use and invest its vast resources and potential.*

Upon what criteria do the ruling elites base their economic decisions? The chief criteria are corporate profit, control, and growth. As we shall discuss in the next two chapters, the big decisions in America are made on behalf of the interests of the giant corporations. Unfortunately, what is in the interests of large corporations is decreasingly in the interests of the population at large—for prices, consumer safety, peace, democracy, race relations, conservation, education, medicine, transportation, aesthetics, housing, urban development, economic welfare, and other social and public spheres of life. In their preoccupation with profit and growth, the ruling class in America annually forces millions of able-bodied men into unemployment, prevents a pliable Congress from passing progressive economic measures, prevails over conservative monetary and fiscal policy, and takes advantage of tens of billions of dollars of self-styled tax privileges. What is among the most ironic aspects of the corporate system's internal dynamic of profit and growth is that, while America faces human and environmental poverty, the corporations and government must continually devise schemes of how to dispose of *surplus* in a profitable way.

While men in high offices reiterate slogans about military humiliation

---

[58] William H. Form and Joan Rytina, "Ideological Beliefs on the Distribution of Power in the United States," *American Sociological Review*, 34 (February 1969), p. 28.

in the eyes of the world, many people of the country increasingly fear social humiliation. What kind of system is it, people around the world ask each other and us, that pours endless billions of dollars into superfluous and redundant research, design, construction, and development of weapons of annihilation, while at the same time tolerating widespread poverty, housing shortages, medical shortages, and urban decay? Or that allows some people to provide better shelter and medical care for their horses than millions of human beings themselves enjoy? Or some men to shoot around the country in personal jet airplanes while others can't even get to a prospective job in their own city?

The cost of wiping poverty from the face of the land will be considerable, much more than the $11 billion deficit between poverty incomes and the federally defined thresholds. It would be impossible to say exactly how much it would cost. But two things are certain when it comes to the cost of eliminating poverty: (1) an economy with a gross national product of well over a trillion dollars can easily afford the bill; (2) the economic and social costs of poverty are much higher than would be the cost of eliminating it. We cannot afford poverty. Poverty is too costly in both economic and human terms. By now, it is very evident that privately incorporated economy cannot be relied upon to produce the jobs. The kind of work that must be done in America today does not seriously interest the corporations, unless the government offers to *guarantee* them sizable profits for their efforts. Besides, much of the work that must be done—as in low-income housing, medicine, mass transportation, education, conservation, and recreation—either is not or should not be open to profit-seeking.

Basic changes in the economic administration of food pricing, health services, education, legal aid, transportation, clothing essentials, disability and retirement insurance, credit, investment, and housing would not only be of great assistance to the stable white- and blue-collar workers, but would help bring the poor back into our society without earmarking them as different or uncommon people, a prerequisite to success. Even more important, the poor and prospective poor must be *involved* in the rebuilding process, also an essential prerequisite to success. Yet, direct income-support programs must for now do a very large part in abolishing poverty. While working-age persons would benefit directly from the creation and upgrading of jobs, dependent, part-time, and underpaid persons require cash support. Until such changes in the availability of economic and social services as those noted above are undertaken, there exists a great urgency for some form of income support as a right.[59] We shall examine in greater detail the proposal of a guaranteed income in connection with our discussion of automation in Chapter 10.

---

[59] A discussion of several strategies for basic economic security in America may be found in Robert Theobald, ed., *Social Policies for America in the Seventies: Nine Divergent Views* (New York: Doubleday & Company, Inc., 1969); for a discussion of the relative value of services as opposed to income support for the poor, see also Robert Theobald, ed., *The Guaranteed Income* (New York: Doubleday & Company, Inc., 1967).

Ultimately, the kinds of basic changes suggested above cannot be achieved within the bounds of the existing economy. For they direct the utilization of production toward human need rather than the acquisition of profit by a single class. Social needs and the needs of corporate capital run in opposite directions; fundamentally this has always been the case, but today this opposition is especially visible. Ours is a system that subsidizes the rich far more than the poor, both via the market and the state (Sentaor James O. Eastland of Mississippi received, for example, $117,-000 in 1968 and $140,000 in 1969 from farm subsidies, Eastland being the senior member of the Senate Agricultural Committee and once voted against a bill to limit the amount of subsidy to $20,000[60]).

As Michael Harrington has written, "So in education, housing, agriculture, welfare and every other area of social life it is necessary to attack the systematic concentration of economic power in order to achieve serious reform." ". . . we insist . . . that the fundamental solution of these problems requires measures that go beyond the limits of the capitalist economy."[61] To an analysis of the concentration of economic power and the class responsible for protecting and preserving the limits of capitalism we turn our attention.

---

[60] Robert G. Sherrill, "Reaping the Subsidies," *The Nation,* November 24, 1969, pp. 561–66.

[61] *Socialism* (New York: The Saturday Review Press, 1972), pp. 279–91.

9

The power structure

TECHNOLOGY, BUREAUCRACY, AND POWER

In Chapter 2 we discussed the relationship between bureaucracy and power, and noted how Weber clarified the manner in which bureaucracy concentrated power in the hands of those who dominated the top of bureaucratic hierarchy. Bureaucratic forms have appeared throughout history, but today they have become the prevailing mode of social organization of advanced industrial society. Bureaucracy is chiefly characterized by its hierarchical division of tasks governed by a set of formal regulations designed to produce efficiency of operation and production. It is a mechanism of social control.

Technology is also a means of control. Technology, as we shall use the term here, refers to the forces of production—the scientific and practical knowledge and techniques, both social and material, applied in the creation of consumption values. The greater the technological development, the more extensive is human control over material production and productivity. What is the relationship between technology and bureaucracy? As Ellul has pointed out, the technological means of material production with its forms of mechanical efficiency may be taken as a prototype or model for social organization as well.[1] The emphasis upon rational technique in material production has itself given rise to the subdivision of labor placed within a bureaucratic form of social organization. The process of alienation has found human beings performing fragmented and regimented tasks in material production, and the fragmentation has been carried over into all aspects of social administration. Further, technology as represented by electronic communi-

---

[1] Jacques Ellul, *The Technological Society* (New York: Random House, Inc., 1967), pp. 4–5.

cations and computers, among other techniques and devices, have greatly facilitated the means of bureaucratic organization and control. The modern state, for example, far exceeds the most highly developed of its pre-industrial predecessors in its ability to exercise social control over both state employees and citizens.

Thus, it would seem that bureaucracy is a necessary companion of technology, and is in many ways identical with it. In defining technology as the systematic application of scientific or other organized knowledge to practical tasks, Galbraith specifies its most important characteristic as the division and subdivision of tasks into component parts allowing knowledge to be applied to performance.[2] Galbraith seems to be saying that modern technology's chief and necessary characteristic is the division of labor into narrow and specialized parts.

While recognizing that technology and bureaucracy have been tied together, we may draw a definite distinction between the two. Technology is preeminently a form of material production, whereas bureaucracy is a form of social organization; they are strictly separable in both definition *and practice.* A society that employs technology, primitive or advanced, need not necessarily also be a bureaucratized society. It need not even be a society with an extensive division of labor in the realm of material production, least of all in social administration and organization. The tasks of a *machine* must be fragmented and repetitive, but the tasks of workers need not necessarily be so; and the more advanced the technology, the more easily can work be arranged so as to enlarge and broaden job responsibility and performance. Even more obvious is the separability of bureaucratic *hierarchies* of regulation and control from the technological forces of production. As Gintis observes, ". . . bureaucratized and routinized tasks do not flow from the nature of 'technology' but from the needs of centralized control."[3] Far from being necessary to efficient production, bureaucracy is highly inefficient and irrational to the realization of full worker productivity and performance, whether the work be material or administrative.

Technology does not require bureaucracy; but to maximize its power and control, bureaucracy requires technology. Ruling elites would convince us that bureaucracy is a necessary component of modern society. They would go even further to convince us that not elites but the imperatives of technology are making the big decisions and deciding the courses of major action. The conclusion would thus be that there *is no* ruling group; only panels of experts following the dictates of technology that reveal the necessary and best courses of action.[4] Also subsumed is the notion that only these experts are competent to interpret

---

[2] *The New Industrial State* (New York: Signet Books, 1968), p. 24.

[3] Herbert Gintis, "Alienation in Capitalist Society," in *The Capitalist System,* Richard C. Edwards et al., eds. (Englewood Cliffs, N.J.: Prentice-Hall, Inc., 1972), p. 280.

[4] See Magali Sarfatti Larson, "Notes on Technocracy: Some Problems of Theory, Ideology and Power," *Berkeley Journal of Sociology,* XVII (1972–73), pp. 1–34.

the demands of technology.[5] It is also evident that the general goals toward which technology is applied can be opened for popular debate and decision. Decisions regarding the use of technology are made on *some* group's behalf, not on the basis of inevitable technological laws. The demands of the capitalist system dictate certain uses and disuses of technology, but all social systems are changeable.

There is still a further way in which the ruling elites argue that large bureaucratic organizations or corporations are necessary to the application of modern technology. Galbraith contends that the enormous costs of modern technology require large organizations both to summon the capital and assure that investment is profitable.[6] Galbraith argues that the risks involved are simply too high to let the competitive market work its will; producers must be big to make production economical and to allow control of prices and profits, and thus, even of consumption. It follows that corporate merger and growth, and massive consumer manipulation, are essential ingredients of the technological society— at least if Galbraith is correct in his assumptions. Galbraith also makes the corollary assumption that technical experts ("the technostructure") control the corporate production process according to the necessities of technology; Galbraith seems to lose sight of the other real necessities of capitalism as an economic and political system, and especially of the capitalist class.

But just as bureaucracy is not necessitated by technology, neither is *big* bureaucracy necessitated by *advanced* technology. Big corporations are more powerful than smaller ones, but they are not necessarily more efficient. As Adams has stated after a review of relevant literature on the subject, "The facts simply do not bear out the contention that firms have to be big to be efficient, or that they are efficient because they are big."[7] The most active area of corporate merger in the past 25 years has been in sectors having relatively simple technologies and low capital intensities such as food, textiles, clothes, lumber, building materials and personal care and toiletries. The needs of control and financial accumulation, not technology, lead to bigness. Efficient production requires units of various sizes depending upon the product produced, but in few cases is the size of any of the top few hundred corporations, which completely dominate the U.S. economy, required to maximize efficiency. In fact, inefficiency in the sense of getting the most out of resources and delivering quality goods at lowest prices is the inevitable consequence of sprawling operations. Bigness means more power and control for those on top and less power and control for those subordinate in society. Technology need not in itself be considered as an unalterable enemy of democracy, even though technology does present a serious danger and current trends are allowing this danger to develop into a reality.

---

[5] See Jean Meynaud, *Technocracy* (New York: The Free Press, 1969).

[6] John K. Galbraith, *The New Industrial State*, p. 16.

[7] Walter Adams, "The Mystique of Bigness," *The Progressive*, November 1972, p. 41.

THE POWER ELITE

Our task in this chapter will be that of analyzing the manner in which the dominant economic and political elites exercise power in contemporary society. The issue of power has long been neglected or ignored. There has been a tendency to define in idealistic terms a popular democracy without dominant elites, or at least elites that respond to the pressures of various interest groups. However, as Kolko has argued, "In American society power responds to power, rather than to the powerless, and . . . competing factions, interests, and elites, none of whom have or depend upon a mass base, define the larger political strategy of the nation."[8] Quite mistaken is Berle's contention that "Power is invariably confronted with, and acts in the presence of, a field of responsibility."[9]

Drawing from the ideas of Weber on bureaucracy, C. Wright Mills wrote what has become a modern classic as well as the definitive study of power in modern America.[10] With careful research and documentations Mills elaborated his theory of the power elite. The dominant bureaucracies in America today, argues Mills, are those of corporation, state, and military. Labor, educational, family, religious, and other institutions are subservient to the interests of corporate, state, and military organizations. Within and around the central hierarchies of power exists a mass society devoid of democratic self-control.

Corporate, state, and military institutions do not represent separate and independent hierarchies of power that might be interpreted as "pluralism" or "counter-vailing power" at the top. Rather, within and between these centers of power exists a considerable coincidence of interests and essential agreement on most major issues. Mills also indicates that, owing to the affinity of interests among the dominant institutions, an elite position in one institution is readily interchangeable with that of another. Thus, top corporate executives move into high federal posts and then back into the corporate world, generals secure high political offices and become corporate officials upon retirement, and ranking federal officers have close ties with large businesses. Often assisting the freedom of movement within and between government and business worlds, but especially within the corporate bureaucracies themselves, is a common psychological and cultural background derived from participation in elite social institutions.

How far down the various hierarchies of power does one go to mark off the elite from the rest of society? The power elite, declares Mills, is composed of those who are in positions to make decisions having national and international consequences. The power elite, then, includes

---

[8] Gabriel Kolko, "Power and Capitalism in Twentieth-Century America," in J. David Colfax and Jack L. Roach, eds., *Radical Sociology* (New York: Basic Books, Inc., 1971), p. 226.

[9] Adolph A. Berle, Jr., *Power* (New York: Harcourt, Brace, and World, Inc., 1969).

[10] C. Wright Mills, *The Power Elite* (New York: Oxford University Press, 1956).

only the very highest circles of men in the dominant institutional hierarchies. What's more, their power does not inhere in them as individuals, but in the offices they hold. Stripped of their institutional bases of power, the power elite would be powerless. Although the power elite shares a common stake in the existing system, Mills makes it clear that the power elite is not a conspiracy or a homogeneous circle of particular men without any internal differences and whose interests prevail against all obstacles.[11] Beneath the top levels of power in Mills's conception of the power structure is a middle range of power. The middle range of power, in particular the Congress, is what Mills refers to as in an organized stalemate. Then comes the mass society, politically alienated and largely powerless. Such in its most brief form is Mills's conception of the power structure.

In opposition to Mills, some observers see the power structure in pluralistic terms.[12] According to the pluralist thesis, no single institution or set of institutions is dominant. Rather, society consists of a plethora of interest groups with conflicting goals, or of many shifting coalitions that temporarily coalesce around specific issues. In pluralist thinking, power operates more or less democratically, as countervailing interest groups contest and veto one another in the political arena. Typically, pluralists tend to be oriented toward community decision-making processes and power structures or include within their analysis organizations and decisions that are of limited impact and scope. This is not to suggest that relatively important decisions of less than national scope, as at the community level, are made democratically. There is convincing evidence that community power also tends to be highly concentrated,[13] though certainly less so and with infinitely less significance than in the national power structure.

Nor should one assume, as many pluralists do, that a case of disagreement or competition between dominant national elites and bureaucracies stands as a refutation of the power elite thesis and partial support of democratic pluralism. Even if there were thoroughgoing and permanent cleavages within the ruling stratum, which there are not, the separate power centers may be as isolated and irresponsible to society as if power

---

[11] Although Mills makes the point very explicit that the elite are not a conspiracy of power in *The Power Elite*, critics have often imputed to Mills a conspiratorial view of history. He unambiguously refutes these critics in a later essay. See his "Comment on Criticism," in G. William Domhoff and Hoyt Ballard, eds., *C. Wright Mills and The Power Elite* (Boston: Beacon Press, 1968), p. 242.

[12] Critical reviews of Mills may be found in Domhoff and Ballard, *C. Wright Mills and The Power Elite*. See also, Arnold M. Rose, *The Power Structure* (New York: Oxford University Press, 1967); and William Kornhauser, "Power Elite or Veto Groups," in S.M. Lipset and Reinhard Bendix, eds., *Class, Status, and Power* (New York: The Free Press, 1966).

[13] For example, see Robert Presthus, *Men at the Top* (New York: Oxford University Press, 1964), and Floyd Hunter, *Community Power Structure* (Chapel Hill: University of North Carolina Press, 1953).

were entirely concentrated in the hands of a definite nucleus of men.[14] In a similar vein, the fact that elites may not be able to exercise complete control over events, such as the inability to stabilize an economy in the face of militarily induced inflation, certainly does not disprove their existence or impotence. As nations have learned before, powerful elites can mess things up quite badly, indeed hopelessly. Power elites are not social physicists able to command society and history as scientists direct their laboratories. The power elite thesis is not based on all-or-nothing criteria. It is based on criteria of the balance of power to decide and to act, to oppose and negate.

Nor does the elite make *all* decisions of importance, virtually an impossible task in a large and complex society. Authority may be delegated and decisions made on the basis of relatively narrow alternatives within the system. Even where authority has not been specifically delegated, the presence of the elite is felt, and use of power in opposition to the interests of the elite must be prepared to reckon with the consequences. If the use of power is not in basic opposition to the interests of the elite, or is of minor import, there is obviously no reason why the elite should be involved or concerned. Indeed, such use of power gives the system a democratic image.

In addition to the pluralist critique of Mills's conception of the American power structure, some scholars have implied that Mills attributed too much power to the military, and even to political elites in comparison to the corporate elite.[15] But it does not seem that Mills underestimated the power of the military, either when he wrote or today, as it is represented by the Pentagon, Department of Defense, and the quasi-public corporations contracting for the military.[16] Nor, in fact, did Mills claim that the military and political elites wielded power equivalent to the corporate elite. Mills argued that corporate, state, and military interests and elites overlapped, making it difficult to assess the relative power of each. Are defense industries with their big government contracts, more a part of the business, government, or military sphere? Is the Department of Defense, with its $80 billion expenditure, a business, political, or military operation?

Mills contended that the keystone of power is the corporate elite or propertied-rich. The corporate elite exercises either direct control over political decisions through placement of corporate executives and corporate lawyers in the government, or indirectly through the control of high-ranking appointed and elected officials and through key advisory councils. In Mills's words, "Not the politicians of the visible government, but the chief executives who sit in the political directorate, by fact and

---

[14] See K. Newton, "A Critique of the Pluralist Model," *Acta Sociologica*, 12 (1970), pp. 209–23.

[15] For example, Kolko, *The Roots of American Foreign Policy*, and G. William Domhoff, *Who Rules America?* (Englewood Cliffs, N.J.: Prentice-Hall, Inc., 1967).

[16] See John Kenneth Galbraith, *How to Control the Military* (New York: Signet Books, 1969).

by proxy, hold the power and the means of defending the privileges of their corporations. If they do not reign, they do govern at many of the vital points of everyday life in America, and *no powers effectively and consistently countervail against them.*"[17] Furthermore, there is little interest within other elites *to* countervail against the business elite. Even as such a semi-pluralist as Robert Heilbroner points out, "On the contrary, a general acquiescence of the business system, when it does not descend to outright sycophancy, describes the general attitudes of the nonbusiness leaders."[18] And one of Mills's central points concerns the interlocking of business and other elites.

A prominent early instance of interlock within the military-industrial complex was that of John Foster Dulles, a chief cold war architect. Before coming to the Eisenhower administration as Secretary of State, Dulles was a senior partner in the law firm acting as attorney to Standard Oil and served as chairman of the board of the Rockefeller Foundation. (His brother Allen, of the same law firm, was for over eight years director of the Central Intelligence Agency.)[19] Among the most conspicuous recent cases of interchangeability within the power elite is that of Robert McNamara. McNamara resigned as president of Ford Motor Company in 1960 to become Secretary of Defense. Ford is, of course, in the middle of military contracting. Another obvious case of interlock is that of Dean Rusk, who went from secondary posts as a protegé to Dulles in the State Department to the presidency of the Rockefeller Foundation (the major stockholder in Standard Oil of New Jersey) and then back to Washington as Secretary of State.

A more recent instance of circulation in the small world of the ruling class is that of David Packard. Packard, one of the founders of the heavily defense subsidized Hewlett-Packard Company, was appointed as Deputy Secretary of Defense in the first Nixon administration. Packard and his wife held some $289 million in Hewlett-Packard shares, which were placed in trust. It would be difficult to imagine how Packard could serve as a neutral public figure—as regards the question of military spending. However, after making a fortune himself off the taxpayers, Mr. Packard may have had some second thoughts about military spending as a good in itself, as indicated in a 1970 speech to defense businessmen (as reported over CBS News): "Frankly, gentlemen," bemoaned Packard, "we have a real mess on our hands. The lesson that comes through loud and clear is that we should buy only what we need, not weapons you or anyone else think they can develop to do something that doesn't need to be done. The Defense Department has been led down the garden path for

---

[17] Mills, *The Power Elite,* p. 125. Italics are mine to emphasize the fact that Mills did locate the greatest power within the corporate elite, and was well aware that corporate interests dominated in the shaping of both domestic and foreign policy. Certain leftist critics of Mills overlook this point.

[18] *The Limits of American Capitalism* (New York: Harper & Row, 1966), p. 57.

[19] See the article of David Horowitz, "Social Science or Ideology," *Berkeley Journal of Sociology,* XV (1970), pp. 1–10.

years on sophisticated systems that you promised would do all kinds of things for some optimistic cost. Too frequently we have been wrong in listening to you, and more frequently you have been unable to deliver on either of these promises—what it would do or what it would cost." (Packard no doubt had foremost in mind General Dynamics' F–111 fighter and Lockheed's C–5A cargo plane.) "Of course," the secretary added, "we share the blame together." Mr. Packard turned down a 1973 offer to become Secretary of Defense in Nixon's discredited and shakey second-term administration.

At least on a par with the Packard "conflict of interests" is the case of Roy Ash, president of major defense contractor Litton Industries, being appointed by Nixon as director of the Office of Management and Budget. Other cases at hand include former presidential aides Clark MacGregor and Dwight L. Chapin, the former taking up a post as vice-president at United Aircraft (eighth largest defense contractor) and the latter as a top executive at United Airlines. At the international level, we might finally note John A. McCone, former head of the CIA and currently a consultant to it, who became a director on the board of IT&T. Mr. McCone and IT&T chief Harold Geneen reportedly tendered an offer of one million IT&T dollars to the government to aid in whatever plans the CIA or Washington might have in preventing Chile's Salvador Allende from assuming the presidency. Rejected through this medium, IT&T and the CIA spent $400 thousand on a covert propaganda campaign to defeat Allende. What later role these organizations had in creating economic chaos in Chile and the final elimination of Allende is uncertain at this time.

Although Mills was essentially correct in relegating education to a service role in the power structure, the major universities—with large corporations influentially represented on the boards of trustees—are also included in the convergence of power. Professors such as Walt Rostow, McGeorge Bundy, Daniel Moynihan and Henry Kissinger have variously found themselves actively working for political or military–industrial interests. As Mills pointed out, "Persons of power do surround themselves with men of some knowledge, or at least men who are experienced in shrewd dealings."[20]

In an affirmation of Mills, *The Nation* observes that "It is striking to what extent government power resides in a small group of men who come and go among the great foundations, prestigious universities, the blue-chip corporations, and the key posts in Washington." "The big aggregates of power—public, private, and quasi-private [military contractors]—are so interlocked today that the circulating celebrities have a near monopoly on certain posts."[21]

The most important form of interlocking power is not between institutional spheres such as government and business, but *within* business, the keystone of power. A study of 74 leading corporations found that

[20] Mills, *The Power Elite*, p. 353.
[21] Editorial, "Circulating Elite," *The Nation*, February 3, 1969.

1,480 directors and managers held a total of 4,428 positions throughout the corporate world.[22] Among 16 recent directors of United States Steel Corporation, one could account for 20 directorships in major industrials, 18 in banks, 11 in insurance companies, nine in railroads, eight in utilities, and three in foundations (and five trusteeships in universities). The selection process for such interlacing tends to weave decision-making cloth of an even texture.

Mills has traced in detail the movement of private capitalism toward an alliance with the state—i.e., toward state capitalism. He documented, as Marx and Veblen had earlier theorized, that state capitalism would assume a predominantly bureaucratic and militaristic posture, involving the society in foreign wars in the pursuit of market control and profit. As we shall subsequently point out, Mills drew our attention to the continued power of the big property owners, despite the profusion of hired managers and public stock. He stressed the existence of a relatively cohesive and self-conscious *social* class as distinct from a mere aggregate of wealthy individuals: "The narrow industrial and profit interests of specific firms and industries and families have been translated into the broader economic and political interests of a more genuinely class type."[23]

THE CONCENTRATION OF CORPORATE POWER

In Chapter 5 we examined the high degree of concentration of corporate wealth and even general wealth in American society at large. In this section, we shall concern ourselves with the extent of concentration of wealth and economic power within the corporate system itself. We shall document Kolko's assertation that, "When discussing the corporate system, it would be more realistic to drop all references to democracy."[24]

During the decades between the Civil War and the Depression, the American economy had moved from a small-unit, competitive system to one dominated by a relatively few large corporate units. Since then, the trend toward economic concentration has continued unabated, but particularly since midcentury. As Marx noted, corporate growth may be the product of two different economic forces. First, certain existing companies may grow at a more rapid rate than other corporations and account for an increasingly larger portion of economic activity (concentration). Second, companies may acquire other companies, be they competitors, suppliers, or completely unrelated (centralization); some of these companies are failing and/or acquired for tax purposes, but the large majority are going and profitable concerns. Owing to the already high degree of feasible horizontal (competitors) and vertical (suppliers) mergers, the recent high rate of concentration is the result of conglom-

[22] H.L. Nieburg, *In the Name of Science* (Chicago: Quadrangle Books, 1966), p. 196.

[23] Mills, *The Power Elite*, p. 147.

[24] Gabriel Kolko, *Wealth and Power in America* (New York: Frederick A. Praeger, Inc., 1962), p. 68.

erate mergers, the merger of companies in totally diverse economic fields. Mergers involving large corporations, even of the conglomerate type, epitomize the driving growth dynamic that variously enhances control of investments, markets, suppliers, aggregate demand, prices, wages, revenues, and profits—all important to long-range corporate planning.

The rate of merger increased markedly throughout the sixties. In 1960 there were 844 mergers involving industrial corporations, and mergers increased to a peak of 2,407 in 1968.[25] In 1968 there were 207 take-overs involving firms with assets of over $10 million. The number of mergers of large firms has since declined. The top 200 corporations must by definition be leading the way in the merger movement (or they probably would not long remain in the top 200). In the interval between 1951 and 1963, before the even more precipitous rise in mergers, the largest 200 companies made 1,956 acquisitions.[26] That such take-overs *do not* involve failing companies suggested by the fact that during the same period the top 200 companies increased their share of all net corporate profits by 17 percent.

The growth of monopolies means an enormous capital concentration. In 1969, less than *one-tenth* of *one* percent of all active U.S. corporations (those with $250 million or over in capital assets) held 56 percent of total assets (up from 46 percent in 1960).[27] The top *one-half* of *one* percent (those with $25 million or over in capital assets) held 75 percent of total corporate assets, and the top one percent ($10 million or over in assets) accounted for 81 percent. The economy is thus completely dominated by a few hundred giant firms, of which the top 100 account for approximately one-half of *total* assets (1970). The legal share ownership of net capital assets (physical plant and property) of the top 100 industrial corporations increased from 44 percent in 1929 to 58 percent in 1962.[28] These are conservative figures, inasmuch as they do not include instances in which the top 100 has less than majority ownership in other firms, and nearly all of the top firms act as holding companies for other corporations. Indeed, many of the largest companies are *nothing but* holding companies of other firms.

In terms of the tens of billions of dollars of after-tax corporate profit, the top *five* manufacturing companies take 20 percent of manufacturing profit; the top 10, 30 percent; the top 50, 48 percent; the top 100, 58 percent; the top 200, 68 percent; and the top 500, 80 percent.[29] (Recent Housing Banking Committee research suggest that today the extent of profit concentration is much greater than this.) This doesn't leave much capital, profit, and power to go around to the remaining mass of smaller

[25] *The American Almanac* (New York: Grosset & Dunlap, 1973), p. 484.

[26] Willard F. Mueller, "Recent Changes in Industrial Concentration, and the Current Merger Movement," in Maurice Zeitlin, ed., *American Society, Inc.* (Chicago: Markham Publishing Company, 1970), pp. 19–41.

[27] *The American Almanac,* pp. 478, 481.

[28] Gardiner C. Means, "Economic Concentration," in Maurice Zeitlin, ed., *American Society, Inc.,* pp. 3–16.

[29] Mueller, "Recent Changes in Industrial Concentration," p. 24.

firms. Foreign investment and profit are even more highly concentrated than are domestic.[30]

Financial corporations are also highly concentrated. In 1971, the 50 largest commercial banks held one-half of all assets and deposits in the nation's 13,687 banks.[31] The 10 largest banks held over one-quarter of all assets and deposits! Bank mergers have been proceeding abreast with industrial mergers, contributing to the 10 percent increase in the share of total bank assets by the largest 50 commercial banks from 1960–1970. Further, 20 large banks hold approximately one-half of the huge private trust assets, and through these trusts influence and control a significant percentage of the top industrial corporations. These same banks control the bulk of the $125 billion (1969) in rapidly growing pension funds, an important weapon in keeping employees in line. Like manufacturing corporations, banks also hold significant percentages of shares in "competing" banks and have convergent interest. The largest banks are increasingly interlocked with nonfinancial firms; 49 large banks hold what could be controlling interests (5 percent or more of the stock) in almost one third of the nation's 500 largest industrials.

Other financial operations follow a similar pattern. For example, 50 out of 1,800 life insurance companies account for 83 percent of 1971 assets, with the top 10 holding almost 60 percent of the total.

In addition to the straight economic aspect of corporate concentration, we might also note that a significant segment of the labor force is employed by the largest firms. In 1971, the 100 largest corporations on the yearly average employed 8.4 million persons and the 500 largest, 14.3 million. To the economic power of productive assets, then, we must add the power of corporations over employment. However, the extent of concentration of employment in large corporations is not the important variable, for increasingly, corporations are becoming organizations of machines rather than people. As we shall discuss, government accounts for an increasing proportion of jobs, as the production of goods becomes more and more automated. Nevertheless, the large corporations easily hold the balance of power when it comes to determining the level of employment.

Ownership and control

Who owns and who controls the big corporations? A thesis generally known as the "managerial revolution" contends that, owing to the public status of modern corporations as opposed to the family-owned firm, ownership has been separated from control. The "people," the thesis asserts, own corporations as stockholders, while the board of directors and the managers control the operation of the corporation and hold its power in trust for the community. Thus, stockholders become the ones

---

[30] Howard J. Sherman, "Concentration of Foreign Investment," in Maurice Zeitlin, ed., *American Society, Inc.* (Chicago: Markham Publishing Company, 1970), pp. 43–45.

[31] The Patman Committee, "The Concentration of Banking," in Maurice Zeitlin, ed., *American Society, Inc.*, pp. 48–76; and *The American Almanac*, 1973, p. 477.

concerned with profit, while the directors and managers are interested mainly in administration and efficiency. Corporate management operates largely independently of the profit motive. Corporate executives and directors, writes Berle, "are in the same boat with public officeholders."[32] But like many theories, the one concerning the separation of ownership and control and the independent operation of the profit motive does not stand the test of empirical data. For as we shall see, the corporate elite *are* among the biggest stockholders. The value of their stocks is not the only reason management is concerned with profit: profit is the *means* of corporate expansion and growth—the real measure of corporate success. (For the mass of small shareholders, "ownership" has quite obviously been separated from control; they can't even control what portion of the companies profits are to be paid out in dividends to them.)

Perhaps the first point that should be stressed is that "family business" in the corporate world is far from dead. Family capitalism, though not entirely of the old robber baron variety with singularly powerful and personally independent entrepreneurs, is as alive as ever and growing with new faces. In 150 of the largest 500 firms, ownership large enough to give control rests in the hands of an individual or members of a single family. Names such as Ford, Mellon, Pew, Rockefeller, Duke, Firestone, Kaiser, McDonnell, Hughes, and Fairchild are heard frequently enough by most Americans. But there are at least 140 more such family names in the largest 500 corporations, some well known and some not so well known (most prefer and seek the latter status –that is, avoidance of press notices, of conspicuous display of wealth, etc.).[33] While families with controlling or large ownership shares may not always be personally represented on boards of directors or in management (meaning that corporate wealth holders—often women and family dependents—and corporate management are not identical), there is really no need or reason for them to act in this elite capacity. There are plentiful loyal and efficient hired executives to oversee firm operations. Moreover, family control tends to be obscured through the placement of stocks in professionally managed trusts and investment companies. Not the individual corporation but the "financial group"—a *coalition* of several families holding controlling blocks of capital and centered in major banks and affiliated industrials—constitutes the vital center of the capitalist system today.[34] Such financial groups dominate the activities of most of the major corporations.

Now, taking the *directors* of the dominant corporations as a group,

---

[32] Adolph A. Berle, Jr., *The 20th Century Capitalist Revolution* (New York: Harcourt, Brace & Company, 1954), p. 60; for the early statement of the separation of ownership and control, see A.A. Berle, Jr., and Gardiner Means, *The Modern Corporation and Private Property* (New York: Macmillan Company, 1933). If corporations are motivated by the public interest rather than growth and profit, the theories explaining the operation of the economy in most textbooks must be seriously questioned, indeed invalid.

[33] See Ferdinand Lundberg, *The Rich and the Super Rich* (New York: Bantam Books, Inc., 1969), pp. 216–19.

[34] See S. Menshikov, *Millionaires and Managers* (Moscow: Progress Publishers, 1969), p. 217.

we find that their share of ownership *in their own companies* is sufficient to give them financial control of at least two thirds of the 232 largest corporations.[35] More importantly, it is not directors as such that hold most of the controlling stock, but only a certain few directors. Villarejo's data indicate, that of the 2,784 directors in the 232 corporations studied, a mere 99 persons completely dominated the holdings ($5.2 billion of $7.1 billion total for individual directors in their own firms). If all family members, trusts, and stock in the other 232 firms are totaled for the 520 propertied-rich directors (those who hold $10 million or were family members with $1 million or more), they accounted for $13 billion of a $14.4 billion directors' total. Almost 200 of these propertied-rich individuals were serving as board chairman or chief executive of a firm, clearly showing the strong family involvement in active management.[36] As a class, directors have a massive stake in the ownership of the dominant corporations, either directly or through holding companies or trusts. Although the share of director ownership in their own companies may compose a relatively small percentage of the total, even 5 to 10 percent ownership may give controlling interest. What's more, a much smaller ownership percentage than 5 percent can provide directors with something more than an impersonal interest in company profit. A fraction of a percent may involve millions of dollars. In 1966, 28 General Motors directors averaged $6 million in GM shares, even though holding an average of much less than one percent of GM stock. However, the focus of analysis must not be narrowed to the matter of ownership by directors in their own companies; the focus should rather be the extent of corporate ownership by directors *as a class*. But regardless of whether the focus is on a particular company or the dominant corporations as a whole, the separation of ownership from control, and profit interests from power, is a myth from the perspective of directors.

Directors need not rely entirely on ownership or their powerful position as director as an avenue of control. For as Kolko has pointed out, at least half of the directors of the largest firms are also key executive officers.[37] The tendency for directors to be members of their firm's management has become more marked since the late 1930s. And again, the total class focus should be kept at the forefront; interlocking directorates assure that the majority of directors in the leading corporations are also active officers in *some* company (some directors are not career businessmen).

To what extent do managers, including director-managers, taken as a group own the corporate property they run? Stock ownership is, in fact, extensive within top management, both within the companies they run and in other corporations. The chief officers of the top 100 corporations are typically enormously wealthy, three-fourths of them being million-

---

[35] Don Villarejo, "Stock Ownership and Control of Corporations," *New University Thought*, 2 (Fall 1961 and Winter 1962), pp. 33–77; 47–65.

[36] Ibid.

[37] Gabriel Kolko, *Wealth and Power in America* (New York: Frederick A. Praeger, Inc., 1962), p. 60.

aires within their own companies only (virtually all are millionaires), and seven being full centimillionaires in their own companies.[38] Executives are interested in company profit not only from the standpoint of capital appreciation on the worth of their stock and as a means to further corporate growth, but salary and bonuses (between $250,000 and $800,000 for the above 100 chief executive officers), dividends, and the exercise of stock options depend upon company profit performance. As a class, then, top management has a huge investment in the dominant firms. Besides, as Mills observes, "Top-level managers are socially and politically in tune with other large property holders."[39]

The distinctions between ownership and control, profit interest and administration, crumble in practice. For the big stock owners as a class *are* predominantly directors and managers. In some instances, director-officer ownership is controlling, while in other instances, their ownership stakes are simply high enough to assume a strong profit motive. Where controlling ownership is not directly represented administratively, hired executives are retained on the basis of profit and growth performance. Owing to the availability of sophisticated technological decision-making techniques and equipment, the media of mass advertising, and market size and control, modern management is in a *better* position to amass profits than the traditional entrepreneur.

Regardless of whether one's concern is with profit or power, ownership or control, research will ultimately lead (often through a maze of complex economic relationships and institutions designed to conceal wealth and power) back to a small elite, accountable to no one other than themselves and, most importantly, to one another in the intracorporate and intercorporate power structure. When we speak of the owners, directors, and managers of the corporate world, we are speaking in large part about persons within the privileged one half of one percent of the adult population that owns the bulk of corporate wealth and one third of the nation's privately owned wealth. As Mills observed, the very rich and the corporate elite are much the same, allowing for major property holders who do not directly hold a corporate office but whose interests are virtually the same as those of officeholders. And as we shall discuss later in the chapter, the very rich and the corporate elite form the center of the upper social class.

Finally, what can we conclude regarding the relationship between property and power? Marx contended that power in capitalist society arises from property ownership, and to the extent that property ownership is concentrated, to a similar extent is power concentrated. We have just substantiated the fact that economic control and the power to decide has not been separated from ownership, suggesting that property and power are still very closely related. In fact, as Mills points out, the power of property is today *more* concentrated than is property ownership.[40]

---

[38] *Forbes*, May 15, 1972, pp. 205–8.

[39] C. Wright Mills, *White Collar* (New York: Oxford University Press, 1953), p. 104.

[40] Ibid., p. 101.

That is to say, a five or ten percent share of ownership may provide 100 percent control or power to decide (this company, in turn, may be holding controlling interests in another company, and so on, giving an upside-down pyramid shape to corporate power). Even more than in Marx's time, then, property ownership determines the distribution of power in capitalist society.

Power to do what?

Given that the power to make the important economic decisions lies within a very small circle of men, what is it that they use their power for? The foremost use of power by the corporate elite is to attempt to maintain the status quo in relevant social, political, and economic institutions, both domestically and throughout the "free world." The direct and proxy influence of the corporate elite on the political directorate has already been noted and will be discussed at greater length presently. Suffice it to note here that, regarding electoral politics, votes are only a nominal source of political power, whereas money tends to be the real underlying source. And only the corporations and corporately wealthy possess the concentration of money to politically indoctrinate the masses, finance major campaigns, support political parties, and bring the full power of wealth to bear on congressional voting (especially on matters of taxation and spending) and administration decision making. A *mass* based and financially supported opposition movement for change forces moneyed elites either to abandon democratic forms (witness the entire Watergate case) and resort to force in an attempt to sustain their predominant position or to yield and make major concessions.[41] History teaches us that the latter alternative is rarely taken.

More specifically, in the area of economic life, the corporate elite determine, in Mills's words, "the size and shape of the national economy, the level of employment, the purchasing power of the consumer, the prices that are advertised, the investments that are channeled."[42] The fulcrum of corporate power, confirms Hacker, is the power to decide how much will be invested, what products and services will be made available and in what quantities, where the products will be made, and who will participate in the production process.[43] In brief, the power of the corporate elite substantially influences what the nation's vast resources are used for, what kinds of jobs are available, how many jobs are available, where jobs are available, how much jobs will pay, what kind of education will be needed, how much profit will be returned in dividends and how much retained, what will be invested in, what people can afford to buy, what the quality of their purchases will be, and how soon they must or think they must buy again.

---

[41] See Paul A. Baran and Paul M. Sweezy, *Monopoly Capital* (New York: Monthly Review Press, 1968), Chapter 6.

[42] Mills, *The Power Elite,* p. 125.

[43] Andrew Hacker, "Power to Do What?" in Irving Louis Horowitz, ed., *The New Sociology* (New York: Oxford University Press, 1964), Chapter 8.

This is obviously not meant to imply, for example, that the directors and managers of the 200 or 500 largest corporations sit down periodically to decide the exact answers to these questions and issues, not to mention their limited capacity to effectively carry them through as desired or planned. In some instances, the answers are given as a result of the *in*decision and *in*action of the ruling elite. But more often, the answers the propertied-rich give to crucial questions such as the above are made on the basis of numerous decisions involving different but overlapping circles of several thousand men. What makes the outcome of the numerous decisions appear as if a specific group consciously makes or attempts to make a single overriding decision concerning the uses of American human and natural resources is that the various decision makers share the same interests in the same corporate economic system so that, in consequence, economic decisions might as well be made by a monolithic clique of economic planners. Indeed, this very tendency is increasingly evident and must necessarily become more pronounced with growing concentration and state involvement. That the pursuit of these policies frequently culminate in economic crises, with all its ramifications on social life, does not detract from the exercise of power. The failure of a system does not mean that somebody was or is not in control. The pursuit of irrational policies leads to trouble, just as rational policies lead to success.

That chief decision makers may not even be fully cognizant of their power or conscious of the direction in which their policies are leading us is alluded to by Mills when he says the elite "are cogs in a business machinery that has routinized greed and made aggression an impersonal principle of organization."[44] Surely the capitalist class would like to lead the way to ever greater heights of self-affluence, but there are insurmountable barriers to economic, social, political, and cultural advance within the currently existing system.

This does not exhaust the limits of corporate power. As shall be discussed in Chapter 14, the large corporations have become internationalized ("multinational" corporations) and act within the world capitalist arena as virtual governments unto themselves. In the process, the conditions of a large portion of the world's population are set by the operations of the capitalist classes of the developed nations.

THE USES OF GOVERNMENT

In defining the modern state, British sociologist Frank Parkin states that "Sociologically, the state could be defined as an institutional complex which is the political embodiment of the values and interests of the dominant class."[45] As regards the U.S., Veblen's summation made earlier in the century stands fast: "Nowhere else does the captain of big business rule the affairs of the nation, civil and political, and control

---

[44] Mills, *White Collar,* p. 109.

[45] Frank Parkin, *Class Inequality and Political Order* (New York: Praeger Publishers, 1971), p. 27.

the conditions of life so unreservedly as in democratic America." "Governments continue to be administered by the gentlemanly delegates of the vested interests and the kept classes."[46]

The role of the state, then, is primarily (it also does many other things, of course) to protect and promote the interests of the propertied class. In its domination of the state, the propertied class assumes the form of a *ruling* class. Since the 1930s, the state has been forced to play an ever increasing role in capitalist society. The state has become the focal point in increasingly broad and varied attempts to maintain economic viability. Economic imbalances have generated periodic mass unemployment and underemployment, price inflations, unused or idle resources and equipment, severe shortages of housing and medical services, military involvements, gross imbalances in family savings and purchasing power, etc. The state has had to enter at more and more points, using mainly its taxation and legislative powers, to attempt to stabilize precarious economic situations while at the same time stimulating the prosperity of the ruling class. The state, in Mandel's words, "becomes the essential guarantor of monopoly profits."[47]

The existing economic relations are such as to create large amounts of surplus wealth available to the big investors, who are already steeped in wealth and with no investment aims in mind other than to further economic expansion. The result is increasingly waste, for waste can in itself be made very profitable. The result is also big government, collecting taxes and spending money, mostly to the benefit—directly or indirectly—of the propertied-rich. The result is also war and the preparation for war, as the state polices the world on behalf of international corporate interests. The state grows larger and larger in its attempts to deal with the chaotic swings of an economy dominated by self-centered corporate giants. As long as the state is dominated by the propertied-rich, not much more can be expected from it. From billion dollar subsidies to big agro-business, to billions for highways (note their importance to the oil and auto interests), to billions in tax write-offs (shouldered then by the average taxpayer), to billions for private medical interests, to billions for defense industries, the stream of social surplus funneled into private profits runs forward in ever new and expanding channels. Social spending for medicine, housing, education, legal services, mass transit, recreation, conservation and recreation, income support, food distribution, and urban rebuilding are fought against and undermined by corporate power—unless there is a way to squeeze profits out of any such programs.

Michael Harrington poses the above issue directly by saying that corporate capitalism "must reconcile increased federal planning and spending with the persistence of private power. It socializes, but only on behalf

---

[46] Thorstein Veblen, *Absentee Ownership and Business Enterprise in Recent Times* (New York: The Viking Press, 1938; 1923), p. 118; and *The Vested Interests and the Common Man* (New York: The Viking Press, 1946, 1919).

[47] Ernest Mandel, *Marxist Economic Theory*, vol. 2 (New York: Monthly Review Press, 1968), p. 502.

of part of the society. Its methods are incipiently non-, or even anti-, capitalist; its purposes are impeccably pro-capitalist."[48] Thus we see the truth in the adage "Socialism for the rich, capitalism for the poor."

The intensity of interest that the corporate elite must have in government spending may be more fully grasped when we note that federal expenditures on a cash basis equal about one fourth of the total national income, meaning the federal government has spent about $240 billion annually ($39 billion more than it collected in 1972). To this may be added $150 billion at state and local levels (1970). Since 1950, government purchases have increased twice as much as private purchases (205 percent and 112 percent, respectively).[49] And over one fourth of the labor force depends directly or indirectly upon state payrolls and contracts. In an effort to shore up sagging prospects for 1974, the Nixon administration set forth a budget proposal of over $300 billion.

With the burden of taxation already great for most people the government (all levels) had piled up $514 billion in debt by 1970. In accordance with expectations, the interest on this debt flows mainly into the hands of the ruling class (who hold most of the securities) and is paid for by the working class (who pay taxes to pay the interest). To the extent that the state is dominated by the rich, they are borrowing from themselves and charging the rest of the population interest.

What all this adds up to is very much what Marxist theory predicts: the capitalist drive for surplus value creating gross imbalances in social as opposed to narrow class uses of resources, concentration of capital and lowered aggregate demand, unemployment, and the use of the state by the capitalist class to preserve high profits and the status quo. Throughout all levels of government, wherever important economic decisions, or political decisions having economic consequences are made, we find members of the corporate elite or representatives of their interests making the key decisions. In James O'Connor's words, "The state is the economic instrument of the dominant stratum of the ruling class—the owners and controllers of the large corporations, who have organized themselves along both interest group and class lines."[50] The result is a government-subsidized private-profit system.[51]

There is a pervasive belief that the federal government is too big and too powerful. That government is big and getting bigger is completely beyond dispute. Whether or not it is too big probably depends on whether government is supportive or oppressive from any given individual or group standpoint. Government must certainly seem too big to Pine Ridge, South Dakota, Indians when they look around and see a ratio of one civil servant to every Indian on their reservation, while government probably seems too small to the directors and officers of Lockheed. As far

---

[48] "Anatomy of Nixonism," *Dissent,* XIX (Fall 1972), p. 577.

[49] James O'Connor, "The Fiscal Crises of the State: Part I," *Socialist Revolution,* 1 (January–February, 1970), pp. 27–30.

[50] O'Connor, "The Fiscal Crises of the State: Part I," p. 18.

[51] H.L. Nieburg, "The Contract State: Government in the Economy," *Dissent,* 13 (September–October 1966), p. 528.

as government being too powerful is concerned, Peter Drucker has provided us with a plausible answer when he wrote that "There is mounting evidence that government is big rather than strong; that it is fat and flabby rather than powerful; that it costs a great deal but does not achieve much."[52] The only qualification to add to Drucker's assessment is that, while government costs the ordinary taxpayer a great deal and doesn't benefit him much, the government costs the large corporations relatively little and benefits *them* a great deal. Government is effective at only two things, contends Drucker, waging war and inflating the currency—both of which work great hardships on the working classes.

THE MILITARY-INDUSTRIAL COMPLEX

On the evening of January 17, 1961, President Dwight D. Eisenhower appeared before the American people to make his farewell address, in which he warned against the unwarranted influence of the military-industrial complex. Said Eisenhower, "In the councils of Government, we must guard against the acquisition of unwarranted influence, whether sought or unsought, by the military-industrial complex. The potential for the disastrous rise of misplaced power exists and will persist." Before Eisenhower's farewell address there was Mills's *The Power Elite,* in which he wrote, "In so far as the structural clue to the power elite today lies in the economic order, that clue is the fact that the economy is at once a permanent-war economy and a private-corporation economy. American capitalism is now in considerable part a military capitalism."[53] Mills later wrote *The Causes of World War Three,* in which he more fully elaborated the nature of the permanent-war economy.

The U.S. military establishment is far and away the largest single organization the world has ever seen. Since 1945, the U.S. has spent over $1.3 trillion on military operations—a sum exceeding in value all of the commercial and residential structures in place in the U.S.[54] The Department of Defense holds property around the globe valued at $215 billion. It recently employed approximately four million persons, military and civilian (one million), almost three-fourths of total federal employment. Department of Defense spending directly accounts for approximately ten percent of all employment, but the multiplier effect easily doubles this figure.[55] As Yarmolinsky has pointed out, "While it seems possible to define and measure the population of the military establish-

---

[52] Peter Drucker, "The Sickness of Government," *The Public Interest,* 14 (Winter 1969), p. 3.

[53] Mills, *The Power Elite,* pp. 275–76.

[54] See the studies by Seymour Melman, *Our Depleted Society* (New York: Holt, Rinehart, and Winston, 1965); and *Pentagon Capitalism* (New York: McGraw-Hill, 1971); See also current data from *The American Almanac,* 1973, p. 255.

[55] See Jeffrey M. Schevitz, "The Militarized Society and the Weapons-Maker," *Sociological Inquiry,* 40 (Winter 1970), pp. 49–58.

ment, the fact is that the list of persons ultimately connected with the military is almost infinitely extensible."[56]

The annual Department of Defense military bill rose sharply during the 1960s, almost doubling from the end of Eisenhower's term to over $81 billion in 1969. Vietnam spending increased from a few hundred million dollars in 1965 to almost $2 billion *a month* in 1968; by 1972 this war was still costing $20 billion. The immediate costs of Vietnam are in all likelihood around $150 billion, and the long-range costs are officially projected at $352 billion (this estimate will quite clearly be far over-run). We may add up overall annual military-related costs as follows for the years of the early 1970s: Department of Defense $80 billion (proposed to reach $87 billion by 1975), veterans outlays $11 billion, interest on militarily incurred debt $21 billion (all debt is essentially military-produced), atomic energy and space almost $6 billion, and $1 billion military assistance (Senator Proxmire estimates the "international affairs" bill to be about $10 billion, the bulk of which is military-related). Between 1950 and 1970, $35 billion was officially dispensed in military aid, excluding Vietnam since 1964. Conservatively put, the federal government has been in dollar terms one-half committed to military spending. U.S. per capita military spending is easily the world's largest. For every dollar of gross domestic fixed investment, the U.S. spends 53 cents on military expenditure compared with 14 cents for Germany and two cents for Japan. It was no surprise that these nations had by 1970 pulled ahead in the area of international consumer trade.

Let us look for a moment at the heart of the military bill, the 80-billion-dollar budget of the Department of Defense. During the past few years, slightly over half of Defense Department money went for the purchase of weapons and other military hardware, the rest for the support of personnel, the operation of bases, military construction, and civil defense.[57] The big corporations are, of course, interested in the entire $80 billion, but their main interest lies with weapons development and military hardware. It is in these latter areas where war industry realizes the largest part of its annual multibillion-dollar profits. The actual extent of war profiteering is unknown to the public for many years after their money has been spent. Not until December 1968 was the issue of "excessive profits" in the big defense industries finally arbitrated for the Korean War.[58] (Boeing Company was found to have amassed $41 million in "excessive" profits during the Korean War alone.)

Where do the billions go? How is it even possible for one organization to spend consistently $80 billion or so a year? Actually it's quite easy. Take sophisticated weapons programs, for example: $6.3 billion for the F–111 fighter-bombers (reportedly shot down by rifle fire in Vietnam),

[56] Adam Yarmolinsky, *The Military Establishment* (New York: Harper & Row, 1971), p. 15.

[57] Richard F. Kaufman, "Pentagon Procurement: Billion-Dollar Grab Bag," *The Nation*, March 17, 1969, p. 328.

[58] Sanford Watzman, "War Profits: The Tax-Court Peephole," *The Nation*, January 27, 1969, p. 113.

$5.4 billion for Minuteman III missiles, $3.8 billion for MK–48 torpedoes, $4.2 billion for antisubmarine defense destroyers, $9.4 billion for B–1 bombers, $7.4 billion for F–15 fighters, $2.1 billion for the airborne warning system, $4.8 billion for nuclear frigates, and $1.7 billion for Sparrow air-to-air missiles.[59]

Significantly, the majority of defense contracts are made without competitive bidding. Nor is there any guarantee that the government will receive the weapons, let alone at the original contracted cost. By the time of delivery, if ever, original estimates may easily double. Lockheed, for example, had delivered by early 1970 only a few of the 81 C–5A transport planes contracted for with the Air Force and had already exhausted the program's funds (the delivered planes have faulty wing structures, to boot). A Pentagon official who made the disclosure of the multibillion-dollar cost overrun on the C–5A was subsequently fired! (He has since been rehired!) More recently the example of Litton's cost overrun on *each* (nine originally ordered, now five) landing helicopter assault ships (LHA) from $133 million to $237 million and possibly nearly $300 million may be cited as an illustration.[60] More frightening, however, than any of the above programs is the fact that there are evidently some 40,000 *nuclear* bombs stored or deployed in the territorial United States alone.

The social cost of military spending is mammoth, for each military dollar spent is also a dollar *lost* to the civilian economy. Seymour Melman calculates that one polaris submarine cost the country the equivalent of 331 elementary schools, or 6,811 hospital beds, or 13,723 low rent housing units. For one TFX airplane the cost has been 13 schools, 278 hospital beds, and 579 dwelling units. But the ruling class cannot afford such social luxuries; the ruling class requires social insecurity and scarcity, and by the same token, profit. As Veblen long ago pointed out to us, "The great business interests are the more inclined to look kindly on an extension of warlike enterprise and armaments, since the pecuniary advantages inure to them, while the pecuniary burden falls chiefly on the rest of the community."[61]

ROOTS OF THE WARFARE STATE

How has it been possible to transform America from a nation entirely suspicious and averse to militarism to one that spends tens of billions annually on a far-flung military force and a massive defense establishment? Does the responsibility rest with foreign enemies? With generals and admirals? With politicians? With big businessmen? With economic necessity? Let's review some facts before we attempt to make a decision

---

[59] "New Nuclear Strategy for America?" *U.S. News and World Report,* April 13, 1970, p. 34.

[60] See Rep. Les Aspin, "Another Pentagon Bailout: The Litton Ship Fiasco," *The Nation,* December 11, 1972, pp. 581–84; and Aspin, "The Case Against Roy Ash," *The Nation,* February 26, 1973, pp. 264–68.

[61] Veblen, *The Theory of Business Enterprise* (New York: Augustus M. Kelley, 1965, 1904), pp. 285–87.

concerning the roots and impetus of the military-industrial complex. Between World Wars I and II, the United States maintained only a small standing military force and spent a negligible portion of the national income for military purposes. All of this changed radically with the onset of World War II. During that war, some $175 billion in prime military supply contracts was issued to private industry. The magnitude of military spending and the military pressures on manpower wiped out depression and massive unemployment, something that the New Deal never even came close to doing. With the end of the war, the economy was apparently eager to convert to peacetime consumption, as it had been following World War I. Demobilization began, and military spending was cut back sharply.

However, the professional military maintained a massive propaganda effort following the war. In 1946, the army was the nation's third largest advertiser.[62] The use of radio, film, public performances, and television by military propagandists continued unabated through the fifties and was greatly accelerated during the Kennedy and Johnson administrations. By 1969, the cost to the taxpayer for military advertising was conservatively estimated at $28 million.[63] But pamphlets, movies, bands, and marching music are not enough to inspire popular acceptance of militarism. An enemy is needed. The ideological enemies were communism and socialism, and the specific enemies were the Soviet Union, China, and any national liberation movement in the world, the latter by definition linked to Moscow or Peking. The efforts of the professional military to preserve their vested interests in a military establishment could not alone have been a sufficient cause in the genesis of American militarism after World War II. Both high-ranking military officers and members of the political elite entered into what was defined as veritably a struggle to the death with international socialism, and the Congress and the people followed. The level of anticommunist propaganda was so intense that the large majority of the American people felt themselves personally threatened and hence approved of the expansion of a permanent military establishment. Congress appropriated billions for European reconstruction and the beginning of the cold war.

Yet, popular approval only gave a facade of democratic actions to what would have eventually developed, irrespective of grass-roots support. The international enemies, communism and socialism, if not threatening to physically and militarily invade the United States, were and increasingly are seen by the economic rulers of capitalism as intolerable threats to their world expansion and dominance. Thus, the giant corporations, with their mounting surpluses, profits, and need for raw materials and markets, held a massive interest in the preservation of the political and social status quo throughout the noncommunist world. The military machine and military aid to other countries (as Baran and Sweezy point

---

[62] See Fred J. Cook, *The Warfare State* (New York: Collier Books, 1964), p. 107. This volume is a classic in its field.

[63] See Derek Shearer, "The Brass Image," *The Nation*, April 20, 1970, pp. 455–64, for a summary of current military propaganda.

out with respect to revolutionary movements throughout the world, "no regime is too reactionary to merit all-out United States backing"),[64] attempt to meet this interest.

The emergence of a permanent war economy was very much in evidence after the Korean War. The Korean War had been fought to save Asia from communism, but it also served to reduce the rising levels of unemployment of the late forties and portended prosperity for American industry. The logic that came to underlie the military-industrial complex began to harden: anticommunism would help sustain popular support of the professional military establishment, justify the expenditure of tens of billions of dollars on employment-stimulating and profit-producing weapons research and procurement, and permit American military intervention any place in the world to protect capitalist interests. From the standpoint of the professional military, the cold war clearly catered to its vested interests; demobilization and disarmament were no longer even mild threats. No less pleased were the bourgeois economists and government officials who could imagine no other means of maintaining employment and "economic growth." The sagging economy of the late fifties was primed by Kennedy (the missile-gap politician) and then Johnson (the no-wider-war politician) with aerospace spending and, finally, another war.

The defense industries, too, became very comfortable with cold and hot wars, whether they involved the United States or other belligerents in any of the 55 big and little wars that have been waged since 1945. The arms companies profit immensely not only from Pentagon orders but also from sales to other governments fighting communism or each other.[65] Assisting in the sales of arms both at home and abroad are over 2,000 retired military officers of the rank of colonel or navy captain or higher, working for war industries such as General Dynamics, Lockheed Aircraft, Boeing Co., McDonnell Douglas, North American–Rockwell, and Ling-Temco-Vought. In addition to their lucrative salaries, the ex-officers receive a five percent commission on all the arms they can sell to foreign governments. In this connection, a private multi-billion dollar arms deal was recently concluded with Iran. Profits are running so high that American arms manufacturers are buying out the big European arms firms. Finally, the American scientific and engineering professions, almost one third of which are performing defense-related work, have grown occupationally dependent on the military-industrial complex. The large majority of the technical *elite*, the top brains, is associated with war-defense industries.

Where, then, does the responsibility for the military-industrial complex ultimately reside? With the political directorate? After all, wasn't it Secretary of Defense Robert McNamara who said in 1966, "Let me assure you that our strategic forces are sufficient to insure the destruction of both the Soviet Union and Communist China, under the worst imagin-

---

[64] Baran and Sweezy, *Monopoly Capital,* p. 201.

[65] See George Thayer, *The War Business* (New York: Simon and Schuster, Inc., 1969). As just one illustration, Thayer points out that the Pakistan-Indian War of 1965 was fought largely with American weapons such as Sherman and Patton tanks. A repeat performance took place in 1971.

able circumstances?"[66] Were not L. Mendel Rivers of South Carolina and Richard Russell of Georgia, when chairmen of the House and Senate Armed Services committees, warhawks interested in billion-dollar bonanzas for military industries and operations in their home states? Has not each president since Kennedy continually uttered statements about this country becoming a "second-rate power"? Certainly it must be the politicians who are responsible.[67]

But then there are the professional military with their vested interests and bombardment of anticommunist and chauvinist propaganda. Was it not General Thomas S. Power who wrote, "The Soviet leadership is irrevocably committed to the achievement of the ultimate Communist objective, which is annihilation of the capitalist system and establishment of Communist dictatorship over all nations of the world"?[68] And General Nathan F. Twining who said, "Red China under its present leadership seems to me . . . to be practically a hopeless case. Naked force seems to be the only logic which the leadership of that unfortunate nation can comprehend"?[69] And General Curtis E. LeMay who sanguinely declared that ". . . I sincerely believe any arms race with the Soviet Union would act to our benefit"?[70]

Or perhaps big businessmen are the promoters of the permanent war economy. Two-thirds of the top one hundred corporations are significantly involved in the military market.[71] A General Motors official, whose company's Allison Division makes jet engines and Hydramatic Division makes M–16A rifles, once commented that "We want to be known as a car and appliance manufacturer, not a merchant of war. But we also want to be ready to profit from the apparently endless series of brushfire wars in which the U.S. seems to involve itself."[72] Or as a vice president for the defense industry of Ling-Temco-Vought once remarked, "We're going to increase defense budgets as long as those bastards in Russia are ahead of us."[73] Isn't it the corporations who every year realize billions in profit from defense spending and entice the Pentagon with fancy new weapons? We have already noted that a top government official recently complained that "The Defense Department has been led down the garden path [by big business] for years on sophisticated systems. . . ." The corporate economy has been "plagued" with surplus profits. What better way is there of safely consuming and expanding them than militarily?

Maybe the American worker has been the culprit? In 1959, aircraft-

---

[66] For an elaboration of the thesis that the Department of Defense stands as the impetus and power center of the military-industrial complex, see Melman, *Pentagon Capitalism*. Quotation from Stuart Chase, *The Most Probable World* (Baltimore: Penguin Books, Inc., 1968), p. 152.

[67] See Michael T. Klare's important study, *War Without End* (New York: Vintage Books, 1972).

[68] Galbraith, *How to Control the Military*, p. 88.

[69] Ibid., pp. 90–91.

[70] Ibid., p. 95.

[71] See Michael Reich and David Finkelhor, "Capitalism and the Military-Industrial Complex," in Edwards, *The Capitalist System*, pp. 392–406.

[72] Thayer, *The War Business*, p. 295.

[73] Galbraith, *How To Control the Military*, p. 32.

missile production accounted for at least 82 percent of San Diego's manufacturing jobs, 72 percent of Wichita's, and 53 percent of Seattle's. Important states such as California, Washington, and Connecticut have found that one quarter of all manufacturing jobs are accounted for by defense contracts. The economic viability of Los Angeles seems utterly dependent on the continuation of the arms race. Millions of workers all over the country, over one quarter of all scientists and engineers, owe their livelihoods to the military-industrial complex. Blue-collar jobs markedly declined between the end of the Korean War and the beginning of the Vietnam escalation, and then sharply increased. And certainly organized labor has tended to support Vietnam policy, at least most union leaders and a portion of the rank and file.

Or isn't it after all the belligerence and aggression of the Soviet Union and Communist China since 1945 that has necessitated the mounting billions for defense? Has not the U.S.S.R. maintained a large military establishment? Has not China over the years been unrelenting in its bellicose and anti-U.S. propaganda? Have not they, too, been preparing for war? While these questions must certainly be raised as precipitating forces in the military-industrial complex, neither the Soviet Union nor China is so utterly dependent upon military and military-related spending for national economic purposes as is the United States. Moreover, they have no international corporations whose interests must be guarded in the face of national revolutionary movements. Finally, when these countries lay war-torn and greatly weakened, the U.S. under Truman was pursuing a militarily aggressive policy in both Europe and Asia.

What do students of power conclude about the wellsprings of the military-industrial complex. Gabriel Kolko is convinced that "The 'military-industrial complex' that exists in the United States is a lopsided phenomenon in which only businessmen maintain their full identity, interest, and commitment to their institution, while the military conforms to the needs of economic interests."[74] John Kenneth Galbraith believes the prime wielders of power within the military-industrial complex are not the businessmen but rather the military and civilian military consisting of the Department of Defense, the armed services, defense scientists and organizations such as RAND, and the Armed Services committees of Congress.[75] However, Galbraith would include under military power the specialized defense contractors such as General Dynamics, McDonnell Douglas, Lockheed, and the defense divisions of diversified corporations such as General Electric and AT & T. Melman focuses upon the Pentagon.

Although Galbraith states that the military is decisive, his inclusion of civilian officials, politicians, and defense contractors brings him very close to the original statement concerning the distribution of power within the military-industrial complex by C. Wright Mills. Mills's view of the military-industrial complex, or the permanent-war economy as he called it, was incorporated into his theory of the power elite. Thus, Mills

---

[74] *The Roots of American Foreign Policy* (Boston: Beacon Press, 1969), p. 31.

[75] Galbraith, *How to Control the Military*, pp. 27–30.

argued that there is, in fact, no operational distinction between the basic interests of military capitalists, military politicians, and military brass. While their priorities may vary slightly from wealth to power to prestige, defense contractors, government officials, and top brass are interested in all of these. But more important, the businessmen, political directorate, and military elite who are tied into the permanent-war economy need one another, their activities being complementary. Mills writes: "In so far as the corporate elite are aware of their profit interests . . . they press for a continuation of their sources of profit, which often means a continuation of the preparation for war. [However,] I am *not* suggesting that military power is only, or even mainly, an instrument of economic policy. To a considerable extent, militarism has become an end in itself and economic policy a means of it."[76] Yet, "A real attack on war-thinking by Americans today is necessarily an attack upon the private incorporation of the economy."[77] Beyond this, Mills would probably agree with Baran and Sweezy that "the need of the American oligarchy for a large and growing military machine is a logical corollary of its purpose to contain, compress, and eventually destroy the rival world socialist system."[78]

The locus of power in the military-industrial complex is the same as where all prevailing power lies in our society: in the ruling class, and the ruling class prevails over *both* government bureaucracy and defense industry. State and corporation are twin facets of ruling class power. The point is moot as to whether one facet is more powerful than the other.

In summary, we might think of the roots of the military-industrial complex in this way: It arose originally to meet the production exigencies of World War II, but began to be dismantled in its immediate aftermath. However, under the influence of formidable military propaganda, the political policy of containment of revolutionary communism and nationalism, and the international status quo interests of expanding capitalism, the logic of the military-industrial complex took shape in the late forties and received considerable definition through the Korean War. Big businessmen, recalling wartime profits, witnessing periodic slumps in civilian production, and facing rising surpluses, developed a dependence upon military spending for prosperity, and defense industry pressed its wares on open-minded politicial officials and military brass. The political elite, too, had discovered a means to sustain economic growth, fairly high levels of employment, and prosperity, while containing socialism and protecting the economic needs of the large foreign investors. The scientific estate had also been nourished through defense spending and consequently became largely dependent upon its continuance. As the epitome of the arms race, and in conjunction with the rise of a military-dependent science and technology, the space race has contributed greatly

---

[76] C. Wright Mills, *The Causes of World War Three* (New York: Simon and Schuster, 1958; published in Ballantine edition in 1960), p. 67.

[77] Ibid., pp. 137–39.

[78] Baran and Sweezy, *Monopoly Capitalism*, p. 190. This does not preclude the possibility of engaging in advantageous or profitable economic ventures in relation to state-planned economies, such as trade deals or certain investments. This latter, complicated development cannot concern us further here.

to the existence of a permanent war economy. Vietnam has been the capstone and logical outcome of political and economic policies pursued during the rise of the military-industrial complex. Instead of this tragic war being a lesson to socialist revolutionaries of the Third World, perhaps it will instead be a lesson to America's counter-revolutionaries of the futility and self-destructive logic of the military-industrial complex. However, there is no assurance that the message will come through, or be acknowledged, in the higher circles.

In seeking a solution, it is doubtful that the people can look to the professional military (though we are aware of sharp criticisms from *retired* generals) or the arms merchants of the corporate world. Perhaps the large corporations without vested interests in war business can press for socially useful production. Perhaps peace-oriented politicians can succeed in forcing a measure of restraint on military dissipation. Men such as Senators McGovern, Church, Mansfield, Fulbright, Hatfield and Proxmire (who learned from a questionnaire received from 12,500 of his Wisconsin constituents that two thirds favored a scaling down of the proposed $74 billion defense budget for fiscal 1971) have already played major roles in bringing pressure to bear on the reduction of military spending. To a large extent, such politicians are translating mounting public dissatisfaction with military waste and war. A 1970 Gallup poll revealed that half of the people queried desired a definite reduction in military appropriations and only one person in ten an increase. In the not too long run, democracy and militarism are incompatible. As Senator Fulbright has argued, "War and conditions of war are incompatible and inconsistent with our system of democracy. Our democratic system is bound to be eroded, and an authoritarian system is bound to take its place. We are in that process now."[79]

TECHNOLOGY AND MILITARISM

"The key to understanding the oppressive class structures now developing in American society," writes John McDermott, "is found less in the maldistribution of the nation's property than in the maldistribution of its knowledge."[80] Among the central themes of Galbraith's book *The New Industrial State* is that power goes to that sector of society commanding the scarce resources. In the 19th century the major source of power was land; in advancing capitalist society, it was financial capital, and in advanced technological society, it is scientific knowledge and technical expertise.[81] Thus, as candidates for inclusion within the power elite some scholars would include the scientific estate.[82]

---

[79] Sen. J. William Fulbright, "The Senate Surrenders," *The Progressive*, January 1973, pp. 30–31.

[80] John McDermott, "Overclass/Underclass: Knowledge Is Power," *The Nation*, April 14, 1969, p. 458.

[81] Galbraith, *The New Industrial State*, especially Chapter 25, "The Educational and Scientific Estate."

[82] See Don K. Price, *The Scientific Estate* (New York: Oxford University Press, 1968).

Conducting sophisticated scientific research requires money, a lot of money. Where does the money come from? The major investor in research and development in science and technology is the federal government—that is, the taxpayer. Upwards of $16 billion a year is spent by government for research and development (R & D).[83] The second biggest R & D spender is private industry, investing about $8 billion annually. Foundations and universities also budget original funds for research, but in very small quantities compared to government and industry. The major role played by universities is the R & D itself, rather than funding. Of the some $25 billion annually spent for R & D only about 15 percent of it goes for basic research. That 85 percent of R & D funds go into development and application should provide us with preliminary hints concerning the largely *military* orientation of sophisticated American technology and scientific research.

Now that we know where the money for R & D comes from we must learn where it goes. Into solving transportation, housing, environmental, and health problems? Some research funds are diverted into these areas of human need, but relatively little. Over four fifths of the federal R & D $16 billion go into military and semi-military agencies, one-half to the Department of Defense, and one-third to space and atomic energy, with space easily coming out on top over atomic energy. In ten years, almost $100 billion has been spent on strictly Defense Department military R & D. Private industry, of course, invests in the development of its own products for civilian use, but much private research is conducted with the ultimate aim of getting the inside track on the bigger federal pork barrel. And once taxpayers' money has been handed over to defense industry for R & D, the financial and technological gains that accrue to the firm rarely find their way back to the original "investors." In short, given the sum of money involved in technological research and development and the uses to which it is mostly put, we are able to see that the scientific estate is an integral component of the military-industrial complex. Since two-thirds of all scientists and engineers engaged in R & D work have been employed with federal funds, and most federal funds for R & D go into military or military-related projects, it is evident that the scientific estate is deeply rooted in the militarism of American society.[84] The concentration of both funds and scientists in military R & D has had the effect of depriving other areas of research that promise a greater human payoff. Although the massive funds and high salaries that have accompanied military research have served to attract much of the nation's best scientific talent into this area, many younger scientists and graduate students are growing increasingly reluctant to enter into militarily related R & D.

What are the agencies or institutions that conduct this largely military-related R & D? First and foremost, there are the big defense and space contractors such as General Dynamics and General Electric; for example, several corporations have spent annually more than a billion each in

---

[83] *The American Almanac,* 1973, pp. 522; 250.
[84] See Klare, *War Without End,* pp. 69–87.

federal tax money. As one might expect in today's lopsided economy, federal R & D funds to business are highly concentrated within a mere handful of giant corporations. Secondly, there are the government facilities run by industrial contractors such as Oak Ridge by Union Carbide and Cape Kennedy by Pan American Airlines. Thirdly, there are the private military research agencies ("think tanks") such as RAND Corporation, Aerospace Corporation, and Systems Development, all heavily oriented toward missile and space programs but not averse to coming down to the study of such earthly things as counterinsurgency warfare. While operating budgets of such think tanks are small compared to the big defense contractors, they may run well over $50 million and tend to attract the scientific elite with the offer of top salaries and prestige (civil service pay grades are, of course, bypassed in the "private" military research agency).

Finally, we have the university-based R & D laboratories such as Johns Hopkins' Applied Physics Laboratory, M.I.T.'s Lincoln Laboratory (recently severed administratively), and Stanford's Research Institute (also now administratively separate). (Student activism has achieved formal administrative changes in university-related military research but the funds, the men, and the work go on just the same.) While university sums are smaller than the R & D allocations to the defense industries, federal funds compose about 70 percent of university research funds and the bulk of certain schools' entire budgets. Single laboratory budgets have counted well over $50 million in federal funds. And again, concentration is the rule as 15 universities account for two fifths ($500 million in 1967) of the federal R & D funds and 100 for nine tenths ($1,166 million).[85] These facts suggest that the educational atmosphere of the nation's most prestigious schools is permeated by military research with all of its ramifications on the nature and type of scientific learning that is available to students. Also within the realm of university operation of government-contracted research are brain-trust installations such as Brookhaven National Laboratory, Argonne National Laboratory, Lawrence Radiation Laboratory, and Los Alamos Scientific Laboratory, combining resources from a number of individual universities in the administration and research process. The latter two organizations, operated by the University of California, counted almost 12,000 employees and a budget of $288 million in 1968.

For top university scientists, federal money, typically from the Department of Defense, is a way of life. For example, government support of university professors doing experiments in high-energy physics recently averaged around $160,000 per year per professor. Instances such as this led Spencer Klaw to comment that the symbol of the new educational order is the academic entrepreneur adept at thinking up big and expensive research projects and persuading government to pay for them.[86] (Government has, in fact, been even more active in inducing university

[85] See James Ridgeway, *The Closed Corporation* (New York: Ballantine Books, 1968), for a critique of university involvement in the military-industrial complex.

[86] Spencer Klaw, *The New Brahmins: Scientific Life in America* (New York: William Morrow Company, Inc., 1969), p. 53; 107.

talent to perform for it.) From developments and techniques created with federal funds in their laboratories, university scientists have set up "spin-off" companies that market mainly defense-oriented products. Large universities, contends James Ridgeway, have been reduced to serving as banker-brokers for the professors' outside interests.[87] Entering the problem-solving and counterinsurgency business on quite a large scale, social scientists, too, see the Department of Defense, Central Intelligence Agency, and other government departments as important sources for research funds and previously unknown feelings of power and prestige.

In the final analysis, all scientists and engineers employed in defense are, of course, university trained, and most maintain close ties with universities, either directly or through periodic university-based or university-operated research. University scientists, in turn, advise and consult for defense agencies and industries. Moreover, many important universities are interlocked with defense agencies and contractors through mutual trustees and directors. As is the case with other elites, the scientific and educational elite cannot be clearly separated out as an autonomous interest group, for they are as enmeshed in government, military, and corporate interests as the latter three are with one another. Each needs the other to accomplish its own ends, and the existing system of cooperation seems to be serving all of the military-industrial-scientific elites quite well.

Are the scientists and technicians, then, full-fledged members of the power elite? While entirely acknowledging the indispensability of the scientific estate to the viability of the military-industrial complex, indispensability is not always a criterion for power. In the case of the American technical elite, whether they be military or civilian, scientific or "social experts," it would be erroneous to assign to them anything more than instrumental and advisory power. They are, in Mills's language, hired technicians.[88] If scientists and engineers had as attractive economic opportunities and employment in the civilian and consumer-oriented economy as they now have in the military-industrial complex, we cannot be certain as to how many would be willing to leave the world of sophisticated military and space technology to work on more mundane things (probably most). But one thing is certain, the technological elite goes where the funds are; they have relatively little to say about what general sector of society R & D funds will be used to support. The technological elite would seem to have a long economic and political route to travel before they are to become much more than advisers and handymen of the corporate and political elite.[89]

WASTE AND SABOTAGE

Strategies for profitable investment of surplus wealth lead in other directions than subsidy and militarism. Veblen laid emphasis upon the "sabotage" of the industrial system, a conscious mode of waste, which

---

[87] Ridgeway, *The Closed Corporation*, p. 193.

[88] Mills, *The Causes of World War Three*, p. 144.

[89] See Noam Chomsky, *American Power and the New Mandarins* (New York: Pantheon Books, Inc., 1969), pp. 323–33.

seeks only profitable ends at the cost of constructive application and use of resources. He suggested that the industrial plant of his day could be utilized with at least three times greater effectiveness in the production and distribution of needed goods and services. Veblen's critique of specious and redundant waste has since become a wave of contemporary popular criticism, especially with respect to the ecological crisis—a logical outcome of waste and sabotage.

Many avenues of waste and sabotage have been utilized by the Vested Interests. Twenty billion dollars are spent each year in bombarding the consumer with advertising, television being the major medium of persuasion. In Harrington's words, "It takes money and ingenuity to convince people to invest in luxuries they do not need and to ignore their necessities."[90] Advertising has become an end in itself, an "industry" supporting a large number of surplus workers. Related to advertising is the cornucopia of brands, labels, outlets, packaging techniques, etc., which contribute to superfluous consumption of value and are intended to increase unnecessary consumption. The cost of duplication is enormous.

Running through the ethos of advanced capitalist society is the belief that increased production and consumption (almost any kind of production or consumption) are themselves nearly absolute and sacred goals. The people are even led to believe that they have almost a moral responsibility to consume, irrespective of whether a need exists. The duty of the consumer has been unambiguously spelled out by Schon: ". . . consumers have a responsibility to accept novelty at the rate corporations produce it, in order to satisfy corporate demands for growth and market expansion."[91]

That profit rather than service is the real aim of the corporation may be suggested in one of many ways by the fact that, according to 1971 Federal Power Commission reports, the electric power companies spent over three times as much on advertising and sales promotion (almost one third billion dollars) than they did on research and development in the power field. Why people need to have electric power advertised and promoted at all is a curious question; the purpose of such advertising and promotion is to *convince* the public how lucky they are to be getting such great service at such low cost, which certainly does require a lot of persuasion.

The chief civilian strategy of the corporate system is to create psychic needs in the consumer for abundant goods and services, thus assuring that men will dutifully work within the system to obtain purchasing power and spend all that they earn. The grander goal of the big merchants is to persuade men to spend *more* money than they actually have (but promise to earn), a virtual guarantee of unswerving commitment to corporate goals.[92] In effect, a person literally cannot afford to con-

---

[90] Michael Harrington, *The Accidental Century* (Baltimore: Penguin Books, Inc., 1966), p. 104.

[91] Donald A. Schon, *Technology and Change* (New York: Delta Books, 1967), p. 44.

[92] Galbraith, *The New Industrial State*, pp. 280–81.

template the pursuit of nonconsumption goals in life. Yet, there is considerable time for leisure. Thus, profit interests must orient production to leisure consumption as well as to other aspects of life. To enjoy their leisure time, Americans spent (including such things as TV sets, newspapers, and sports supplies) over $40 billion in 1970. This is *in addition to* the massive sums spent on new and used cars, gasoline and oil, alcohol, and tobacco. Not all of these expenditures can be chalked up to leisure (such as necessary transportation costs), but a significant proportion certainly can. In brief, Americans have been led to believe that fun and leisure must be purchased, and that it necessarily comes at a high price. The relationship between consumption and leisure use is much greater in the United States than elsewhere in the world, owing to our belief in both the relationship and the means of realizing it.[93]

In leisure consumption as in every other type of personal consumption, a primate strategy of the corporate system is to render its products obsolete as soon as possible. Obsolescence through the actual improvement of products may have some justification. But what late-model American automobile is superior to and more durable than any number of makes in the 1940s? In most cases, obsolescence involves poor quality (the product breaks down and must be replaced or repaired) or style (the product is defined as outmoded).[94] The consumer has paid a high price for style obsolescence. For example, by sticking to its basic design, Ford reduced the cost of some of its early models by half but subsequently lost the lead to style-changing General Motors and so joined the fashion parade. The model changeover in Detroit now costs the consumer an average of $700 for each new car he buys. The built-in and style obsolescence of automobiles has created a monumental disposal and environmental problem, not to mention the waste of materials and capital. But as ex-General Motors chief James M. Roche has declared, "Planned obsolescence, in my opinion, is another word for progress."[95] And progress it has been for GM, $22 billion profits worth from 1947 to 1969 and $2 billion in 1971 (among the costs to the public were 55,000 killed in car crashes that year and millions injured).

Or take the style consciousness and waste of AT & T with the Bell invention. A Bell System advertisement reads:

> Will the plain black phone ever stage a comeback? NEVER. This is not to say that the plain black phone doesn't work as well as its newer, brighter cousins. It's just that people want more telephone variety for their money: phones that dial automatically, phones that hang *on* the wall, phones that fit *in* the wall, phones with a dial in the receiver, phones with buttons, phones that light up, phones in color . . . we could go on and on. And we do . . .

Have you ever wondered why your telephone bill is so much? Now you have part of your answer. American Telephone & Telegraph heads the

---

[93] See Paul Hollander, "Leisure as an American and Soviet Value," *Social Problems,* 14 (Fall 1966), pp. 179–88.

[94] See Vance Packard, *The Waste Makers* (New York: Pocket Books, 1963).

[95] Cited in Colman McCarthy, "The Faulty School Buses," *Saturday Review,* March 11, 1972.

top of the list in corporate profits, netting well over $2 billion annually.

Finally and tragically in view of widespread individual and social poverty, if consumers cannot be mesmerized and cajoled into consuming or when even high levels of consumption by those with money cannot maintain a level of demand high enough to assure sizable profits, the corporate system cuts back production and the supply of goods (some $60–$70 billion worth annually in the sixties). One fourth of existing capacity has stood idle for several years, not to mention the massive waste of human resources. Only then can demand for goods be kept near or preferably above the supply of goods, the necessary balance for corporate success. But cutting back production below capacity may also erode profit levels—unless prices are greatly inflated to compensate—just another of the contradictions giant corporations must deal with and the public must suffer with.

Production for use

Corporate capitalism produces for profit, and only secondarily for use. The consequences of elevating profit above use have been responsible for much of the waste and misallocation of resources in American society. Even the broader goal of economic growth cannot be assumed as a good in itself, asserts Theobald, but only insofar as it helps to solve the problems and increase the meaning of the life of each man, woman, and child. Unexamined economic growth creates more problems than it solves, and destroys meaning in life more than enhance it. As Marx once quipped "Too many useful things make too many useless people."

Profit and growth for their own sake are the leading contributors to domestic and foreign problems. In effect, the corporate system has turned people into a means, rather than allowing them to live their life as an end in itself. Economic necessity and outmoded assumptions are preserved at a time when social needs could be openly dealt with.

If homes, hospitals, and recreational facilities are needed—as they desperately are—the United States has the technical know-how, the material resources, and the manpower to build them. There is no logical reason to not do so simply because the profit calculations of private interests discourage investment in these areas or render their production prohibitively expensive. Must millions of Americans go without homes they need just because Japanese businessmen can render American businessmen higher profits for the country's timber? Must highly educated manpower be used up in the production of profitable but useless military gadgets when it could be applied to problems of mass transit or pollution? Production for use produces what is specifically needed and preserves what is not needed; it is not moved to action or inaction by the promise of profits.

THE POWER ELITE AND THE UPPER CLASS

One final question remains to be discussed concerning the American power structure. To what extent, if any, are members of the power elite and capitalist class members of a self-conscious social class? Before we attempt to answer that question, we might ask what difference it makes whether all or part of the power elite are members of a social class. As Marx pointed out, awareness of common interest, class consciousness, and organization are essential steps in the consolidation and perpetuation of power. Isolated individuals, each pursuing personal ends, regardless of whether or not they happen to be in similar objective circumstances, can never materialize into an effective social power. Given the fact of association, consciousness, and organization, the power of an objective class will be immeasurably strengthened. To the extent that members of the American power elite are also members of an upper class, their grip of power is strengthened.

Mills clearly states his agreement that members of the power elite form a national upper social class: "They [the power elite] form a more or less compact social and psychological entity; they have become self-conscious members of a social class. People are either accepted into this class or they are not, and there is a qualitative split, rather than merely a numerical scale, separating them from those who are not elite."[96] The extensive research by E. Digby Baltzell on the overlap between business-political elites, and on the upper social class as a group of families descended from elite individuals, lends support to Mills's view.[97]

However, Baltzell's concern with the power structure has not been with the concentration and misuse of power by the elite or upper class; in fact, as a traditional conservative, Baltzell argues that an aristocracy or upper class provides an autonomous power in society, serving as protection against totalitarian power. Instead of charging that the upper class has acted narrowly and irresponsibly, as does Mills, Baltzell will only go so far as to admit the upper class has been "possibly guilty of somewhat conservative and narrow conception of the duties and obligations of wealth."[98] Baltzell has evidently overlooked the possibility of an upper class itself becoming a monolithic elite of power. Rather than directing *economic* criticism at the upper class, Baltzell charges that the upper class has become *ethnically* unrepresentative of the people and, increasingly, of the various institutional elites. Instead of assimilating the families of new members of the elite into its social institutions, the white Anglo-Saxon Protestant upper class has chosen to preserve its ethnic integrity, threatening to degenerate into a closed caste. As institutional elites find less and less representation in the upper social class, the elite, contends Baltzell, must increasingly resort to coercion and manipulation as a means of rule as opposed to rule based on legitimate authority and respect, as with a representative upper class. (Baltzell must feel his arguments for rule by a hereditary aristocracy fully confirmed after the conduct of many *nouveau* elites within the Nixon administration.)

Mills, too, directed our attention to the white Anglo-Saxon Protestant composition of the ruling class. Whether a different ethnic composition

[96] Mills, *The Power Elite,* p. 11.

[97] E. Digby Baltzell, *An American Business Aristocracy* (New York: Collier Books, 1962), and *The Protestant Establishment* (New York: Random House, Inc., 1964).

[98] Baltzell, *An American Business Aristocracy,* p. 81.

of the elite or upper class would make by itself any real differences in the uses of power is doubtful. There are persons of all ethnic backgrounds who disagree radically with the policies of the ruling class and would institute changes if they could do so, while there are also people of all ethnic backgrounds who essentially agree with ruling-class policies and would perpetuate these policies as members of the elite. The crucial point is that *access* to the elite is controlled by incumbent members, and the recruitment process tends to produce almost mirror social and ideological images of the existing elite. The chances of a Jew, Mexican, or black of entering the upper class elite are poor, both from a purely statistical standpoint and an ideological one. Cultural and social differences would also weigh against members of these groups. White Catholics naturally might be expected to fare somewhat better, and they do.

A psychologist, G. William Domhoff, has taken the necessary step of empirically tying the upper social class to the decision-making elite.[99] Using such criteria for upper class membership as the *Social Register,* attendance at an exclusive private preparatory school, millionaire status, and membership in one or more leading metropolitan men's clubs (easily the most reliable and valid indicator of upper class membership, as well as the most important upper class social institution), Domhoff discovered that members of the national upper social class composed a majority of the directors of the top 20 industrials, top 15 banks, and top 15 insurance companies. The major group of non-upper class directors consisted of hired executives, whom Domhoff argues are in the process of being assimilated into the upper class and must share goals with members of the upper class. Domhoff also found upper class dominance and control or delegated control in foundations, prestigious universities, the Department of State, the Department of Defense, the Central Intelligence Agency, the diplomatic corps, the secretaries of the armed services, and the nomination of presidents. The upper class is, then, a ruling class.

But what of the military elite as such? What is their status vis-à-vis the upper class? Domhoff argues that, while the military brass themselves are not members of the upper social class, the military is subservient to upper class interests as expressed through the president, the Department of Defense, and other civilian military departments dominated by the upper class. More important, Domhoff found that *half of the directors of the leading defense contractors were members of the upper class.*[100] This is indeed a grim fact for those who see the potential for an ideological split between the largest civilian and military-oriented corporations. For the two sectors are not only interlocked through directors, management, and ownership, but they are interlaced with members of the upper class. Members of the national upper class, with the assistance of co-opted and mobile executives (who probably outnumber their upper class counterparts), both own and control the large civilian and defense corporations and shape major domestic and foreign policy.

---

[99] G. William Domhoff, *Who Rules America?* (Englewood Cliffs, N.J.: Prentice-Hall, Inc., 1967); and *The Higher Circles* (New York: Vintage Books, 1971).

[100] Ibid., p. 123.

Is power in American society, then, located within bureaucracy or within the upper class? Power is *located* within bureaucracy, but power is *held* by the upper or ruling class. The upper class holds the bulk of corporate wealth and thus controls, through both its own members and hired representatives, the vast manpower, communication and decision making, and financial resources of the corporate bureaucracy. And the corporate bureaucracy and the upper class are the chief suppliers of top elites in the political bureaucracy as well as in others such as the elite universities and major foundations. Analytically speaking, then, there are property-holding members of the upper class not *directly* involved in the power elite of bureaucracy, and there are power-holding members of bureaucracy who are not members of the upper class (though their children may well be so in the future). However, both of these groups are very much akin (sometimes literally), in both economic and social interest, to ruling members of the upper class (see the following diagram).

POWER ELITE AND UPPER CLASS

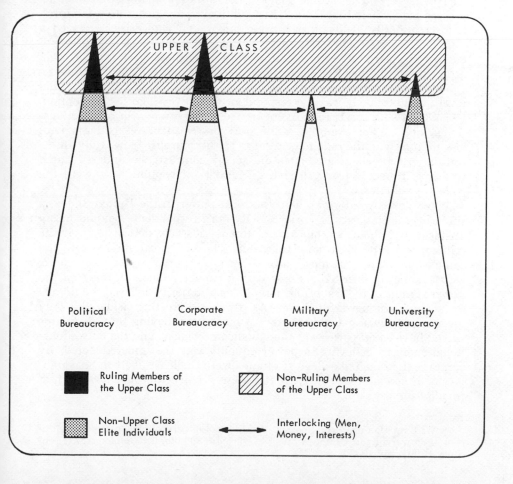

Popular views of the power structure

How much difference it makes what the people believe concerning the power structure is not certain; probably not much difference in the way power is actually used nationally and internationally by the ruling class. (A very sizable segment of the population believes the ordinary American is, in fact, powerless.) Be that as it may, it may be of interest to examine the findings of a study that asked residents of a Michigan industrial community how they perceived the distribution of political power in the United States. Form and Rytina queried their respondents as to whether they felt "no one group really runs the government of this country" ("pluralist" position), "a small group of men at the top really run the government of this country" ("Millsian" power elite position), or "big businessmen really run the government of this country" ("Marxist" position).[101] Overall, almost two-thirds held to the pluralist position, and about one fifth each to the Millsian and Marxist positions. Surprisingly, differences among respondents along income and racial lines were relatively minor regarding the majority agreement on pluralism, with the exception of *middle*-income blacks. Less than a majority of middle-income blacks held that the nation's political power structure was pluralistic; a majority of all other income and racial categories perceived a pluralist power structure. However, variations in the perception of political power distribution were found with regard to *level of education* attained; the higher the educational level the more likely was the respondent to report a pluralist perception, and the lower the educational level the more likely was the respondent to report a Marxist perception. (The Mills elite thesis found support from about one-fifth of all educational levels.) For example, while only one-third of respondents with less than an eighth-grade education held the pluralist view, fully three-fourths of the college graduates did so; by contrast, the undereducated were five times as likely to give a Marxist interpretation as were the college graduates.

When asked what *group* held the most power in the United States, a slight overall majority of Form and Rytina's respondents pointed to big business and about one quarter to unions; scarcely one in ten felt the military to be the most powerful group. The major variation within the sample concerning the most powerful group was that white respondents with incomes of over $25,000, or with a college education, *reversed* the power ratings of the rest of the sample, as a majority believed the unions to be the most powerful group. As a very interesting aside, the only income and racial category to have a majority believing that all groups *should* have *equal* power was the low-income blacks, and the only educational category believing in power equality was the undereducated. By contrast, the rich and college graduates were the least likely to be equalitarian, *although almost two-fifths of these privileged groups were in fact equalitarian.*

---

[101] William H. Form and Joan Rytina, "Ideological Beliefs on the Distribution of Power in the United States," *American Sociological Review*, 34 (February 1969), pp. 19–31.

In reacting to Form and Rytina's findings concerning popular conceptions of the distribution of political power, a number of things seem to stand out: (1) the ideology of classic liberalism persists despite drastic shifts in the organization of modern society; (2) rather than serving to clarify the dynamics of power in the United States, education often seems to inculcate pluralistic myths and feelings; (3) objective condition and material interest substantially influence ideological beliefs; and (4) a large minority of Americans do, in fact, realize that their country is run by a small elite. Perhaps at least on one score the affluent could stand to learn from the American underclass. Crude though the latter's perception of power may be, it is no more crude than the power that makes them the underclass.

10

Work and freedom

WHO WORKS?

At the center of several discussions thus far has been the question of position within the means of production, and the role of occupation in shaping a person's life situation. We have drawn attention to the manner in which wage labor creates surplus wealth and how the ruling class maintains deep interests in the perpetuation of these relationships. The overarching need of the power elite is to promote a wage labor system yielding profits and to stimulate spending and consumption within the population. There is a contradiction here, for profits call for holding wages down while consumption calls for increased purchasing power among employees. This contradiction has been met with continual extensions of credit and inflation, but these cures only create new difficulties in the end. It would be possible to reduce the amount of work done and still meet normal human consumption needs. But corporate capitalism *must* have wage workers to create profit and *must* stimulate all sorts of novel needs (even while neglecting many essential needs) to realize financial expansion. In this chapter, we examine more closely questions relating to work and the ties between work and free time.

In a population of some 210 million persons, approximately 83 million of these are members of the *paid* labor force. Of the same 56 million persons 16 years old and over not in the paid labor force, 35 million are "keeping house" and nine million are in school. The large majority of adult males are in the paid labor force, 80 percent of those 16 years old and over and 96 percent of those between 25 and 44. For women the figures are 43 and 53 percent, respectively. In all, for those 16 and over, 60 percent are paid labor force; if the entire population is taken as the base, only 40 percent are paid labor force. This fact alone would suggest a serious reevaluation of the heavy emphasis placed upon work role as the income medium, not to mention property ownership as an income source.

Despite the efforts of a work-oriented system, the volume of non-workers keeps on increasing, though the availability of free time to the working-class labor force has been fought off quite successfully. Most wage earners and salaried employees work forty hours a week or more, fifty weeks a year. In a boom period, it is not uncommon to find many people working twelve hours a day and six days a week. Under a rationally ordered economy that placed essential needs and free time above all else, the working time of much of the paid labor force could be halved immediately.

Unemployment

The government defines an unemployed person as one who has not actively sought work in the four weeks previous to the given survey date. Obviously, then, to say that 5 or 6 percent of the labor force (those working or seeking work) are unemployed is to greatly underestimate the extent of idle human resources. The young person who lingers on in school for lack of job prospects, the housewife who would like nothing better than to enter an interesting job but sees no hope of finding one or the middle-aged man who has been rebuffed so many times that he has given up or lost self-confidence, these kinds of people are not counted as unemployed. Idle people are very much a necessary part of the system. Idle people are the unusable industrial reserve army, ready to step into low wage jobs and threatening any drive for higher wages among the employed.

Let us look at the real extent of unemployment. At the start of 1971 the official rate of unemployment was 6.2 percent of the labor force. This figure represented over 5.1 million individuals. This is only the beginning of the unemployment story. As Gross and Moses state, "Labor force definitions have been constructed so as to exclude millions of people in order to understate the dimensions of unemployment and the extent to which the economic system has failed to generate adequate and suitable job opportunities."[1] Pursuing their definition of unemployment as "all those who are not working and are able and willing to work for pay," Gross and Moses calculate the real rate of unemployment to be 24.6 percent. Their figures include a 1971 officially unemployed category of 4.7 million, 7.1 million government-counted underemployed and part-time individuals seeking full-time work together with job-wanters not officially counted, five million housewives (only one-seventh of women at home), three million students who would prefer to work (one-third of working-age students), four million persons aged 55–64 not working, 1.5 million hidden and uncounted unemployed and unemployables who could work given opportunities, and .3 million persons in manpower programs—for a total of 25.6 million out of a real labor force of 104 million.

---

[1] Bertram Gross and Stanley Moses, "Measuring the Real Work Force: 25 Million Unemployed," *Social Policy*, September/October 1972, pp. 5–10.

The U.S. Labor Department has itself estimated the real rate of unemployment, counting only officially unemployed, labor force drop-outs, and part-time seeking full-time, to be well above 30 percent in many major cities. With just this more limited group of categories the national rate runs to almost twice the usually given figure. In all accuracy, the full-time *working poor* should also be added to the above calculations, since this employment is not earning them a living wage.

An additional fundamental point regarding unemployment in the U.S. has been made by Sweezy: by adding to 8.1 million officially and dropped-out unemployed in December 1970 the 2.9 million active military personnel, 1.2 million Department of Defense civilian employees, 3.0 million direct defense industry employees, and 7.1 million jobs created by the military multiplier effect, a grand total of unemployed and military employed reaches 22.3 million persons, over 25 percent of the official labor force.[2] Even granting a 50 percent increase for hidden joblessness to the 1930s unemployment levels, without the military-industrial complex and its global activities the economy of today would be doing no better in employing the population than it did in the 1930s. Combining the Gross-Moses and Sweezy calculations, we may total some 14.2 million military-dependent employed with the 25.6 million real civilian unemployed to obtain nearly 40 million persons out of a real labor force of 104 million who are either military-dependent or out of work.

While exclaiming the virtues of work and expanding upon the immorality of those who don't work but "could work if they wanted to," the authorities are well aware that it is a blessing that so many housewives are not out on the job market and students linger on in school and frustrated men drop out of the labor force. The sermonizing on work is a strategy to encourage those on the job to work harder and justify minimal or no income support to those not working (and to stir up opposition against income support). Given their virtual exclusion from welfare programs, most adult males who are unemployed are involuntarily unemployed. We need not enter into a thorough documentation that the unemployed are not "lazy good-for-nothings."

One concrete illustration of system-produced unemployed might be well-taken: Litton Industries bought Royal Typewriter Company of Hartford, Connecticut, which also had a plant in Hull, England. The wages at the Hull plant were $1.20 an hour and at the Hartford plant $3.60. Naturally more concerned with profit than with unemployment in Hartford, Litton shut down its Hartford facility and moved its production to England.[3] This example could be repeated hundreds of times; the Big Three auto corporations are moving production abroad on a large scale, now employing over one-third of all their employees overseas.[4]

---

[2] Paul M. Sweezy, "Economic Stagnation and Stagnation of Economics," *Monthly Review*, 22 (April 1971), p. 9.

[3] Robert Sherrill, "Invisible Empires: The Multinationals Deploy to Rule," *The Nation*, April 16, 1973, p. 491.

[4] See Leo Fenster, "Small Car Imports: Detroit Goes Multinational," *The Nation*, March 12, 1973, pp. 326–29.

If unemployment were so desirable, the unemployed would not experience such social and psychological difficulties when they are out of work (omitting for the moment the fact that their unemployment compensation, if such is received, is only one-third the size of their normal paychecks and will eventually be exhausted). The impact of unemployment upon blue-collar workers has been extensively documented.[5] The trauma is no less severe upon the new working class. Powell and Driscoll have provided us with an account of how scientists and engineers degenerate through a cycle of unemployment: "The image of competent and energetic men reduced to listless discouragement highlights the personal tragedy and the loss of valuable resources when there is substantial unemployment."[6]

THE UNIONS

In the 1940s it appeared as if unions were to become the center of power in American society; Mills had written ". . . new men are accumulating power in America. Inside this country today, the labor leaders are the strategic actors: they lead the only organizations capable of stopping the main drift towards war and slump."[7] The ideology of the union leaders increasingly paralleled that of the big corporations and their government allies, with men such as the late Walter Reuther (killed in the crash of a light aircraft in May 1970) standing out as unique exceptions; Reuther was an articulate and outspoken critic of American domestic and foreign policy. Instead of becoming men of independent power, the large part of top union leadership settled down into a secure and subservient relationship with the corporations. Mills was quick to reassess union leadership; by the early 1950s he sees this leadership as "would-be members of the national elite" and as giving consideration only to programs "realizable alongside present corporations and within the present state framework."[8] Aronowitz carries the identity of labor and management further: "With few exceptions . . . employers regard labor leaders as their allies against the ignorant and undisciplined rank-and-file workers."[9]

Big labor leaders hold stakes in the status quo almost as deep as management. For example, Joseph Curran, president of the 50,000-strong National Maritime Union during its entire 33-year existence, receives a salary of $92,050 a year and has a retirement benefit of

---

[5] See, for example, Michael Aiken, Louis A. Ferman, and Harold L. Sheppard, *Economic Failure, Alienation, and Extremism* (Ann Arbor: University of Michigan Press, 1972).

[6] Douglas H. Powell and Paul F. Driscoll, "Middle Class Professionals Face Unemployment," *Society,* January–February 1973, pp. 18–26.

[7] C. Wright Mills, *The New Men of Power* (New York: Harcourt, Brace, and Company, 1948), p. 3.

[8] *Power, Politics, and People,* ed. I.L. Horowitz (New York: Oxford University Press, 1963), p. 108.

[9] Stanley Aronowitz, "Which Side Are You On? Trade Unions in America," *Liberation,* 16 (December 1971), p. 24.

$650,000.[10] Not to be outdone by Curran, George Meany raised his own salary from $70,000 to $90,000—during the wage freeze of 1972!

Leading the way in the conservative labor movement are the building or craft trade unions. Lenin labeled the craft unions as "labor aristocracy" and defined them as "narrow-minded, selfish, case-hardened, covetous, and petty-bourgeois 'labour aristocracy,' imperialist-minded, and imperialist-corrupted."[11] A contemporary sociology student agrees: "Skilled trade unions are reluctant to admit disadvantaged people into their training programs, are in the vanguard in stifling any sort of cross-trade or cross-industrial solidarity, are politically very reactionary and interested in doing whatever is necessary in maintaining the status quo."[12] Nixon's appointment of conservative New York building trades boss Peter J. Brennan as Secretary of Labor in 1972 epitomizes the labor aristocracy idea. From the very beginning, Samuel Gompers's AFL had been racist rather than radical. As Hill has remarked, "How different American life might have been if organized labor had not repeatedly acted against the interests of non-Caucasian workers, both Oriental and black, who could have joined in a racially unified struggle for the equal rights of all working people."[13]

Marx had early pointed out this problem with regard to the English workers' attitudes toward the Irish. Capitalists naturally exploit this ethnic cleavage to their own advantage. The racial division has been exploited throughout the country, but nowhere has it been used for so long and with so much success as in the South, where poor whites are told by the elites what great status benefits are theirs, owing to the color of their skin. Simply being white is supposed to dissolve labor militance, and to a large extent skin color has proven an effective tranquilizer.

Unions have been weak in the broad social sense; they do not often bind members into close social and political association and obtain commitment to collective working class goals. Workers tend to view unions as distant insurance companies at best and enemies of labor progress at worst. So in speaking of unions it is necessary to maintain a distinction between the upper bureaucracy and the plant committees and membership. It is also necessary to maintain distinctions between the various unions, some of which are supportive of the status quo and some of which are progressive. Without entering into a listing, we may cite the United Auto Workers as an example of the latter and the building trades and Teamsters (at least in upper bureaucracy) as examples of the former. The differences between UAW President Leonard Woodcock (Mc-govern supporter in 1972) and Frank Fitzsimmons of the Teamsters (Nixon supporter in 1972) are as sharp as were those between McGovern

---

[10] Editorial, "Viva Curran!" *The Nation*, October 27, 1969.

[11] V.I. Lenin, " 'Left-Wing' Communism—An Infantile Disorder," *Selected Works*, vol. 3 (Moscow: Progress Publishers, 1971), p. 374.

[12] "Comments by a Teaching Assistant," review to author of first edition of *Toward a New Sociology*, p. 12.

[13] Herbert Hill, "Anti-Oriental Agitation and the Rise of Working-Class Racism," *Society*, January–February, pp. 43–54.

and Nixon themselves—on military spending, war, taxation, corporate profits, income support programs, workers' rights, racial equality, etc. The black caucases, the walk-outs and wildcats, the youthful resistance to authority, the outside union organizing activities among the unorganized, and the unprecedented strike activity suggest that there is much unrest and instability in the contemporary labor movement.[14]

Labor organization has stagnated since 1950, save for some energetic organizing activities among public employees, hospital workers, farm workers, and a few other white collar and service occupations.[15] Less than one-half of *manufacturing* workers are organized, and only about one fourth of the total labor force belongs to unions (in marked contrast to many European countries where the large majority are organized). Of the some 20 million new labor force entrants since 1950, barely one fourth were unionized. While the blue-collar work force is proportionately less well organized today than in 1955, the white-collar or non-manual work force has made notable gains. Though only one-sixth of the white-collar work force is organized, this represents a 50 percent gain since 1960. Mills presaged the white-collar unionization movement over 20 years ago when he pointed to their proletarian placement in large organizations, reduction in "middle class" status claims, limited individual mobility potential, and the increasing threat of unemployment and economic insecurity.[16]

The government sector has created the vast majority of additional jobs during the past 20 years. Whereas federal civilian employment rose from 2.1 million in 1950 to 2.9 million in 1971 state and local figures increased from 4.3 million to 10.4 million. Local government accounts for 7.6 million of the latter total, 4.3 million accountable to education. Adding federal military personnel to the government figure, we obtain 16.2 million government employees, or almost 20 percent of the labor force.

Federal employment has leveled off since 1967 and evinces no signs of absorbing significantly greater numbers at the moment. State and local employment has continued to increase in recent years, but here, too, an employment bottleneck may be approached. Not only are funds for payrolls in a squeeze, but the number of entering school children is now leveling off and even decreasing (not that student-teacher ratios couldn't be lowered). With jobs being exported by the tens of thousands to East Asia, Latin America, and Europe, and plant modernization pressing as a necessity at home, the private sector cannot be expected to yield much of a job harvest in the future. Unemployment will be an increasing problem, and unions must necessarily be affected by the abundance of available labor.

Of special importance to union vitality is that labor address itself to much broader societal issues than are contained within the plant gate.

---

[14] See Chapter 6.

[15] For one account, see Everett M. Kassalow, "Trade Unionism Goes Public," *The Public Interest,* 14 (Winter 1969), pp. 118–30.

[16] Mills, *White Collar* (New York: Oxford University Press, 1951), p. 312.

Income, at least in amounts the unions can obtain for workers, cannot solve the pressing concerns and needs of the working class. The standard of living is eroding underneath the working class, "economic prosperity" notwithstanding. A broad range of social and public needs must be confronted by organized labor in the political arena so that the nation's priorities are reversed from military construction to social rebuilding, from profit accumulation to the delivery of health and welfare services, from productivity to worker safety and satisfaction.

AUTOMATION

Automation has been referred to as a "silent revolution."[17] Automation consists of a revolution in the means of production which promotes the conditions for a revolution in the social relations of production. Automation is one development in a long history of development of the forces of production, albeit an extremely important one. Indeed, automation presents such a major development in society's productive forces that we may speak of a qualitative change in production as opposed to one of degree. As discussed in Chapter 4, automated production alters the creation of value from human labor toward value created freely by machines. It alters the measurement of value from labor time to free time, and creates the conditions for material security and a voluntary association of labor.

Thus, automation brings out the contradictions of capitalism much more than previous industrial processes. It pushes questions and problems of surplus utilization, material reward, necessary labor, and free time to the fore. It magnifies the problems of private ownership, and enlarges perception of the social nature of production.

What *is* automation? Automation refers to the use of a whole range of electronically regulated machinery to control production processes, monitor the quality of the product, and adjust production to correct for deviations.[18] In effect, whereas men were required to control and operate industrial machines, automated machines control and operate themselves. What's more, automated machines are more efficient, accurate, and safe than industrial machines (U.S. industry, quite aside from normal dangers, is notoriously dangerous, and results in 25 million annual worker injuries, 14,500 deaths, and 10,000 occupationally caused deaths[19]). We usually think of automation mainly in terms of "Detroit automation," the integration and linking of machines by means of electronically controlled transfer mechanisms. The reduction of an assembly operation to the push of a button, originally utilized in the automobile

---

[17] Donald N. Michael, "Cybernation: The Silent Conquest," in Morris Philipson, ed., *Automation: Implications for the Future* (New York: Random House, Inc., 1962), pp. 77–128.

[18] John Diebold, "Congressional Testimony," in Philipson, ed., *Automation*, pp. 27–38.

[19] Franklin Wallick, "Good Laws, Dangerous Shops: Paying Lip Service to Safety," *The Nation,* January 22, 1973, pp. 114–16.

industry but soon applied in meat-packing, baking, and many other industries involving transfer processes, is an important but not the only type of automation. Also important are process control systems—computerized operation of process plants in oil, mineral, and chemical industries. A further type of automation, numerical control, allows programmers to change tapes and produce different products with the same machine. Basic to all automation, but specialized for the automatic handling of information and data in administration and decision making, is an assortment of computers.

The number of blue-collar workers required to produce a given amount of goods has declined sharply as a result of automation. In a seven-year period, the meat-packing industry lost 40,000 jobs, while output per man-hour increased over 50 percent.[20] Steel employment fell 28 percent between 1951 and 1963, but steel production did not drop. Automobile employment fell 20 percent during the same period, but a million more cars and trucks were produced. The story is the same for mining, railroads, communications, food processing, and food producing. (The highly mechanized top three percent of the nation's farmers produce more food than the bottom 74 percent.) The rise in efficiency and decline in a work force might be further illustrated with data from the West German textile industry, where from 1958 to 1966 production increased by 48 percent and productivity per working hour by 86 percent, while the number of employed dropped by 87,000 (14 percent), and the working time of those on the job dropped by eight percent.[21]

Nor are white-collar and service workers immune from the inroads of automation. Sales, clerical, administrative, supervising, cleaning, and repair, among other tasks in management and service, are directly amenable to automation. The ranks of American business and government already seem to have a surfeit of office manpower. One suspects that a sizable segment of the white-collar work force is now a superfluous luxury without which operations would go on as usual. In the automated office, it will become increasingly difficult to continue make-work duties with any real belief in their utility. As perhaps a good indication of substantial "diminishing returns" of employees even at the upper white collar level, a study of British industrial managers and executives disclosed that frequent reference was made to the tolerance by the organization of "deadwood"; more significantly, about one fourth felt that they were being underutilized and another fraction felt they were incorrectly placed.[22]

Just how much of the work force can be displaced by technological advancements? Even such an ardent disbeliever in the disruptive potential of automation as *Fortune* editor Charles Silberman has declared that "Sooner or later, of course, we shall have the technical capacity to substi-

---

[20] See Ben B. Seligman, *Most Notorious Victory* (New York: The Free Press, 1966), p. 136.

[21] Dennis Gabor, *Innovations: Scientific, Technological, and Social* (London: Oxford University Press, 1970), p. 49.

[22] Cyril Sofer, *Men in Mid-Career* (Cambridge: Cambridge University Press, 1970), pp. 10; 223.

tute machines for men in most of the functions men now perform."[23] The RAND brains says that two percent of the labor force will produce everything the country can consume. We should not allow "futurists" too much latitude in this regard, for it is fairly evident that the larger portion of the industrial work force will be on the job for a long time to come. Nevertheless, the percentage of technologically displaced persons is already high and certain to grow in many sectors of the economy.

Percentages are abstract; individuals are not. Technological displacement was concrete to an unemployed West Virginia coal miner who looked up from his sagging porch at the stripped mountain across the way and said, "Mechanical machinery is ruining this country."[24] (Workers should realize that it is the *misplaced* use of machinery that is ruinous, and not machinery per se.)

Automation, or cybernation, as Norbert Weiner has referred to the phenomenon of self-regulating machinery,[25] usually takes its toll more silently than through plant closures and layoffs. Automation takes its toll on employment mainly through *attrition*. Instead of layoffs and dismissals, employers simply do not hire new people, or hire at a much slower rate than the labor force is expanding. *In an age of automation, the economy may grow while unemployment levels rise.* The social challenge is that of taking hold of the automated mode of production and applying it to the gradual elimination of wage labor, rather than allowing the ruling class to utilize (or not utilize) the potential of automation for its own financial ends.

Alienation and automation

The question may be raised as to the impact of automation upon worker alienation. We may note at the outset that automation does nothing in the way of eliminating alienation in the basic sense so long as workers do not both own *and* control the entire organization of production. Automation changes nothing in this regard.

However, researchers have raised the empirical question as to whether automated production illicits greater worker satisfaction than machine labor. A body of research exists which suggests that people involved in automated, computer-oriented, or continuous process systems are more satisfied with their work, feel great independence, and express greater involvement in their work than assembly line operators or office machine operators (not at all surprising).[26] It wouldn't take much to score lower

---

[23] Cited by Robert Theobald, *An Alternative Future for America* (Chicago: The Swallow Press, Inc., 1968), p. 105.

[24] Ben H. Bagdikian, *In the Midst of Plenty* (New York: Signet Books, 1964), p. 52.

[25] See Weiner's essay on cybernetics, *The Human Use of Human Beings* (New York: Avon Books, 1967).

[26] For example, Robert Blauner, *Alienation and Freedom* (Chicago: University of Chicago Press, 1964); John Goldthorpe et al., *The Affluent Worker: Industrial Attitudes and Behavior* (Cambridge: Cambridge University Press, 1968); Michael Fullan, "Industrial Technology and Worker Integration in the

on a scale of "alienation" than an auto assembly line worker or a mimeograph machine operator. Yet, evidence is also available that indicates that men who previously worked in a steel fabricating machine plant and were switched over to a new automated fabricating operation felt less control, less interest, greater boredom, a loss of skill and status, social isolation, and a flattening of opportunities on the new job.[27] They reported being "tired" even though not exerting physical effort. Most agreed, however, that the quality of the work was an improvement over the more physically exhausting and dangerous manual labor.

In an empirical study of alienation among French workers, both new and old working class, Melvin Seeman discerned prominent indications of alienation.[28] The majority of respondents, except for non-manual employees with higher education, reported that they don't really enjoy work (one-third of the non-manual higher education were negative towards work). Rather substantial numbers felt their work to be too fast, routine, and that they lacked control over pace. The French respondents evinced considerable feelings of political powerlessness regarding internal social affairs (though they were such more optimistic about preventing international wars) and felt that personal events were difficult to control. It was the workers who were involved in some kind of work union or organization that expressed the most feelings of personal and social control. The degree of alienation was quite constant across blue- and white-collar lines, though greater amounts of education brought smaller percentages of alienated respondents.

Still, on work-specific questions of challenge, innovation, and interest, only a minority of both manual and non-manual workers were negative in response, especially the non-manual persons. Thus, work content itself did not seem to be a disrupting or alienating force; primarily the roots of alienation were to be found in the lack of control over the work process and moreso, lack of control over social events outside of the work setting. The French working class expressed strong feelings of political powerlessness, a remoteness from the societal decision-making apparatus, an unresponsiveness of officialdom. While the majority of those with less education felt the lot of the average man to be getting worse, one third of the more highly educated thought so.

The conclusion to be drawn here may be that advanced technological

---

Organization," *American Sociological Review*, 35 (December 1970), pp. 1028–29; Jon S. Shepard, *Automation and Alienation* (Cambridge, Mass.: M.I.T. Press, 1971); Lewis Carliner, "The White Collar on the Ex-Blue Collar is a Cool Collar," *Dissent*, Winter 1972, pp. 260–63; and Barbara A. Kirsch and Joseph L. Lengermann, "Alienation in Work as Applied to Different Type Jobs in a White-Collar Setting," *Sociology and Social Research*, 56 (January 1972), pp. 180–94.

[27] See J.K. Chadwick-Jones, *Automation and Behaviour* (London: Wiley-Interscience, 1969).

[28] Melvin Seeman, "The Signals of '68: Alienation in Pre-Crisis France," *American Sociological Review*, 37 (August 1972), pp. 385–402. For an account of the upheaval itself, see Henri Lefebvre, *The Explosion* (New York: Monthly Review Press, 1969).

or skilled work is not so much the source of alienation as the bureaucratic organization, the drive for profit (too fast pace), and the concentration of power among elites. In contrast to the French workers, who not long after the study were to revolt on a large scale in May 1968, a comparative sample of U.S. workers displayed significantly less alienation on many dimensions. (However, on the possibility of the prevention of war they easily exceeded the French in pessimism.) Nevertheless, the same symptoms were present in the U.S. as in France, and we should expect a maturation process over time (today, six years later, Seeman may find a U.S. working class much less sanguine than that of 1967).

In order to maximize fully the reward and interest in work, whether fully automated, partially, or not at all, production must be under workers' control so that their insights, ideas, innovations, needs, and desires are foremost rather than those of financiers. The task of rendering work as enjoyable or as tolerable as possible must be up to those directly involved. The very activity of trying to improve upon the production process and the efficiency of work organization is enough to bring an intensified participation on the part of the worker. The worker must decide when he or she shall work and for how long, what the structure of the job shall be, how rewards shall be distributed, and above all, what shall be produced in the first place. Such is the model of associated labor. Perhaps such groups of self-governing people will decide to build quality housing units in their community instead of "tiger cages" for military dictators abroad (the U.S. Agency for International Development contracted a U.S. construction firm to build 4' × 6' underground pens to contain some of the 200,000 *political* prisoners of the Thieu regime in South Vietnam).

Emancipated labor

In addition to the work involved in building, organizing, and maintaining even a highly automated economy, and the political responsibilities required of all, the demand for personal services would continue to grow—even when the service can be automated without destroying the nature of the institution it serves. While teaching machines may be valuable instructional aids, no machine can serve as a model for curiosity or scholarship. While computers may vastly increase the accuracy of medical diagnosis and save many lives, no computer can express the concern and compassion that disabled, sick, or dying people often desperately need.[29] No pitching machine can create the anticipation with which one awaits the thrown ball, no instructional film can duplicate the conviviality of a golf or ski pro, no tape recorder can inspire like live musicians, and no instant dinner can match the taste of one by a good chef. The entire range of artistic, intellectual, and crafts occupations

---

[29] See the prognostication of the physician role within advanced technology by Jerrold S. Maxmen, "Goodbye, Dr. Welby," *Social Policy,* December/January 1972–73, pp. 97–106.

may be assisted by technological advance, but never displaced. As standardized products come to predominate everywhere, interests in crafts and arts may increase and the demand for handmade products grow. The elimination of structured and repetitive work leaves the kinds of creative work that men find satisfying and personally rewarding; i.e., working with social and material challenges. The ideal of craftsmanship, gradually lost through mechanization, may again have the opportunity to flourish precisely as a result of liberating technological advance.

Yet, there are no guarantees that people will invest in the full development of, for example, educational, medical, recreational, and social services. We may allow unemployment rates to rise, or attempt to reduce them by involving people in make-work military programs or bureaucratic nonsense. Nor is there any assurance that people freed from repetitious labor will find themselves prepared to use time in ways other than packaged thrills and distracting, passive entertainment. The model of craftsmanship may have already become an irretrievable anachronism for many.[30] Yet, a renewed interest in the development of personal skills is very much in evidence.

Emancipated labor brings new definitions to leisure. People working in personal service, intellectual, arts, and crafts occupations often do not distinguish between work and leisure. Their work is what they enjoy doing, and they pursue work-related activities in leisure. Recreation is work itself, and the work-leisure dichotomy vanishes. Such people are fortunate, for the work they do is not threatened by machines, nor do they feel a need to escape from work into programmed or distracting leisure. We must, of course, exercise caution in making statements about rewarding and unrewarding, constructive and unconstructive leisure; leisure styles vary greatly from person to person, and there are really no criteria with which to objectively assess the quality or worth of leisure use. Reading, gardening, picnicking, bowling, home projects, moviegoing, travel, conversation, and endless other activities or inactivities carry widely different values, and no one can really issue a judgment concerning their worth (chasing deer with snowmobiles is a different story).

In fact, rather than people complaining about having too much leisure time and not knowing what to do with it, a more frequent complaint, among adults at least, is that they are short on leisure time. The large majority of men between 21 and 65 are in the labor force working at least 40 hours a week, and often much more; and while many may be bored and insecure in their *jobs*, few consider *leisure* a problem. However, the unemployed are a different story, insofar as they have less resources with which to pursue leisure; and the onus of involuntary idleness seriously dampens the enjoyment of leisure. The involuntarily unemployed therefore do not offer a valid test of how men might handle an abundance of free time. Whether the ordinary person on a 20-hour workweek with a fully supporting wage would eventually grow restive

---

[30] See Mills's classic discussion of craftsmanship in *White Collar,* pp. 220–24.

under a surfeit of leisure time remains to be seen. The independently wealthy seem to find things of interest to do, but then, these aren't ordinary people.

Before continuing with our examination of the impact of automation on work and free time we might take note here of the view that there is insufficient work aspiration in American society to meet the occupational openings or needs that exist.[31] Thus, instead of seeing the main problem as one of technological displacement and unemployment this view argues that the work and achievement ethic has so badly deteriorated, especially among youth, that important segments of the occupational structure threaten to go unmanned.[32] The eschewing of college training or professional employment by groups of "drop-outs" from the nation's colleges and universities, and their residence in such experimental communities as rural communes, is taken as indication of this antiwork trend. Aside from the fact that making a living off the soil requires at least as much self-discipline, hard work, and (with practice and experience) skill as a white-collar urban job, this interpretation of work and the occupational structure is unconvincing for other reasons.

In the first place the "founders" and majority of participants of what is really an *antitechnological, antibureaucratic* antiwork ethic (there are, of course, *other* kinds and *other* types of work that can and *need* to be done) represent a privileged minority of young people typically raised in relatively abundant and liberalized homes. Many of these people *desire* kinds of work in mainstream society for which there exist no or insufficient outlets. Rather than enter rural communes some of these persons have organized so-called work-communes within which they can pursue industrial professions with greater autonomy and freedom. Some do pick-up jobs in selected desirable locations. The point is here that the antibureaucrats could disappear from the job market almost without notice inasmuch as their numbers are quite small relative to the vast sea of capable youth who desire the kinds of college education that would lead them into the economic and social security of the upper professional, business, and technical worlds. Not only do most of these young people fear underemployment and seek solid jobs, few of them are able to fully comprehend the ostensibly carefree orientation of the cultural rebels. Granted that the latter's numbers are growing, but then so is the pace of productivity, which more than compensates for their absence from the world of salaried and wage employment.

As we are arguing in this chapter, the real danger lies in the waste of human capacities rather than in an unfilled void within the upper levels of bureaucratic and technological employment. And, to the cultural rebels, it is precisely bureaucratic and technical employment that constitutes the waste. Joy, not grief, would be their response to the atrophy of the establishment occupational structure due to lack of interest in

---

[31] See John Porter, "The Future of Upward Mobility," *American Sociological Review,* 33 (February 1968), pp. 5–19.

[32] Lewis M. Andrews, "Communes and the Work Crises," *The Nation,* (November 9, 1970), pp. 460–63.

such careers. For the near future, however, labor surplus rather than shortage is the pressing issue. Ask any graduating education major, social worker, chemist, or engineer, black or white. Better still, ask any of the approximately 45,000 unemployed scientists, engineers, and technicians.

FREE LABOR AND FREE LIVING

The industrial era has cemented the tie between work and income. As the means of livelihood, it is believed, income can ultimately be justified only through work. The assumption that in order to live a person must work is as deeply ingrained in the American mind as belief in God, if not more so. God, many believe, has Himself ordained the relationship between work and income. Dependent women, children, elderly, and disabled persons have been excepted from the work-income imperative, but only reluctantly and with minimal enthusiasm. Even the unemployed are widely suspected of sloth and lethargy, though the realities of technological displacement and economic breakdowns are starting to make their impact on popular thought.

Carried to its full potential, technology is capable of displacing the larger portion of today's industrial workers. What, then, is the status of the categorical imperative concerning work and income? What are today's millions of unemployed workers, who have ordinarily relied upon the work-income equation to function smoothly for them, doing about life chances. Even those who are covered for and still receiving unemployment compensation find their family's life chances badly undermined. And what of tomorrow's millions of displaced persons? What will their life chances be?

In considering the precarious future of the work-income tie, Robert Theobald has devoted much of his scholarly career to the study and debate of a guaranteed income, or basic economic security. When machines do the work, how can men earn their living, other than by virtue of their membership in society? As Theobald has phrased the issue, "Human dignity in a cybernated era can only be guaranteed through a constitutional right to share in the production of machine systems.[33] The actual levels of guaranteed income are up for debate (they would vary with the number of persons in the household), but the necessity for a guaranteed income, argues Theobald, is increasingly urgent. A guaranteed income as a right of every citizen would at least put an end to the indignities, inadequacies, inefficiencies, and stigma of the welfare system. As Cole and Lejeune have documented, the stigma of welfare is so deeply internalized by the majority of recipients that many define their health as poor and evince chronic symptoms of illness in order to better deal with the indignities to self suffered as a result of receiving welfare.[34]

---

[33] Theobald, *Free Men and Free Markets* (New York: Doubleday & Co., 1965), p. xiv; also see Theobald, ed., *The Guaranteed Income* (New York: Doubleday & Company, Inc., 1967) for several analytic and critical essays by Theobald and others.

[34] Stephen Cole and Robert Lejeune, "Illness and the Legitimation of Failure," *American Sociological Review,* 37 (June 1972), pp. 347–56.

Would a guaranteed income of, say, $4,000 for a family of four inter-fere with work incentives? Incentives are not at issue, or should not be at issue, when retired, dependent, disabled, or unemployed persons who can't find work are involved. But what about the employed worker? Wouldn't he be tempted to quit work and live on the guaranteed income? First of all, few people holding jobs paying more than the minimum in-come would choose to quit work. The median family income in the United States is more than double even the boldest proposals for a minimum income. Not only would few people be willing to cut their standard of living in half or worse, few would find themselves socially or psychologically prepared to retire in the prime of life at even their current wage, to say nothing of a proposed $4,000 guaranteed income. In addition to money, most men depend upon their jobs for self-respect and social acceptance and would work irrespective of the level of guaran-teed income. In response to the question "If by some chance you had enough money to live comfortably without working, do you think that you would work anyway, or would you not work?" over four fifths of a sample of blue-collar men studied by Tausky reported that they *would work anyway*. Nearly all would take a job as a car washer rather than get the same pay on welfare. (Note that this strong desire to work, even as a car washer, for reasons of self-worth and social respect is *not* neces-sarily to gain intrinsic satisfaction and personal meaning from work.) Tausky has also found that white-collar workers are equally dependent on their jobs for self-respect and feeling of social acceptability as are blue-collar workers.[35] In a more recent investigation, Kaplan and Tausky learned essentially the same thing concerning strong commitment to work regardless of guaranteed comfort among a sample of chronically unemployed workers.[36] The unemployed workers placed a high value upon the respect from friends earned as a result of satisfactory job per-formance, and the majority valued the idea of promotion more for the respect generated from friends than the increased money.

Moreover, almost certainly the professional, scientific, managerial, and social service workers who gain intrinsic satisfaction from their voca-tions would be exceedingly unlikely to drop out to accept the minimum income standard. For example, a study of British industrial managers and executives disclosed that very few would leave the world of work if independently supported (presumably well above the minimum stan-dard), for work was too important to them as a medium for social inter-action, performance challenges, time flow, and identity.[37]

Finally, as a further inducement to work, guaranteed income pro-posals usually incorporate built-in incentive measures that allow for

---

[35] See Curt Tausky, "Meanings of Work among Blue-Collar Men," *Pacific Sociological Review*, 12 (Spring 1969), pp. 49–55; and Curt Tausky, "Occupa-tional Mobility Interests," *The Canadian Review of Sociology and Anthropol-ogy* 4 (November 1967), pp. 242–49.

[36] H. Ray Kaplan and Curt Tausky, "Work and the Welfare Cadillac: The Function of and Commitment to Work Among the Hard Core Unemployed," *Social Problems*, 19 (Spring 1972), pp. 469–83.

[37] Sofer, *Men in Mid-Career*, p. 193.

progressive improvement upon the income base until topping out into the break-even or lowest tax bracket.[38] Anyway, given substantial material security and growing opportunities, more and more people would move into positions of voluntary and cooperative production outside the limits of necessary wage labor.

Theobald points out some interesting by-products we might expect from a guaranteed income, and eventually free goods and services, in a cybernated era of increasingly voluntarily associated labor. The introduction of free goods and services and a sustaining income (ultimately unneeded) would erode the power of privileged groups over the labor force and other bases of economic power. Economic power is based to a considerable extent on artificially created scarcity, wage labor, and maldistribution of resources. Moreover, people would tend to move into areas of work and activity they could freely choose and enjoyed and preferred. Wages in the pleasant and preferred jobs would decline or even disappear and thus automation would be slowed down in them. Unpleasant jobs would demand higher wages and hence automation would be pushed ahead in them.[39] Theobald also alludes to the reason why so many affluent people are so vociferous in their opposition to basic economy security: the affluent are worried that the persons who are, in effect, subsidizing affluence with their low wages will walk off their jobs, leaving the rich to do their own dirty work. Little wonder, then, why the higher one goes in the class system the greater is the opposition to basic economic security; for the higher one goes in the class system the more does one stand to benefit from being subsidized by low wages among workers and service people toward the bottom.

The anarchist Murray Bookchin declares that "In attempting to uphold scarcity, toil, poverty and subjugation against the growing potential for post-scarcity, leisure, abundance and freedom, capitalism increasingly emerges as the most irrational, indeed the most artificial society in history."[40] The artificiality (some would say insanity) of modern society, in the widest sense, has been increasingly evident to ever larger numbers of people. New courses of action await their imagination and initiative.

---

[38] See James Tobin, "The Case for an Income Guarantee," *The Public Interest,* 4 (Summer 1966), pp. 31–41.

[39] Theobald, *An Alternative Future for America,* p. 55.

[40] *Post-Scarcity Anarchism* (Berkeley: The Ramparts Press, 1971), p. 15.

11

Ethnic groups

THE NATURE OF ETHNIC GROUPS

While man may be a mongrel lot, most people nevertheless recognize divisions between themselves and other people, based on ethnic background. The word "ethnic" stems from the Greek *ethnos,* meaning people. Men who share a sense of peoplehood or identify with one another, who feel an irrevocable affinity with persons who have common roots in a meaningful historical tradition, are members of an ethnic group.[1] The idea of ethnic group carries implications of "we" and "they," the in-group and the out-group.[2] In the strong sense, the idea of an ethnic group connotes an interdependence of fate, a common destiny, for its members.[3]

What shared phenomena have served as bases for ethnic solidarity? For 99 percent of human history, or as long as man was in a food-gathering state, ethnicity was based on membership in a small tribal unit.[4] Even today, the tribal unit, with its distinct territorial limits, language, culture, and often appearance, serves as the basis of ethnicity for many groups in every continent of the world: Indians of North and South America, Laplanders in Scandinavia, Aborigines in Australia, and myriad societies in Africa, Asia, and Oceania compose tribal ethnic groups. In an age of nation-states, tribal units are subsumed within national political boundaries such as are the Sioux and Hopi in the United States, Yoruba and Ibo in Nigeria, the Mongols and Tibetans in China,

---

[1] See Milton M. Gordon, *Assimilation in Amerian Life* (New York: Oxford University Press, 1964), especially Chapter 2.

[2] Peter Rose, *They and We* (New York: Random House, Inc., 1964).

[3] Kurt Lewin, *Resolving Social Conflicts* (New York: Harper and Brothers, 1948), pp. 163–66.

[4] See Arnold J. Toynbee, *Change and Habit: Challenge of Our Time* (New York: Oxford University Press, 1966), p. 102.

and the Tatars and Uzbeks in the Soviet Union. In some instances, existing tribal units consist of only several hundred persons, while in other cases several millions of persons may be included. The term "nationality" tends to be applied to the larger tribal peoples, since tribe connotes a group of smaller size. Tribal divisions may be found within the larger tribe or nationality, such as Oglala, Teton, and Yankton Sioux.

Nation-states may themselves serve as a basis of identification and belonging, especially in the smaller or homogeneous countries. Religion may serve to reinforce ethnic belonging, as Lutheranism in Norway, Catholicism and Presbyterianism in Northern Ireland, Judaism in Israel, Islam in Egypt, and Buddhism in Japan. In religiously and racially diverse countries such as the Soviet Union and the United States, the nation-state is usually not the most important ethnic focus among the people, although it may nevertheless serve ethnic purposes at times.

Within the United States, or any nation-state that subsumes within its political boundaries diverse tribal, religious, racial, nationality, or national-origin groups, ethnic belonging may have several different bases for given members of the population. An American of Italian descent may anchor his ethnic group membership in national origin, religion, race, or nation state. Whether he thinks of himself as being an Italian-American, Catholic, white person, or American may depend upon his past experiences, the time, the place, and any other of a number of contingencies relating to ethnic behavior. Often the implicit or explicit goal of large and diverse nation-states is the *assimilation* of all ethnic groups, whatever their bases might be, into the core or dominant ethnic group, which usually views itself as the true ethnic group of the nation-state. In the Soviet Union, Russians may assimilate Ukrainians, Belorussians, and Central Asians; in the United States, Anglo-Saxon Protestants may assimilate German Protestants or Catholics, Italian Catholics, or Jews; in China, Chinese may assimilate Mongols, Tibetans, or Koreans. The assimilation of other ethnic groups by the dominant or host society is never an inevitability, for ethnic groups may persist indefinitely alongside one another within the same country. Assimilation is an important social process, and we shall examine it further in the context of American society.

Are ethnic groups desirable?

A valuational question might be raised before we examine further the process of assimilation: Are ethnic groups desirable or undesirable? From the standpoint of individuals, ethnic groups evidently must be desirable insofar as most people claim or participate in ethnic groups. Full ethnic awareness may not surface among people immersed in a relatively isolated homogeneous agricultural society, as among the 19th-century peasant immigrants who came to America from places like Poland or Norway, but living in the ethnic maze of the United States soon stimulated strong feelings of ethnic belonging in Poles, Norwegians, or whatever the immigrant group. And most of the descendants of the immigrants continue to locate themselves within the boundaries of ethnic groups. As Milton Gordon has observed, "As though with a wily cunning of its own, as though there were some essential element in man's nature that demanded it—something that compelled him to merge his lonely individual identity in some ancestral group of fellows smaller by far than the whole human race, smaller often than the nation—the sense of ethnic belonging has survived."[5]

Tribal belonging is as old as man himself, and the habit of immersing oneself in an ethnic group is deeply ingrained in tradition, if not biology. Ethnic groups, we might argue, are thus desirable, for they provide people with a sense of identification, a social group, and, usually, a way of life. By contrast, we might argue that ethnic groups are undesirable, for they serve as a point of prejudice, discrimination, and conflict. Imagine the equanimity of American society if we were all Anglo-Saxon Protestants. Or can you imagine it? Protestant-Catholic, British-Irish, and white-black have not been the only points of animosity and conflict. Ethnic conflict is but one form of conflict; political and economic conflict would still be with us in the event of complete assimilation. Indeed, ethnic groups, by crosscutting social classes, have served to *prevent* the formation of hardened political and economic conflict. Thus, assimilation could give rise to more intense forms of political and economic conflict rather than lowering the level of conflict in American society. To the extent assimilation has already occurred, we are perhaps witnessing a commensurate degree of heightened political and economic conflict.

Moreover are not ethnic groups parochial, narrowing, and stultifying? Would not society be improved and the individual freed if everyone moved freely and openly from group to group, regardless of ethnic backgrounds? To some people, enclosure within an ethnic group may indeed seem restricting and limiting. But to other persons, the ethnic group is the only milieu within which he can relax, be comfortable, and open up. Only in the ethnic group can he really dare to be himself. To such people, the ethnic group is liberating rather than restricting. In the judgment of the cosmopolitan sophisticate, people who depend upon the familiarity of the ethnic group for relaxation and conversation may appear to be deadly provincial in life style. To the ethnic group member, the cosmopolitan sophisticate may appear rootless and without meaningful cultural and social ties. Desirability of ethnic groups on the issue of self-realization and satisfaction is thus an entirely personal value judgment.

However, unless there exist adequate substitutes for ethnic belonging, such as political or occupational community, the presence of ethnic groups in American society serves an important integrative purpose, even while recognizing their very divisive potential. Ethnic groups may themselves serve as foundations for political organizations, particularly for minority ethnic groups.

THE PROCESS OF ASSIMILATION

Assimilation refers to the absorption or disappearance of one ethnic group into the life of another ethnic group. Assimilation results in the

---

[5] Gordon, *Assimilation in American Life*, p. 25.

loss of the identity and separate existence of an ethnic group. It may result in the loss of the original identity and separate existence of *both* ethnic groups involved and the creation of a fundamentally new social and cultural entity, as occurred in the assimilation of Spanish and Indians in Mexico. (Fusion is perhaps a better word here than assimilation, allowing assimilation to refer to the loss of identity of one group only.)[6] In the United States, the process of assimilation has been largely one way, that is, one ethnic group has lost its separate identity while the other dominant group, the Anglo-Saxon Protestant, has preserved its original social and cultural identity.

Assimilation is a multistage process. Gordon has detailed several stages or subprocesses of assimilation, and we shall follow his analysis closely.[7] When two ethnic groups come into contact, the first step in the assimilation of one to the other involves language, norms, values, and general life styles—in a word, culture. Cultural assimilation, or acculturation, may or may not take place when two groups are juxtaposed. For example, American Indians, while being forcibly stripped of much of their traditional culture, have not as a group taken over the dominant or mainstream culture. Mexican-Americans have also retained considerable cultural separation. However, substantial cultural assimilation of American ethnic groups to the Anglo-Saxon Protestant norm has been the rule rather than the exception. German, Scandinavian, Irish, Slavic, and most other European national-origin groups were largely, though not entirely, acculturated within two or three generations. Yet, American society is not strictly homogeneous culturally speaking; national origin, religious, and minority groups variously contribute to a moderate level of cultural pluralism along ethnic lines.[8]

The reduction of linguistic, life-style, and normative differences between ethnic groups far from concludes the process of assimilation. Ethnic groups bearing the same culture may coexist as separate social entities indefinitely. How much difference is there, in terms of life styles, between white-collar Jews, Catholics, Protestants, blacks, Mexican-Americans, or Japanese-Americans? While cultural differences are certainly present within classes, differences do not seem sufficiently marked or important to in themselves sustain the identity and independence of the various ethnic representatives. Nevertheless, separate ethnic groups survive intact.

The second step in assimilation concerns interaction rather than culture. To continue the process of assimilation, a group must not only take on the culture of the dominant group but also enter on a large scale the dominant group's primary groups and social organizations

---

[6] Walter P. Zenner, "Ethnic Assimilation of the Corporate Group," *The Sociological Quarterly*, 8 (Summer 1967), pp. 340–48.

[7] Gordon, *Assimilation in American Life*, Chapter 3.

[8] See, for example, Nathan Glazer and Daniel P. Moynihan, *Beyond the Melting Pot*, revised edition (Boston: M.I.T. Press, 1970); Michael Novak, *The Rise of the Unmeltable Ethics* (New York: Macmillan, 1971); and Andrew Greeley, *Why Can't They Be Like Us?* (New York: Dutton, 1971).

(*structural* assimilation). A certain amount of interaction with members of the dominant society would, of course, be required in acculturation. But the process of acculturation can occur through more formal contacts in schools, businesses, and civic activities, and through acculturated members of one's own ethnic group. Only the subtleties of primary-group culture cannot be absorbed without direct participation in the informal social life of the dominant ethnic group. Such is the general state of assimilation in the United States: cultural assimilation has largely taken place, with important exceptions, while structural assimilation has not. However, some large-scale melting down of ethnic group social boundaries has occurred; for example, Protestant national origin groups such as British, German, and Scandinavian have by today largely merged socially with one another,[9] as have to a lesser extent the American-born generations of Catholic national-origin groups such as Irish, Italian, and Polish.[10] Moreover, white native-born Catholics and Protestants cross ethnic boundaries quite often in primary interaction and very often in voluntary associations and clubs. Jews and Gentiles also belong to one another's cliques and informal social circles,[11] but with considerably less regularity than do Catholics and Protestants. Even black and white occasionally find social lines breaking down. However, aside from the considerable structural assimilation that has occurred between national-origin groups of the same religion, resulting in the larger ethno-religious collectivities of Protestant, Catholic, and Jew, American society remains importantly divided by religion and race in primary-group life.[12] Even in secondary groups or voluntary associations, such as schools, special-interest groups, recreational and social clubs, and business affiliations and patronage, ethnic group status may figure in important ways.

The strength of religious communalism (the opposite of structural assimilation) is attested to by the fact that over two fifths of white Protestants and Catholics have been found to have only coreligionists among their closest friends, and for another one third, predominantly coreligionists, greatly exceeding what one would expect on a chance

---

[9] Charles H. Anderson, *White Protestant Americans: From National Origins to Religious Group* (Englewood Cliffs, N.J.: Prentice-Hall, Inc., 1970).

[10] Paul Wozniack, "Assimilation into Pan-Catholicism: A Sociological Study of Structural Assimilation among Catholic National Origin Groups," Ph.D. dissertation, University of Massachusetts, 1967.

[11] Benjamin Ringer, *The Edge of Friendliness* (New York: Basic Books, Inc., 1968).

[12] See Robin M. Williams, Jr., and Edward Suchman, *Strangers Next Door* (Englewood Cliffs, N.J.: Prentice-Hall, Inc., 1964), pp. 144–67; Edward O. Laumann, "The Social Structure of Religious and Ethnoreligious Groups in a Metropolitan Community," *Amerian Sociological Review*, 34 (April 1969), pp. 182–97; Charles H. Anderson, "Religious Communality among White Protestants, Catholics, and Mormons," *Social Forces*, 46 (June 1968), pp. 501–8; Gerhard Lenski: *The Religious Factor* (New York: Doubleday & Company, Inc., 1963), pp. 37–42; and James L. Christensen, "Values in Conflict: Religious Views among Catholics," Ph.D. dissertation, University of Utah, 1970.

basis.[13] Ethnic community is not only for the average working-class person. Top professionals are as communally oriented as the rest of the population; a study of lawyers and engineers by Wilensky and Ladinsky disclosed that religion was far stronger than occupation as a basis for social ties.[14] Among Jews, Mormons, and non-Anglo minority groups, enclosure at the primary-group level is much more complete than among white Protestants and Catholics.

Ethnic communalism may or may not involve ethnic group conflict. Protestants and Catholics have engaged one another in violent conflicts in American history, but today Protestant-Catholic conflict, where it exists, is routinized and usually of low intensity. Jewish communalism has rarely been the source of intergroup conflict, except as an object of outgroup hostility; anti-Semitism itself seems to be on the decline.[15] There remain the intergroup conflicts between white and black, white and Indian, Anglo and Mexican, black and Puerto Rican, and other racially defined ethnic antagonisms.

A third important step in the assimilation process involves intermarriage between members of different ethnic groups (marital assimilation). Conversely, an important indicator of ethnic communalism is a high in-marriage rate. Given extensive interethnic contact at the primary-group level, intermarriages tend to increase—for obvious reasons. Thus, the Protestant-Catholic intermarriage rate is higher than the Jewish-Gentile rate, which is, in turn, higher than the white-black rate. Concerning religious intermarriage, we might note the distinction between the intermarriage rate as based on the religious upbringing of partners and the intermarriage rate as based on the couple's current religious affiliations. These affiliations reflect religious *conversions* of one partner or another, thus yielding a lower intermarriage figure than that referring to religious *upbringing* of spouses. While Protestant-Catholic marriages are much less frequent than would be expected by chance, the number is quite substantial—at least one-fourth of all marriages involving a Catholic—and is in all likelihood increasing.[16] Gentile–Jewish matings

---

[13] Anderson, "Religious Communality among White Protestants, Catholics, and Mormons," p. 504; Lenski, *The Religious Factor,* pp. 37–42; Wozniack, "Assimilation into Pan-Catholicism," pp. 119–20. Wozniack's Buffalo, New York, data indicate that 80 percent of Catholic respondents limited primary contacts mainly to other Catholics.

[14] Harold L. Wilensky and Jack Ladinsky, "From Religious Community to Occupational Group," *American Sociological Review,* 32 (August 1967), pp. 547, 557.

[15] Charles Stember et al., *Jews in the Mind of America* (New York: Basic Books, Inc., 1966); and Charles Y. Glock and Rodney Stark, *Christian Beliefs and Anti-Semitism* (New York: Harper & Row, Publishers, 1966).

[16] Paul J. Reiss, "The Trend in Interfaith Marriages," *Journal for the Scientific Study of Religion,* 5 (Fall 1965), pp. 64–67. Protestant–Catholic religious communalism in Holland, Germany, and Switzerland is also attested to by the relatively high in-marriage rates in these countries for Protestants and Catholics. Johan Goudsblom, *Dutch Society* (New York: Random House, Inc., 1967), p. 56.

are relatively infrequent, between five and ten percent of all marriages involving a Jew, though increase is evident here as well. Interracial marriages are much rarer than even this, but counting all types, it is a measurable phenomenon.

If primary-group and family solidarity are braced by ethnic factors, we might also expect self-identification to contain a significant ethnic component. A majority of Americans do, in fact, identify strongly with their ethnic group, more so than their occupational group. Identification is quite strong not only among the racial minorities, but with white religious groups as well. Will Herberg early stressed the prominence of religion as a locus of identity subsequent to the assimilation of national origin groups within a multiple religious melting pot.[17] However, a fourth stage of assimilation, identificational assimilation, is reached following extensive ethnic intermarriage. Subsequent generations find ethnic ties too diluted to identify with. Intermarriage and loss of identity removes the social visibility of an ethnic group and therewith the possibility of prejudice and discrimination.

Thus, the assimilation process tends to follow through to completion if the structural or primary-group step is bridged: intermarriage, submergence of ethnic identity, and, with the absorption of the ethnic group, the disappearance of prejudice and discrimination against the ethnic group. As Gordon has emphasized, structural assimilation is the keystone to the arch of assimilation.

Ethnic conflict

Ethnic conflict has early and deep roots in the U.S. Overlapping with class position, higher status native-born Americans clashed with immigrants, first other Protestants and then increasingly Catholics. Anglo-Saxons picked out Irish targets for attack, and the Irish fought back; conflict was especially bitter between Ulster Protestants and Irish Catholics, a battle that continues to the present day in Northern Ireland. Later in the 19th century and on into the 20th, workers of British origin, typically having higher occupational status and incomes, clashed with Eastern and Southern European workers in the coal fields of Pennsylvania and in the coastal mill towns as the unskilled immigrants used to undercut wages and break strikes. On the West Coast and in the Mountain states, Anglos attacked Oriental labor with even more vengeance. Mexican-Americans faced harsh discrimination throughout the Southwest by the advancing forces of Anglo capitalism, and are today engaging Anglo power on a variety of fronts. The conflict between the invading white and the native (Indian) American is legendary. Race riots between whites and blacks erupted several times in the first half of the 20th century, and the ghettos burst into flames in the mid-sixties.

While ethnic conflict in the U.S. has been defined mostly in ethnic

---

[17] Will Herberg, *Protestant—Catholic—Jew* (New York: Doubleday & Company, Inc., 1960); also see Ruby Jo Reeves Kennedy, "Single or Triple Melting Pot? Intermarriage Trends in New Haven, 1870–1940," *American Journal of Sociology,* 49 (January 1944), pp. 331–39.

terms, it is easy to decipher an important measure of distinctly class content to much of it. In nearly every case of non-Anglo minority conflict, the minority has been a dispossessed segment of the working poor; and even in 19th century Protestant–Catholic conflict, more established segments of the population clashed with economic marginals. Black–white race riots were perhaps more clearly ethnically incensed prior to mid-century, but the ghetto riots of the 1960s were outbursts of an oppressed minority. Further, the conflict between Mexican-American farm workers and the big growers in California is clearly a case of class struggle, although the ethnic factor contributes a binding influence among the organizers (the Teamsters collusion with the corporate-controlled agro-businesses is an instance of white establishment cooperation against Mexican-American labor power[18]).

THE ROLE OF RELIGION

Sociology has always given considerable attention to religion. Max Weber conducted extensive analyses of the role of religion in society. His thesis regarding the impact of Protestantism upon the rise of capitalism exemplifies the sociological imagination.[19] Weber's chief premise was that religious ideas may exert an independent influence upon behavior and the organization of society; he set out to challenge the Marxist contention regarding the causal primacy of the economic factor. Actually, modern students tend to portray the differences between Weber and Marx in this regard as much broader and decisive than they really are. Weber contended that Protestantism encouraged methodical work and the accumulation of savings, and hence, material accumulation. However, he never attributed to religion any stronger role than that of a stimulation to capitalism, much as the industrial revolution was a stimulation of another kind. The emergence of capitalism is embedded in a complex of economic, political, and social forces, of which religion is, according to Weber, only one. Nor would Marx deny the possibility of culture (superstructure), of which religious beliefs are a part, influencing economic life; much of his analysis is directed toward this very fact. Weber's point was that religious ideas and interests were important and could override material and class interests, though he pointed out how people tend to gravitate toward religious ideas that are congenial to their economic interests. Weber found the purely independent religious force in prophetic individuals possessing charisma or extraordinary power of personal appeal, and whose religious ideas attracted followers congenial to the economic thrust of these ideas.

Emile Durkheim has also written a classic study of religion.[20] Durk-

---

[18] Ronald B. Taylor, "Teamsters & Growers; A Romance Rekindled," *The Nation*, March 19, 1973, pp. 366–70.

[19] Max Weber, *The Protestant Ethic and the Spirit of Capitalism* (New York: Charles Scribner's Sons, 1958); and Max Weber, *The Sociology of Religion* (Boston: Beacon Press, 1963).

[20] Emile Durkheim, *The Elementary Forms of Religious Life* (New York: Collier Books, 1961).

heim looked upon religion as an integrating and cohesive social force; the group reaffirms its legitimacy through the practice of religious rituals and strengthens bonds between members through commitment to religious beliefs. Religion itself, contended Durkheim, is a projection and deification of the human group, the spiritualization of mankind. In attributing to religion a stablizing and integrating influence, Durkheim was not only interpretating social reality, but enunciating his own social preferences.

Marx would not disagree with Durkheim's view of religion as a social projection and social reaffirmation. Marx would, of course, take sharp issue with Durkheim's view of the *positive* function of religion. Although Marx recognized the manner in which religion eased the suffering of the dispossessed, he similarly recognized how by the same token religion stood in the path of revolutionary reconstruction of society. According to Marx, religion epitomizes human alienation, the cleavage of man from himself, from others, and from nature. Marx viewed religion as an escape mechanism, an opiate: "*Religious* suffering is at the same time an *expression* of real suffering and a *protest* against real suffering. Religion is the sigh of the oppressed creature, the sentiment of a heartless world, and the soul of soulless conditions. It is the *opium* of the people."[21] Thus, Marx was not openly hostile toward religion, at least in terms of the balm it provided for the oppressed or the confused. Rather, religion represents a human tragedy.

The longstanding incompatibility between religious fundamentalism and political radicalism would tend to confirm the Marxist interpretation of religion. Research by Gary Marx indicates that in civil rights, for example, religious belief exerts a dampening effect upon militancy.[22] Leftist movements have typically been anti-clerical or hostile toward the organized church; religious fundamentalism is either aloof from politics or actively supportive of the status quo. Nor must the conservative influence of religion be limited to the organized church. Various outcroppings of mysticism and cultism furnish the same social function; they seem to provide explanations for complex questions, comfort in an era of anxiety and impersonality, and common interests within an alienated society. Religion must be couched in diverse terms to meet both social and psychological needs of affluent and poor, old and young, educated and uneducated.[23] Hence, religious denominations tend to have some correlation with class status of the membership.

Historically speaking, and continuing into the recent period, religion

---

[21] *Contribution to the Critique of Hegel's Philosophy of Right,* in *Karl Marx: Early Writings,* trans. and ed. by T.B. Bottomore (New York: McGraw-Hill, 1964), pp. 43–44.

[22] Gary T. Marx, *Protest and Prejudice* (New York: Harper & Row, Publishers, 1967), pp. 94–105.

[23] See H. Richard Neibuhr, *The Social Sources of Denominationalism* (Cleveland: The World Publishing Company, 1962); and Liston Pope, "Religion and the Class Structure," *The Annals of the American Academy of Political and Social Science,* CCLVI (March 1948), pp. 84–91.

in the U.S. has been associated with political voting.[24] Protestants have leaned toward the Republican Party and Catholics and Jews the Democratic Party. The relationship has long been attached more to ethnic ties than any affinity between religion and political ideology. White Protestants have been the insiders and identified their interests with the more conservative Republican Party, whereas Catholics, Jews, and minorities have considered the Democrats as the party of the underdog or the outsider. While to a certain extent these interpretations still hold, the mix up of religious affiliation and party preference is so extensive as to greatly reduce religion as a reliable predictor of voting.

MINORITIES

The U.S. contains numerous ethnic minority groups, but we shall have space to touch upon only a few of them here; the following chapter deals with by far the largest minority, blacks.

Jews

The over 5.6 million Jews in the United States compose almost three percent of the population.[25] The Jewish community in this country had its origins in a small group of Iberian Jews who settled in New Amsterdam in 1654. From a few thousand Jewish persons living in America at the turn of the 19th century, immigration, mainly from Germany, had raised the total to one-quarter million by 1870. Between 1870 and the end of immigration in 1929, about two and one half million Jewish immigrants arrived, over half of them coming from Russia and much of the remainder from Austria-Hungary. Most of the immigrants from Eastern Europe were religiously and ideologically orthodox. While the German Jews who had arrived earlier were becoming well-established economically and socially, the inundation of poor and dispossessed Eastern European immigrants radically altered the image of American Jews. Although there was some early resentment from the Jewish middle class, the support and cooperation of the established Jewish community proved to be of immeasurable value in the adjustment and mobility of the newcomers. The small-family norm (an average of only slightly over two children per family) is limiting the Jewish annual population increase to one percent; therefore the Jewish percentage in the population decreased from a high of 3.7 percent in the 1930s to slightly below three percent in 1970.

Partially as a result of the small family norm and the extended family support, partially due to the high valuation placed upon values that

---

[24] Robert Alford, *Party and Society* (Chicago: Rand McNally & Company, 1963), Chapter 8; and Charles H. Anderson, "Religious Communality and Party Preference," *Sociological Analysis*, 30 (Spring 1969), pp. 32–41.

[25] For a general sourcebook on Jews, see Peter I. Rose, ed., *The Ghetto and Beyond* (New York: Random House, Inc., 1969).

stimulate learning, and partially owing to their exclusion from corporate businesses, American Jews have experienced marked educational and occupational mobility. A large minority are college graduates, and a high proportion of the graduates go on to graduate school; in the younger generation, college plans are almost universal. A recent study of the Jewish population of Providence, Rhode Island, disclosed that 21 percent of the males were professionals, 41 percent managers, 21 percent in sales, 12 percent in clerical or skilled labor, and only four percent in semi-skilled and one percent in service or unskilled labor.[26] One-third were college graduates and one-fifth had attended graduate school. Among females, 90 percent of those working were white collar, and overall almost 20 percent were college graduates. Following the general trend toward salaried employment, the proportion of self-employed Providence Jews declined from a large majority in the older generation to a minority in the middle-aged group and a small minority in the young generation. In a suburban community, nearly all Jewish respondents reported some college, and one third postgraduate work; one-third were professionals, and one-half were in management.[27] In brief, American Jews have had a remarkable record of upward mobility within two to three generations.

Anti-Semitism has evidently declined markedly since World War II, although the Nazi genocide did not in itself arouse much sympathy for Jews in America during the war. Evidence suggests that no more than one-fifth of the Gentile population is anti-Semitic or believes that Jews as a group have objectionable traits, as compared to possibly two thirds in 1940.[28] Indeed, about one-third of Gentiles regard Jews positively (philo-Semitism). Over one-half of the population believes Jews have no distinctive traits as a group. However, most Gentiles in frequent contact with Jews evidently consider them to possess distinguishing traits.[29] In negative terms, Jews are considered as aggressive, clannish, material-istic, and crude; in positive terms, they are considered ambitious, family-oriented, intellectual, and astute in business. Obviously, the outsider places his own interpretation on what he thinks he sees; aggression or ambition, clannishness or family loyalty, materialistic or successful.

The decline in anti-Semitism, or at least in the willingness to express it, is further evidenced by the fact that, while in 1940 one-fourth would object to a Jewish neighbor and two-fifths to a Jewish employee, virtually no one in 1962 expressed such sentiments.[30] Social class, rural-urban, and Protestant and Catholic differences in attitudes toward Jews are relatively minor. And while much is often made over black anti-

---

[26] Sidney Goldstein and Calvin Goldscheider, *Jewish-Americans* (Engle-wood Cliffs, N.J.: Prentice-Hall, Inc., 1968), pp. 65–78.

[27] Marshall Sklare and Joseph Greenblum, *Jewish Identity on the Suburban Frontier* (New York: Basic Books, Inc., 1967).

[28] Stember et al., *Jews in the Mind of America*, p. 8; and Glock and Stark, *Christian Beliefs and Anti-Semitism*, p. 129.

[29] Stember, *Jews in the Mind of America*, pp. 54–56; Ringer, *The Edge of Friendliness*, p. 182.

[30] Stember, *Jews in the Mind of America*, pp. 226–28.

Semitism, blacks tend if anything to view Jews in a better light than they do other whites.[31]

Despite their general similarities in cultural behavior to Gentile society, there exists a sharp cleavage between Jews and Gentiles in primary-group life. Although substantial numbers of both Jews and Gentiles may deny feeling any strains in social relations, Ringer concludes on the basis of his extensive research in a mixed suburb that "fairly strained" would be a better estimate of intergroup relations.[32] While relations may usually be tranquil on the surface, observes Ringer, they may be very delicate underneath. As is often the case with minority groups, Jews frequently find it difficult to define interpersonal conflict or differences with Gentiles in individual rather than ethnic group terms. Thus, half of Ringer's suburban subjects felt ill at ease among Gentiles, fearing prejudice, uncertainties of judgment, and differences in expectation.

The majority of Jews live in mixed neighborhoods and prefer to do so, often giving reasons having to do with familiarizing their children with out-group attitudes and behavior toward Jews. Some, however, prefer the familiarity of a predominantly Jewish neighborhood. Social contact between Jew and Gentile is frequent on a work, community, and neighborhood basis, but very limited in the confines of more intimate primary groups. Although many Jews may express no preference regarding religion of close friends, perhaps as many as half have no close Gentile friends, and most of the remainder belong to primary groups in which Jews are the majority.[33] And many of the Jewish cliques with Gentiles in them are mixed via an intermarriage. It is the ability to be oneself, to be secure and relax, that predisposes Jews to their own group, as it is among any ethnic group: "You can give vent to your feelings. If you talk to a Christian and say you don't believe in this, you are doing it as a Jew; with Jewish friends you can tell 'em point blank what you feel."[34]

Departing from the strong communalism of mainstream Jewish society are the majority of Jewish academics and intellectuals.[35] Jewish academics and intellectuals tend to participate in ethnically mixed primary groups, intermarry in large proportion, and wear their ethnicity lightly.

---

[31] Marx, *Protest and Prejudice*, p. 138.

[32] Ringer, *The Edge of Friendliness*, Chapter 2.

[33] Sklare and Greenblum, *Jewish Identity on the Suburban Frontier*, pp. 272–75.

[34] Herbert J. Gans, "The Origin and Growth of a Jewish Community in the Suburbs," in Marshall Sklare, ed., *The Jews: Social Patterns of an American Group* (New York: The Free Press, 1960), p. 229.

[35] See Allan Mazur, "The Socialization of Jews into the Academic Subculture," in Anderson and Murray, eds., *The Professors;* Charles H. Anderson, "The Intellectual Subsociety Hypothesis: An Empirical Test," *The Sociological Quarterly* (Spring 1968), pp. 210–27; and Norman L. Friedman, "The Problem of the 'Runaway Jewish Intellectuals,'" *Jewish Social Studies*, 31 (January 1969), pp. 3–19.

Mexican Americans

Largely situated in the border states from Texas to Southern California are some five million Mexican Americans, who constitute almost three percent of the nation's population but at least 12 percent of that of the Southwest.[36] The Mexican American minority did not have its initial origins in the U.S. as immigrants, but rather through annexation. The Southwest was Mexican territory until 1836, and held some 75,000 "Spaniards," mostly in New Mexico. American inroads into the area culminated in virtual conquest by 1848, and the bulk of the natives were treated in the same manner as Indians whose land had been stripped away. Only in New Mexico did a small nucleus of established Spanish-speaking families preserve their material position, and only then by collaborating with the American invaders in the exploitation of the Mexican underclass.[37] Militant movements all eventually failed. By the turn of the century, nine-tenths of the Mexican-American people were completely impoverished and surviving on the rural fringes of the society.

The border had always been relatively open, and the passage of Mexicans into the U.S. increased markedly from the time of the Mexican Revolution in 1910. By 1920 as many as 800,000 had crossed the border; many returned to Mexico, but the majority stayed on to attempt to scratch a living as agricultural laborers or in war industries. Even many of those who stayed intended to return home, and so continued to live in the U.S. as aliens. The flow of the decade from 1910 to 1920 became a much broader stream during the boom years of the 1920s, increasing to approximately 1.5 million during that decade. The Spanish-speaking population, although still predominantly rural, had begun congregating in "Mextowns" within the urban areas. Their poverty persisted. The Depression cut the number of border crossings to a relative trickle, but the tempo again began to rise slowly through the 1940s with the increased demand for unskilled labor in the fields and factories. The jobs paid poverty wages in this country, but the goal of many was to save enough money here to make a successful start at home (in this sense no different from large numbers of European immigrants). The flow of Mexicans into the U.S. attained a post-War peak in the mid-fifties—almost matching that of the twenties—and subsided somewhat through the sixties until Congress, with the McCarron-Walters Act, clamped tight restrictions on Western hemisphere immigration.

Labor organizations had historically been opposed to the migrant flow from south of the border, just as they had fought against the importation of Oriental workers. In the post-War period special efforts were under-

---

[36] For general references on Mexican-Americans, see John H. Burma, ed., *Mexican Americans in the United States* (San Francisco: Canfield Press, 1970); Joan Moore, *Mexican Americans* (Englewood Cliffs, N.J.: Prentice-Hall, Inc., 1970); and Leo Grebler, Joan W. Moore, and Ralph C. Guzman, *The Mexican-American People* (New York: The Free Press, 1971).

[37] See John Womack, Jr., "The Chicanos," *New York Review of Books,* August 31, 1972, pp. 12–18.

taken by the U.S. government to limit the number of Mexicans entering and residing in the country, and in a five year period in the 1950s some 3.8 million Spanish-speaking persons were expelled ("Operation Wetback"); the majority were illegally established in the U.S., but many were, in fact, citizens. The longstanding exploitation of Mexican agricultural labor in the Southwest and as migrant labor throughout the Western states has been the traditional reason for the allowance of a relatively open border by U.S. authorities.

The large number of Mexican nationals entering the U.S. since the 1940s was greatly stimulated by the *bracero* farm labor program, terminated in 1968 but without completely stemming the inflow. The influx and exploitation of *bracero* labor by rural capitalists served to depress subsistence wages even lower, encourage employers to ignore laws governing wages and working conditions, and undermine the leverage of Mexican-American labor organizers and strikers.[38] In recent years, however, farm labor in California has achieved notable success in organizing against the abuses of the big growers, despite desperate and violent opposition (the California courts have upheld the right of agricultural labor to organize and strike, but Arizona has passed legislation making such activity illegal!). Caesar Chavez and the United Farm Workers have written a new page in the history of the American labor movement.

But as among blacks in the South, mechanization has displaced large numbers of agricultural laborers in the West, thus shifting the chief locus of poverty from farm to city. Following the more recent generations of Spanish-speaking people into urban poverty have been many long-established independent farmers and artisans whose Spanish-American villages were undermined economically by government expropriation of land and destruction of land by Anglo capitalists.[39] The Alianza movement, began in 1963 and inspired by the former evangelist Reies Lopes Tijerina, has been a rural revolt demanding the return of such expropriate land.[40] Spanish-Americans and Indians have both contested the U.S. government in New Mexico for the return of expropriated land, but with only minor successes thus far.

On nearly all indicators of class status, the contemporary Mexican American, or Chicano, population is among the very worst off, standing at a level comparable to blacks and Puerto Ricans (Table 9). The Mexican American population is very heavily concentrated in lower-blue-collar occupations (including farm labor), reports a median family income of roughly two-thirds the national average, has three times as many persons in poverty as whites, falls significantly behind the educational attain-

---

[38] Sheldon L. Greene, "Wetbacks, Growers and Poverty," *The Nation*, October 20, 1969, p. 404.

[39] See Clark S. Knowlton, "Changing Spanish-American Villages in Northern New Mexico," *Sociology and Social Research*, 53 (July 1969), pp. 455–74.

[40] See Clark S. Knowlton, "The Guerrillas of Rio Arriba: The New Mexican Land War," *The Nation*, June 17, 1968, pp. 792–96; and Joseph L. Love, "La Raza: Mexican-Americans in Rebellion," *Trans-action*, 6 (February 1969), pp. 35–41.

ment norm, and suffers a high rate of unemployment.[41] Complicating these deficits is an extremely young population structure and a relatively high birth rate. However, an advantage of the Mexican Americans over blacks and Puerto Ricans is the markedly lower percentage of broken families, a percentage only slightly higher than that of whites.

In Albuquerque, Merkx and Griego report that approximately one third of Mexican-American family heads are unemployed.[42] Whereas

Table 9

COMPARATIVE SOCIAL AND ECONOMIC STATISTICS OF WHITE, NEGRO, MEXICAN, AND PUERTO RICAN FAMILIES AND PERSONS, MARCH 1971

	White	*Negro*	*Mexican origin*	*Puerto Rican origin*
Number (millions)	177.6	22.8	5.0	1.5
17 years old or under (percent)	34	44	49	49
4 or more own children in family (percent)	9	17	26	16
Female-headed families (percent)	9	31	12	34
Less than 5 years of school (percent)	4	14	26	24
4 years high school or more (percent)	57	35	26	20
All white collar, male employed (percent)	44	22*	18	20
Operatives (percent)	18	27*	28	33
Unskilled labor, service, and farm workers (percent)	15	37*	34	33
Unemployed (percent) ...	6	10*	10	10
Family income (median) ..	$10,236	$6,279	$7,117	$5,975
Head full-time-year-around	$12,016	$8,880	$8,946	$8,829
Persons below low income level (percent)	10	34	28	29

* Negro and other races

Source: U.S. Bureau of the Census, *Current Population Reports,* Series P-20, No. 224, "Selected Characteristics of Persons and Families of Mexican, Puerto Rican, and Other Spanish Origin: March 1971," U.S. Government Printing Office, Washington, D.C., 1971, pp. 3–7; 10–12; 14.

44 percent of the Anglo population is upper white collar, only 11 percent of the Chicano population is so; 41 percent of the latter, however, are unskilled laborers and another 13 percent semi-skilled. In terms of in-

[41] See also, U.S. Bureau of the Census, *Current Population Report,* "Persons of Spanish Origin in the United States: November 1969," Series P-20, No. 213, U.S. Government Printing Office, Washington, D.C., 1971.

[42] Gilber W. Merkx and Richard J. Griego, "Crises in New Mexico," in *Majority and Minority,* Norman R. Yetman and C. Hoy Steele, eds. (Boston: Allyn & Bacon, Inc., 1971), pp. 599–610.

come, one-third of Albuquerque's Chicanos are under $4,000 and four-fifths are under $7,000; the comparable figures for Anglos are 13 and 43 percent. The bulk of the urban Mexican-American population is crowded barrios of the largest cities in the Southwest. What the Alianza movement and the United Farm Workers are to the rural population, the Brown Berets are to the urban poor. Beginning their organizational activities in Los Angeles, the Brown Berets have spread into other urban centers of the Southwest. United Mexican-American Students have brought together the college and university population having organizational goals of ethnic activism.

As a group, Mexican Americans have been slow to acculturate, though trends suggest that the process of cultural assimilation has greatly accelerated in recent years. After all, it wasn't until well into the 20th century that Anglo-Americans achieved numerical ascendance in New Mexico, an area until then dominated by the village community, the patriarchal extended family, a patron–peon system, and folk Catholicism.[43] The Spanish-speaking people of the Southwest were, in short, firmly and securely embedded in a highly integrated cultural system much different from that of their Anglo-American neighbors—a folk as opposed to an urban society. As noted, the economic basis (land) of the traditional Spanish-speaking society of the Southwest was undercut by the U.S. government and Anglo capitalists, and traditional culture patterns, like much of the land, eroded away. Mexican villagers became small-plot farmers, migrant laborers, and urban slum dwellers.

Mexican Americans differ widely among themselves in social class, length of residence, racial composition, and degree of acculturation. Middle-class persons may strive to conform to Anglo behavioral norms and are frequently accepted in Anglo organizations and neighborhoods. Close friendship and marriage with "high-type" Mexican Americans is in some instances considered acceptable by Anglos.[44] Yet full acceptance is rarely offered. The Anglo-oriented Mexican tends to be a marginal person who may resent less acculturated counterparts, while being denied social equality by Anglos.

Anglos frequently hold assumptions and stereotypes about Mexican Americans that are similar to the ones they hold about blacks. For example, Mexicans are considered inferior beings suited primarily for manual and especially "stoop" labor. Despite socioeconomic gradations, most Anglos consider all Mexicans to be alike, making exceptions when necessary and convenient. Mexicans are stereotyped as unclean, deceitful, musical, romantic, and irresponsible. To a large extent, there has in the past been a strong tendency on the part of Mexican Americans to accept the superiority of Anglo culture and society, despite widespread dislike of Anglo ways as impersonal, arrogant, and inconsistent. However, Chicanos have come to emphasize the positive aspects of their

---

[43] Knowlton, "Changing Spanish-American Villages in Northern New Mexico."

[44] Ozzie G. Simmons, "Mutual Images and Expectations of Anglo-Americans and Mexican-Americans," *Daedalus*, 90 (Spring 1961), pp. 286–99.

heritage and to stridently denounce Anglo prejudice; growing numbers of Mexican-American students, veterans, migrants, villagers, and barrio dwellers are rising in protest against poverty and discrimination and are urging organization and group pride.

Interestingly, the peer-group orientation and person-centeredness of Mexican-American attitudes toward work and leisure, family, interpersonal relationships, and individual social mobility are much closer to those of working-class Italian-Americans in Eastern cities than those of their Anglo neighbors in the Southwest. Mexican-American rejection of bureaucratic and economic manipulation by the dominant society is also in accord with the response of the urban villagers.

Indians

Nearly a million strong before their decimation by white diseases, persecution, and guns, the over half a million American Indians are again on the numerical increase.[45] Approximately three-fourths are located on reservations. A mere handful of persons are left to represent some tribes; others such as the Navaho (75,000), Sioux (32,000), Chippewa (25,000), and Cherokee (17,000) count substantial membership. As in the case of many Spanish-speaking communities in the Southwest, the economic bases and cultural integrity of most Indian tribes were systematically destroyed by white society. The majority have never accepted white ways of life. Indian patterns of culture range from the traditional and integrated styles of life among the Navaho to the demoralized and disintegrated life of the Plains tribes, among whom alcohol is commonly used to shore up sagging confidence and a vacuum in meaning. For example, on a South Dakota reservation in 1967 there were some 2,600 arrests involving Indians for disorderly conduct— drunk, out of an adult Indian population of 4,600.[46]

The bureaucratic regulation of reservation Indians is nearly monolithic. The Bureau of Indian Affairs is the closest thing to a total institution that any group of American citizens has ever experienced. The government's *Indian Affairs Manual* fills 33 volumes, standing six feet high. On the bureaucratically top-heavy Pine Ridge Reservation in South Dakota (site of Wounded Knee), the ratio of civil service bureaucrats to Indians is approximately one to one. The Pine Ridge budget, if divided among Indian families, would provide each with incomes of $8,040, yet their median income is only $1,910! Writes a student of Indian affairs, "Behind every official looking over every Indian's shoulder, there are several layers of officials looking over each others' shoulders."[47]

---

[45] For a comprehensive sourcebook on the Indian, see Howard M. Bahr, Bruce A. Charwick, and Robert C. Day, eds., *Native Americans Today: Sociological Perspectives* (New York: Harper & Row, 1972); see, also, Murray L. Wax, *Indian Americans: Unity and Diversity* (Englewood Cliffs, N.J.: Prentice-Hall, Inc., 1971).

[46] Eileen Maynard, "Drinking as Part of an Adjustment Syndrome among Oglala Sioux," *Pine Ridge Research Bulletin,* 9 (June 1969), pp. 35–51.

[47] Edgar S. Cahn, ed., *Our Brother's Keeper: The Indian in White America* (New York: World Publishing Company, 1969), p. 7.

The majority of the Indian labor force is without job opportunities much of the year. Housing facilities range from abandoned car hulks, jerry-built mud huts, broken trailers, and dilapidated, unserviced wood frame houses to modest standard dwellings for the fortunate few who have been allowed into the paying side of the bureaucratic apparatus.[48] Without access to financial capital to develop land and mineral resources, Indians frequently lease their lands to whites for small fees. The flooding of Indian lands by dams such as the Garrison in North Dakota has destroyed the foundations of stable Indian tribes. The state of Washington, which spends up to $2,000 a year per salmon, has not allowed its Indians to fish the Columbia River, despite the rights granted to them by the U.S. government after it had expropriated Indian land. As has always been the case, whenever Indian land has interfered with or held economic promise for government or white interests, Indians are the losers. Even when mineral royalties have been paid over to them, white lawyers cream off huge sums for their favors.

The majority of Indian children attend integrated public schools, but many are in Indian boarding and day schools. Education is frequently made singularly irrelevant or desultory to Indian children. In one classroom, Indian children were asked to write compositions on "Why we are all happy the Pilgrims landed."[49] Punitive white administrators resort to such animalistic disciplinary measures as dunking children's heads in unflushed toilet bowls. Indian peer-group values of courage, loyalty, generosity, passion, luck, and integrity are systematically undercut by school authorities with emphasis on narrow respect for rules, routine, discipline, and academic competition.[50] Thus, while young Indian children tend to start off ahead of whites, the gap progressively widens.[51] The Indian high school dropout rate is the highest in the nation. Indian students who do go on to college are isolated by whites, culturally threatened, and frequently referred to as "bucks" and "squaws."

In cultural values, generosity is the supreme Indian virtue. "Don't be so stingy," or "Don't be a *wasicu* (white)," are common admonitions from Sioux parent to child. The quality of interpersonal relationships is more important than worldly success, treating all men justly and as equals more important than status achievement. Peer-group loyalty and a strong communal orientation characterize many Indians. But as a result of the forcible repression of Indian culture in the 19th century, few traditional and integrating traits have survived. The extended family with its strong social controls has been replaced by a weak matrifocal one. Native religion, the most severely repressed institution, has been channeled mainly into Roman Catholicism and Episcopalianism. Indigenous political leadership and authority was dealt a crushing blow

---

[48] See Robert G. Sherrill, "Red Man's Heritage: The Lagoon of Excrement," *The Nation,* November 10, 1969, pp. 500–503.

[49] Cahn, *Our Brother's Keeper,* p. 2.

[50] Rosalie H. Wax, "The Warrior Dropouts," *Trans-action,* 4 (May 1967), pp. 40–46.

[51] A.D. Fisher, "White Rites Versus Indian Rights," *Trans-action,* 7 (November 1969), pp. 29–33.

through the paternalistic reservation system.[52] Mixed bloods tend to lose command of the native dialect. Small chance, then, that Indian self-acceptance, mutual trust, and group pride could be sustained. Among many tribes, a non-Indian ancestor is a source of prestige and a legal marriage to a white a way to modify the stigma of belonging to Indian society and for children to possibly escape it. Ironically, in a South Dakota sample of high school students, there were far fewer Indians who blamed white discrimination for their problems than whites who were willing to shoulder the blame for the tragedy of the red man.[53] Moreover, many Indian students tended to trust whites more than each other.

Social intercourse between mixed bloods and whites is rather common; a small minority intermarry. Full bloods are much more isolated. The Indian suffers as many degrading stereotypes among whites as other racial minorities, and the imagery tends to be as bad if not worse among neighboring and reservation whites as those far distant. A few Indians successfully relocate to urban areas, but a return to the reservation is frequently the outcome for those who have sought a life among whites in the outside world. Indian shantytowns have taken shape on the fringes of several Western communities, and, in several instances, in inner-city ghettos. The native Americans are, in short, the furthest removed from the core society—culturally, socially, and economically.

There are, however, indigenous movements for change gaining momentum within the Indian community.[54] The American Indian Movement (AIM) has dramatized the Indian condition in the U.S. in several encounters with the white establishment in western South Dakota in 1973, most importantly at Wounded Knee. Whether Indians can yet mend a shattered way of life and self-image into a successful experiment hinges on the determination of whites to cooperate only where needed and allow the Indians a new chance at ethnic self-respect and dignity.

Puerto Ricans

The newest additions to the ethnic landscape of the mainland are the Puerto Ricans.[55] The main influx came in the postwar period, with the peak in the early fifties. Men came for economic reasons, women with their families. In the early 1940s, Puerto Ricans began working extensively as contract agricultural laborers along the East Coast, and continue to work farms and orchards from Florida to New England. Working

[52] Robert K. Thomas, "Powerless Politics," *New University Thought*, 4 (Winter 1966–67), pp. 44–53. This is a report on the Pine Ridge Reservation, site of AIM efforts to strengthen the Indian political voice.

[53] Eileen Maynard, "Negative Ethnic Image among Oglala Sioux High School Students," *Pine Ridge Research Bulletin*, 6 (December 1968), pp. 18–25.

[54] See Stan Steiner, *The New Indians* (New York: Delta Publishing Company, 1967).

[55] See Joseph Fitzpatrick, *Puerto Rican Americans* (Englewood Cliffs: Prentice-Hall, Inc., 1971).

and living conditions are typically deprived and unregulated. Presently, about 1.5 million Puerto Ricans live in the United States, the largest concentration in New York City. The largest concentration of New York's Puerto Ricans is in East Harlem, overlapping with the nation's largest black ghetto.[56] A very small minority of Puerto Ricans themselves are black, but close friendships and what mainlanders would consider interracial marriages between light and dark Puerto Ricans occur without note.

Puerto Rican aspirations duplicate those of earlier European immigrants in that they envisage gradual intergenerational mobility out of the slums and into middle America. The second generation has in fact considerably improved its socioeconomic status over the first as significant numbers, especially females, have moved out of semiskilled and personal service jobs into lower white-collar positions. The largest occupational group among Puerto Rican males, however, remains lower blue collar (see Table 9). Poverty is extensive. A young Puerto Rican population is on the whole handicapped by large and fragile families—a detriment confronted by American Indians and blacks as well (mothers in all of these groups *desire* smaller families).

There are few ethnic organizations, and no Puerto Rican Catholic parishes as such, to help replace the institutional lacunae left when the extended family moved from Puerto Rico.[57] While religious in their own fashion, Puerto Ricans are not nearly so active in the church as other Catholics; some are Protestants. Attempting to countervail organizational, occupational, and demographic liabilities among Puerto Ricans is a strong desire for educational achievement and mobility.[58] A high value is placed on school performance, and children receive considerable encouragement in Puerto Rican homes, the major focus of communal life. But most school authorities set low levels of expectation for Puerto Rican children, again a problem faced by American Indians, Mexicans, and blacks. Puerto Rican arrivals have had little education, contributing to comparatively lower level of educational attainment. Language difficulties have also been present.

Social relations between Puerto Ricans and black Americans are often infused with considerable tension, although there is a notable amount of cordial intergroup contact in friendship cliques. Anglo-Americans are the most preferred group among Puerto Ricans, blacks next, and the newest Puerto Rican immigrants least! Few Anglo-Americans return the compliment. Puerto Ricans, it would seem, have the least amount of ethnic pride and nationalism of any American ethnic group, though the Spanish language is a value in most homes. Blacks, in fact, rate Spanish-speaking people far above Anglos and seemingly have a higher estimation of Puerto Ricans than Puerto Ricans do of themselves. Evidently, Puerto Ricans identify with and plan to benefit from the success system

---

[56] For a study of East Harlem, see Patricia Cayo Sexton, *Spanish Harlem* (New York: Harper and Row, Publishers, 1965).

[57] See C. Wright Mills, Clarence Senior, and Rose K. Goldsen, *The Puerto Rican Journey* (New York: Russell & Russell, Publishers, 1950).

[58] Ibid., p. 157; and Fitzpatrick, *Puerto Rican Americans*, pp. 130–54.

of white America, whereas blacks, and increasingly Mexican-Americans and many younger Indians, tend to stress group pride and nationalism as compatible and even necessary to group advance. Should Puerto Rican strategies for mobility and assimilation fail to materialize, militance and nationalism may grow. Perhaps then Puerto Ricans will recognize the need for group solidarity and organizational strength.

Japanese-Americans

"Scratch a Japanese American and find a white Anglo-Saxon Protestant." Such an aphorism mirrors the belief that Japanese-Americans closely approximate the ideal type of the Protestant ethnic: hard work, thrift, and asceticism.[59] On the other hand, traditional Japanese-American culture in the United States has strong strains of passive conformity, unquestioning deference to authority, and preoccupation with rules. Today's generation, however, is accepting a more flexible and open world view.[60] The Japanese American often represents in the eyes of the white majority the ideal minority group: economically stable and politically nonmilitant.

Despite the idealization of the half million Japanese Americans (two-fifths annexed with Hawaii and a third in California) as a cultural minority, they lack full social acceptance among mainland whites. Feelings of ethnic community run high, however, and there have been cases of Japanese excluding Caucasians from organized groups. Indeed, Japanese organizational life, in sharp contrast to the history of other nonwhite minorities, has been very strong. Ethnic strength and identity have been enhanced through business and property ownership (though much was wantonly confiscated in the 1942 relocation to concentration camps throughout the Western states—one of the most despicable acts committed by white society against a minority), professional and business organizations, women's and children's clubs, a strong family system, and a variety of festivals and celebrations.

An economic strategy of low expectations, assiduous training, full utilization of public education, and capitalization on occupational opportunities as they have appeared has served the Japanese Americans rather well. The chief involvement of Japanese in the economy has historically been in agriculture, but they have also developed a small-business base and are increasing their numbers with white-collar and professional categories. Most of the latter, however, are not in the mixed economy but are dependent on a Japanese clientele.

Why have the Japanese Americans as a nonwhite minority progressed quite abreast with the European national origin group in educational attainment, occupational achievement, and median income? In some ways, the Japanese resemble the Jews in their adaptation to the U.S.

---

[59] Harry Kitano, *Japanese Americans* (Englewood Cliffs, N.J.: Prentice-Hall, Inc., 1969).

[60] See Stanford M. Lyman, "Generation Gap," *Society*, 10 (January–February 1973), pp. 55–63.

Both began largely as unskilled and impoverished laborers or agriculturalists (in the Japanese case). A strong family and ethnic support system helped group members to make adjustments to the external society. A small business base was developed within which intra-ethnic employment and services would be rendered on an independent basis. The kind of prejudice and discrimination faced by Japanese, while clearly more intense than that confronted by Jews, did not attain the debilitating levels consistently faced by Mexicans, Indians, and Negroes. But perhaps most important to Japanese (and Jewish) economic adaptation was a strong family and ethnic community structure (the Japanese have a special name for each American generation) and an independent financial base in small business and agriculture. Finally, certain cultural and psychological attributes seem to have meshed better with the dominant culture, particularly within the context of public education, as compared with the cultural backgrounds of other non-Anglo minorities. The Japanese Americans did not have to abandon fundamental values and identities to adapt to the dominant society.

12

Black Americans

BLACKS IN MOTION

More than any other ethnic group of the modern period, black Americans have been caught up in the throes of social change. Entering the 20th century as an overwhelmingly southern, rural, and illiterate people, blacks today are approximately equally divided between South and North, predominantly urban, and largely literate.[1] In the North, and increasingly in the South, nearly all blacks reside in cities, the large majority in central cities. No major American urban ethnic group has been residentially concentrated or segregated to such an extreme and for such a long period of time as have the millions of black southern migrants and their children living in the ghettos of large northern and western cities.

Many of the blacks who streamed north and west since the time of World War I to work in war and other industrial efforts were high school graduates, possessing more social skills than those who remained behind. However, like most European immigrants before them, the majority of black southern migrants were unskilled laborers who entered the labor force at the lowest wage levels. Although the mass migration of blacks north and westward achieved for most of them real gains in economic and educational opportunities over previous conditions in either the rural or the urban South which they left behind, migration out of the

---

[1] For general references on blacks, see Sidney Willhelm, *Who Needs the Negro?* (Cambridge, Mass.: Schemkman Publishing Company, 1970); Alphonso Pinkney, *Black Americans* (Englewood Cliffs, N.J.: Prentice-Hall, Inc., 1969); Thomas F. Pettigrew, *A Profile of the Negro American* (Princeton, N.J.: D. Van Nostrand Company, 1964); Kenneth B. Clark, *Dark Ghetto* (New York: Harper & Row, Publishers, 1965); Arnold Rose, *The Negro in America* (New York: Harper & Row Publishers, 1964); and *Daedalus*, 94 (Fall 1965) and 95 (Winter 1966).

South today no longer promises a brighter future. Economically, the opportunities for industrial laborers in the North have declined as a result of declining and transplanted industry, automation, and cyclical stagnation almost as rapidly as opportunities arose as a result of war industry and the consumer build up of postwar periods. Socially, the opportunities for blacks and their children seem to have been repressed by the relatively hard lines of Northern segregation, presenting few rights and privileges that cannot be found in the contemporary South. And while the promise of the North has faded, the South itself has been advancing industrially and educationally. The mechanization of agriculture, which has displaced millions of rural laborers, stimulated black urbanization in the South as well as in the North. The modern South has also been one of the chief benefactors of federal military spending, although blacks have been and continue to be systematically and entirely illegally discriminated against in employment by defense contractors.

Despite the fact that at the time of the first census in 1790 blacks composed almost 20 percent (three-quarters million) of the population, their approximately 11 percent (22 million) representation of 1970 is inestimably more conspicuous and important. Blacks constituted a declining portion of the population from 1790 until the end of large-scale European immigration in 1930, reaching a low of 9.7 percent, but owing to a slightly higher natural growth rate formed a very slowly rising proportion since that time. The greater conspicuousness and importance of blacks today as opposed to, say, 1900 are a result of their urbanization, socioeconomic mobility, and political activism. America's vital nodes are its large cities, and numerically speaking its largest cities contain majorities, near majorities, or large minorities of blacks, who thus weigh more heavily in the disposition of American society than their 11 percent representation would indicate.

What they do not have is a fair share of America's income, wealth, and occupational careers. Blacks do not have their fair share of housing space insofar as they are packed by segregation and unequal economic opportunity into ghetto densities that are five times higher than the density of the metropolitan area in which the ghetto is located. And despite constitutional amendments and over half a dozen civil rights acts, blacks still have a substantial distance to travel in the South before they are able to consistently cast their share of votes. Blacks do not even get a fair share of life itself, for black babies die before they are one year old twice as often as white babies, and as adults they cannot expect to live as long. By contrast, when convicted of similar crimes, blacks get by several years more than their share of prison sentences, as compared with whites.

But black Americans are on the move psychologically and politically, their predominant motion today being social rather than geographical. This is not to imply that the black protest movement is of recent origin. As we shall point out below, it has a long and venerable history. However, the scale of the protest movement is relatively new and its aims and strategies more diverse.

RACE

The concept of race is laden with ambiguity. What constitutes a racial group? How is it possible to determine who belongs to what race? The fact that criteria of race are so subjective and variable has led most anthropologists to abandon the whole idea of race as a useful scientific concept. Few students of physical man can agree as to how many subgroups of Homo sapiens there might be. The human mix of genes is due to the mobility and intermingling of peoples throughout human history. While it is possible to observe a number of physical similarities within specific groups of people or geographical regions, due to selective mating or inbreeding, the similarities are only tendencies and not uniformities. It is a truism that all men share innumerably more physical traits in common than they differ in. In comparison to what they share, genetic differences among human groups are almost negligible. Genetic variations within groups, psychological and behavioral predispositions in particular, are far larger than variations between groups.

Ultimately, then, race is only as important as the people of any given society define it to be. Race becomes extremely important and dangerous when a society posits a causal relationship between physical characteristics and cultural behavior—that is, the way a person acts, thinks, and feels is explained by his physical appearance.[2] In such a culture, biology is frequently used as a shortcut account for most intergroup differences. The name for people who evoke biological explanations or justifications for group behavior or treatment of a group is *racist*. When an entire set of social institutions channels expectations and interaction in ways that imply biologically or physically determined differences in cultural behavior, we are dealing with racist society. As Noel argues, "A society is racist—or, more accurately, its structure is supported by a racist ideology —only if the idea of group [biological or genetic] superiority-inferiority is incorporated into the institutional structure."[3] Noel points out that a racist ideology serves to justify a racist social order, and such institutionalized racism made its first appearance in the 16th century as a corollary of colonialism and was pervasive by the 18th century; in effect, institutionalized racism grew up alongside the imperialist phase of capitalist development.

This conception of racism suggests that a society may have racist institutions without everyone being racist or even prejudiced; conversely, prejudice and discrimination may be held and practiced in a non-racist society or by a non-racist person. But as is pointed out in Chapter 3, institutions are ultimately made up of individuals. Thus, while racist institutions may and do make it easy for bigots to act in racist ways and make it difficult for free men to act in nonracist ways, the disease of

---

[2] See Pierre van den Berghe, *Race and Racism* (New York: John Wiley & Sons, Inc., 1967).

[3] Donald L. Noel, "Slavery and the Rise of Racism," in *The Origins of American Slavery and Racism,* Noel, ed. (Columbus, Ohio: Charles E. Merrill Publishers, 1972), p. 158.

racism has its *final* locus in individuals as such. Only individual persons can *act* as racists.

To say that group differences in attitudes and behavior cannot be explained by genetics is *not* to say that a group with physical similarities will not evince cultural similarities or systematically differ in cultural behavior from another group. As W.I. Thomas observed some time ago, if we define a situation as real it tends to be real in its consequences; or in Robert K. Merton's language, there are self-fulfilling prophesies. If, as white Americans have done for centuries with blacks, one group defines another as intellectually inferior and thereby excludes that group from full participation in the educational system, then in terms of the measures of intelligence of that educational system definitions of inferiority will be self-fulfilled. The poor, both black and white, are perpetually faced with the self-fulfilling behavior of more affluent whites. As a result, over an extended period of time, racial differences in attitudes and behavior may indeed arise. Despite the operation of racial self-fulfilling prophesies, *class* differences in cultural behavior *within* black America are much greater than those between black and white.

We might again note, as we did in Chapter 2, that a group may consider itself *culturally* superior to other groups without being racist. Ethnocentrism or, in Noel's words, "in-group glorification," should not be considered racist unless the feelings of superiority are rationalized in biological terms. Although the distinction between ethnocentrism and racism may appear to be purely academic or superfluous, it is not. The ethnocentric person or group considers members of an out-group or minority to be fully capable of equal performance if only the out-group would give up its inferior ways of life and adopt those of the dominant society. By contrast, a racist person or group considers members of an out-group as genetically incapable of equal performance or unworthy of equal treatment or acceptance. These different definitions of out-groups have contributed significantly to the better (though rarely good) racial relations in Latin as opposed to Anglo-dominated areas of the world.

In Chapters 5 and 7 we discussed the attempt by certain social scientists to link racial inequality to intelligence. According to our definition of racism, it is racist to argue that any racial minority (or majority) is genetically inferior in cognitive capacities and hence "explain" social inequality on that basis. It is also bad social science, whether one has in mind psychology, sociology, or economics. As we have pointed out, racial inequality—or inequality of any kind—is not founded upon genetics but upon the economic (including political) structure of the society.

RACE RELATIONS AND INTEGRATION

The majority of blacks are primarily concerned with economic opportunities rather than integration per se, though most realize that greater economic opportunities require integration. But let us consider for a moment some logically possible types of race or ethnic relations. First, two racially defined groups may exist in a social condition of separation or nonseparation; secondly, the choice of separation or nonseparation may be either voluntary or involuntary. Arranging these two factors of separation and choice in the form of a fourfold table, we can observe four types of race relation situations:

| | | CHOICE | |
		Voluntary	Involuntary
RELATIONS	Separation	Communalism	Segregation
	Nonseparation	Integration Assimilation	Racial Quotas

Involuntary separation of racial groups involves segregation and is usually enforced by both legal and extralegal means. Desegregation, or the elimination of legal and extralegal (de facto) obstacles to the freedom of movement in education, housing, employment, public facilities, and so forth, sets up the voluntary choice for separation as either ethnic communalism or integration. Note, however, that integration does not imply assimilation. Schools, neighborhoods, and jobs may be integrated without primary groups, clubs, and families being so. By the same token, then, the choice is not strictly between communalism and integration, for people may be integration-oriented in work, education, and neighborhood while being highly communal in primary-group life. We have already noted that Jews tend to occupy such a position both in preference and fact; and we shall note in a moment that blacks tend to occupy such a position in preference but not in fact.

Where there is an element of coercion or formal intervention in bringing two racial groups together, racial quotas exist, such as in hiring or busing to attain a representative proportion of both groups. Coercion or formal intervention has been necessary to achieve much of the integration that now exists, racial quotas themselves being a means of integration.

Black attitudes

America has its black and white proponents of all variations on the race relations theme. There are both black and white segregationists who disagree radically regarding the worth of one another but fundamentally agree that blacks and whites should have nothing whatsoever to do with each other economically, politically, or socially. These are the extremists or "radicals" in race relations. Significantly, whether they be black or white, the separationists tend to be explicitly or implicitly *conservative* in terms of economic change, siphoning off their energies against one another instead of against inequitable economic institutions. Racial extremists usually say little about programs for economic change and are often the unwitting allies of the economic status quo.[4]

[4] See Paul Feldman, "The Pathos of 'Black Power,'" *Dissent,* 14 (January–February, 1967), pp. 69–79.

Racial extremists may experience personal psychological gains in driving for separation and race superiority, but these types of gains do less to raise wages, construct housing, or provide jobs than do even civil rights acts. The large majority of blacks want to become a part of the economic mainstream of American society rather than withdraw from it. Black separationists who would like to set up their own country have the support of only a very small minority of the black community.[5] Even the type of black separatist who goes only so far as to advocate such things as an all black civil rights movement, avoiding whites if at all possible, having mostly black teachers in schools with mostly black children, and limiting business ownership to blacks in black neighborhoods has the support of rather a small minority of the black population.[6]

On the other hand, nearly all blacks think black children should go to the same schools as whites, the large majority prefer to work on mixed jobs, and a majority prefer to live in mixed neighborhoods.[7] Very few prefer all black schools, workplaces, or neighborhoods, though many naturally prefer to be in the majority. Like Jewish and other minority group thinking on the subject, strict separation would seem to restrict or preclude the possibility of equality of opportunity. Thus, hardly any blacks feel that the federal government is pushing integration too fast. In general, northern blacks are more integration oriented than southerners and, in both North and South, better educated blacks are more integration oriented than lesser educated ones. Even at more intimate levels of interaction, there are differences within the black community regarding integration. Only a minority would prefer an all black social club to an integrated one, and many would approve of marriage to a white.[8]

The black separatist position tends to be associated with antiwhite hostility. However, greater numbers of blacks harbor at least some antiwhite hostility than are black nationalists or separatists. Data presented by G. Marx suggest that about one fourth of black Americans are definitely antiwhite, one fourth are not antiwhite, and the rest are low in antiwhite hostility.[9] Northern blacks tend to be less antiwhite than southerners, older persons less than younger ones, those of higher status less than those of lower status, those informed less than the uninformed,

[5] Joe R. Feagin, "White Separatists and Black Separatists: A Comparative Analysis," *Social Problems,* 19 (Fall 1971), pp. 167–80; Gary T. Marx, *Protest and Prejudice* (New York: Harper and Row, Publishers, 1967), p. 28; Angus Campbell and Howard Schuman, "Racial Attitudes in Fifteen American Cities," National Advisory Commission on Civil Disorders (Washington, D.C.: U.S. Government Printing Office, 1968).

[6] Campbell and Schuman, "Racial Attitudes in Fifteen American Cities."

[7] Marx, *Protest and Prejudice,* pp. 21; 176; William Brink and Louis Harris, *Black and White* (New York: Simon & Schuster, Inc., 1967), pp. 232–34; Lewis Killian and Charles Grigg, *Racial Crises in America* (Englewood Cliffs, N.J.: Prentice-Hall, Inc., 1964), pp. 41–43.

[8] Robert B. Johnson, "Negro Reactions to Minority Group Status," in Bernard Segal, ed., *Racial and Ethnic Relations* (New York: Crowell Company, 1966), pp. 251–70.

[9] Marx, *Protest and Prejudice,* p. 177.

those with high morale less than those with low morale, and those with high self-image less than those with low self-image. Finally, blacks most militant in civil rights are the *least* antiwhite, whereas separatists are the most antiwhite.[10] In brief, the large majority of blacks neither hate whites nor are attracted to them; whites are simply viewed as members of the dominant society who must be dealt with frequently on an educational, occupational, political, and, especially, economic basis.

The relative openness of black attitudes toward whites is frankly astounding, considering the history of white discrimination. Indeed, a majority of blacks feel that whites either want to keep them down or don't care at all about blacks.[11] A majority of blacks also feel that many or almost all whites dislike blacks. Yet, about one-third feel whites are neutral or favorable toward blacks, and a majority that blacks will in the future be fully accepted by whites. Significantly, the sharpest difference of opinion within the black community concerning beliefs about white attitudes towards blacks is between younger and older college graduates; black college graduates over 39 years of age are twice as likely to perceive white attitudes as favorable compared to those 39 or under.[12] Paradoxically, the white counterparts of the young blacks are more favorable toward blacks than the white counterparts of the older black generation.

Part of the explanation of black tolerance of whites may be found in the often overlooked fact that, like the American Indians we noted in the previous chapter, many blacks (one study reported one-half)[13] blame not whites but themselves for black socioeconomic problems. However, self-blame does not imply self-deprecation. The same study which found that one-half of black respondents blamed themselves for their lower economic position also found that most were proud to be black and approved of race pride, while disapproving of whitewardly mobile blacks and Uncle Toms.[14] But that many blacks are willing to shoulder the blame for their lower socioeconomic status instead of pinning it on whites or the system they dominate is a form of black self-criticism many whites, in a day of charge and countercharge, are not aware exists.

Younger blacks of the right (separationists) and left (civil rights militants and economic radicals) are increasingly likely to attack whites and white institutions for black difficulties. White academic conservatives have taken this as an opportunity to argue that many blacks are unwilling to work hard educationally and occupationally for economic gains, inasmuch as they have exonerated themselves from intellectual and physical effort on the basis of previous white discrimination. While a few blacks may expect lifetime compensation for a history of white discrimination, we know that virtually all desire self-help avenues to change, the only avenue that can provide genuine returns.

---

[10] Ibid., pp. 185–99.

[11] Ibid., p. 171; and Campbell and Schuman, "Racial Attitudes in Fifteen Cities."

[12] Campbell and Schuman, "Racial Attitudes in Fifteen Cities."

[13] Johnson, "Negro Reactions to Minority Group Status, p. 263.

[14] Ibid.

We should keep in the forefront of discussion the fact that separation or integration is not the primary concern of the average black American. In focusing on issues of race relations or how blacks and whites relate to one another socially, we become unwitting conservatives; the concern of the majority is primarily with wages, jobs, housing, education, and personal safety. There is the awareness by blacks, however, that gains in these areas will require integration. The crucial challenge confronting advocates of change is the implementation of radical economic programs and the redistribution of power. Race relations as such is today the *dependent* variable, reacting positively or negatively with changes in economic and political institutions.

White attitudes

The large majority of whites are not segregationists, at least in expression of attitude. (The fact that a very substantial minority of whites in the study by Feagin cited above responded yes to a question regarding the desirability of blacks having a separate state or county should keep us alert to questions of respondent validity of the subsequent data.) The majority are now willing to accept integrated politics, public facilities, jobs, schools, and many even neighborhoods.[15] The majority of whites accept blacks as intellectual equals and, for example, would go to a black doctor for medical care. The majority of whites approve of equal political, employment, educational, and housing opportunities for blacks, and a sizable minority favor the enforcement of laws to back up the opportunities. Whites are nearly equally divided on the question of neighborhood integration, and from that issue on toward the more informal aspects of group life involving social clubs, cliques, and family, they become increasingly opposed to racial mixture. But blacks are themselves communally oriented and few desire integration (assimilation) at the level of informal group life. And while social acceptance by whites in schools, jobs, public facilities, and neighborhoods would be a natural human concern, the interest in integration among blacks has largely to do with life chances or material well-being.

The general posture of whites toward blacks runs the entire gamut from concern to neutrality to prejudice and racism. For example, as a white survey respondent commented about black Americans, "They're tired of being the underdog. This country is very prosperous, and too many Negroes have not shared in this prosperity."[16] By contrast, we have extremist attitudes toward blacks with which black extremists tend to agree, but for different reasons, such as "They should be treated like Jews and put in a country of their own. They are egged on by the Communists." A study of Florida junior high school students disclosed that 31 percent of white students were shocked, grieved, saddened, or angry

[15] See Angus Cambell, *White Attitudes Towards Black People* (Ann Arbor: Institute for Social Research, 1971); Paul B. Sheatsley, "White Attitudes toward the Negro, *Daedalus*, 95 (Winter 1966), pp. 217–38; and Brink and Harris, *Black and White*, pp. 122–31.

[16] Brink and Harris, *Black and White*, pp. 122–23.

at the murder of Martin Luther King, but 59 percent were indifferent or pleased.[17] Female students were much more likely to be disturbed by King's death than males, and upper white-collar children much more likely than lower white-collar and working-class children. In striking contrast to a mere 15 percent of white students who felt loss of some one close in King, 81 percent of black students expressed such a loss in the death of John F. Kennedy, a greater proportion than among whites themselves.

As alluded to above, the new middle class, especially professional workers, is the most prointegration; in the North, there is throughout the rest of the occupational structure relatively minor variation by broad background. Higher educated persons are more prointegration than those with lower levels of education, and Jews more so than Gentiles. However, easily the largest variation on integration within the white population is regional, the North and West being approximately twice as prointegration as the South. However, white attitudes toward integration are continually shifting, and regional differences are narrowing. Compared with 1960, whites have reportedly liberalized their attitudes toward integration, probably reflecting a combination of the passage of federal civil rights legislation, rising levels of education, and some socio-economic mobility of segments of the black population.

Despite the gradual increase of prointegration sentiment (which has interestingly followed closely behind the decline of anti-Semitism) and the fairly pervasive belief in equality of opportunity for blacks, whites have thus far been for the most part unwilling to push through the kinds of important economic changes that are necessary for integration and equality of opportunity, not to mention the elimination of gross inequality of condition. In fact, the majority of whites feel that blacks are asking for *too much* and are strongly and increasingly opposed to black activism (white conservatism here is not primarily racial but ideological, inasmuch as the large majority of white adults feel that white students are asking for too much and strongly oppose student activism).

The dilemma that American society faces, then, is that while the white majority believes in equality of opportunity and increasingly that integration is a prerequisite to equality of opportunity, the majority does not recognize how distant equality of opportunity really is and that it is growing *more distant* all of the time. The impasse is an inability to recognize the growing incompatibility of corporate capitalism with equality of opportunity and material justice, and the consequent passivity and acquiescence to the status quo.

ECONOMIC REALITIES

Like all other members of the working class, blacks have always found their condition in the U.S. determined by their position in the organization of production. Brought to America as slave labor for the enrichment

---

[17] James W. Clarke and John W. Soule, "How Southern Children Felt about King's Death," *Trans-action*, 5 (October 1968), pp. 35–40.

of the planter aristocracy, blacks have been pushed and pulled by the needs of the dominant bourgeoisie. "Emancipated" by the needs of Northern capitalists for an industrial as opposed to an agricultural-aristocratic South, blacks were only to sink into wage slavery at a poverty level.[18] From that point on, the black population saw its fortunes hinge on the demand for manual labor, rising momentarily in "boom" periods (especially and almost entirely war stimulated) and sagging the rest of the time.[19] Blacks have served the needs of the ruling class by providing cheap labor, constituting an industrial reserve army with which to threaten wage demands of white labor, working in the most degrading and menial jobs (most of which could be automated but at a greater cost), and maintaining a weakening cleavage in the working class.

Although the black labor force increased in the proportion of white-collar jobs from 1960 to 1970, nearly all of the gain can be accounted for by low-paying clerical and salaried professional (social work and teaching) employment (see Table 10). And whereas the white work

Table 10

CURRENT OCCUPATION OF EMPLOYED PERSONS BY RACE AND SEX

	Black		White	
	1970	1960	1970	1960
Male				
Professional and technical	5.8%	3.3%	14.8%	11.6%
Managerial	4.1	1.4	15.4	12.2
Clerical	8.6	6.1	7.4	7.7
Sales	1.6	1.6	6.1	7.5
Craftsmen	14.2	10.0	20.6	21.3
Operatives	30.6	27.0	18.9	20.5
Nonfarm laborers ..	18.9	24.3	5.7	5.6
Service workers	11.7	15.6	6.0	5.5
Farm	4.5	10.6	5.2	8.1
Total employed	100.0%	100.0%	100.0%	100.0%
Female				
Professional and technical ...	10.0%	7.0%	15.5%	14.6%
Managerial	1.4	0.7	4.7	4.4
Clerical	18.9	8.1	36.1	34.9
Sales	2.5	1.3	7.3	8.8
Craftsmen	0.8	0.9	1.1	1.4
Operatives	16.8	14.0	14.5	16.7
Nonfarm laborers ..	0.9	0.8	0.4	0.5
Service	48.1	63.7	18.8	17.2
Farm	0.5	3.6	1.5	1.5
Total employed	100.0%	100.0%	100.0%	100.0%

Source: U.S. Bureau of the Census, *Current Population Reports*, Series P-23 No. 37, "Social and Economic Characteristics of the Population in Metropolitan and Nonmetropolitan Areas: 1970 and 1960," U.S. Government Printing Office, Washington, D.C. 1971, Table 14, pp. 60–62.

[18] See Eugene Genovese, *The Political Economy of Slavery* (New York: Pantheon Books, 1965).

[19] Willhelm, *Who Needs the Negro?*

force is two-thirds white collar or skilled blue collar, the black work force is only one-third white collar or skilled. Compared with whites, blacks are greatly overrepresented in low-paying personal service and unskilled jobs. The higher paying the job, the poorer is the ratio of actual to expected employment of black persons: social workers, 1.17 (over-represented); teachers, .77; skilled workers, .50; sales, .19; lawyers, .12; engineers, .10; salesmen in manufacturing, .06; and salaried managers in manufacturing, .05.[20] At the rate of change during the fifties and sixties, scores of years, indeed centuries, would be required for blacks to catch up with whites in the categories of professionals and managers, owing not only to the slow progress of blacks but to the continuing advancement of whites. The occupational gap itself has narrowed very little if at all over the past generation.

Much fanfare surrounded the Nixon administration's slogan of "black capitalism." The fact of the matter is that black business has been in the past stronger than it is today and is coming to be. For example, there used to be 68 black-owned banks compared with today's 21.[21] The number of black-owned businesses in Harlem itself has dropped by one-third over recent years. In the ghettos themselves, blacks own only one in five of all businesses, the majority of these being marginal personal services establishments.[22] The perennial discrimination against blacks in the sales, skilled, and construction trades has long blocked one of the common avenues of entrance into small business—salesman into store owner, plumber into shop owner, and construction worker into building contractor. Indeed, the systematic discrimination against blacks in skilled, building, construction, and most manufacturing trades has pulled a crucial rung out of the mobility ladder, the step bridging the gap between ordinary labor and the business and professional world. Further, business loans or credit to blacks, especially ghetto prospects, are strictly limited or unavailable, while insurance may be impossible to obtain and exorbitant in cost if available.[23]

But today discrimination is not the chief obstacle to black capitalism. The chief obstacle is the fact that 500 white-owned and white-controlled corporations monopolize the economy, stacking the odds against the independent small businessman, black or white (three out of four small business fail within their first three years).

Within their own community, blacks are faced with a severe shortage

---

[20] Leonard Broom and Norval Glenn, *The Transformation of the Negro American* (New York: Harper and Row, Publishers, 1967), p. 113.

[21] George Eckstein, "Black Business—Bleak Business," *The Nation*, September 15, 1969, pp. 243–45.

[22] Albert J. Reiss, Jr. and Howard Aldrich, "Absentee Ownership and Management in the Black Ghetto," *Social Problems*, 18 (Winter 1971), pp. 444–61. See, also, Arthur I. Blaustein and Geoffrey Faux, *The Star-Spangled Hustle: White Power and Black Capitalism* (New York: Doubleday & Co., 1972).

[23] Louis L. Knowles and Kenneth Prewitt, *Institutional Racism in America* (Englewood Cliffs, N.J.: Prentice-Hall, Inc., 1969), pp. 16–17.

of professional personnel, most importantly doctors, dentists, and lawyers. The educational system and the political and economic powers that guide it are doing next to nothing to rectify these shortages. For example, while blacks represent about one percent of the legal profession, they represent only 1.3 percent of today's law students.[24] The urgent need for legal services within the black community, and among the working class at large, cannot be overemphasized. And though blacks have made quite notable gains in such areas as social work and primary and secondary teaching, the wages are low and the opportunities in these areas, race aside, have already been sharply cut back by surplus labor and financial austerity. In other areas of government service, blacks have realized their best progress, but again at the lower ratings.

Black underrepresentation in the legal profession is paralleled by underrepresentation in law enforcement. Considering riot cities such as Detroit, Newark, Cleveland, and Baltimore, where blacks compose about one-half of the populations, black representation on the police force has been less than 10 percent.[25] As in the professions and other government service, black policemen are uniformly of low rank; it wasn't until 1968 that the city of San Francisco so much as named a black sergeant on a force of nearly 1,800 men.

To the black laborer, writes participant observer Elliot Liebow, "the job is not a stepping stone to something better. It is a dead end. It promises to deliver no more tomorrow, next month or next year than it does today"; what's worse, "A man's chances for working regularly are good only if he is willing to work for less than he can live on, and sometimes not even then."[26] Thus, whereas a highly paid skilled worker may not value his work in an intrinsic way, he places very high value on it as a means of family support, family authority, and social respect. The low-paid laborer, especially the black laborer, cannot value work even on these extrinsic counts. Little wonder, then, that Liebow declares that for the black laborer the man-job relationship is a tenuous one. And little wonder also that dead-end "job training" and menial dead-end jobs may offer slight stimulus or hope to low-income persons already fully acquainted with the mechanics of the bottom end of the American economic system.[27] Liebow believes that "jobs alone are no longer enough."[28] Many blacks, Liebow argues, must undergo psychological change to achieve self-confidence in the realm of work. While this may be true for some, the large majority of the unemployed need only decent and promising opportunities; and even for those most demoralized, we might well expect rapid response to genuine challenge.

---

[24] Ibid., p. 64.

[25] Ibid., p. 60.

[26] Elliot Liebow, *Tally's Corner* (Little, Brown and Company, 1967), pp. 50–51, 63.

[27] See David Wellman, "The *Wrong* Way to Find Jobs for Negroes," *Transaction,* 5 (April 1968), pp. 9–18.

[28] Leibow, *Tally's Corner,* p. 224.

The extent of real unemployment among blacks is much greater than the official rate of 10 to 12 percent (the official rate for teenagers and many central cities is at least double this). The real rate of unemployment and underemployment could well run to one-half of the potential black labor force.

Income

We have already pointed out the wide gap between black and white income (Table 1), but we shall examine the differences in greater detail here. The most important point to make regarding black income levels is that, like white real income and purchasing power, they rose substantially from World War II to the mid-sixties, but they have not risen *relative* to white levels. Occasional relative gains such as from 1965 to 1968 are erased by unemployment and growing income discrepancies between the skilled and the unskilled (among whom blacks are overrepresented and thus more affected). Given existing differences, the arithmetic of income differentials alone makes it difficult to close the black-white gap. With median black income for full-time, year-around male workers ($6,435) only about two-thirds of white income ($9,447),[29] a hypothetical 10 percent annual increase for blacks and a 5 percent increase for whites (a rare actual case over the past 25 years) does very little to alter the absolute income difference.[30] Indeed, the actual annual percentage increases since 1950 have usually been quite similar and, given base differences, have more often than not *widened* rather than narrowed the black-white absolute income gap. The white-black female income gap for full-time workers is much more narrow at a rate of about .80 compared to the male .66.

With all black workers in the labor force as the universe, and not just full-time workers, the ratio of black to white individual income drops from .66 to .57. Owing both to discrimination and a lower occupational distribution, southern blacks are much worse off relative to whites in purely income terms than are northerners; for example, Indiana blacks earn four-fifths the amount of white Indiana income, but Mississippi blacks earn only one-third as much as Mississippi whites. Black females in the North earn almost as much as their white counterparts, but a wide female income gap exists in the South.

Focusing on specific jobs, we find that in those in which blacks are mainly dependent upon a black clientele, the ratio of black to white income is worse than in salaried jobs, and considerably worse than in government salaried jobs. For example, the ratio of black to white income for physicians is .39 and insurance agents, .63, but for professors and airplane mechanics, .77 and .88, respectively, and for police and mail

[29] *The American Almanac* (New York: Grosset & Dunlap, 1973), pp. 93–94.

[30] Aaron Wildavsky, "The Empty-head Blues: Black Rebellion and White Reaction," *The Public Interest*, 11 (Spring 1968), pp. 3–16.

carriers, .95 and .96, respectively.[31] Differences in specific government jobs mirror the lower GS or civil service pay-scale ratings of blacks.

In examining black-white income differentials, we discover at least a partial explanation for the greater militancy and activism of higher educated blacks: the higher the educational level attained, the greater is the relative difference between black and white income. College-educated blacks earn only about two-thirds of the income of college-educated whites, whereas blacks with an eighth-grade education or less earn three-fourths of the income of similarly educated whites. Thus, not only are college-educated blacks confronted with greater feelings of relative deprivation from the standpoint of their comparative or equity reference group, they also have a better vantage point from which to assess and perceive their situation. Viewed otherwise, a black family headed by a *college* graduate has a median income of only $500 more than a white family headed by a *high school* graduate; but to terminate at high school graduation would mean that the black family would fall $3,000 *behind* the white high school-headed family.

In effect, blacks in the very same occupations as whites, and with the same formal education as whites, must still pay a high price for their color. Despite these kinds of liabilities, nearly 40 percent of all blacks, liberally interpreted, may be considered as economically at or above subsistence levels; but another 40 percent are marginal or near-poor, and 20 percent are impoverished. Black economics are, relatively speaking, bleak economics.

Education

Underneath some of, though certainly far from all, the occupational and income deficits experienced by blacks lies an educational deficit (blacks with similar levels of education still face occupational and income deficits). Although the gap in the median number of years of completed education between black and white has narrowed over the past two generations, the broad distribution of educational resources is inequitable and has not changed appreciably in recent years. The median education of black and white are closer together now than in previous generations, but the absolute gap between the best and worst educated thirds of the black and white male population is wider in the 1930-born generation than in that born in 1910.[32] More blacks are finishing high school and entering college, but also more whites are finishing college and entering graduate school.

The quality of most black education is markedly inferior to that received by the majority of whites. In the mid-sixties, fully 85 percent of black student intelligence test scores were below the white average, the differences in scores increasing from the early grades upward and being

---

[31] Broom and Glenn, *The Transformation of the Negro American,* p. 114.

[32] See Christopher Jencks and David Riesman, "Class in America," *The Public Interest,* 10 (Winter 1968), pp. 65–85.

much greater in the South than in the North and West.[33] Five times as many black as white youths are rejected for military service for mental reasons. An ex-dean of Harvard College working as director of freshman studies at a black college in the South writes that students entering the college seem to be, on the average, at about the 9th- or 10th-grade level in mathematical and language skills.[34] In 1968, the U.S. Civil Rights Commission found that in Clarke County, Alabama, virtually all white schools were valued and insured for more than $100,000, whereas no black school was valued above $20,000 and two were insured for $750. In asking the state superintendent of education why Clarke County has white schools worth $100,000 and black schools worth $750, the commission received the following reply: "Well, I would assume that the building which is assessed for $100,000 is a more expensive building than the one that is assessed for $750. That would be a reasonable assumption. Now, the state has nothing to do with the building of either one of the buildings. All the plans were promulgated by the local school system. It is a little something that we call democracy and we think it has worked pretty well."[35]

We have previously (Chapter 7) discussed at length the significance of college education for economic mobility. It is precisely in the matter of college degrees where black-white inequality is the greatest and evinces the fewest signs of change. Proportionately, between two and three times as many whites as blacks have graduated from college, and the ratio of black to white graduates in 1970 (.38) is unchanged from 1960 (Table 11). The disparity is as great for the age bracket 25–29 as for older brackets, although the black to white ratio among

Table 11

YEARS OF COLLEGE COMPLETED BY PERSONS 25 YEARS OLD AND OVER, BY RACE

	Black	White	Ratio
1960 (25 years old and over)			
4 years or more of college	3.1%	8.1%	.38
1 to 3 years of college	4.1	9.3	.44
1970 (25 years old and over)			
4 years or more of college	4.5	11.6	.38
1 to 3 years of college	5.9	10.7	.55
1971 (25–29 years old only)			
4 years or more of college	6.4	16.9	.38
1 to 3 years of college	11.0	16.7	.65

Source: *Statistical Abstract/American Almanac* (New York: Grosset & Dunlap, 1973), p. 112.

---

[33] James S. Coleman et al., *Equality of Educational Opportunity* (Washington, D.C.: U.S. Government Printing Office, 1966).

[34] John U. Monro, "Negro Colleges: Escape from the Dark Cave," *The Nation*, October 27, 1969, p. 434.

[35] Ibid., p. 438.

those with one to three years of college has improved. As on other indices, the relative position of southern blacks is worse than elsewhere. Only 15 percent of young black men and women residing in the South will get to college, as compared with 50 percent of young whites. Yet, more than half of all blacks attending college are enrolled in southern schools, some 120 junior and senior all-black schools. As Monro has pointed out, these "black colleges are reaching a seriously disadvantaged population that no other colleges even know about, much less can reach."[36]

In addition to the relatively inferior physical plant, academic facilities, staff educational background, and curriculum, black students have the benefit of fewer college-oriented reference groups or models, both in the school environment and the home. In fact, the comprehensive national survey conducted by social scientists for the federal government indicated that variation in educational achievement accounted for by variation in school facilities, equipment, and staff over and above that accounted for by family background and characteristics of student peers is relatively minor.[37] (See Chapter 7.) However, in regard to this research finding, we might point out that it is difficult to separate the handicaps of inferior school facilities and instructional level from those of background and general social context. And survey data (Coleman, Jencks) clearly reveal that the primary school has a significant effect upon cognitive development, though the independent impact of the school is not nearly so marked in later years once self-concept and aspirations have been rather firmly established.

James Baldwin has succinctly expressed the meaning of education to a black youth from the perspective of his own experience; "School began to reveal itself . . . as a child's game that one could not win, and boys dropped out of school to work. My father wanted me to do the same. I refused, even though I no longer had any illusions about what an education could do for me; I had already encountered too many college-graduated handymen."[38]

The Supreme Court decision on school integration in 1954 heightened the debate on whether the aim of the black movement should be that of integrating schools or improving black schools. That segregated schools promote economic inequality is a fact challenged by some, but agreed upon by most. For example, Crain has recently shown that blacks graduated from integrated schools have better jobs and higher incomes than those with the same level of educational attainment and from the same class background educated in segregated schools.[39] The greater economic success of blacks from integrated schools, argues Crain, is probably not

---

[36] Ibid., p. 437.

[37] Coleman et al., *Equality of Educational Opportunity.*

[38] James Baldwin, *The Fire Next Time* (New York: Dell Publishing Company, 1963), p. 31.

[39] Robert L. Crain, "School Integration and Occupational Achievement of Negroes," *American Journal of Sociology*, 75 (January 1970), pp. 593–606.

linked to formal education at all but to more contact with and trust in whites which has provided information about employment opportunities through types of informal social contacts which segregated blacks don't have. Thus even if occupational discrimination were eliminated, educational segregation would lower the incomes of blacks insofar as they are denied access to resources of information about opportunities in employment. As Crain correctly points out, the best jobs are usually not advertised to begin with, since they can be filled without incurring the cost of advertising. Moreover, blacks and whites alike have long tended to *define* black schools as inferior, regardless of their physical and academic characteristics; and definitions are often self-fulfilling.

But asking for the improvement of black schools does not necessarily mean opposition to integration. Only a small minority of extremists of both races feel that segregated schools can ever result in equality. The building up of ghetto or black schools must move ahead concurrently with efforts of integration. The extreme residential segregation of the black community necessitates the reconstruction of ghetto schooling, irrespective of integration ideologies. Central-city schools would often be predominantly black even if all central-city schools were "integrated"; for example, Manhattan's public schools are 80 percent nonwhite. The exodus of central-city whites to private schools or to the suburbs and the racial or economic exclusion of blacks from the suburbs have often made integration of central-city schools on a neighborhood basis a logical impossibility. School segregation and integration hinge largely on residential segregation and integration, though busing and proposals for centralized educational complexes may circumvent residential segregation. (The busing uproar of 1972 should be interpreted in the light of the fact that fully 44 percent of public school enrollment rode a bus to school in that year and only one percent of it was due to integration efforts.) In the South, where black neighborhoods are often separated from one another, the gerrymander is a common technique of maintaining segregation.

Segregated education is still a predominant fact of American life, and nearly a generation after the desegregation ruling. Overall, about four-fifths of white students attend schools that are nearly all white, and two-thirds of black students attend schools that are nearly all black.[40] In the South, the percentage of blacks attending desegregated schools varies from about seven percent in Mississippi to nearly 40 percent in Texas, the average from the Deep South being about 14 percent and for the rest about 25 percent. These figures represent headway since 1954, but with a few districts excepted, largely of the token variety. The federal government has only weakly stood behind its constitutional pledge to black America to desegregate schools; rarely has it used its potent financial levers to enforce integration and only half-heartedly has it assigned a mere handful of overworked Justice Department lawyers to the entire spectrum of civil rights—far too few to even deal with educational prosecutions alone. But then, federal civil rights action is unpopular with most

---

[40] Coleman et al., *Equality of Educational Opportunity.*

southern political bigwigs, and administration leaders are careful not to offend these valuable allies (the Humphrey-Maddox bear hug being the symbolic epitome of this long-standing fact of American politics).

Ghetto as colony

Certain students of race relations in the U.S., Blauner and Tabb in particular,[41] have likened the black ghetto to an imperialized colony much as those of Africa or Latin America. Tabb enumerates the following similar traits shared by poor nations and black ghettos: low per capita income, small middle class, low technological development and labor productivity, outside ownership, credit defaults, unskilled labor and high unemployment, privileged positions held by outsiders, local leaders dependent upon outsiders, occupying military or police, and low rate of economic growth. The list could be extended to such things as higher birth rates, young population structure, higher infant mortality rates, deterioration of physical structures and housing, etc.

The parallels are those which any region or people come to display when in a subordinate relationship to external financial powers. The ghetto is underdeveloped and grows increasingly morose, while the surrounding society feeds in any way it can off what resources the ghetto has to offer. The same relationship of underdevelopment and development exists between Latin America and the U.S.[42] Further, so long as colonies or ghettos maintain a subordinate relationship with an external profit-oriented system, they can never rise out of their underdeveloped condition. The evidence in support of this view is overwhelming.

What would it mean to say that the black ghetto breaks away from the control of "foreign" capital? There are no plantations, mines, refineries, and modern factories in the ghettos. What are the forces of production the ghetto has to "nationalize"? Certainly the residents could take charge of the administrative apparatus, land use, schools, small businesses, etc. But none of these are direct sources of material production as such. Thus, while external conditions may be similar in many ways, the solutions to colonization and ghettoization are very different. The underdeveloped societies must themselves socialize the means of production within their respective countries, whereas the people of the black ghetto —living *in* a developed society but not being fully part *of* it—must join with the larger working class in the establishment of a new social and economic order. As Proctor points out, "Black liberation and working-class liberation are inseparably linked."[43]

---

[41] Robert Blauner, "Internal Colonialism and the Ghetto Revolt," *Social Problems,* 16 (Spring 1969), pp. 393–404; and William Tabb, *The Political Economy of the Black Ghetto* (New York: W.W. Norten and Company, 1970). On ghetto formation, see Robert E. Forman, *Black Ghettos, White Ghettos, and Slums* (Englewood Cliffs: Prentice-Hall, Inc., 1971).

[42] See Andre Gunder Frank, *Capitalism and Underdevelopment in Latin America* (New York: Monthly Review Press, 1969).

[43] Roscoe Proctor, "Black Workers and the Class Struggle," *Political Affairs,* LI (January 1972), p. 17.

In this vein, the black ghetto is much more class conscious and industrially advanced in education and experience than most Third World peoples, suggesting that they are in an historically different position than the underdeveloped countries. For while the bourgeoisie and capital development within the ghetto is small, the ghetto is an articulated part of the largest, richest, and most powerful bourgeoisie in the world. The ghetto is preeminently urban and stands within a highly industrialized society; the colonial world is preeminently rural and even its cities are made up in large part of rural-oriented, peasant-derived people.

In short, although the ghetto has external traits of a colony, structurally and historically it has very little in common with the underdeveloped world. The paths out of oppression and poverty must take different courses.

FAMILIES

Although middle-income black families tend to be paragons of family unity and stability by comparison, the fact that the black population has an overall high rate of family dissolution is today pervasively known.[44] About nine in ten white families are biparental, compared with seven in ten black families (at the same class levels, however, the black-white differences are considerably reduced). Nearly all of the one in ten white families and three in ten black families that contain a single parent are female-headed families.

The comparatively high number of female-headed families in the black population has often been attributed to the legacy of slavery. However, statistics contradict this view. Throughout the postbellum era black people were successfully establishing a biparental family system, so that by 1917 nearly 9 in 10 children were born in wedlock.[45] From that point forward, however, the rate of family break-up and of illegitimate births increased. The rise of illegitimacy and female-headed families has coincided with 20th-century urban ghettos and industrial economic insecurity. These figures strongly suggest that the female-headed family is a response to the economic pressures of industrial America.

While black illegitimacy is substantially higher than white (31 percent of all births versus five percent of white), the white *rate* has been increasing and the black rate declining.[46] Further, the difference is magnified by the fact that black unwed mothers more often marry after the

---

[44] See Jessie Bernard, *Marriage and Family among Negroes* (Englewood Cliffs, N.J.: Prentice-Hall Inc., 1966), and Andrew Billingsley, *Black Families in White America* (Englewood Cliffs, N.J.: Prentice-Hall, Inc., 1968).

[45] Bernard, *Marriage and Family among Negroes*, p. 3.

[46] Reynolds Farley and Albert I. Hermalin, "Family Stability: A Comparison of Trends Between Blacks and Whites," *American Sociological Review*, 36 (February 1971), pp. 1–17; and U.S. Bureau of the Census, *Current Population Reports*, Series P-23, No. 36, "Fertility Indicators: 1970," U.S. Government Printing Office, Washington, D.C., 1971, Table 23, p. 44.

birth of a child compared with whites who more often marry prior to giving birth;[47] there is also a differential reporting in statistics whereby white illegitimacy is more often officially unreported. Differential access to birth control information and abortion also contributes to the lower white rate. Whether illegitimate or even legitimate, the proportion of unwanted births within the black population is extremely high, well over one-third of the total of legitimate births and the large majority of illegitimate births.[48] The white population differs on this point only by a matter of degree, for it, too, has a very substantial number of unwanted children. We have yet to see what effect will come from the recent liberalization of abortion laws.

Employment and money lie at the core of family dissolution, black or white. American family norms have traditionally placed the entire or major responsibilities of providing family food, clothing, shelter, and economic dignity on the husband and father. No able-bodied man, black or white, can hold the full authority and respect of family, relatives, or friends if he is unemployed, sporadically employed, or even underemployed. Authority and respect decline if the male does not serve as an adequate breadwinner. In concrete terms, the inability to provide for rent or house payments, food, clothes, medicine, education, and other family needs stimulates internal family tensions and generates interpersonal conflict. As Liebow points out regarding low-income urban blacks he studied in depth, "Money is chronically in short supply and chronically a source of dissension in the home."[49] Thus, continues Liebow, "In self-defense, the husband retreats to the streetcorner. Here, where the measure of man is considerably smaller, and where weaknesses are somehow turned upside down and almost magically transformed into strengths, he can be, once again, a man among men."[50] Rainwater's extensive research on ghetto families confirms the strain on family life engendered by financial shortages.

The mother often assumes the dominant socializing role within the working class and low income black family (although she probably does so to a somewhat lesser extent in the suburban white family as well). A large survey disclosed that in 51 percent of the cases behavioral codes were primarily taught by the mother; 33 percent, by both mother and father; and in only six percent, by the father.[51] An in-depth study of seven low-income young black men by Gift disclosed that five considered their mother as the most significant person in their lives and a sixth, an

---

[47] Frank F. Furstenberg, Jr., "Premarital Pregnancy Among Black Teen-agers," *Trans-action*, May 1970, pp. 52–55.

[48] Leslie Aldridge Westoff and Charles F. Westoff, *From Now to Zero* (Boston: Little, Brown and Company, 1971), p. 272; Furstenberg, "Premarital Pregnancy Among Black Teen-agers"; and Lee Rainwater, *Behind Ghetto Walls* (Chicago: Aldine Publishing Company, 1970), p. 216.

[49] Liebow, *Tally's Corner,* p. 131.

[50] Ibid., p. 136.

[51] Brink and Harris, *Black and White,* p. 268; Rainwater, *Behind Ghetto Walls.*

aunt.[52] The reasoning behind their choice is typified in the following comments by one of the respondents:

> To me the most significant or valued person in my life is definitely my mother. I write this because I am certain that had it not been for her reasoning and constant suggesting, I never would have made the effort to better myself. The reason I am making an effort to be someone now, is because she feels that I have the potential to be someone important. All of the time when I was in school she did all that she knew how to help me; such as proper clothing, lunch money (by many times neglecting herself). She really stressed the importance of being well-educated. She explained how it is that I should do without many of my whimsical desires and pleasures in order to be successful. . . .

The data we have examined in this chapter and previous ones on occupational, economic, and educational inequality ultimately account for any differences between black and white family stability and for differences *within* the black and white populations. In an urban industrial setting, economic security is virtually a prerequisite to, though not a guarantee of, family stability. It is not the rate of family dissolution among the economically deprived that is phenomenal, but rather the rate of family success, white and black.

The average size of the black family, like that of the white, has recently declined and continues to do so. A significant factor in the decline has been the increased effective use of contraception, though the day of planned parenthood seems still to be some distance off for all groups in the population.[53] According to recent statistics, the middle-income black couple desires and has on the average fewer children than middle-income whites, whereas the low-income black couple tends to desire and be slightly larger than the low-income white. Although smaller families will help alleviate financial pressures on the black population, we should not expect significant changes in the material situation of the black community simply as a result of lower fertility, particularly in terms of the near future. Nor is a biparental family any assurance of improved material circumstances; we have noted previously that Mexican Americans do not have an extraordinarily high proportion of female-headed families, yet their poverty equals that of blacks.

STRATEGIES OF CHANGE

Blacks have traveled an arduous route to achieve their present socioeconomic status. Most of the journey has been made possible by a combination of black determination, labor shortages during war, and technological change, though the latter has worked against the blacks almost as much as for them and could seriously worsen their condition in the future.

Five generations of black Americans have lived through amendments to the Constitution, alternating adverse and favorable Supreme Court

---

[52] Mac D. Gift, "Self-Concept and Social Change among Black Youth," Ph.D. dissertation, University of Utah, 1969.

[53] Westoff and Westoff, *From Now to Zero*, Chapter 7.

decisions, a half dozen civil rights acts, alternate segregation and integration ideologies, passive and militant leadership, legal battles and street battles, boycotts, sit-ins, freedom rides, voter registration drives, and marches.[54] They have faced Jim Crow, the Ku Klux Klan, White Citizen Councils, Orval Faubus, Ross Barnett, George Wallace, police, state troopers, and the National Guard. They know the meaning of a noose, billy club, cattle prod, mace, tear gas, shotgun, and rifle. Major events of violence against blacks should not overshadow the day-to-day threats and violent actions, especially against low-income blacks, by the representatives of the white power structure. Blacks have also heard concrete proposals for economic change in A. Phillip Randolph's Freedom Budget and unfulfilled promises in Lyndon B. Johnson's Great Society.

Legal equality, while not complete, is far in advance of economic equality. Legal equality itself remains more of a formality than a fact of daily life, since enforcement of civil rights legislation has been halfhearted. The civil rights movement as a legal strategy served to set the stage for the elimination of the insults and degradations of separate facilities and segregation, but it took direct action against volatile white resistance to achieve most of the actual gains that have been made in these areas. Voter registration and school integration have taken a high toll in human life and injury—both bodily and psychologically. Yet, the civil rights movement in its direct action stages brought black individuals into the movement on an unprecedented and massive scale, cementing commitments and heightening aspiration and hope.

However, civil rights overlap only partially with economic rights, such as in discrimination in employment. Even here, city ordinances against discrimination in employment, fair employment practice commissions, national labor relations acts, Department of Labor regulations, civil rights acts, and executive orders are all ineffectual if not enforced, and they tend not to be enforced. More to the point, none of these civil rights measures do anything in the way of staging economic change, that is, providing services, directly creating jobs, or raising income levels. Voting rights would seem to suggest the possibility of legislating economic change, but we have already witnessed the evident immunity of the corporate system from incursions via the voting booth.

Yet, for many blacks, change in legal status and civil rights progress has resulted in some socioeconomic advance. As of 1966 at least, a majority of blacks felt their situation to be improving, though only about one-fourth of low-income persons in the North felt so.[55] For example, a television repairman believes, "There has been much progress. The Negro has progressed faster in a given period than any other people throughout the world."[56] And a housewife in Georgia contends that "The

---

[54] For an analysis of the history of the black liberation movement, see Lewis Killian, *The Impossible Revolution? Black Power and the American Dream* (New York: Random House, Inc., 1968); also, Louis H. Masotti et al., *A Time to Burn* (Chicago: Rand McNally & Co., 1969).

[55] Marx, *Protest and Prejudice,* p. 6; and Brink and Harris, *Black and White,* pp. 222–23.

[56] Marx, *Protest and Prejudice,* p. 7.

kids are getting along fine in white schools. I am making more money than I ever have, and when I ride the bus, I sit where I want."[57]

Many disagree. A Chicago housewife asserts, "If things were getting better young people should get their share of jobs, but this isn't happening. My children have not been successful in getting jobs."[58] A Cleveland janitor states, "Four hundred years, and it's [improvement] much too slow. They could get together up there in Washington, D.C. I don't see what could be holding them back. All we want is some decent jobs like the white man."[59] A Louisiana farmhand declares, "Just look at this house. One side of it is falling down. Every time I ask 'The Man' to do something about it, he say that maybe he will if I do better in the fields."[60] And a New York ghetto resident claims that "Things are the same. I'm still forced to raise my family in inadequate surroundings and there is still discrimination in the white man's attitude."[61]

The careful research by Willhelm of the prospects for the black community on a variety of social and economic fronts suggests that there is really no hope of progress for the vast majority of blacks within the present system.[62] Only a small minority have benefited much at all from the past 15 years of activism.

Degrees of protest

Few Americans need be informed that blacks are incomparably more militant today than they were 20 years ago or that black militancy is growing. Whereas probably a large majority of blacks would not have participated in a demonstration 20 years ago, today the majority would do so (yet, two-fifths of a Newark sample would *not* sit-in or demonstrate).[63] The large majority approve of non-violent demonstrations, and a greater number would like to see more demonstrations than would like to see less. Although those living in the metropolitan areas of the North report somewhat greater militancy than southerners, the direct-action phase of the black rights movement originated in the South with boycotts and sit-ins. The rise of black militancy is no mere response to a decline in white resistance; an increasing majority of the white population disapproves of even nonviolent forms of mass protest and black activism, though a majority have tended to sympathize with black occupational and social rights.

The critical question at this juncture is not whether blacks are going

---

[57] Brink and Harris, *Black and White,* p. 26.

[58] Marx, *Protest and Prejudice,* p. 7.

[59] Ibid., p. 13.

[60] Brink and Harris, *Black and White,* pp. 27–28.

[61] Ibid., p. 26.

[62] Willhelm, *Who Needs the Negro?* Rather than view blacks as another ethnic group on the mobility ladder in the fashion of European ethnic groups, Willhelm sees far more similarities of the black condition with that of the Indian.

[63] Marx, *Protest and Prejudice,* p. 20; and Penn Kimball, *The Disconnected* (New York: Columbia University Press, 1972), p. 94.

to pursue actively racial equality, but the means through which their goals will be pursued. Locally organized boycotts, pickets, strikes, and demonstrations may bring some concessions and changes affecting certain groups within the local black population. The ballot box theoretically offers a mechanism for change. Even though proportionately almost as many blacks as whites in the North now vote for president (which doesn't take a great deal), of what significance have their votes been? And of what significance is it to major economic change that several dozen blacks sit in state legislatures and a dozen in the national Congress? The urban ghetto and the rural slum persist with all of their occupational, income, educational, medical, transport, diet, and housing deficiencies, and absolutely no major program of social change is officially even in the conceptual or experimental stage.

Understandably, then, the oppressed have considered and employed violent means of protest. Violent attacks against white supremacy and black impoverishment are not recent inventions. In the early 19th century slave insurrections were instigated by Gabriel, Denmark Vesey, and Nat Turner, the first two exposed by house servants but the latter culminating in the death of 55 whites. Although riots and violence in St. Louis, Washington, and Chicago at the time of World War I, Tulsa during the Great Depression, and Detroit at the time of World War II were mainly white-instigated racial battles, Harlem violence of 1935 and 1943 was outbursts of black frustration against oppressive economic conditions.[64]

The ghetto riots of the sixties, Watts, Detroit, Newark, Cleveland, Chicago, Cincinnati, Buffalo, and elsewhere, have all been violent protests against the injustices and inequities of economic conditions, although police incidents and their treatment of blacks have triggered most major riots. That economic and political rather than racial targets underlie ghetto violence is evident from the fact that in Newark, for instance, where 3,000 national guardsmen, 1,400 police, and 500 state troopers moved about in the open, only one policeman was killed—possibly by a stray government bullet (most of the injuries incurred by police and troops during riots are self-inflicted; wild police fire from the street killed three Newark women in their homes).[65] Rioters tear up and loot the stores having trick contracts and installment plans, phony scales, inferior meat and vegetables, and other economically deceiving and exploitative practices. Institutions rather than individuals have been the object of attack.

Violence and radicalism

Have the advocates of violence driven their point home to the black population? Available evidence suggests that on the whole they have not.

---

[64] See the materials in Rodney F. Allen and Charles H. Adair, eds., *Violence and Riots in Urban America* (Belmont, Cal.: Wadsworth Publishing Company, 1969); and Joseph Boskin, ed., *Urban Racial Violence in the Twentieth Century* (Beverly Hills, Cal.: The Glencoe Press, 1969).

[65] See Tom Hayden's account of the Newark riot in *Rebellion in Newark* (New York: Random House, 1967).

The majority of blacks still feel that violence is not the solution to the problems of black America; however, a substantial and very likely growing minority view violence as an effective tool of change.[66] Thirty percent of a Newark sample would resort to violence, and one-third would risk jail.[67] The fact that the majority of blacks remain opposed to violence as a means of social change does not imply that they see no possible good in the wake of violence. Northern metropolitan blacks are quite evenly split on the issue of whether riots can accomplish any good; but Chicago residents are considerably more optimistic over the outcome of violence than New Yorkers, as well as more violence-prone. Southern residents also lean more toward the optimistic interpretation of rioting.

Soon after the Los Angeles riot in 1965, the majority of both riot participants and spectators reported holding favorable attitudes as to the riot's outcome.[68] However, as to the riot event itself, only a small majority of even the participants were favorable toward it, and only one-fourth of the spectators. Sample surveys indicate that about 15 percent of the black population would actually join a riot,[69] probably a close estimate inasmuch as about 15 percent (30,000 persons) of the Watts ghetto rioted.[70] In addition to those who would join a riot, another approximately 25 percent report that they are uncertain as to what they would do (about 30 percent of the Watts population were close spectators of the riot).

The chief point of division within the black community on willingness to use violence to gain rights is between younger and older persons. Regardless of educational level achieved, persons 39 and under are significantly more likely to be ready to use violence than those over 39. The young and old *with college degrees* are the most widely separated on the issue of violence; one-fourth of the former but very few of the latter argue for violence as a ready weapon.[71]

Research conducted by Ransford in Los Angeles and the Watts area following the riot specified further variables in addition to age that predict willingness to use violence in gaining black rights.[72] Ransford learned that blacks who are isolated from whites are more violence-prone than those in communication with whites, those with feelings of powerlessness more so than those with feelings of control, and those expressing racial dissatisfaction more so than those racially satisfied. Whereas only one in ten blacks who were not racially isolated, did not feel powerless,

[66] Marx, *Protest and Prejudice*, p. 32; and Brink and Harris, *Black and White*, p. 266.

[67] Kimball, *The Disconnected*, p. 94.

[68] David O. Sears and John B. McConahay, "Participation in the Los Angeles Riot," *Social Problems*, 17 (Summer 1969), pp. 3–20.

[69] Campbell and Schuman, "Racial Attitudes in Fifteen American Cities"; and Brink and Harris, *Black and White*, p. 266.

[70] Sears and McConahay, "Participation in the Los Angeles Riot."

[71] Campbell and Schuman, "Racial Attitudes in Fifteen American Cities."

[72] H. Edward Ransford, "Isolation, Powerlessness, and Violence: A Study of Attitudes and Participation in the Watts Riot," *American Journal of Sociology*, 73 (March 1968), pp. 581–91.

and were not racially dissatisfied would resort to violence, fully two out of three of the isolated, powerless, and dissatisfied persons would do so. Nearly all of the persons studied by Ransford who admitted to riot activity were among the alienated. Ransford's findings suggest that susceptibility to racial violence is perhaps as much explainable in terms of personal consciousness as in terms of objective economic conditions. While other data presented by Ransford clearly indicated that violence proneness among individuals was markedly lower in a middle-income integrated black community than in low-income Watts, the sociopsychological characteristics of his respondents helped account for violence willingness over and above economic conditions of the neighborhood. This suggests the separability of objective and subjective aspects of class status.

A study by Spilerman of 673 cities that experienced racial violence in the 1960s indicated that such objective factors as black occupational, income, and educational status within a given city were poor predictors of a city's violence proneness.[73] Spilerman's analysis suggests that the best guide to a city's racial explosiveness was simply the absolute size of its black population: the larger the black community the greater the chances for disorder. The larger the city, the better off socioeconomically is its black population, so racial violence was more likely to occur in cities where the objective conditions of blacks were somewhat better than in cities where conditions were somewhat worse. But, contends Spilerman, this relationship is simply incidental to black population size (blacks have over the years moved into areas holding greater economic promise). Thus, Spilerman and, elsewhere, Tomlinson[74] argue that pervasive national influences such as the role of the federal government, television, and black consciousness and solidarity gave rise to a "riot ideology" that superseded individual communities and their specific objective socioeconomic conditions. Riot propensity is the sum of the aggregate individual riot values.

While agreeing with the thesis that every black individual has been influenced by government, mass media, and in-group communication on strategies and means of change, it is hard to believe that simply by adding up individual black persons and their respective "riot ideologies" we can arrive at an accounting of why black communities rebel or revolt. Granted that an ideology is a crucial action catalyst, but are we to believe that blacks are so uniform that a "riot ideology" is ingested by each like a blanket inoculation program for measles? Though government and the media have stimulated and facilitated the development of black consciousness and solidarity, government and media are *reflec-*

---

[73] Seymour Spilerman, "The Causes of Racial Disturbances: A Comparison of Alternative Explanations," *American Sociological Review*, 35 (August 1970), pp. 627–49.

[74] T.M. Tomlinson, "The Development of a Riot Ideology among Urban Negroes," *American Behavioral Scientist*, 2 (March 1968), pp. 27–31; and Vincent Jeffries and H. Edward Ransford, "Interracial Social Contact and Middle-Class White Reactions to the Watts Riot," *Social Problems*, 16 (Winter 1969), pp. 312–24.

tions of and communication channels for specific interest groups and the needs and objectives of these groups. To pin the origin of "riot ideology" on government or television is to confuse symptoms with causes. The very term "riot ideology" is grossly misleading inasmuch as it infers blacks riot due to externally induced impulse rather than as part of a strategy of social, political, and economic change. Why don't the black bourgeoisie riot? They are exposed to the same sources of "riot ideology." Certainly we must finally look to individuals, but to individuals within a specific social, political, and economic context, as, for example, Ransford has done with segregated, low-income and integrated, middle-income blacks within the same city.

Black opponents of violence might be typified by a Buffalo housewife who argues that "It can't help because we are outnumbered. In fact with all the people that are against us, we couldn't possibly win any type of battle. We would be beaten before we started." Or a Brooklyn electrical worker who contends that "By riots you put a fear in people which takes you further away from them." (The electrician's thesis is borne out by the fact that white Los Angeles residents tended to report increasing estrangement from blacks as a result of the Watts riot.)[75] A Brooklyn clerk is sharper in his opposition to riots: "Rioting is just an excuse to be a thief and liar. I feel that when you demonstrate it is for the good, to help someone. You are trying to build a foundation, but when you riot you are destroying the foundation you have not yet built."[76]

Advocates of violence and riots make the following points: "People get scared in riots. So we get action and the government tries to find out why we riot. White people are afraid of getting hurt" (Buffalo welder). And, "They have to get out there and show these people we mean business. If we set back like our foreparents we will never get anywhere" (Detroit housewife). And, in the extreme, "Less demonstrations and more shooting of the white man. Mass black violence must be organized" (New York worker).[77]

While riot participants were most likely to be under 30 years old, they were not simply teen-agers raising hell. Ghetto rioters were more often men frustrated by unemployment or underemployment than boys seeking thrills and easy loot, as likely to be high school graduates as dropouts, and more often racially and politically aware than indifferent and uninformed.[77] Militance as such tends to be more intense among the politically aware and informed.[78]

The most evident trend with regard to the use of violent strategies of change within the black community is that among the college educated and college students. Although they tend to come from middle-income backgrounds, to interact in integrated social settings, to feel influential, and to be racially satisfied—factors which we previously noted are associated with nonviolence—they are also tending to move from civil rights

[75] Marx, *Protest and Prejudice*, p. 34.
[76] Ibid., p. 33.
[77] Boskin, *Urban Racial Violence in the Twentieth Century*.
[78] Marx, *Protest and Prejudice*, pp. 49–93.

militancy to advocacy of violent and radical change. What could be emerging, then, is a coalition of educated middle-income and under-educated lower-class youth, quite different in objective economic condition but very similar in political and psychological outlook.

A sizable minority of this youth coalition is already firmly committed to violent means of change; the rest tend to be undecided at the moment; but with every passing day that portends no change in the black condition, more are converted to a strategy of violence. The undecided are under continual pressure to make a political commitment. As one young black points out, "A black man today is *either* a radical or an Uncle Tom. It so happens that I'm a radical or militant or whatever you call a black man that is tired of getting the ass-end of things. I'm a member of the new Black generation. I feel that the black aggressive youth in the slums and in the colleges are the real holders of the Black man's future in this racist society."[79]

Several observers of black student radicalism would take issue with the view that middle-income youth and student militants are seeking revolutionary change.[80] Obatala contends that, radical rhetoric aside, there was "never much of a genuine revolutionary conviction on the part of most black students." Obatala perceives a significant cleavage between the student elite and the ghetto poor:

> For the masses, the struggle for power had truly revolutionary implications, in that such a struggle must necessarily concern itself with a redistribution of goods and income and a change in the ownership of productive capacity. On the other hand, when the Afro-American middle-class—including the black student elite—spoke of power, it was, with few exceptions, speaking mainly in terms of social recognition and social mobility within the present system.[81]

Some would argue that not only is student militance devoid of real radical content, but that black violence in general is reactionary rather than revolutionary. For example, Larner argues that there is aggression, threats, tough rhetoric, and speeches, "but no sustained, organized revolutionary action, perhaps even less than among white children of the middle class."[82] Larner points out that the known assassins of Medgar Evers, Emmett Till, Goodman, Schwerner and Chaney, the four little Birmingham girls, and others walk around the South free from retribution; and instead the ghetto teacher, cab driver, shop owner, and other such persons are the more likely target of black violence. Not radical politics, suggests Larner, but "religion is the survival program of black

---

[79] Gift, "Self-Concept and Social Change among Black Youth."

[80] Harold Cruse, *The Crisis of the Negro Intellectual* (New York: William Morrow, 1967); Irving L. Horowitz and William H. Friedland, *The Knowledge Factory* (Chicago: Aldine Publishing Company, 1971), pp. 198–99; and J.K. Obatala, "Black Students: Where Did Their Revolution Go?" *The Nation*, October 2, 1972, pp. 272–74.

[81] Obatala, "Black Students."

[82] Jeremy Larner, "To Speak of Black Violence," *Dissent*, Winter 1972, pp. 70–73.

people." Thus, the legacy of Malcolm X is seen as that of a religious prophet rather than a political revolutionary.

Yet religion as an opiate and random aggression is no more characteristic of blacks than of whites; the working and under-classes have in general failed in the majority to politically conceptualize their oppression, though as we have argued, a substantial and increasing number have done so. For example, the Black Panthers have long enunciated a radical political interpretation of oppression and sought inter-racial working class alliance and action (in contrast to past "black power" leaders and most Afro-American cultural nationalists).[83] That the Panthers sponsor self-help programs and have entered electoral politics is entirely in keeping with their stated aims.

Blacks and power

Certainly the condition of black Americans is an artifact of their powerlessness, just as the condition of the upper class is an artifact of their powerfulness. That blacks are powerless in the sense of being excluded from the dominant economic, political, legal, educational, and labor institutions of American society is beyond doubt. Baron's research in Chicago, for example, revealed that, out of 6,838 decision-making positions in business corporations, blacks occupied only 42, most of these being in all-black insurance firms. None of the 757 policy-making positions in the top law firms was held by blacks, only five of 380 top university posts, and 58 of 1,088 top government posts. Blacks held 108 of 819 union offices studied, mostly at the lower echelons.[84] Ironically, black Americans do not tend to perceive themselves as an especially weak or powerless interest group in the nation's political structure.[85] Low-income whites tend to be more alienated in terms of power than blacks.[86]

Indeed, blacks are *not* a weak or powerless group in an ultimate sense, or any weaker or more powerless than the white working class. Power in the United States is neither black power nor white power but ruling class power. Placing representative numbers of blacks in top corporate management or on boards of directors of the top 500 corporations, making them rich and politically influential, would in all likelihood do little in the way of changing the condition of the black poor. For these hypothetical black executives, millionaires, and officials would still be racially far outnumbered by whites. More important is the fact that capitalism as a formal system is largely impartial to race, as any of the large

---

[83] See Philip S. Foner, ed., *The Black Panthers Speak* (Philadelphia: J.B. Lippincott, 1970), pp. 41; 43; 50–51; 151–52. Compare with the statement by Stokely Carmichael and Charles V. Hamilton, *Black Power* (New York: Random House, Inc., 1967).

[84] Harold M. Baron, "Black Powerlessness in Chicago," *Trans-action*, 6 (November 1968), pp. 28–31.

[85] William H. Form and Joan Rytina, "Ideological Beliefs on the Distribution of Power in the United States," *American Sociological Review*, 34 (February 1969), p. 26.

[86] Brink and Harris, *Black and White*, p. 135.

majority of poor who are white will tell you. Whether whites or blacks, Protestants or Catholics, northerners or southerners, Ivy Leaguers or Bush Leaguers are predominant in the power structure is not especially crucial to the outcome, so long as all are equally committed to the existing system and adept at managing it.

The unwillingness to deal theoretically and strategically with the dynamics of the capitalist system was the central weakness of many of the "black power" advocates. White student radicals tend to share a similar aversion to a hard and realistic examination of power and property, but somewhat less so. Black power moved more on emotional than radical wheels, but then so do the forces of sanctioned violence, the protectors of law, order, and the system. Few of the black power spokesmen were or are prepared for a revolution altering the structure of the society. Nor are they experimenting with a counterculture which would undermine profit capitalism by default. An extreme materialism is often present in their views and values. The challenge of changing the corporate system and its hold on economic institutions and political life is not a new one, and the failure of the black power movement to have any real impact was not surprising nor unprecedented. To fail to understand the new industrial state is to fail to understand one's condition in society, and to fail to understand one's condition is to be unable to change it.

Moreover, the skeptic might ask, how is it possible that a movement such as the Black Muslim, with its code of Puritanism, rationality, individualism, punctuality, and asceticism could if successful escape the outcome of its Protestant ethic forebears in stimulating black capitalism and attendant inequality? Is there any reason to believe that black capitalism would be any more equalitarian and humane than white capitalism?

White response

Throughout the sixties white sympathy with black protest declined from a slight majority early in the decade to a constantly dwindling minority toward the end. While fairly widely favoring racial progress in education, jobs, and housing, whites increasingly felt blacks were pushing too hard or trying to move too fast. The tone of dominant feelings toward minorities is importantly conditioned by the inter-group atmosphere created by presidential administrations, and the atmosphere has deteriorated badly. Administration decisions to commit the nation's resources and energies to Southeast Asia instead of American cities seriously worsened the race situation, setting the stage for urban disorder and riot, which in turn heightened white resentment of blacks. The comparatively strong showing of George Wallace in the 1968 presidential election and 1972 campaign among both white-collar and blue-collar persons in both North and South attested to the strength of white fear and resentment.

White analysis of the precipitants of riots and violence in the ghettos of their cities is sheer guesswork, placing as much causative importance on riffraff and communists as on institutionalized problems of American social structure. A Detroit researcher, Donald Warren, concludes that "For the vast majority of persons in satellite communities, the Detroit riot was as likely to be the work of social undesirables or agitators as that of more enduring social forces."[87] While there is considerable overlap between black and white agreement on housing, jobs, and poverty as riot causes, a serious misunderstanding exists concerning the role played by police. Blacks tend to rank police brutality as the single most important riot precipitant, whereas whites isolated from blacks tend to completely ignore police action as a cause.[88] Rather, among those whites who lack regular personal contact with blacks, police action is viewed as the *cure*.[89] Whites lean heavily upon police or military action as an immediate solution to racial problems, but tend to liberalize their thinking somewhat regarding longer range solutions.

The editor of *Fortune*, Charles E. Silberman has written that "Nothing less than a radical reconstruction of American society is required if the Negro is to be able to take his rightful place in American life.[90] James Baldwin agrees: "Now, there is simply no possibility of a real change in the Negro's situation without the most radical and farreaching changes in the American political and social structure."[91] But Baldwin argues that whites are neither willing nor ready for structural change: " . . . it is clear that white Americans are not simply unwilling to effect [radical] changes; they are, in the main, so slothful have they become, unable to envision them."[92] Sociologist Lewis Killian agrees: "Given the choice between a massive freedom budget and a police state, the American electorate is more likely to choose the latter."[93]

---

[87] Donald I. Warren, "Suburban Isolation and Race Tension: The Detroit Case," *Social Problems,* 17 (Winter 1970), p. 331.

[88] Ibid., p. 332.

[89] Jeffries and Ransford, "Interracial Social Contact and Middle-Class White Reactions to the Watts Riot."

[90] Charles E. Silberman, *Crises in Black and White* (New York: Random House, Inc., 1964), p. 10.

[91] Baldwin, *The Fire Next Time,* p. 115.

[92] Ibid.

[93] Killian, *The Impossible Revolution?,* p. 173.

13

Family change and population problems

POPULATION AND PRODUCTION

Without in any way distracting from the seriousness of worldwide population problems, we might first draw attention to some facts concerning the relationship between population, the organization of production, and the standard of living. That is, when making a critical examination of the quality of life in the advanced countries and the conditions of life and prospects for industrialization in the underdeveloped countries, we are suggesting that one look first, but certainly not only, at the nature of the class system and secondarily at a country's population situation.

Western Europe and Japan are among the most densely populated land areas in the world, having 150 and 283 persons per square kilometer.[1] We all know that these areas are also among the most highly industrialized ones. Conversely, Latin America and Africa have population densities of 14 and 12, respectively (about the same as the United States). Yet, Latin America and Africa are underdeveloped and their masses are impoverished. No one who knows the natural resources of South and North America would hold that South America is poor in resources and North America is rich in resources, thus accounting for the differences in the standards of living. South America has been and continues to be abundantly rich in a wide range of mineral and agricultural resources. South American resources have, in fact, been the object of plunder by North America for many decades. Oil, copper, precious minerals, industrial ores of all sorts, timber products, agricultural raw materials, feeds, and more have been extracted for the indus-

---

[1] *Demographic Yearbook 1971*, Statistical Office of the United Nations, New York, 1972, p. 111.

trial development of advanced nations from around the entire under-developed world.

At the moment and at all moments past, the most decisive factor in human well-being is the organization of production and not the number of people within a given territory or societal boundary. The underde-veloped world has over two thirds of the earth's population but only one-seventh of its economic production, an imbalance which has steadily deteriorated in recent decades (despite the sharp increase in foreign-owned industrial operations). Such an imbalance in population and production lies at the bottom of the population problem of the world. Within a brief span of twenty years, revolutionary Shanghai was trans-formed from a sea of misery to a developing city whose inhabitants are all individuals with material security and hope for the future. A colo-nized Calcutta was and still is a sea of misery, and so is every other urban area in the underdeveloped world, at least as far as the masses are concerned. So long as these areas remain the objects of foreign domi-nation, and function for the benefit of the national bourgeoisie, there is no hope for their masses. The crucial point in the population-resources equation is how the two are brought together, not necessarily the balance of people versus land. If resources were developed by and for the ma-terial advancement of a country's inhabitants, there is not a country on earth that has so many people that the least of its citizens could not be adequately clothed, fed, housed, employed, and educated.

From the standpoint of sheer ability of any given country's resources to support its own people, including the possibility of fair and balanced trade with other countries, not population but the organization of pro-duction is the root of poverty and oppression whether it be found in underdeveloped *or* developed countries. Americans generally don't con-sider the deprived of their land to be a result of overpopulation, and neither should they consider the Mexican, Peruvian, Nigerian, Indian, or Filipino poor to be impoverished because of overpopulation. We too often regard world poverty primarily in terms of overpopulation.

This is not to at all diminish the importance of the problem of popu-lation. As we shall observe, high birth rates and rapid population growth in the underdeveloped countries have greatly complicated survival prob-lems for millions. Even as developing state-planned countries, both China and Cuba have recognized the need for reduced rates of popula-tion growth and the benefits of a rational population policy. They are realizing the relevance of Engels' observation that "the number of people will become so great that limits will have to set to their increase."[2] Most European countries have, in fact, voluntarily set limits to population growth rates, but most are well beyond the densities and population to resource ratios of the large majority of underdeveloped countries.

Nor is population the central problem of pollution. The U.S. has only one-fourth of China's population, but pollutes the earth at an immeasur-ably greater rate. The U.S. has an economic system which, as Bookchin

---

[2] See *Marx and Engels on the Population Bomb,* Ronald L. Meek, ed. (Berkeley: The Ramparts Press, 1971). Citation p. 120.

points out, is inherently anti-ecological;[3] profits and consumption must be endlessly pursued regardless of the impact upon environment. Again, we must look at the organization of production for an accounting of the problem.

A rationally constituted society requires *both* democratic organization of production and a sensitivity to the importance of population control. And at least as far as the underdeveloped countries are concerned, it is absolutely essential that economic independence and population control be combined. Conditions are such to make it exceedingly difficult if not impossible to institute population control as long as a country remains an impoverished link within the world capitalist system. For example, China would today be faced with overwhelming population problems of the same magnitude found in India if there had not been a revolution. By the same token, India can expect population chaos as long as it persists in a condition of underdevelopment. In a condition of underdevelopment, especially in the rural areas where the bulk of the population is located, a large family is frequently a defense against starvation and a resource for a slim margin of security from the standpoint of both old and young. A developed society generates its own rationale for family limitation and conveys to its members the advantages of having fewer children.

In reading the next series of pages on family, population, and industrialization, we should thus keep in mind the foregoing discussion as general background assumptions. In the subsequent presentation, we shall focus at a lower level of analysis and attempt to sort out a few of the internal questions and issues relating to population and industrial development. The related question of industrialization itself is a separate topic reserved for the next chapter. We could leave a description of family types to the next chapter, but since family organization has bearing upon population growth and industrialization, it is best introduced here. We also might be cautioned that the questions surrounding the relationship between type of family organization and population on the one hand and industrialization on the other, is open to much debate and questioning. Nevertheless, the questions and issues should be raised.

FAMILY TYPES

Extended families

Among the most common generalizations in the sociology of the family is that agricultural societies contain *corporate* or *extended* family

---

[3] Murray Bookchin, *Post Scarcity Anarchism* (Berkeley: The Ramparts Press, 1971), p. 16. Bookchin points out that "Any attempt to solve the environmental crisis within a bourgeois framework must be dismissed as chimerical." See, also, E.J. Mishan, *Technology and Growth: The Price We Pay* (New York: Praeger Publishers, 1969); and Mishan, "Ills, Bads, and Disamenities: The Wages of Growth," *Daedalus*, 102 (Fall 1973), pp. 63–87.

structures, and industrial societies, *nuclear* ones.[4] The extended family ideally encompasses several nuclear families and any unmarried or dependent kin, usually under the rubric of paternal headship. Thus, an example of an extended family might be a husband and wife, their married sons and wives and children, unmarried daughters (rare instances, since all eligible females tend to marry early and leave the household), and possibly other older dependent kin of the paternal head. An extended family such as this may count 30 or 40 members living in contiguous dwellings and working commonly held land. In a sense, the corporate or extended family is a "corporation," a social security system, meeting the social, political, and economic needs of members. It is "extended" in the sense that it reaches out from a single paternal headship to integrate into a cooperating social and economic network numerous related individuals. The extended family is usually the dominant institution of a traditional agricultural society. Whatever the human needs, be they protective, supportive, or regulatory, the extended family attempts to meet them. It must, for an agricultural society usually does not sustain specialized institutions to accommodate specialized human needs. The extended family, and its various linkages with clan and tribe, is *the* social, economic, and political center of life in most preindustrial societies.

The extended family system tends to be a rigid social structure, carefully defining reciprocal rights and responsibilities and unambiguously placing men above women and adults above children. Families as such fit into an equally rigid social structure within the larger society, each unit tending to inherit status positions ascribed for life. Often the rigidity of the social status hierarchy is formalized and legitimized through religious belief systems. However, the main points of inequality and stratification may be *within* families, as between male and female, old and young, rather than between societywide status levels, for most people live at or near subsistence levels. Greater class differentiation and mobility arise with commerce, cities, and, of course, industrialization.

Wealth or position in agricultural societies obviously rests on land ownership and productivity. Except for a small number of artisans, nearly everyone could be classified as agricultural workers, or in terms of preindustrial stratification systems, peasants. Thus, whether it concerns a strictly subsistence-barter economy or one drawn into a cash economy (as most now have been), we may see the purely economic incentive for a large family, especially for male children: to administer and work the land, provide security in parents' old age, and carry on the family estate and tradition. Strength and security then, tend to reside in family numbers.

While the extended family may be the ideal in traditional societies, only the more well-to-do landowners could expect to fully attain the ideal. At a point soon reached by most families, the number of persons living within the household exceeds that that can be supported by the amount of land owned or that can be profitably applied to agricultural production. Plots of land are usually too small to support all of the sons and

[4] See William J. Goode, *World Revolution and Family Patterns* (New York: The Free Press, 1963); also, Dorothy R. Blitsten, *The World of the Family* (New York: Random House, Inc., 1963).

their families, so all but the oldest tend to leave eventually in search of land or, when available, wage work.[5] Thus, as Goode points out, the extended family is today typically only a stage in the life cycle of any given person rather than a permanent ongoing system, so that at any given point in time only a minority of families are operationally extended.[6]

When the economy within which the family is located offers wage labor on plantations, in mines, or cities, the families of villagers and peasants are presented with an alternative to scratching around for land. However, the level of wage labor available to the displaced rural migrant may offer less economic stability and security than the village or land. But young people in rural areas have a diminishing choice concerning migration, for the land, if any land is owned at all, is in too short supply to support burgeoning rural populations. In this context, we are able to envisage the strong political appeal of revolutionary movements advocating land reform, the confiscation and redistribution of large estates and plantations from a small circle of often absentee landlords to landless peasants and small farmers, or to collectives of such.

Nuclear families

The nuclear family consists of only the elemental family members: parent(s) and children. While the nuclear family is a formal unit within the complex extended family, the nuclear family as an independently operating unit is clearly definable only when it is residentially and more or less socially separated from related nuclear family units and parental families. We should keep in mind that extended and nuclear families are ideal types; most actual families contain elements of both types. We have noted the social and supportive role of close relatives in even highly industrialized societies. In urban areas of countries such as the United States, the Soviet Union, and Japan, families tend to be largely autonomous nuclear units but often sustain social and occasionally economic ties with kin in rural areas or with other related urban families.[7] And in rural areas of industrial societies where tradition is strong (as in Soviet Central Asia) or welfare systems have not been extensively developed (as in Japan), the nuclear family is often firmly socially and economically anchored in kin networks.

Nor does the relocation of rural families to urban areas of underdeveloped societies necessarily mean the dissolution of extended families ties. In addition to sustaining ties with the village, related nuclear family units may frequently engage in joint protective and supportive activities and

---

[5] S.C. Dube, *Indian Village* (New York: Harper & Row, Publishers, 1967), p. 133.

[6] Goode, *World Revolution and Family Patterns*, p. 124.

[7] See, for example, Robert F. Winch, Scott Greer, and Rae Lesser Blumberg, "Ethnicity and Extended Familism in an Upper-Middle-Class Suburb," *American Sociological Review*, 32 (April 1967), pp. 265–72; Thomas Fitzsimmons, Peter Malof, and John C. Fishe, *Some Aspects of Contemporary Russian Society* (New Haven, Conn.: HRAF Press, no date); and Ezra F. Vogel, *Japan's New Middle Class* (Berkeley: University of California Press, 1967).

even reside in the same household.[8] Yet, while the correlation is far from perfect, the overall tendency has been for the corporate or extended family to break down into more autonomous nuclear units in the process of urbanization and, especially, industrialization. In underdeveloped urban areas without the resources to support social insurance and welfare programs, ethnic, religious, occupational, and caste groups and benefit societies frequently subsume traditional corporate family protective, supportive, and social roles.

FAMILY TYPES AND INDUSTRIALIZATION

Insofar as autonomous nuclear families tend to emerge within urban industrial society we might be inclined to conclude that industrialization *causes* the dissolution of the extended family and the emergence of the nuclear family. We might even be disposed to argue that the extended family is economically and politically *incompatible* with industrialization.

On the one hand, it is evident that urbanization has uprooted masses of people from rural and village locales, tearing them away from the confines of extended family organization. Moreover, some political elites have implemented legislation aimed at breaking up extended family systems that directly compete with state power, economic planning, and loyalty. Expropriation of land and inheritance taxation are the most direct means of undermining the economic viability and, hence, the power of the traditional family over its members. Laws governing the age of marriage may prevent family interests from binding through matrimony young members to each other and the extended family, thus encouraging individualism and a mobile labor force. Legislation governing the rights of women help undermine the system of patriarchal dominance and the confinement of women to the household for purely domestic and child-bearing purposes. Other statutes dealing with marriage, divorce, abortion, legitimacy, taxation, and education variously undermine the rigidity and control of the extended family. It is also true that an industrial society requires a geographically mobile labor force free of family and landed restraints and a socially open occupational system relatively free of transmitted family status ascription. Thus, industrialization would seem incompatible with the immobility, both geographical and social, of the traditional corporate family system.

Yet, the relationship between family organization and industrialization is not as simple as it might initially seem to be. We have already pointed to the existence of considerable kin activity in urban industrial centers of underdeveloped societies. We might also note that, rather than be the *effect* of industrialization, changes in family behavior may precede or enhance the progress of industrialization. For example, democratic beliefs regarding the role of youth in freely choosing their own mates, individual autonomy, and female equality may be forerunners or correlates rather

---

[8] Joan Aldous, "Urbanization, the Extended Family, and Kinship Ties in West Africa," in Pierre L. van den Berghe, ed., *Africa: Social Problems of Change and Conflict* (San Francisco: Chandler Publishing Company, 1965), pp. 107–16.

than consequences or effects of industrialization. Furthermore, in a society such as Japan where the family has traditionally been considered as an extension or replica of the larger social order (rather than society being considered an extension of the family as in traditional China), the extended family may serve a salutary function in state economic and political administration by mediating wider social duties and responsibilities. Finally, rather than restricting geographical and social mobility, the extended family may facilitate the process of urbanization and industrialization by contributing to the economic support of younger migrating members.[9]

In the final analysis, however, the traditional viability of extended families is contrary to the attainment of greater social equality and even industrialization itself. That extended family systems clash with industrialization and goals of social equality is suggested by the reactionary politics of nearly every landed aristocracy, whether in premodern Europe, the Soviet Union, and China, or today's Southeast Asia, Middle East, and Latin America. The poor have the weakest extended family systems, the least to protect, and are the first to be swept into the currents of industrialization; the landed aristocracy has the strongest extended family systems, the most to lose, and are the most vigilant protectors of the status quo.

The fact that landed aristocracies transmit a system of family privilege and are the guardians of the status quo has historically been tied to the process of revolutionary change, as industrializing classes overthrew agrarian bureaucracies and aristocracies. In many underdeveloped areas of the world today, aristocratic families having both rural and urban bases manage to maintain the economic status quo with considerable American counterrevolutionary military aid. Politically, the outcome is increasingly military dictatorship. We shall deal in some detail in the next chapter with American involvement in the underdeveloped world and the role of the national military. Suffice it to point out here that wherever aristocratic extended family systems are found behind an economic status quo, revolutionary activity—democratic or totalitarian—is always present or threatening. For industrialization *is* a revolution, be it bloodless or bloody. Whether a given historical process of industrialization achieves greater equality is an empirical question; but it nearly always results in a shake-up of the class structure and turnover of elites, a shake-up and turnover that inevitably threaten entrenched extended family power.

Family size and economic mobility

Students of population of *industrial* society have for some time recognized the relationship between family size and economic mobility.[10]

---

[9] Joel M. Halpern, *The Changing Village Community* (Englewood Cliffs, N.J.: Prentice-Hall, Inc., 1967), p. 86.

[10] Jerzy Berent, "Fertility and Social Mobility," *Population Studies*, 5 (March 1952), pp. 244–60; and Ronald Freedman, *The Sociology of Human Fertility* (Oxford: Basil Blackwell, 1963), pp. 95–97.

Households having fewer children tend to be situated higher in the class structure than those having larger families. That the tie between family size and economic position is but a tendency and not a law may easily be seen in the fact that certain high-status groups at certain times tend to have *larger* families than groups beneath them in the class structure (for example, Catholic white-collar college-educated families now tend to have larger families than Protestant blue-collar families).[11]

The implied dynamics of the relationship between family size and economic mobility in urban areas or countries is evident enough: unlike a preindustrial agricultural family that must depend on surplus children for hand *labor*, success for an urban industrial family requires surplus *capital* or financial assets to invest in medical care, diet, and, especially, schooling of children. The urban family also requires surplus *time* to invest in the socialization and preparation of each child to compete successfully in education and occupation (recall earlier discussions of inequality and education). Aside from the declining economic value of children in urban areas, a critical variable here is education: the preindustrial agricultural family educates their children informally to engage in agricultural activity, whereas the urban industrial family must assume the major responsibility of financing indirectly or directly, say, 16 years of schooling for one child, 32 years for two, 48 years for three, and so on for additional offspring, if their children are to succeed occupationally and economically. At any given class level (apart from the very affluent and wealthy), the larger the family the less likely the chances of each child attending college. Rearing a child to age 18, with no frills or additional education, costs well over $35,000 in the U.S. today.

Also influencing the economic success of an urban industrial family is the *rate* of family growth: the longer is the interval between marriage and first birth and between births the better situated will the family tend to be economically.[12] Rapid family growth is deleterious for the life chances of both parents and children, and for the same social and economic reasons that large families are deleterious to life chances. (Higher income and education groups, in turn, space their children more advantageously.) Thus, while two groups of people may have similar average family sizes, one group may still hold mobility advantages over the other if one more widely spaces its births.

The cause and effect relationship implied in the foregoing is that of smaller and well-spaced families are an asset to the economic circumstances of an urban industrial household. The influence, however, is two way, since families higher up in the economic and educational hierarchies have smaller and more widely spaced offspring. For example, for

---

[11] Pascal Whelpton, Arthur A. Campbell, and John E. Patterson, *Fertility and Family Planning in the United States* (Princeton, N.J.: Princeton University Press, 1966); and Leslie Aldridge Westoff and Charles E. Westoff, *From Now to Zero* (Boston: Little, Brown & Company, 1971), p. 228.

[12] Ronald Freedman and Lolagene Coombs, "Childspacing and Family Economic Position," *American Sociological Review*, 31 (October 1966), pp. 631–48; and U.S. Bureau of the Census, *Current Population Reports*, Series P-23, No. 36, "Fertility Indicators: 1970," U.S. Government Printing Office, Washington, D.C., 1971, Table 23, p. 39.

women 35–44 years old in 1969 in middle-income, college-educated families, the average number of children was slightly less than three compared with slightly less than four for low-income and primary education families.[13] Among blacks the family size differences vary more sharply by income and education than among whites (2.1 versus 4.7). Yet, among Catholics (1965) college-educated women have more children than those who leave high school before graduation (4.6 versus 3.7), for an average similar to low income blacks.[14] The average number of children *wanted* is fewer than the number a family actually ends up with, and the lower the income and education the greater is the gap between wanted and actually expected, suggesting more effective family planning or contraceptive use among those higher in economic and educational status.[15] In fact, the number of children wanted is quite consistent throughout the class structure, with the chief exceptions being the higher status Catholics desiring slightly larger families than the average and higher status blacks desiring smaller families.

With the exception of Catholics, among whom religious variables reverse the general pattern (middle-income Catholics are more devout than lower-income Catholics), advances in socioeconomic status conditions a lower rate of birth. In brief, we may observe an interaction between family size and economic status in urban industrial society. This is not to suggest that purely class influences are not substantially more important in setting life chances than family size. Among the propertied-rich, family size makes little difference on life chances; $50 million is obviously enough to cover the complete demands of ten children. And four children in a middle-income, college-background family have better prospects than a single child of an unskilled laborer. The point is that for the majority of families and children, family size and economic resources bears a noteworthy relationship.

Population and industrialization

Though not a strong analogy, the economic advantages that accrue to a family with a low birth rate and a slow rate of growth may similarly accrue today to a society with a low birth rate and a slow rate of growth.[16] There are, of course, great differences between family and national economies. For example, we could not technically speak of a

---

[13] Ibid., Tables 15–17, pp. 29–31; and Westoff and Westoff, *From Now to Zero*, pp. 225; 231.

[14] *From Now to Zero*, pp. 228; 267.

[15] Ibid., p. 231; Frederick S. Jaffe, "Family Planning and Poverty," *Journal of Marriage and the Family*, 26 (November 1964), pp. 467–70; and see Lee Rainwater and Karol K. Weinstein, *And the Poor Get Children* (Chicago: Quadrangle Books, Inc., 1960).

[16] See David M. Heer, "Economic Development and Fertility," *Demography*, 3 (1966), pp. 423–44; Richard A. Easterlin, "Effects of Population Growth on the Economic Development of Developing Countries," *Annals of the American Academy of Political and Social Science*, 371 (January 1967), pp. 98–108; and Gayle D. Ness, ed., *The Sociology of Economic Development* (New York: Harper & Row, Publishers, 1970), Section 3.

labor shortage or labor surplus in an urban industrial family, whereas labor shortages and surpluses are among the most critical aspects of industrial economies. The degree to which population growth affects economic growth depends on a number of other factors, such as population density and the level of industrialization.

For example, a society with a relatively low population density in the early stages of industrialization, as the United States in the last century or the Soviet Union in the present century, would usually have labor shortages and would economically benefit from population growth. On the other hand, an advanced technological society with a relatively high population density, as Japan, England, or the Netherlands, would tend to suffer culturally if not economically from additional population growth (albeit they may have shortages of certain types of *skilled* labor).

With some exceptions, a country's birth rate is roughly inverse in relation to its position in world economic stratification; countries with lower birth rates rank high economically and those with higher birth rates rank low economically. Most of the world's poor countries have birth rates that are twice as high as those of the rich countries. Family sizes vary enormously; for example, 52 percent of families in the Philippines and 45 percent of those in the United Arab Republic have seven or more persons per household compared with only five percent in Sweden.[17] Birth rates as such obviously cannot account for successful or unsuccessful industrialization. The impact of population growth on economic growth must be considered in the context of a number of other factors, in particular the type of economic and political system and its ties with the rest of the world. Population growth is a contextual factor that may impede or enhance economic progress, depending upon certain other social conditions. However, given the social conditions existing in virtually all countries of the world today, population growth either impedes industrialization or restricts the quality of life and creates difficulties in areas already industrialized.

Underdeveloped countries find themselves in the bind of having meager rates of annual economic growth nullified by rates of annual population growth. It is as if entire countries were running on a treadmill; some are barely holding their own, while others are slipping backward. The high rates of fertility found in underdeveloped areas are creating young populations and high dependency ratios. To have between 40 and 45 percent of the population under 15 years of age (compared with under 25 percent in Europe) is not uncommon. The high proportion of young dependents places heavy strains on already inadequate food, water, housing, clothing, medical, and educational resources.[18] When population doubles within a generation or so, as is now common throughout much of the Third World, so must a country double existing social facilities just to break even.

---

[17] Thomas K. Burch, "The Size and Structure of Families: A Comparative Analysis of Census Data," *American Sociological Review*, 32 (June 1967), pp. 355–56.

[18] Ansley J. Coale, "Population and Economic Development," in Philip H. Hauser, ed., *The Population Dilemma*, 2nd ed. (Englewood Cliffs, N.J.: Prentice-Hall, Inc., 1969), pp. 59–84.

To the poor countries, the numbers of young are far too large to permit providing any but a minority with more than four to six years of education, and expenditure per child is usually miserably small. Moreover, the pyramid-shaped age structure of Third World countries portends high absolute increases in the coming decades, as today's children become tomorrow's parents. With rural labor already frequently in surplus for arable land, and urban unemployment and underemployment at high levels, employment futures are grim and capital investment per worker low. Low capital investment per worker means low productivity per worker, which, in turn, means low income and poverty.

As we shall point out in the next chapter, the underdeveloped countries have not had a shortage of resources per person or even of potential capital investment per person—at least not such a shortage as to inhibit the process of development and produce mass poverty. The fundamental problem has been the foreign appropriation of resources and the misuse and unequal distribution of wealth by the national elites. The oil-producing countries of the Middle East are only the most obvious examples.

How is it possible for underdeveloped areas to escape the population trap and raise standards of living? How did population growth reach such peaks in the first place? And what happened with population and industrialization in the West? We shall address ourselves to the question of escaping the population trap in a subsequent section. First, let's examine the roots of the population problem and then the Western case of population and industrialization.

THE POPULATION EXPLOSION

From the time of the Roman Empire to the colonization of America, the world population intermittently grew from approximately a quarter billion to a half billion persons, for an average growth rate of less than 0.1. Then in only 200 years, at about a .5 percent growth rate, the population roughly doubled to one billion. By 1930 with a growth rate approaching one percent, the Earth's population again had doubled to two billion persons. A third billion was then added between 1930 and 1960 at a 1.7 rate. Since 1960 another three quarters billion persons have been added at a two percent rate, making a total population of over 3.7 billion.[19] By the year 2000, world population may be well over six billion, an addition of possibly one billion per decade. Each month the world must make room for enough people to populate a large American metropolitan area, and each year, room for more than enough people to populate a nation the size of Great Britain.

In world terms, a crude birth rate of 34 persons per 1,000 population per year and a death rate of 14 is yielding a two percent annual increase (compared with 0.3 in 1750).[20] From Table 12 we may see that the

---

[19] For general works on population, see Shirley Foster Hartley, *Population Quantity vs. Quality* (Englewood Cliffs: Prentice-Hall, Inc., 1972); and Ralph Thomlinson, *Demographic Problems* (Belmont, Cal.: Dickenson Publishing Company, 1967), p. 16.

[20] *Demographic Yearbook,* 1971, p. 111.

Table 12

WORLD, REGION, AND SELECTED COUNTRY DEMOGRAPHIC CHARACTERISTICS

	Population (millions)		Rate of increase	Birth rate (most recent data)	Death rate (most recent data)	Density per sq. km (most recent data)
	1950	1971	1965–71			
World	2,586	3,706	2.0	34	14	27
Africa	217	344	2.6	47	21	12
Latin America ...	162	291	2.9	38	10	14
East Asia mainland	536	779	1.8	33	15	70
South Asia	698	1,158	2.8	44	17	73
North America ..	166	230	1.2	18	9	11
Europe	392	466	0.8	17	10	94
Japan	83	105	1.1	18	7	283
Australia-New Zealand ..	10	16	1.9	21	9	2
U.S.S.R.	180	207	1.0	18	8	11
Selected countries						
Algeria			3.5	49	17	6
Egypt			2.5	35	15	34
Ghana			3.0	47	18	37
Kenya			3.1	48	18	20
Nigeria			2.5	50	25	61
Argentina			1.5	22	9	8
Bolivia			2.6	44	19	5
Brazil			2.8	38	9	11
Dominican Republic			3.0	49	15	86
Cuba			2.3	27	7	76
Peru			3.1	42	11	11
Mexico			3.2	43	10	26
China			1.8	33	15	82
India			2.2	43	17	168
Indonesia			2.8	48	19	84
Iran			3.0	45	17	18
Pakistan			2.1	51	18	123
Philippines			3.0	45	12	127
South Korea			2.2	36	11	324
Thailand			2.7	43	10	69
Austria			0.5	14	13	89
England and Wales			0.5	16	12	323
Hungary			0.5	14	10	111
Italy			0.8	17	10	180
Netherlands			1.2	19	8	323
Scotland			0.0	17	12	66
Sweden			0.8	14	10	18
Canada			1.8	17	7	2
United States			1.1	17	9	22

Source: *Demographic Yearbook*, 1971, Statistical Office of the United Nations, 1972, pp. 111; 112–18, 125–29.

underdeveloped regions of the world have birth rates of at least double those of the developed regions, and growth rates of more than double. Focusing upon selected countries we may more clearly perceive the marked demographic differences between developed and underdeveloped countries. At current rates of increase, the majority of underdeveloped countries will double their population in 25 years or less, compared with between 70 and 100 years for most developed nations. Even this is still a *short* time interval in historical perspective.

What has caused the phenomenal upswing in world population since the 18th century and is sustaining high rates of increase throughout much of the world? World population—and, excluding migration, national population—is determined by the rate at which people are born and the rate at which they die. If more people are born during a given period of time than die, then the population increases. If more die than are born, population decreases. If the number that are born and die is the same, population remains stable (that is, on the average, people only replace themselves).

Now, as we have already noted, the population level of the Earth has remained quite stable or shown only very nominal increases throughout most of man's history. In terms of human reproductive capacity, birth rates have traditionally and consistently been high (around 40 annually per 1,000 population—a ratio known as the crude birth rate, since it does not take into account important variations in the number of women in reproductive ages of the population). But death rates, too, have been high, near or just slightly below birth rates. Especially high have been infant death or mortality rates (the number of deaths per 1,000 children born under the age of one). In the language of Thomas Malthus, positive

THE DEMOGRAPHIC TRANSITION. THE WEST

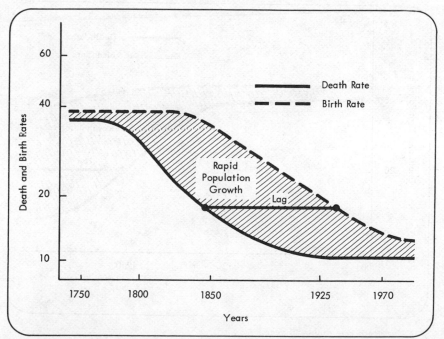

Major death rate drop—125 years.
Death rate—birth rate lag—75 years.
Major birth rate drop—100 years.

checks in the form of war, starvation, but especially disease (plague, dysentery, cholera, smallpox, malaria, etc.) held population down. Population fluctuations were determined mainly by variations in the death rate, but the death rate has historically varied insufficiently to produce marked changes in world population. Insufficiently, that is, until about the time of industrialization in the West, when advances in agriculture, a rising standard of living, and particularly major advances in sanitation and preventive and curative medicine (as in the handling of food and drink, inoculations, and drugs) began to make gradual but irreversible inroads on the death rate.

Thus, over a period of about 175 years, say from 1750 to 1925, death rates in industrializing countries of Northern Europe slowly declined from natural highs of near 40 to around 10, reductions in infant mortality leading the way but increased longevity contributing notably. Whereas hardly more than half of a family's children could be expected to survive beyond age 10 at the onset of industrialization in Northern Europe, today most survive. Birth rates, however, continued at a high level at the same time death rates were falling. For example, while the English death rate was 21 in 1850, the birth rate did not lower to 21 until 1925, a lag of some 75 years. From a birth rate of 31 in 1800, about 130 years elapsed before the rate lowered to 14 in Sweden. It is during the lag of birth rates behind death rates that population grows;

THE DEMOGRAPHIC TRANSITION: THIRD WORLD

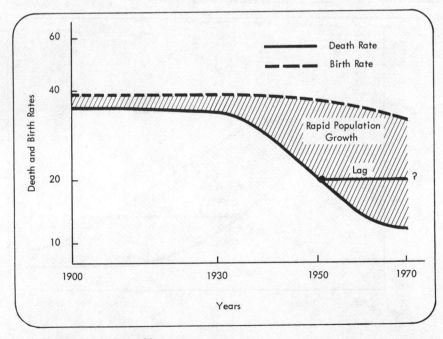

Major death rate drop—20 years.
Death rate—birth rate lag—?
Major birth rate drop—?

and the wider the gap between birth and death rates and the longer the lag of birth rates behind death rates the sharper and longer is the increase in population growth.

The movement of a population from a condition of high birth rates and high death rates, to one of high birth rates and low death rates, and finally to one of low birth rates and low death rates has been referred to as the "demographic transition."[21] To date, the transition from slow growth to rapid growth to slower growth has followed the sequence in all industrialized countries. The time that elapsed in getting the birth rate down to levels nearer the death rate was well over 100 years in the West; Japan, the only non-Western nation to thus far have fully industrialized, also made the demographic transition but at a different time and in a much shorter time period. The Japanese transition was accelerated, particularly the drop in the birth rate, declining from 34 in 1947 to 17 in 1965, fortunately accomplishing in less than 18 years what required 130 years in, for example, Sweden. Thus, with death rates approaching bottom levels, the immediate future of population growth has been transferred to the behavior of the birth rate, or in Malthusian terms, to preventive checks. By preventive checks, Malthus meant birth control, actually sexual abstinence, since he was opposed to contraception.

As in the West, the Third World population explosion has been the result of declining death rates and continuing high birth rates. However, the timing and conditions of population changes in the Third World are different, drastically different. Underdeveloped regions received considerable modern sanitary and medical techniques veritably in one fell swoop, frequently witnessing drops in death rates in 10 to 15 years that took almost the full course of industrialization in European countries. As in the West before, much of the drop in death rates is attributable to sharp declines in infant and child mortality, resulting in an even more accelerated rate of population growth than if death rate decline came gradually, due to slowly increasing longevity among adults. Due to the young age structure of the population, death rates in many underdeveloped regions are as low as those in the most advanced countries, with their older populations. The death rate in Mexico, for example, is about the same (10) as that of the fairly young U.S. population.

Meanwhile, birth rates in the underdeveloped world have mostly continued at high traditional levels. Indeed, with improvements in sanitation and health, birth rates have substantially risen in many Third World countries. The Mexican birth rate, for example, was up to 46 in 1964 from 32 in 1911, and in Ghana up to 56 in 1960–64 from 33 in 1945–49.[22] Elsewhere, birth rates have been in the vicinity of 40 at least since the turn of the 20th century, while death rates have fallen in recent

[21] See George J. Stolnitz, "The Demographic Transition: From High to Low Birth Rates and Death Rates," in Ronald Freedman, ed., *Population: The Vital Revolution* (New York: Doubleday & Company, Inc., 1964), pp. 30–46; and Dennis Wrong, *Population and Society* (New York: Random House, Inc., 1967).

[22] United Nations *Demographic Yearbook, 1964* (New York: The United Nations, 1965).

decades to about 15. Hence, the gap between birth rate and death rate in most underdeveloped areas is larger than it ever was in the West and developed with much greater rapidity, both factors thus promoting greater population explosions.

The United States

The United States has approximated the European experience in the demographic transition. However, the U.S. birth rate since World War II has been consistently higher than those of most European countries, and the percentage of annual population increase two to three times as great. "Prosperity," a younger age at marriage, a higher rate of marriage, fewer childless and one-child families, and an increase in family size variously contributed to the postwar U.S. population boom.[23] Since 1960 the rate of U.S. population growth has slowed, but it still stands above most European countries. In the sixties, the United States added some 35 million persons to its population for a 1971 total of about 208 million, reflecting an annual growth rate of 1.6 percent. In 1971, the birth rate stood at 17 (down from 23 in 1960) and the death rate at 9 (the same as in 1960).

The U.S. population is growing at 1.1 percent (1971), or two million persons a year. Owing to the high birth rates following World War II, women in child-bearing years will have increased from 36 million in 1960, to 43 million in 1970, to 54 million in 1980. But despite the unprecedented potential for growth, U.S. fertility rates have been diminishing overall since 1950, and thus the absolute number of births have been holding rather steady. The U.S. birth rate is now at or below the all-time Depression level lows of the 1930s. Average number of children has been reduced from over three to slightly over two; 56 percent of women aged 25–29 said they intended to have no more children compared with 33 percent in 1955.[24] The greater number of employed women (non-working women have 27 percent higher fertility than working women), higher educational levels, and smaller ideal family size, and improvements and increased use of contraception have contributed to smaller families and lowered fertility. Still, population estimates range from 240 to 258 million by 1985 and 271 to 322 million by the year 2000.[25] The land can certainly support this number, but with rising concern for ecology and life-quality sheer physical support is not the issue.

With no assurance that the fertility level will not again turn steadily upward, the U.S. is faced with a 30 percent population increase over the next 70 years even given the continuation of the 1972 replacement

[23] William Petersen, *The Politics of Population* (New York: Doubleday & Company, Inc., 1965).

[24] "Fertility Indicators: 1970," p. 48.

[25] U.S. Bureau of the Census, *Current Population Reports*, Series P-25, No. 470; "Projections of the Population of the United States, by Age and Sex: 1970 to 2020," U.S. Government Printing Office, Washington, D.C., 1971, p. 1.

level low of 2.1 children per family.[26] To achieve zero population growth within a generation of reproductive age women, it would be necessary for child-bearing women to have on the average about 1.4 children—or as Davis observes, a mean that could be reached if 60 percent had one child and 40 percent two.[27] (This calculation excludes immigration and assumes a certain minority of childless women.) Such is a conceivable but highly unlikely state of affairs.

Now and in the immediate future, the quality of life is at stake in America—what individuals may aspire to and attain in terms of self-realization and social participation. As the Days have put it, "How much . . . will we have to sacrifice—materially, ethically, politically, aesthetically—here, and in the rest of the world, before population growth is halted?"[28]

HALTING POPULATION GROWTH: THE WESTERN CASE

How *do* we halt population growth? How were birth rates lowered in today's industrialized nations? As noted previously, except for Japan, birth rates throughout industrialized regions have exhibited a rather gradual decline. Western birth rates were lowered through the self-conscious and voluntary efforts of parents who desired to have fewer children and took necessary measures to attain their desires. Cultural definitions of the ideal family size have commensurately declined, and with increasing concern over population, group sanctions may operate against persons who voluntarily exceed the norms. Rising levels of living, education, communication, and urbanization have generally preceded or run concurrently with falling birth rates in industrial societies. While the slowing of population growth in industrialized areas appears to have taken place quite automatically and spontaneously (the United States government has no population policy or program as such and the U.S. Population Commission's report has been largely ignored by government elites[29]), the matter has not been that simple, and permanently stabilizing the population is seemingly going to be more difficult than slowing it down has been.

In the first place, the forces that have encouraged or influenced Westerners to limit their family size—rising economic position, high levels of education, mass media, and industrial cities—are obviously not auto-

---

[26] Kingsley Davis, "Zero Population Growth—The Goal and the Means," *Daedalus*, 102 (Fall 1973), pp. 15–30.

[27] See Tomas Frejka, "Reflections on the Demographic Conditions Needed to Establish a U.S. Stationary Population Growth," *Population Studies*, 22 (November 1968), pp. 379–97.

[28] Lincoln H. and Alice Taylor Day, *Too Many Americans* (New York: Dell Publishing Company, 1965), p. 7; also see Daniel O. Price, ed., *The 99th Hour: The Population Crisis in the United States* (Chapel Hill: The University of North Carolina Press, 1967).

[29] *Population and the American Future* (Washington, D.C.: U.S. Government Printing Office, 1972).

matic or spontaneous events or phenomena. These historic developments have taken place under extremely propitious conditions, especially when considered in the context of the rapid population growth that accompanied the process of industrialization. Western countries were able to industrialize and continue to raise their standard of living *at the same time* their populations were rapidly growing, because food production was vastly increased, population densities were relatively low to begin with, millions of persons emigrated to new and richly endowed continents, colonial empires returned raw materials, and there was a gradual reduction in the death rate that allowed for social adjustments.[30] These developments and conditions tended to provide forerunners in industrialization with the demographic latitude or margin to achieve rapid economic growth despite large-scale population growth; indeed, in many ways, the additional population stimulated economic development. Once achieved, the forces that accompany economic development such as education and urbanization exercised the influences that helped lower birth rates in the West.

Now, few underdeveloped countries have the set of conditions enjoyed by the West that would provide the margin for rapid economic development at the same time death rates are low and birth rates high. Agriculture is stagnating, densities are often high, there are no new continents to be settled or colonies to exploit, and death rates came down with a veritable crash, allowing little time for even minimal adjustments in social organization. The Third World seems inextricably caught in the population trap, limited economically due to population problems and unable to reduce population growth by way of the forces of economic growth that accompanied declining birth rates in industrial nations. Unlike the West, birth rates must be lowered *before* any substantial gains in the standard of living will be made in most countries.

Declining birth rates offer immediate and direct support to developmental efforts. In addition to food considerations, the dependency ratio is lowered, freeing capital for industrial purposes. Later, lowered birth rates have the consequence of increasing employment opportunities; increasing capital investment per worker and, hence, worker productivity; raising wages; and lowering fertility potential.

Returning to the efforts that have been required in lowering the birth rates of advanced countries, we should recall that among many low-income families in the United States, achieving the *desire* for small families is far from realizing the deed. Successful family planning or contraception is neither automatic nor spontaneous. Even given existing levels of contraception technology, unwanted third, fourth, and more pregnancies are common and a reason for much of the continued U.S. population growth. The knowledge and practice of contraception even in a highly literate society such as the United States, though practically universal in some form, is not yet up to the point of desired effectiveness. Although the United States still stands in need of considerable improve-

---

[30] See Wrong, *Population and Society.*

ment in lowering the ideal family size, our first objective should be to see that the actual average family size gets down to the ideal.

When knowledge or the practice of contraception (sterilization aside) is inadequate or fails, as it so often does even among highly industrialized peoples, birth is not inevitable. Indeed, induced abortion has played a major role in the reduction or at least limitation of birth rates (most notably in Japan and Eastern Europe) but has had a very palpable impact in many other countries. The Japanese birth rate plummeted as the number of *recorded* abortions rose from 102,000 in 1949 to 1,170,-000 in 1955 (data estimated to be only 50 to 75 percent complete). In the same period, births declined from 2,697,000 to 1,727,000.[31] In 1961, legal abortions in Hungary totaled 145 per 100 births. Despite the traditional (but declining) opposition among American people to abortion for social or economic reasons,[32] a few states had passed liberalized abortion laws by 1970. Then in 1973 the U.S. Supreme Court struck down restrictive abortion laws in some 40 remaining conservative states. (Rather than promiscuous young girls seeking a reprieve for errant ways, about 85 percent of the estimated 850,000 to 1,200,000 illegal abortions that were performed annually prior to liberalization in the United States involved married women.) To be equitable and reach those most in need of economic help, not only must abortion be legal upon demand, but free to everyone.

THIRD WORLD OBSTACLES

What stand as the major impediments to a reduction in the birth rate in underdeveloped countries? A number of interrelated incentives to having children, or at least disincentives to control family size, are embedded in the structure of the extended family and agrarian society itself. In the extended family, biological parents are able to share the economic and personal costs of raising children with other members of the kin group; thus, child responsibilities do not fall solely upon biological parents, an important consideration in having children. Conversely, parents in old age tend to rely on children for support. In societies with highly developed welfare systems strong disincentives to having children have been created; children are no longer assets for family security, economic strength, and parental old age. From this standpoint, social welfare systems might be expected to reduce birth rates, but poor countries cannot under present circumstances develop economic surpluses and afford welfare. And one of the reasons they have insufficient welfare surplus is because of underdevelopment and overpopulation, in turn conditioned by the need of security through

---

[31] Kingsley Davis, "The Theory of Change and Response in Modern Demographic History," in Thomas R. Ford and Gordon F. DeJong, eds., *Social Demography* (Englewood Cliffs, N.J.: Prentice-Hall, Inc., 1970), p. 25.

[32] Alice Rossi, "Public Views on Abortion," Committee on Human Development, University of Chicago, February, 1966; and data presented by Hazel Gaudet Erskine published in the Fall 1966 issue of *Public Opinion Quarterly*.

large families—another of the numerous cyclical traps of underdevelopment.

Also owing to the corporate nature of the extended family, children are able to marry at a very early age, have their own children, and not assume direct responsibility for them. Thus, several additional and highly fecund childbearing years are added to the course of marriage. The level of age at marriage is a complex matter, but it typically rises during industrialization as young people face the prospect of having to sustain economically independent nuclear families, thus preparing themselves educationally and occupationally before risking marriage. Hence, while marriage for females in the midteens has long been common in India, in Ireland marriage has been postponed until the mid- or late twenties. However, in an era of economic surplus, when material security is sufficiently great so that young people can afford to marry after high school, while attending college, or before a permanent job or career has been set, the age of marriage for women tends to again turn downward to the very early twenties and late teens. Such a situation has contributed to the high postwar birth rate in the United States. As Western norms of free mate selection (as opposed to parents contracting marriages for young children) have gained currency in many urban areas of the Third World, young men and women are increasingly entering into courtship and marriage markets, which also encourages later marriage.

In addition, the traditional family system has stimulated birth rates through its value emphasis on male virility as demonstrated through procreation and female worth as demonstrated through early and consistent childbearing. The wife's status and acceptance in her husband's household depends on her childbearing, especially male childbearing, performance. The strictly subordinate and family work role of the female in the traditional family allows her little option or alternative to the domestic scene. Activity as a field or household laborer in no way competes with also having numerous children. In an urban industrial family, especially if it has a modern or democratic orientation, the female may choose other roles, such as paid occupation, community activities, or self-development in education and arts, which directly compete with domestic and childbearing activities. But even the modern mother role, as opposed to the traditional one of letting the children run free as the mother labored for the household, stresses the importance of spending a lot of time with a *few* children. Greater general female equality per se may also slow population growth. Research into fertility in urban Latin America indicated that employed women had fewer children than non-employed women, though the limiting influence seemed to be differences in socioeconomic status, personal motivation, and preferred role rather than employment per se.[33]

Religion is often cited as an obstacle to population control. As a social institution, religion throughout the world has contributed to values of high fertility. Of major world religions, however, only Catholicism is ex-

---

[33] Paula H. Hass, "Maternal Role Incompatibility and Fertility in Urban Latin America," *The Journal of Social Issues*, 28 (2, 1972), pp. 111–27.

plicitly and doctrinally opposed to mechanical means of birth control. Other world religions all tend to consider contraception or artificial birth limitation as at least doctrinally acceptable. With the exception of Latin American countries, religious leaders have posed no opposition to government programs of contraception. Catholicism as such does not seem to be an insurmountable obstacle to the reduction of birth rates, as Ireland, France, and Italy document (the fact of later age at marriage aside). However, a cooperative Church could be a valuable asset in government efforts at birth control, and an uncooperative Church, as today, a serious impediment. But whether Latin American Catholicism is cooperative, uncooperative, or neutral regarding birth control, contraception programs will move ahead.[34]

The ideal family size in Third World areas, even where more or less autonomous nuclear families are concerned, remains at substantially high levels. Samples of married women in seven Latin American capitol cities, the majority of whom were using contraception and evinced modern social attitudes, still preferred on the average over four children.[35] Throughout the underdeveloped world ideal family sizes range from four to five.[36] As the Paddocks have simply put it, "People *love* children."[37] Two thirds of lower class respondents of a Bogota, Colombia, sample agreed to the statement, "The happy family has many children."[38] Thus, concern over family size tends to develop only after four or five children are already present. As Stycos points out, this is not family planning at all, but a desire to *stop* having children.[39] Yet any concern at all is a point of optimism, for too often there has been and is simple indifference to family limitation. The idea of family limitation through contraception has often never even been considered. Children have flatly been defined as valuable, and too often the more the better.

Along with traditional indifference to family planning or contraception comes a profound ignorance of sexual physiology. The biology of sex and reproduction tends to be misunderstood and sexual superstitions may inhibit the practice of contraception, even if child limitation is desired. Vasectomy, for example, may be equated with castration. Group norms defining "good" and "bad" women may find their definition in whether a female has been sterilized or fitted with a contraceptive device.

Despite much indifference and ignorance in regard to sex and contraception, available evidence suggests that a large portion of people in

---

[34] See Margaret Larkin, "As Many as God Sends? Family Planning in Mexico," *The Nation*, November 14, 1966.

[35] Hass, "Maternal Role Incompatibility," p. 116.

[36] Hartley, *Population Quantity vs. Quality*, p. 253.

[37] William and Paul Paddock, *Famine—1975!* (Boston: Little, Brown and Company, 1967), p. 23.

[38] Robert C. Williamson, "Social Class and Orientation to Change," *Social Forces*, 46 (March 1968), pp. 317–28.

[39] J. Mayone Stycos, "Obstacles of Programs of Population Control—Facts and Fancies," *Marriage and Family Living*, 25 (February 1963), pp. 5–13.

many Third World countries are aware of birth control possibilities and would agree to their use to prevent unwanted birth.[40] Yet, only a small portion of Third World peoples have had actual exposure to birth control information, and even a smaller minority regularly practice birth control. The regular practice of birth control tends to be almost entirely limited to a small minority of middle-income urban residents who have at least high school educations.[41] The steps from awareness of birth control, to the approval of it, to the desire to use it, to the education in its use, and to the regular practice of it are long, difficult, and far from an inevitable sequence. While awareness and approval of contraception may currently encompass large portions of Third World peoples, the desire to use it consistently *and* early is largely lacking, and the steps of education and application are even more remote.[42]

When we speak of practice or application of contraception we imply availability. Availability itself represents a giant operational step, especially when trained medical personnel are required (China has made effective and extensive use out of medical assistants and "barefoot" doctors in family planning[43]). And how much do contraceptives cost? Certainly few families in the poor nations could afford to pay retail prices of condoms or pills. For many this would require a significant portion of their income. Sterilization is also expensive in cash terms. Within financial limits of poor peoples and countries, however, are a variety of penny-cheap intrauterine rings (IUD's), which prevent maturation of fertilized ova. When properly fitted, the IUD is highly effective and requires only periodic attention, unlike the regular motivation that must underlie the use of pills or condoms. Then, too, an M.D. would not ordinarily be required for its use. But whatever the form of contraception that is most acceptable or amenable to those in need, any failure in provision, when placed in worldwide perspective, cannot be excused on account of economic deficiencies. Rather, international value priorities and political expediences would be held accountable.

Before the application and practice of contraception must come birth control information or education. By education here is not necessarily meant requiring so many years of formal education. As Americans should well know, finishing 12 years of school means very little in terms of birth control knowledge or even knowledge of sexual physiology and behavior. People may be educated in the practice of contraception without being able to read or write, although literacy is an extremely valuable

[40] See Donald J. Bogue, "The End of the Population Explosion," *The Public Interest*, 7 (Spring 1967), pp. 10–20; and, especially, Bernard Berelson et al., *Family Planning and Population Programs* (Chicago: University of Chicago Press, 1966).

[41] Williamson, "Social Class and Orientation to Change."

[42] For a survey of the practice and means of contraception, see Elizabeth Draper, *Birth Control in the Modern World* (Baltimore: Penguin Books, Inc., 1965).

[43] Committee of Concerned Asian Scholars, *China! Inside the People's Republic* (New York: Bantam Books, 1972), pp. 228–46; and Maria Antonietta Macciocchi, *Daily Life in Revolutionary China* (New York: Monthly Review Press, 1972), pp. 266–99.

if not indispensable asset in successful birth control.[44] Japan's almost universal literacy greatly facilitated her remarkable performance of halving the birth rate in 15 years.

Despite its usual substantive irrelevance to sex education and birth control, the more years of school a woman completes, the fewer number of births she is likely to have. Stycos has shown that the number of births among Puerto Rican women drops rather sharply for those who have completed seven or eight years of education and continues to drop with years of additional schooling.[45] However, as he further points out, there is a considerable time lapse between rising national levels of education and a drop in the birth rate; and the level that most countries can economically aim at is little more than four to six years, a level that evidently is not in itself high enough to have a very marked lowering effect. Yet, revolutionary societies such as China and Cuba have placed education high on development programs and within a relatively short time have greatly increased levels of educational attainment among youth and almost eliminated adult illiteracy. Cuba has achieved one of the lowest birth rates in Latin America, while China has done the same with respect to mainland Asia. Furthermore, birth control education, as the Japanese and now the Chinese can testify, may also occur by way of contraceptive clinics, volunteer workers, midwives, drugstores, and mass media.

A final obstacle may be cited which concerns the view of many Third World idealogues that family planning is a white man's scheme to weaken their people. The Chinese once took this stand, as have many Africans. But the western powers have other schemes to maintain dominance, and they don't involve family planning. Like the Chinese today, the proponents of development must come to realize that a rational population policy can be a valuable asset in development strategy.

Prospects

What, then, are the prospects of halting population growth in underdeveloped regions? Some observers, such as the demographer Donald J. Bogue, are optimistic.[46] Optimism must be an essential ingredient to the solution of population problems; to define the situation as hopeless would inevitably be a self-fulfilling prophecy. Bogue is optimistic only under the condition that both advanced and undeveloped countries engage in an "all-out crash program" of medical, psychological, and economic research and aid. Others, such as agricultural specialists William and Paul Paddock, would disagree strongly with Bogue's optimism.[47] Like Bogue, the Paddocks anticipate widespread famine in the near

---

[44] B. Alfred Liu, "Population Growth and Educational Development," *Annals of the American Academy of Political and Social Science*, 371 (January 1967), pp. 109–20.

[45] J. Mayone Stycos, "Education and Fertility in Puerto Rico," in Ford and DeJong, *Social Demography*, pp. 453–549.

[46] Bogue, "The End of the Population Explosion."

[47] Paddock and Paddock, *Famine—1975!*

future but are much less hopeful with regard to the adoption and application of contraception. For each form of birth control—abortion, sterilization, pills, condoms, and IUD's—they see serious difficulties. The Paddocks' chief concern is how the billions in the world's poor countries are going to be fed, and we shall deal with the problem of agriculture in Chapter 14.

Japan stands as a model to the Third World for major and rapid progress in slowing population growth. However, very few of the non-revolutionary underdeveloped countries enjoys many of the conditions that accompanied Japan's fertility decline: universal literacy, advancing level of education, mass media, industrial urbanization, a relatively large medical profession, open attitudes toward abortion, a small family norm, and a determined government population policy. (Argentina and Uruguay are exceptions to some of these conditions and their birth rates are the lowest in the Third World.) Most important, Japan had already attained a comparatively high level of industrialization and standard of living from which its people could weigh the value of small families.

Any all-out population program that is going to hope to succeed must initially place abortion high on the list of priorities. Large-scale abortion is an emergency measure used while a population is in the process of acquiring effective contraceptive habits. Also necessary is going to be a much more militant attitude on the part of political officials with respect to family limitation, not only in underdeveloped regions but in the majority of industrialized nations as well.[48] Making contraceptive information and contraceptives available is not enough. Many economically advanced and most traditional peoples still *want to have* too many children. Governments could, for example, attempt to exert pressure on childbirth by penalizing through taxation third and subsequent children. Daris suggests the possibility of legal limitation to two children. A more immediately plausible and quite effective alternative is social coercion; i.e., popular resentment against persons who abuse the privilege of having children or exceed a rational community norm. Japan has put to use precisely such social and informal coercion. A direct and forthright attack on excessive family size by society and government would presuppose, of course, the unrestricted use of and access to any and all safe means of preventing childbirth.

In the final analysis, the prospects for halting the most excessive and threatening aspects of world population growth hinges largely upon the economic development of the Third World. Such development cannot take place without social revolution, an event the U.S. has consistently opposed.

ON FEMALE INEQUALITY

Going hand in hand with ancient precepts regarding the value of large families is the norm of male superiority and female subordination.

---

[48] See Kingsley Davis, "Population Policy: Will Present Programs Succeed?" in Ness, *The Sociology of Economic Development,* pp. 357–81.

Working full-time as veritable baby factories and household laborers, women have traditionally been consigned to a position of disprivilege, although males have often done all in their power to glorify and sanctify motherhood and housewifery as the highest earthly virtues. Women have themselves contributed strong support to the deification of the domestic role. In a premodern era of high mortality rates, systematic reproduction has tended to be the inescapable lot of females. But when two children can be delivered within a five- or six-year period, placed in school, and expected to reach adulthood, there is little reason for women to continue to produce children and/or accept lifelong domesticity, unless they continue to do so out of habit and their husband's wishes.

Herbert Spencer's anthropology holds that "The slave class in a primitive society consists of women."[49] While doubtlessly an exaggeration Spencer's mythical primitive society does allude to the distinctly inferior status of women in probably an easy majority of human societies.[50] From his Social Darwinist perspective, Spencer felt that any attempt to upgrade women through education to prepare them for such things as business or professional work "would be mischievous." Marx charged that women were treated as chattels or prostitutes under the capitalist system, bought, sold, and used for bourgeois interests. Marx, however, would do something about sexual inequality. Child rearing, a foremost obstacle to sexual equality, would be done on a communal basis. Women would be equally trained and educated and drawn into the sphere of social production, and family relations would be freed from economic tensions and exploited unpaid labor.

Where Marxist revolutions have taken place, such as in Russia, China, and Cuba, the status of women has indeed been quite radically transformed.[51] Early Soviet legislation elevated female legal equality and greatly liberalized laws governing marriage, divorce, abortion, and illegitimacy (finding that the effect of the latter statutes was to cut down the birth rate and that it was socially disruptive, the Soviets returned to somewhat more controlled family regulations). Nurseries and kindergartens have relieved some of the burdens of child rearing for large numbers of Soviet mothers, but the great majority of children are still *mainly* raised by mothers and grandmothers. Partially due to labor shortages and partially due to ideological beliefs, Soviet women have been drawn into higher education and the labor force on a massive scale. Almost 80 percent of all available Soviet women work, composing

---

[49] Jay Rumney, *Herbert Spencer's Sociology* (New York: Atherton Press, Inc., 1965), p. 102.

[50] See Stuart A. Queen and Robert W. Habenstein, *The Family in Various Cultures* (Philadelphia: J.B. Lippincott Co., 1967).

[51] See H. Kent Geiger, *The Family in Soviet Russia* (Cambridge: Harvard University Press, 1968); Janet Weitzner Salaff and Judith Merkle, "Women in Revolution: The Lessons of the Soviet Union and China," *Berkeley Journal of Sociology*, XV (1970), pp. 166–91; Nancy Milton, "Women in China," *Berkeley Journal of Sociology*, XVI, 197–72, pp. 106–19; *China! Inside the People's Republic,* pp. 266–92; and Petur Gudjonsson, "Women in Castro's Cuba," *The Progressive*, August 1972, pp. 25–29.

half of the work force. They work in occupations that would startle Westerners, such as road repair, heavy construction, mining, and machine operation. Over three fourths of Soviet doctors are women, almost three fourths of the teachers, and about one third of the engineers and scientific workers.[52] Women have made major advances in political and managerial posts as well.

Indeed, Soviet norms do not permit a woman to be "only" a housewife; a strongly negative image is purveyed in official propaganda of women who do not work if they have no children or even one child, especially if they have received higher education at the expense of the state.[53] However, Geiger notes that the strain on women from *both* running a household and working seems to be growing high, as indicated in part by a rising disability rate among Soviet women. And despite what most observers would consider radical gains for women, men continue to dominate top political and managerial decision-making positions. Considering the shortage of child care centers (greatly expanded in recent years) and the continuing domestic and child-rearing load of women, the fact that Soviet women are also working at a variety of jobs may be taken as an indication not of liberation but of greater life pressures. Polish women, too, have complained about the double loads they often carry.[54] In China, major strides toward female equality have been taken in education, politics, work, and income. Yet, observers have noted the under-representation of women in the more highly esteemed and rewarded positions, while Chinese women have had to assume most domestic as well as their social tasks.

In other industrialized countries the status and expectations of women vary from the rather advanced equalitarianism of Swedish society to the restrictive and conservative posture regarding the female role in Japan.[55] In the latter country, men have with considerable conviction opposed the entrance of even highly educated women into the independently employed (as opposed to family enterprise) labor force, not allegedly because men consider their wives and daughters inferior and incapable, but because of belief in women's traditional domestic rights and responsibilities. Men prefer their wives to have an orderly house, well-behaved and educated children, and a prompt dinner prepared when they arrive home from the office—often via the bar with its young female embellishments. But feminist currents exist in Japan as well, particularly among the young, single, and educated.

The feminist movement in the United States has renewed momentum after a half-century lull.[56] Political indications include the liberalization

---

[52] *Women in the Soviet Union* (Moscow: Progress Publishers, 1970), pp. 17–47.

[53] Geiger, *The Family in Soviet Russia*, p. 182.

[54] Krystyna Wrochno, *Women in Poland* (Warsaw: Interpress Publishers, 1969).

[55] Frederic Fleischer, *The New Sweden* (New York: David McKay Co., Inc., 1968), and Vogel, *Japan's New Middle Class.*

[56] Marlene Dixon, "Why Women's Liberation—2?" in Milton Mankoff, ed., *The Poverty of Progress* (New York: Holt, Rinehart and Winston, 1972);

of abortion and the passage of the Equal Rights Amendment in the House and Senate and (to date) thirty of a required thirty-eight states (several states, however, have voted it down). A greater level of social awareness regarding women's condition and rights exists today than perhaps any other point in modern history.

Economic position

Yet, women's status continues to lag far behind that of men on numerous fronts.[57] Although one third of women are in the paid labor force and they compose well over one-third of the active labor force, they are heavily concentrated in low-paying clerical, service, semiskilled, and professional jobs (see Tables 3 and 10). In some higher level occupations, women are not as well represented as they were in the past.[58] In income, white females working full time earn only six-tenths of white male income and black females earn but seven-tenths of black male income. Women are paid less relative to men than blacks are to whites; for example, females working full-time, year-around with a college education earned $1,411 less than a male high school graduate, whereas a black male college graduate earns $500 more (1970). At the high school level the female earns $4,000 less than the male compared with the black's $3,000 less than the whites.

That women are largely confined to jobs rather than improving careers is attested to by the fact that female college graduates in the age cohort 24–34 have a median income of $8,116 increase by only $1,000 to the age 45–54 cohort compared with a male increase of $5,000.[59] A small part of this difference is accounted for by the greater representation of men holding advanced degrees: in 1970, 60 percent of master's degrees were awarded to men and fully 87 percent of doctorates.[60] Even at the bachelor's level women earn only two-fifths of the degrees each year. The

---

Alice S. Rossi, "Equality between the Sexes: An Immodest Proposal," *Daedalus*, 93 (Spring 1964), pp. 607–52; Robin Morgan, ed., *Sisterhood Is Powerful* (New York: Random House, Inc., 1970); Mary Lou Thompson, ed., *Voices of the New Feminism* (Boston: Beacon Press, 1970); Edith Hoshino Altbach, ed., *From Feminism to Liberation* (Cambridge, Mass.: Schenkman Publishing Company, 1971); and Mari Jo Buhle, Ann G. Gordon, and Nancy Schrom, "Women in American Society," *Radical America*, 5 (July–August 1971), pp. 3–66.

[57] For general documentations, see Cynthia Fuchs Epstein, *Women's Place* (Berkeley: University of California Press, 1971); and Jesse Bernard, *Women and the Public Interest* (Chicago: Aldine Publishing Company, 1971).

[58] Dean D. Knudsen, "The Declining Status of Women," *Social Forces*, 48 (December 1969), pp. 183–92; and Cynthia F. Epstein, "Encountering the Male Establishment: Sex-Status Limits on Women's Careers in the Professions," *American Journal of Sociology*, 75 (May 1970), pp. 965–82.

[59] U.S. Bureau of the Census, *Current Population Reports*, Series P-60, No. 80, "Income in 1970 of Families and Persons in the United States," U.S. Government Printing Office, Washington, D.C., 1971, Table 49, p. 102.

[60] *Statistical Abstract/American Almanac* (New York: Grosset & Dunlap, 1973), pp. 133; 112.

ratio of female to male college graduates in the population was .60 in 1970, the same as in 1960. Still, women with Ph.D.s can expect to earn no more than men with bachelor's degrees. Women are largely working much below their level of education, and a large percentage of college-educated women are not in the labor force. This underutilization of women in social and economic production constitutes a great waste of human resources.

To employers, however, the underutilization of women may be profitable. Female labor is often cheaper than investment in new machinery. As Agassi observes, "As long as women are willing to fill these demanding, high-speed, mind-dulling, and nerve-racking dead-end jobs for wages lower than those of most male workers, management will not invest in modernization."[61] Women may serve the same function as that of any minority labor force in the maximization of surplus wealth for the capitalist class.

Paid employment is a major step in the direction of equality of the sexes. But an important distinction should be drawn between the employment of women as a measure to meet emergency labor shortages, to cut labor costs, or strictly to supplement husband's income and the employment of women in a voluntarily chosen vocation. The great majority of married working women and their husbands view female labor as strictly supplementary or temporarily supporting, and the great majority of single women view their work as simply a precursor to dependent status in marriage. However, there are indications of serious occupational interests, especially among new working class women, though considerably less than the extent of career orientations found among young Scandinavian women.[62] Working women have not necessarily eschewed motherhood. We may be quite confident, however, that a minority of those having serious vocational interests have any intentions of trying to blend three or four children with work. That women with vocational interests or a deep interest in cultivating personal development will make an effort to limit their number of children to less than three is one of the main assets in coping with population problems. The industrial poor tend to want to limit their families due to economic necessity, but the affluent can argue to themselves and others that they have plenty of money to support three or four children, and they often tend to have them. Female interest in career and personal development militates against the four-bedroom home.

Before married women can entertain thoughts of freedom to pursue a vocation or extrafamilial activities their child-rearing and domestic responsibilities must be eased. Day care facilities for children are among the more urgent needs. (Six million children under six years old with full time working mothers have only 900,000 places in licensed day care centers—the large majority of children coming from families whose well-being depends upon mothers working.) These facilities should be avail-

---

[61] Judith Buber Agassi, "Women Who Work in Factories," *Dissent*, Winter 1972, p. 235.

[62] Vance Packard, *The Sexual Wilderness* (New York: David McKay Co., Inc., 1968), p. 101.

able around the clock all year and certainly beyond a 24 hour period for a given stay. For the present such facilities should be paid for in part according to size of family income and in part by the state. Low income families would have minimal or free access, while upper income groups would pay at least half the cost. The facilities should be controlled on a community or neighborhood basis with national guidelines regulating charges and minimum quality control. To date, the child day care idea as developed by the federal government and corporations has had a strategy of taking responsibility for children of low-paid, working mothers rather than child day care as a general need for all women.[63] The day care center advocated and used by the large employers is intended as a device to control working class and poor women and their children in both an economic and ideological manner (teaching the women the work ethic, children respect for authority, etc.). The Nixon administration has been especially involved in this strategy, and vetoed the Child Development Act that would have provided general day care facilities at free or moderate graduated costs.

Another essential change is that women at work be considered equal in every way to men, and that includes such things as not *always* being the person to have to quit work to take care of household emergencies or of *always* being the person to have to assume responsibility for meals and domestic chores.[64] Men must relent in their aloofness from domestic chores and learn the household tasks to be shared with women. This holds true not just for husbands of working women but for all husbands regardless of whether a wife is in the paid labor force or not. For family and domestic duties are often 18 to 24 hour a day propositions when small or sick children are in the house. When both partners are working full-time, domestic chores should be split down the middle in terms of both time and repugnance. If the wife is not employed, the husband still has the responsibility to assume, say, one-fourth of family duties (which does not include cleaning out a fishing tackle box). Domestic duties themselves must be recognized as unpaid and necessary *labor* supportive of material production.

Some women's liberationists argue for the abandonment of the family, at least in its present nuclear form.[65] They contend that the family is the oppressor of women, that it restricts, degrades, and narrows the

---

[63] Katherine Ellis and Rosalind Petchesky, "Children of the Corporate Dream: An Analysis of Day Care as a Political Issue under Capitalism," *Socialist Revolution*, 2 (November–December 1972), pp. 8–28; see, also, Elinor C. Guggenheimer, "When Mothers Work: The Battle for Day Care," *The Nation*, May 7, 1973, pp. 594–97. The fact of employment of mothers itself does not seem to significantly influence either marriage or family relationships (child development) one way or another, though on individual basis the effect may be profound. F. Ivan Nye and Lois W. Hoffman, *The Employed Mother in America* (Chicago: Rand McNally & Co., 1963).

[64] See Rose Laub Coser and Gerald Rokoff, "Women in the Occupational World: Social Disruption and Conflict," *Social Problems*, 18 (Spring 1971), pp. 335–54.

[65] For example, Evelyn Frankford and Ann Smitow, "The Trap of Domesticity: Notes on the Family," *Socialist Revolution*, 10 (July–August 1972), pp. 83–99, including critical comments by Ann Farrar and Peggy Somers.

life of women. We could certainly agree with the notion that the contemporary family may be a medium of oppression, but not that the family per se is a reactionary institution.[66] The contemporary family is not the universal family; family relationships may assume personally rewarding and self-fulfilling forms. Even in its present form, the family is not to be considered as the chief oppressor of women, no more than the school is to be considered as the chief oppressor of children. Both family and school are shaped by much more powerful external economic and political interests. A variety of family forms may be imagined and tried,[67] but as long as they must function within the prevailing economic milieux, not much additional success can be expected. In any event, the family today is considered to be a source of security and satisfaction by far more people than consider it oppressive. If they do consider it oppressive, they are usually not judging the family but the people in it and so make another try at it.

Sex-role stereotypes

Sexual equality also requires a change in male attitudes towards women. Despite the greater awareness of women's rights, it would be an exaggeration to state that the majority of men consider women their equals. The male superiority complex is as strong among youth as among the older generation, perhaps even stronger in many masculinity-conscious circles.

Linked to the required changes in male attitudes is the stereotyping of sex roles. Unequal sex role learning stems from early childhood and is reinforced throughout life.[68] Males are rewarded for rationality, aggression, individual initiative, and competence, while females are encouraged for emotion, expressiveness, dependability, and reserve. Females are thought to be intuitive and expressive and males achieving and instrumental. Vance Packard thinks men have a "special genius for analytical thinking" and females a "special genius for harmonizing."[69] The consistency of sex-role learning tends to give the impression that differences between male and female roles have an innate or biological origin, an illusion exposed by the fact that, while most activities in most societies are assigned to one sex or the other, there is almost no activity that has not been assigned to both sexes.[70]

That sex role stereotypes are deeply ingrained has been documented

---

[66] Frederick Engels, *The Origin of the Family, Private Property and the State*, in Marx and Engels, *Selected Works*, vol. 3 (Moscow: Progress Publishers, 1970), pp. 191–334.

[67] See Michael Gordon, ed., *The Nuclear Family in Crises: The Search for an Alternative* (New York: Harper & Row, 1972).

[68] Paul H. Mussen, "Early Sex-Role Development," in David Goslin, ed., *Handbook of Socialization Theory and Research* (Chicago: Rand McNally & Co., 1969), pp. 707–41.

[69] Packard, *The Sexual Wilderness*, p. 306.

[70] J. Richard Udry, *The Social Context of Marriage* (Philadelphia: J.B. Lippincott Co., 1966), p. 29.

by Broverman and associates.[71] Their data indicate a strong concensus among both men and women regarding differing characteristics of the sexes. A competence-rationality trait complex is ascribed to males and a warmth-expressiveness one to females. Characteristics ascribed to men are positively evaluated more often than those felt to belong to women; and while women rarely claim the positive male traits, men frequently identify with positively valued female traits. Women were found to incorporate into their self images the negatively valued traits of relative incompetence, irrationality, and passivity.

The incorporation into self-concept of such negative traits has been a source of serious difficulties for many women and hedge against their full personal effort and development. Horner learned in her research that the most highly competent and motivated young women adjusted their behavior toward the female sex-role stereotype when confronted with a conflict between the feminine image and pressing forward their competencies and aspirations.[72] Such women fear success in competition with men and rejection of their femininity. In Horner's words, "The anticipation of success is anxiety provoking and as such inhibits otherwise positive achievement-directed motivation and behavior. In order to feel or appear more feminine, women, especially those high in fear of success, disguise their abilities and withdraw from the mainstream of thought, activism, and achievement in our society."[73] However, the sex-role typing, including specific roles such as men are to be doctors and women are to be nurses as well as the general stereotyping of role traits, displays some signs of weakening in certain countries.[74]

Women and class

The "sisterhood" or feminist movement should not obscure the fact that women belong to social classes with conflicting interests the same as do men.[75] Female liberation is as dependent upon working-class liberation as is black or brown liberation. Women are as well represented in the upper class as are men, though they play different parts. The feminist movement has had a psychological, social, and sexual emphasis that leaves working-class women cold; it has been a movement of rela-

---

[71] Inge K. Broverman et al., "Sex-Role Stereotypes: A Current Appraisal," *The Journal of Social Issues*, 28 (2, 1972), pp. 59–78.

[72] Matina S. Horner, "Toward An Understanding of Achievement-Related Conflicts in Women," *Journal of Social Issues*, 28 (2, 1972), pp. 157–75.

[73] Ibid., p. 173.

[74] Scandinavians (including Finns) display a comparatively flexible perspective on women's roles, while the participation of men in household and child care responsibilities is very much in evidence, especially among younger couples. See Olof Palme, "The Emancipation of Man," *The Journal of Social Issues*, 28 (2, 1972), pp. 237–46; and Elina Haavie-Mannila, "Sex Role Attitudes in Finland, 1966–70," pp. 93–110. Nevertheless, sexual stratification and traditional unequal roles remain very much in evidence.

[75] See Marlene Dixon, "Public Ideology and the Class Composition of Women's Liberation," *Berkeley Journal of Sociology*, XVI, 1971–72, pp. 149–67.

tively secure middle-income people who have not thought in the necessary economic terms. There are, of course, many fronts upon which to conduct the fight for women's liberation, but the one with top priority deals with changes in the relations of production.[76] Only from this point can genuine gains be achieved for all women.

---

[76] For a critique of women's liberation movement strategy, see Jo Freeman, "The Tyranny of Structurelessness," *Berkeley Journal of Sociology*, XVII, 1972–73, pp. 151–64.

14

The Third World

IMPERIALISM

In a classic statement on the subject, Lenin referred to imperialism as the final stage of capitalism.[1] Imperialism is, in effect, an international system of capitalism; it is a process whereby the ruling classes of the advanced capitalist states extend the scope of their economic and political powers beyond their own societies to those of other nations of the world. Imperialist relations may be consolidated within other advanced capitalist states, such as the United States has done in Canada. Our main concern in this chapter, however, is with the relationship between imperialism and underdevelopment, the penetration of Latin America, Asia, and Africa (the Third World) by the advanced capitalist states. As Lenin pointed out, "The world has become divided into a handful of usurer states and a vast majority of debtor states."[2]

Over fifty years ago, Veblen rendered the following definition of imperialism:

> In recent time, owing to the latterday state of the industrial arts, this national pursuit of warlike and political ends has come to be a fairly single-minded chase after unearned income to be procured by intimidation and intrigue. It has been called Imperialism; it might also, in a colloquial phrasing, be called national graft.[3]

Veblen pointed out that the presence of a powerful and aggressive

---

[1] V.I. Lenin, *Imperialism: The Highest Stage of Capitalism,* in *Selected Works,* vol. 1 (Moscow: Progress Publishers, 1970), pp. 667–768.

[2] Ibid., p. 746.

[3] Thorstein Veblen, *Absentee Ownership and Business Enterprise in Recent Times* (New York: The Viking Press, 1938; 1923), p. 442. Also available as Beacon Press paperback edition, 1967.

national government allows foreign investors and corporations greater latitude of action and larger profits, "particularly in their dealings with helpless and backward peoples."[4] He also observed that the cost of imperialist activities, especially in building up the necessary armed forces and waging war against other imperialist competitors and against rebellious subjugated peoples, outweighs the profit gained by businesses through imperialism; "but the costs are not paid out of business gains, but out of the industry of the rest of the people."[5]

A quarter of a century ago Paul Sweezy wrote the following prophetic lines: "The greatest danger to world peace, and indeed to much that is best in human civilization itself, is that the rulers of America will seek to put off the day of reckoning by embarking on a career of unlimited militarism and imperialism."[6] This is precisely what the rulers of America have done; the costs thus far have been too extensive to describe fully or to calculate in anything but the most general terms. The costs have been most high to the victims of war, but nearly everyone involved has paid a high price—including the perpetrators themselves. The latter have weakened and undermined their own position in the process, so that ultimately they, too, will have to pay the price of their actions.

Imperialism in its economic aspects is a system of international expansion and intervention whereby raw materials are taken cheaply, wages paid to the laborers are miniscule, manufactured goods are sold at huge profits, taxes and tariffs are evaded, obsolete equipment is exchanged with subsidiaries to maximize profit, operations are transferred abroad to save labor costs, loans and credit are extended at high interest rates with political strings attached, high shipping charges are assessed, royalties and service charges are appropriated, and enormous profits are earned from foreign-owned oil wells, mines, plantations, and factories.[7] Military hardware is both sold and given away to regimes set upon repression of nationalist or revolutionary forces in their own countries. As Heilbroner remarks, we [the U.S.] "have ranged ourselves against nearly every movement that might have led men toward a better life, on the grounds of our opposition to communism."[8] Thus, with Great Britain, France, Portugal, and South Africa, the U.S. voted against 99 other states of the United Nations in 1972 to recognize the legitimacy of anti-colonial armed struggles.

---

[4] Thorstein Veblen, *The Vested Interests and the Common Man* (New York: The Viking Press, 1946; 1919), p. 131.

[5] *The Theory of Business Enterprise* (New York: Augustus M. Kelley, 1965; 1904), p. 297. Also available as Mentor paperback.

[6] *The Present as History* (New York: Monthly Review Press, 1953), p. 73.

[7] See Paul A. Baran, *The Political Economy of Growth* (New York: Monthly Review Press, 1957); Harry Magdoff, *The Age of Imperialism* (New York: Monthly Review Press, 1969); Pierre Jaleé, *The Third World in World Economy* (New York: Monthly Review Press, 1969); and Jaleé, *Imperialism in the Seventies* (New York: The Third Press, 1972).

[8] Robert Heilbroner, *Between Capitalism and Socialism* (New York: Vintage Books, 1970), p. 78.

Imperialism both creates and perpetuates underdevelopment.[9] While imperialism has taken the lives and wealth of the working classes in the U.S., it has preserved a system of backwardness and oppression in the Third World. The national bourgeoisie collaborates with the foreign governments and corporations in the appropriation and export of wealth, assuring themselves handsome dividends of money and power. They sell out their countries, and repress opponents with the military technology provided by the foreign powers. The rural masses struggle for survival on small plots or as landless laborers, while the big landowners grow fat on inefficient use of acreage. The urban masses remain illiterate, unemployed or underemployed, unskilled, underfed, and rotting in squalor, while the government elites and bourgeoisie send their children to the finest schools, hoard royalties and large salaries, invest money abroad, purchase expensive durable goods and travel around the world, and maintain extravagant estates, villas, and townhouses at home and in world resorts. Riches circulate amid unparalled poverty. Billions of dollars of wealth are created in the underdeveloped countries, but the mass of people subsist on a few dollars.

The working class back home is worked into a patriotic fervor over "communism," and so sees its civilian technology lag, its taxes rise, its jobs go overseas, its currency inflated, its living conditions neglected, and many of its sons lost. It sees its political leaders lie as a matter of policy, its military engage in murder of civilians and maintain itself on drugs, and it sees the international respect of its country vanish into distrust and condemnation.

THE COLONIAL LEGACY

The term colonialism refers to a form of imperialism whereby the foreign power not only is involved in the extraction of wealth but in the direct political rule of the subjugated nation. Colonialism attaches itself primarily to an earlier period and to European powers, England, Spain, Portugal, and France in particular. The U.S. also was very active in the colonizing field, although it didn't really enter the field as the dominant imperialist power until well into the present century. "Independence" for Third World colonies from imperial powers has not meant economic or even political autonomy. Rather, foreign administrations have simply been replaced by national elites.[10] A changeover from foreign to domestic elites opened up a handful of bureaucratic posts, but the vast majority continued in a manner quite like that under colonial domination.

Thus, *neo*-colonialism has been used to describe the contemporary period of foreign intervention through and with the national elites. Foreigners hold much of the real power; i.e., they dominate the large organizations of finance and production and through these means exer-

---

[9] See André Gunder Frank, *Capitalism and Underdevelopment in Latin America* (New York: Monthly Review Press, 1969).

[10] See Gail Omvedt, "Towards a Theory of Colonialism," *The Insurgent Sociologist,* 3 (Spring, 1973), pp. 1–24.

cise pervasive influence upon government and foreign policy. The debtor states ($30 billion unamortized in the sixties) are economically at the mercy of foreigners, and to a large extent, militarily as well. Revolution has been proven possible—in Russia, China, Indochina, Algeria, and Cuba, but the cost in every case was high. Yet, underdeveloped societies have learned that if they are to realize full national independence and material progress, they must cut loose from neo-colonialism and the system of international domination. Without the military and financial backing of the capitalist powers, the national bourgeoisie of many Third World countries would be overthrown by revolutionaries. The system of neocolonialism specializes in financial dealings which yield interest on loans, buying out or driving out local competition, starting subsidiary assembly operations which import finished parts and export complete products, and extraction of foods and raw materials—especially oil. Oil has been at or near the core of U.S. foreign policy and shall be of increasing importance in the future.[11]

Colonialism itself left a ripe situation for neo-colonialist intervention. The colonialist system was geared toward rough extraction of materials, and created very little industrial labor force or industrial plant. What "infrastructure" (rail lines, power grids, port facilities, roads, etc.) was established had a narrow self-serving focus and was essentially useless for the society at large. The financial and commercial responsibilities were largely or entirely in colonialist hands, so that the skills of administration and trading were not cultivated in a native white-collar or managerial stratum.

The colonial legacy was also that of a single crop or limited products emphasis. There was never any intention of trying to help establish a diversified economy of goods and services for the people, to promote economic independence, or to build a balanced national product capable of successful trade. Tied to a single commodity or two, underdeveloped countries are defenseless on the world trade market as foreign powers deal them inferior terms of trade (except where nationalization of an especially scarce and needed resource has occurred), constantly raising the price of manufactured products and forcing down the relative price of Third World exports. This forces the poor countries to obtain credit and loans, and increases their dependency. Underdevelopment means growing trade imbalances, domestic inflation, and a chronic shortage of foreign exchange with which to purchase industrial supplies. Frequently, foreign exchange earnings are used to purchase luxury goods for the wealthy, while much of it is siphoned off into repayment of loans. The unskilled status of the underdeveloped regions is reflected in the fact that 90 percent of their exports to the developed nations are unfinished or semi-finished products, whereas 80 percent of their imports from developed nations are manufactured products.[12] And what exports are finished goods are largely *assembled* in the Third World only, and not manufactured as such.

---

[11] Paul M. Sweezy and Harry Magdoff, "The Importance of Calling a Defeat a Defeat," *Monthly Review*, March 1973, pp. 1–9.

[12] See Jaleé, *The Third World in World Economy*.

Also tied to the commercial nature of the economy was the Westernization of one or a few urban centers and ports, a development that has created a sharp cleavage between these cities and the surrounding countryside. As we shall later note, this internal cultural cleavage between urban and rural, educated and uneducated has been carried to further extremes in the modern day. Accordingly, there has developed a lopsided distribution between urban and rural areas of what medical, educational, transport, and economic services do exist (and within urban areas as well).

Politically, the legacy of the colonial period has been that of shattering traditional bases of power, imposing Western forms of administration, and often creating political states that had no cultural or linguistic bases. As noted, the end of colonial political rule has meant very little, materially speaking, for the vast majority of people; Westernized nationals have simply stepped into and added onto government bureaucracies inherited from the colonial era. Entrenched Western economic elites often persist after political power is in native hands.[13]

In sum, the colonial period took much and left little of value for industrialization. What is left has been far more debilitating and impeding to economic development than enhancing. Colonialism was designed to enrich foreign states and investors. While gains for the advanced countries do not by definition imply or require losses for the underdeveloped countries, colonialism meant just that. And neocolonialism is also meaning just that.

THE AMERICAN EMPIRE

U.S. corporations count about $50 billion net profit annually (plus about $60 billion in depreciation money) and, of course, expectations are that in the decades ahead the sum will be higher. As noted in Chapter 9, the bulk of these profits belongs to a small handful of firms. These large corporations continually need places within which they can invest these profits and markets to consume their products; for without investment and markets, growth and expansion are impossible, and growth and expansion are the lifeblood and yardstick of success of corporate capitalism. Although the domestic economy is, of course, far and away the chief locus of investment and largest market, 208 million Americans are proving now, and will do so even more in future, to be an insufficient market (not that all needs are being met) for the big corporations. More important, raw materials are needed from outside the United States in ever greater proportions. As big Latin American investor Nelson Rockefeller put it back in 1951, "With critical shortages developing rapidly a quickened and enlarged production of materials in the underdeveloped countries is of major importance."[14] Thus, the large corporations have turned with rising interest to foreign countries. In Marx's words, "Urged onward by the need for an ever-expanding

---

[13] On the West Indian case, see Charles C. Moskos, *The Sociology of Political Independence* (Cambridge, Mass.: Schenkman Publishing Company, 1967).

[14] Cited in Baran, *The Political Economy of Growth*, p. 192.

market, the bourgeoisie invades every quarter of the globe." Moreover, "It forces all nations, under pain of extinction, to adopt the capitalist method of production; it constrains them to accept what is called civilization, to become bourgeois themselves. In short, it creates a world after its own image."[15]

The world capitalist economy has a vested interest in underdevelopment. Underdevelopment means low prices on Third World food exports, low-cost raw materials, cheap labor, lopsided economies that must import consumer goods, and commercial economies that do not themselves have a demand for their own raw materials and mineral products.[16] The latter point is especially important and is linked to all of the others; for example, if the Middle East or Venezuela began using their own oil for industrial purposes, the advanced nations would have to pay higher prices for it.[17] Michael Harrington has observed that Western politicians and businessmen need not be diabolical or evil in order to do incalculable harm to the Third World; they only have to rationally pursue the ends of the corporate system.[18] The United States, far and away the world's leading foreign investor and Third World investor, has the greatest single interest in underdevelopment and has demonstrated this in Indochina. As Kolko points out, "In short, the United States is today the bastion of the *ancien regime,* of stagnation and continued poverty for the Third World."[19] And, as Baran and Sweezy add, "it is only by increasingly direct and massive intervention by American armed forces that the old order can be held together a while longer."[20]

Thus, in this context much of the anti-Americanism that has been so pervasive throughout the underdeveloped world may be understood. Take Africa, about which Ferry writes, "No one acquainted with the behavior of Western corporations on their pilgrimages for profit during the last fifty years can really be surprised to read that African explosions now taking place are doing so in an anti-American, anti-capitalist, anti-Western context. For many years these continents have been happy hunting grounds for corporate adventurers, who have taken out great resources and great profits and left behind great poverty, great expecta-

---

[15] From C. Wright Mills, *The Marxists* (New York: Dell Publishing Company, 1962), pp. 49–50.

[16] See Gabriel Kolko, *The Roots of American Foreign Policy* (Boston: Beacon Press, 1969). As the author of a widely used economics text phrases the question with regard to cheap labor, "If, then, everyone in this country remains fully employed at his most suitable occupation, is it not to *our selfish advantage* for the workers of other countries to be willing to work for very little?" Paul Samuelson, *Economics* (New York: McGraw-Hill Book Company, 1970), p. 672.

[17] See Michael Tanzer, *The Political Economy of International Oil and the Underdeveloped Countries* (Boston: Beacon Press, 1969).

[18] Michael Harrington, *Toward a Democratic Left* (New York: Macmillan Company, 1968), p. 178.

[19] Kolko, *The Roots of American Foreign Policy*, p. 78.

[20] Paul A. Baran and Paul M. Sweezy, *Monopoly Capital* (New York: Monthly Review Press, 1966), especially Chapter 7.

tions, and great resentment."[21] Take Latin America, about which Mills writes, "Latin America is enormously rich—in soil, timber, oil, all the metals, the chemicals; it is rich in virtually everything men need to live well. Yet in this plundered continent there exist today some of the most hopelessly impoverished and consistently exploited people in the world." Thus, Mills' Cuban asks, "Well, Yankee, do you want soldiers and capitalists—and tourists, of course—do you want just them to represent you in the world? Is that now all that Yankee means? We don't know the answer for the whole world, but we are pretty sure about it for Cuba. That *is* the answer; that and not much else."[22]

The United States embodies very well Marx's "under pain of extinction" description of exporting the capitalist system. In 1967, the U.S. armed forces were represented in 19 Latin American, 21 Asian and Near Eastern, and 11 African countries (plus 13 European countries).[23] Counterrevolutions seem often to occupy the main energies of American foreign policy makers. Making the world a resource and a market for corporate capitalism is proving extremely costly, and inevitably the price is going to go up. Americans, who are going to have to pay the price, whether with their dollars or their lives, benefit the least from the high cost. About 40 corporate giants in oil, aviation, chemicals, steel, automobiles, electronics, and rubber reap the bulk of the payoffs on foreign investment—$6 billion in income receipts from direct corporate investment in 1970.[24] A mere one percent of all American corporations investing abroad takes approximately 60 percent of the net profits.[25] Oil corporations easily dominate foreign investment, accounting for 40 percent of all direct U.S. investment and 60 percent of all earnings.[26] While the overall rate of corporate earnings on foreign investment is 15 percent, the oil companies net 20 percent. Thus, returns on foreign investment typically exceed those on domestic investment.

The percentage of foreign investment of all corporate investment (plant and equipment) rose steadily throughout the sixties and now accounts for about one-fifth of the American total. The U.S. had $78 billion in direct corporate long term investment abroad in 1970, almost 30 percent of it in the Third World.[27] Similarly, foreign sources of earnings have also increased to the point of accounting for over one-fifth

---

[21] W.H. Ferry, "Irresponsibilities in Metrocorporate America," in Andrew Hacker, *The Corporation Take-Over* (New York: Harper & Row, Publishers, 1964).

[22] C. Wright Mills, *Listen, Yankee: The Revolution in Cuba* (New York: McGraw-Hill Book Company, 1960), pp. 160–69.

[23] Magdoff, *The Age of Imperialism*, p. 42.

[24] *Statistical Abstract/American Almanac* (New York: Grosset & Dunlap, 1973), p. 767.

[25] Howard J. Sherman, "Concentration of Foreign Investment," in Maurice Zeitlin, ed., *American Society, Inc.* (Chicago: Markham Publishing Company, 1970), pp. 43–45.

[26] Tanzer, *The Political Economy of International Oil and the Underdeveloped Countries.*

[27] *American Almanac*, 1973, p. 777.

of domestic nonfinancial corporate profits.[28] While Canada and Europe account for the large majority of U.S. foreign investments (about $1 billion more in Canada alone than in the entire Third World), the majority of the *income* on this investment capital has come from under-developed countries. In fact, whereas the U.S. flow of direct investments from 1950 to 1965 into Europe and Canada was greater than the income earned, U.S. corporations took three times as much value out as was put into underdeveloped regions. From 1950 to 1965 $25.6 billion in income on capital investments was transferred from the Third World to the United States, compared with $11.4 billion from Europe and Canada. For example, U.S. corporations took over $1 billion from Chile's copper mines from 1953–68, but new investment and reinvestment of profits only totaled $71 million.[29] One of the reasons for this fact is that investments in advanced countries tend to be in manufacturing and finance, whereas investments in underdeveloped regions are largely extractive. Moreover, underdeveloped economies mean low labor and overhead costs and tax concessions. In 1970 the underdeveloped countries yielded $3.1 billion in direct investment income compared with $2.7 billion from the developed world, though investment capital in that latter exceeded by two to three times that in the former.

The multinational corporations have as one of their central strategies that of buying up local industries and marketing goods from abroad. Of the some $200 billion in U.S. products delivered to foreign markets (making the U.S. *foreign* sector the third largest economy in the world), only one-sixth is exported *from* the U.S. The rest is marketed from U.S.-owned subsidiaries abroad. This trend has been greatly accentuated in recent years and portends to increase, especially in such major areas as automobiles and electronics. Among the fastest growing foreign operators (though far from the largest) is IT&T. It operates in 60 countries with $3 billion in foreign assets, has 47 percent of its assets and sales abroad, and earns 59 percent of its profits off foreign markets.[30]

A large number of Western hemisphere countries are literal U.S. economic colonies. Canada and Mexico find the controlling ownership of their corporate economies in U.S. corporate hands. In Brazil, foreign corporations control three-fourths of the capital goods and durable goods production, with the U.S. accounting for at least half.[31] The largest profit earnings in Brazil are taken by foreigners, while production is oriented toward luxury and durable goods for domestic consumption by the rich and for export. "This means," writes Alves, "that though some are riding in more and better automobiles than ever, most Brazilians have less food and less clothing."[32] Shortages of consumer necessities have contributed

[28] Magdoff, *The Age of Imperialism*, pp. 182–83.

[29] Dale L. Johnson et al., "ITT and the CIA: The Making of a Foreign Policy," *The Progressive*, May 1972, p. 16.

[30] Ibid., p. 15.

[31] Marcio Mereira Alves, "Stalinism for the Rich," *The Progressive*, March 1973, pp. 36–39; and Joao Quartim, *Dictatorship and Armed Struggle in Brazil* (New York: Monthly Review Press, 1971), p. 101.

[32] Alves, "Stalinism for the Rich," p. 38.

to inflation that has eroded the purchasing power of workers by 30 percent since 1964. In many host countries, single foreign corporations dwarf the government itself; for example, Firestone's sales are ten times the national income of Liberia, which hosts some of Firestone's rubber plantations. The international (mostly U.S. based) corporation has become a government unto itself capable of independent activity against the interests of almost any single national state.

One of the interesting ironies of imperialism is that the American military machine that protects capitalism in the underdeveloped areas and the arms manufacturers who sell weapons to Third World governments require minerals that depend exclusively or heavily on Third World mines.[33] One half of the sixty-two strategic materials listing by the Defense Department require 80 to 100 percent importation, and five-sixths require at least 40 percent. Three-fourths of these materials are taken from underdeveloped areas.[34] The American aluminum industry, for example, imports nearly all its bauxite. Concerning critical materials used for the manufacture of jet engines, aerospace contractors depend exclusively on Third World countries (e.g., Turkey and the Philippines) for chromium, and depend heavily on these countries (e.g., Congo) for cobalt; (e.g., Brazil) for columbium; (e.g., South Korea) for tungsten; and (e.g., New Caledonia) for nickel. (Canada is also an important supplier of aerospace metal.) U.S. defense and civilian industry alike must import a large portion of such basic and essential metals as zinc, copper, lead, and iron ore. U.S. industry gets manganese from Brazil; bauxite from Jamaica and Guyana; copper from Chile and Peru; tin from Malaya, Thailand, and Bolivia; iron ore from Venezuela, Brazil, and Africa; and, of course, petroleum from the Middle East, North Africa, and South America. Moreover, of equal importance to the fact that the United States is fully self-sufficient in only a few industrial materials, such as coal, sulphur, magnesium, and molybdenum, is the related fact that corporations are so rapidly depleting the high-quality ore reserves of the United States that their dependence on foreign sources today is relatively small compared to what it will be in the near future. Paying low prices for this increasing dependence is a key component in maximal corporate profits.

Some observers of American foreign policy have a difficult time reconciling the fact that the $150 billion expenditure in Vietnam was not worth protecting the some $250 million in annual profits taken by American corporations from East Asia.[35] Most taxpayers would agree that it is not. However, there is much more to the economic argument for American military involvement in Vietnam than the annual $250 million. As was stressed in Chapter 9, military spending has become a crucial supporting factor within the domestic economy. The money all does not literally go up in fire, smoke, and blood in Vietnam, though a very substantial

---

[33] Kolko, *The Roots of American Foreign Policy,* pp. 51–53.

[34] Adam Yarmolinsky, *The Military Establishment* (New York: Harper & Row, 1972), pp. 110–52.

[35] Steven J. Kelman, "Youth and Foreign Policy," *Foreign Affairs,* 48 (April 1970), p. 424.

sum does go directly into the hands of the Vietnamese and to pay for their imports. The sum paid for the war in the procurement of materials from defense industries and the support of a half million men. It was a major factor in the reduction of unemployment and the economic "prosperity" of the mid to late sixties. More important, the $250 million taken from East Asia is but a symbol of what monopoly capitalism is concerned with on a world-wide scale, now and particularly for the future. To keep the Third World free from revolution is to keep it safe for monopoly capitalism. Nationalist revolutions disrupt and threaten the "foreign sector" of the economy with its expansionist goals and economic needs. A nationalist revolutionary success in one part of the world gives moral strength to movements in other parts. Vietnam was supposed to be a major lesson to revolutionaries everywhere that imperialism is here to stay. As noted above, the United States depends increasingly on both strategic and nonstrategic materials from the underdeveloped world. Strategic materials may be relatively cheap (especially if taken from an underdeveloped country) and required in only small quantity per manufactured unit, but they are by definition *necessary*. Finally, Southeast Asian shorelines are rich in low sulfur oil deposits. Why should the big corporations concern themselves with the costs of counterrevolution when *others* pay the costs and *they* reap the profits?

American foreign aid to Third World countries has been predominantly military to help shore up antisocialist regimes, irrespective of their attitudes toward democracy and change, and has been heavily concentrated in client states and military dictatorships such as Formosa, Thailand, South Korea, the Philippines, Brazil, Greece, Turkey, and South Vietnam. Pakistan and, especially, India have been heavily dependent on U.S. agricultural surpluses, which owing to high government price supports and excess productivity, would rot in the United States if not dumped abroad (recently a changed situation). U.S. economic and technical aid to underdeveloped countries, including client states, composes an almost negligible percentage of gross national product, smaller than that of many less prosperous European nations. American foreign aid, whether in the form of guns or wheat, is unabashedly used as an instrument of control. Among the purposes of U.S. foreign aid and loans, observes Magdoff, are the implementation of worldwide military and political policies, the enforcement of an open-door policy for freedom of access to raw materials and investment opportunities, the assurance that such economic development that does take place is firmly rooted in capitalist ways, the acquisition of immediate economic gains for U.S. businessmen, and the creation of dependency on U.S. and other capital markets.[36]

The power structure of foreign policy

As has been argued in Chapter 9, decision-making power is highly concentrated in top corporate and government circles. The concentration

---

[36] Magdoff, *The Age of Imperialism*, pp. 116–36.

of foreign policy decision making is even more extreme than in domestic decision making, but the two spheres cannot in reality be clearly separated. National corporate interests are but the center of world corporate interests, and decisions that affect one directly influence the other. The foreign objective of corporate capitalism is to exceed or at least to duplicate abroad its successes at home. The objective of foreign policy, then, is to provide the political atmosphere in which the objectives of the large corporations can be pursued.

Foreign policy is determined in the federal government mainly by ex-corporate employees or big businessmen on loan to the government (see the empirical data in Kolko),[37] and is advised by men who have long studied and espoused a corporate capitalist world view. A very small group of men who have backgrounds mainly in big business, investment, and law fills the large majority of foreign policy posts; that is, like the corporate directorate itself, there is a great amount of overlap in positions involving the same men. Many of these men are also members of what we described in Chapter 9 as members of the upper class. Although oil and financial interests might be expected to predominate, whether rubber, iron ore, fruit, fiber, or strategic metal interests are at stake is not especially important; for the big foreign investors and buyers have basically similar foreign policy interests, that is, those listed at the end of the previous section. That these men are moved by self-interest rather than an understanding of the aspirations and needs of Third World peoples hardly needs mention. As Mills's Cuban remarked, "They [U.S. officials] don't have the slightest glimpse of what we're really all about, and why, and what kinds of men and women we really are."[38]

Mills clearly perceived the forces that underlie U.S. foreign policy (again from Cuban eyes): "So it seems to us you're up against this: You've got to make your Government change its whole line of policy. . . . But to do that you've got to change drastically the whole economic system of your big corporations, at least as they operate outside the U.S.A." Economist James O'Connor puts it in the following way: "In short, it is precisely the men who control the largest and most powerful corporations who have the greatest stake in economic expansion abroad, together with the maintenance of a worldwide military network to protect their far-flung economic interests. Thanks to the recent work of radical historians and sociologists, we know that these are also the men who constitute the U.S. upper class, dominate nearly all of the country's major institutions, and effectively control the executive branch of the federal government. So long as these men continue to rule there can be no major changes in either foreign or domestic policies of the federal government, precisely because these policies are formed by the corporate ruling group on the basis of their own *interests*."[39] And the elimination of that American hegemony," writes Kolko, "is the essential *precondition*

---

[37] Kolko, *The Roots of American Foreign Policy*, Chapters 1 and 2.

[38] Mills, *Listen, Yankee*, pp. 158; 165.

[39] James O'Connor, "The American Economic Empire," *The Nation*, July 14, 1969, pp. 53–55.

for the emergence of a nation and a world in which mass hunger, suppression, and war are no longer the inevitable and continuous characteristics of modern civilization [italics mine]."[40] (Kolko is obviously not saying here that the elimination of American hegemony will somehow automatically produce a free and well-fed Third World; but at least the conditions will be set).

U.S. foreign policy relies largely upon military force. As Baran observed 15 years ago, "And the larger and more permanent the military establishment, the greater the temptation to 'negotiate from strength'—which means to serve ultimata to smaller and weaker nations and to back them, if need be, by force."[41] How familiar this strategy has become under recent U.S. presidents. Veblen early described the manner in which foreign policy is conducted:

> It is to be presumed that, for the good of the nation, no one outside of the official personnel and the business interests in collusion can bear any intelligent part in the management of these delicate negotiations, and any premature intimation of what is going on is likely to be "information which may be useful to the enemy."[42]

Foreign policy, noted Veblen, is largely "administrative prevarication and democratic camouflage." How painfully true Veblen's words ring today, a time when deceit and lies have become incorporated into the executive branches of government; when President Nixon and his top foreign policy advisor Henry Kissinger order wire taps on the telephones of State Department employees and vindictively attempt to persecute those who would bring the truth to the public. Baran's words are more glaring today than when he wrote them:

> A spiderweb of corruption is spun over the entire political and cultural life of the imperialist country and drives principles, honesty, humanity, and courage from political life. The cynicism of vulgar empiricism destroys the moral fibre, the respect for reason, and the ability to discriminate between good and evil among wide strata of the population.[43]

From the meddling and coup-designing interventionism of the CIA, to the special counterrevolutionary army units, to economic blockades, to the Michigan State University intelligence project in Vietnam and the Army's aborted Latin American information survey Project Camelot, to the carpet bombing of Hanoi and Haiphong—these have been among the characteristic ingredients of U.S. foreign policy. Unfortunately, it has taken a long time and a costly toll for the American people to begin to realize that what is good for big foreign investors is not necessarily good for them, indeed detrimental to their own standard of living and physical survival. A person need not be a radical to sense that corporate expansion

---

[40] Kolko, *The Roots of American Foreign Policy,* p. 87.
[41] Baran, *The Political Economy of Growth,* p. 133.
[42] Veblen, *Absentee Ownership,* pp. 443–45.
[43] Baran, *The Political Economy of Growth,* p. 130.

and interventionism in all of its forms has been a leading force in the undermining of American society itself.

ECONOMIC PROBLEMS OF UNDERDEVELOPMENT

Underdevelopment has generated a mass of economic difficulties, and we have enumerated many of these. Among the most visible problems are those concerning inequality and the unequal distribution of resources within the country itself. The Third World is for the majority a rural world that depends upon the use of land for its day to day survival. The first domestic problem of the underdeveloped world is the vastly unequal distribution of land ownership. In Brazil, for example, less than one half of one percent of the adult population holds one-half of private lands.[44] In Jamaica, one percent of the farms account for 56 percent of the land, and much more of the best land, while 71 percent of the farms divide up 12 percent of the acreage. The picture is the same all over Latin America, where the large majority of the some 114 million rural persons are impoverished small holders or landless workers.[45] One half of the rural population is chronically underemployed or unemployed and millions continually migrate seeking wage labor. The big landowners raise export crops such as cacao or graze livestock or let the land lay idle, while the peasants suffer malnutrition and attempt to scratch out subsistence on marginal land. In a large Brazil cacao area, large estates (latifundios) hold one half of the land and have only 0.5 percent of it in annual crops, 13 percent in permanent cacao crop, 62 percent in pasture, and the rest unused. The minifundios are much more efficient producers than the backward big landholders, who produce only one-half of the agricultural product of what their portion of the land represents. Yet, the small holders can't obtain credit and are frequently driven off their land.

The large family and multifamily farms are the backbone of the old oppressive society. As Feder argues, "Latifundismo has been and still is an agriculture of oppression and arbitrariness."[46] The rural population is held in poverty as a means of maintaining insecurity, dependence, fear, and passivity. When militance is shown it is met with intimidation, terrorization, and corporal punishment. Land and housing rents are designed to take what income the peasant or laborer earns, debt is used as a leverage, and organization is smashed at all costs. The plantation system exploits laborers and peasant tenents in the same manner. Beckford observes that "Government policies . . . soak the poor to help the rich within plantation society," and that "the plantation system must be destroyed if the people of plantation society are to secure economic,

---

[44] Quartim, *Dictatorship and Armed Struggle in Brazil,* p. 128.

[45] George L. Beckford, *Persistent Poverty* (New York: Oxford University Press, 1972), p. 23. This book is essential reading for an understanding of the agricultural situation; and also Ernest Feder, *The Rape of the Peasantry* (New York: Doubleday & Co., 1971).

[46] Feder, *The Rape of the Peasantry,* pp. 65–67; 109.

social, political, and psychological advancement."[47] But even the weak land reform measures promulgated in the early sixties have been largely dropped, and expectedly so.

In Chapter 5 we noted the extreme inequality of income distribution in underdeveloped countries. Throughout most of the Third World, a tiny fraction of landowners and bourgeoisie (state, industrial, commercial, and imperialist-tied), frequently overlapped in person and family, control the bulk of national wealth and take the lion's share of the income. Latin American and Asian investors have $13.5 billion in short term U.S. bank investments alone,[48] capital that has been creamed off their own society and the payoffs from foreign investors. These funds could be applied toward diversified industrialization and agricultural modernization. Oil rich Venezuela has had oil revenues of $500 million a year, or an average of $3,000 per family. Yet, 30 percent of the Caracas population dwell in slums, the urban unemployment rate exceeds 20 percent, and over one-half of the rural population lacks supporting work.[49] The oil sheikdom of Kuwait has a per capita income equal to that of the U.S., yet squalor and poverty are everywhere. Saudi Arabia has billions of dollars of oil royalties, yet most of the country's ten million persons are impoverished. Pakistan has achieved moderate gains in economic growth indicators, but all of the per capita income increases have gone to the top 20 percent of the population.[50]

Western economists speak of the shortage of capital in the underdeveloped world, but usually fail to point out such things as the above, or that some $12 billion a year (1965 calculation) is gleaned from the Third World by the advanced capitalist states.[51] If all of the existing resources generated in the Third World were today applied to development, a major stride could be immediately taken. The potential capital surplus is, of course, far greater.

Developmental goals

The central goal of revolutionary societies and nationalistic movements have been the economic independence of the people and the forces of production. This is itself only a means to human goals, such as raising the level of education in the population, expanding medical facilities, providing adequate clothing and shelter, creating employment and developing agriculture—which we shall examine later. In addition to developing human and agricultural resources, a major prerequisite to economic development is the establishment of a socially oriented industrial infrastructure of such things as roads, railroads, communications, dams, and electrical grids. Some developmental prerequisites, such as

---

[47] Beckford, *Persistent Poverty,* pp. 182–215.

[48] *The American Almanac,* 1972, p. 756.

[49] Salvador de la Plaza, "Foreign Exploitation of Oil and National Development," in I.L. Horowitz et al., *Latin American Radicalism* (New York: Vintage Books, 1969), pp. 292–313.

[50] Timothy and Leslie Nulty, "Pakistan: The Busy Bee Route to Development," *Trans-action,* 8 (February 1971), pp. 18–26.

[51] Jaleé, *The Third World in World Economy,* p. 116.

education, medicine, housing, dams and irrigation, and primitive roads, do not always or necessarily require heavy machines and industrial equipment but rather can utilize labor-intensive techniques.

Building a structure of industrial equipment and facilities and most of the more advanced transportation and communications needed to serve such an industrial structure requires heavy and light machines in addition to human labor. The machines, which may subsequently accommodate and produce additional machines and goods, require in the first place financial capital for purchase abroad. The problem of economic development and industrialization, then, boils down to a need for foreign exchange or assistance with which to purchase or start at least the germinal core of industrial equipment. Upon the establishment of an industrial structure, a developing nation would be able to work toward diversified production, greater self-sufficiency, and trade, and away from the vagaries of a raw material export and the import of consumer items.

We might take Cuba as an example of the dilemmas of economic development and the shortage of foreign exchange. Cuba has long been a typical case of a lopsided, one-crop (sugar cane) economy run mainly for foreign profit. Conversely, Cuba had to import practically every essential or luxury item she consumed, an economic system that kept the vast majority of Cubans poor and usually hungry. As in many other Third World countries, the same system that keeps the masses poor and hungry supports a small middle class or elite in considerable affluence. The revolutionary government first turned to a diversification of agriculture and industry to avoid the crippling effects of the one-crop economy, but could not move far in this direction due to the shortage of foreign exchange required to import the necessary machinery of production. And it would take too long for the new products and crops to pay off loans or credit for industrial investment. Inheriting all the illiteracy, poverty, unemployment, medical, and housing shortages from the past, the new government was also faced with pressing social needs and the development of human resources. Thus, the government reversed its strategy of diversification and concentrated on the sugar crop as a source of foreign exchange. (The United States has done its best to devalue Cuban sugar exports and, of course, has not bought any Cuban sugar.) Once urgent social needs had been met and an industrial core established, investment could then be directed toward diversification. The Cuban government has pushed sugar production goals to increasingly higher levels. It is at this point that socialist critics of Cuban policies become concerned that Castro's drive for higher and higher sugar yields is increasingly coming at exorbitant social and overall wasteful economic costs.[52]

Getting the necessary capital to launch a self-sufficient industrial economy may come from other sources than the purchase of machines from abroad with exchange earned through the export of raw materials

---

[52] Leo Huberman and Paul M. Sweezy, *Socialism in Cuba* (New York: Monthly Review Press, 1969).

or surplus agricultural products. Among the possible alternatives would be low-interest control-free loans from an internationally supported United Nations bank. Direct open aid from the developed countries could be another important source. In most cases there is a substantial amount of cash or wealth available but it is now in the hands of landed aristocrats and bourgeoisie interested in private consumption and savings rather than domestic capital investment.

Much of the industrial building in Third World countries to date has been through that of foreign investment. Foreign investment as a source of industrial structure has been dimly viewed by many Third World reformers and revolutionaries precisely because of the previously noted fact that three times as much value is taken out of underdeveloped countries as is invested, not a very favorable equation for recipient nations. Although proponents of foreign investment argue that a time-table for the turnover of industrial facilities to an on-the-job-trained native work force, a profit ceiling on repatriated earnings, or partnership could avoid the kind of economic exploitation that has been traditionally tied to foreign investment, agreement on such stipulations and restrictions would seem difficult to achieve effectively, given the customary investment and profit guidelines of corporate capitalism. Yugoslavia has invited and received similar investments, but it has a substantially different government and society than that of the underdeveloped world.

Whatever the source of investment capital, the long-range key to successful industrialization is the voluntary or forced saving and rational reinvestment of national income, and the elimination of waste and the postponement of nonessential consumption. At what point a society can turn from preoccupation with the plowback of national income into further industrial capital toward meeting consumer demands for more goods and services is a critical juncture in the political life of a nation.

Moving an economy in the direction of light or small-scale production, sometimes referred to as cottage industry, is yet another partial alternative to dealing with the problem of shortage of heavy industrial capital.[53] Proponents of light industry argue that their approach would conserve scarce capital while at the same time utilizing local handicraft skills and would put idle or underemployed men to work; it would avert the necessity for large capital outlays and the required advanced industrial and administrative skills. Heavy industry is capital-intensive and employs far fewer people per dollar invested than labor-intensive small-scale operations, and thus may leave untouched or even worsen the problems of unemployment. Moreover, light industry has the additional virtue of not requiring the advanced infrastructure of transportation, communications, and power grids. The cottage approach can directly alleviate the need of importing essential consumer items such as clothes, shoes, soap, furniture, and other personal and household goods, helping to diversify

---

[53] See William McCord, *The Springtime of Freedom* (New York: Oxford University Press, 1965); and Irving Louis Horowitz, *Three Worlds of Development* (New York: Oxford University Press, 1966, Second Edition, 1972).

the economy at the level of essential consumer goods. Small-scale production could be decentralized, thus helping to hold the population in rural areas and avoiding the problems of overurbanization. Workers' control would also be enhanced. Small-scale, decentralized industry would also minimize the cultural disruptions that accompany large-scale industrialization and urbanization and the political discontent that arises where enclaves of heavy industry are surrounded by tradition-bound village society. Finally, light industry and a mixed economy would tend to avoid the irreversible decisions and cumulative errors that are problematic to large capital outlays, placing economic decision making on a more decentralized and democratic basis. China has utilized many of these advantages.[54]

However attractive the strategy of cottage industry might be, most concerned elites favor the route of heavy industry with perhaps some amount of accompanying small goods production. Advanced industry, the argument runs, can produce more goods more efficiently than labor-intensive production; it also accelerates capital accumulation, whereas light production only leads to the increased demand for consumer goods and hinders the process of capital formation. Reversing the arguments for light industry, proponents of heavy industrial development contend that only through heavy industry can a country gain economic self-sufficiency. Finally, they contend that government can centrally plan and efficiently administer a concentrated heavy industrial economy, but not dispersed small units. The latter point is not disputed by advocates of small-scale production; the dispute revolves around the desirability of heavy, concentrated industry and central planning as such. The Soviet Union has been the model of centralists, whereas China is emerging as the model of the decentralists.

Decision making

The problem of who is to lead a nation in its developmental efforts has received considerable comment from proponents of both "centralized authoritarians" and "decentralized democrats."[55] The authoritarian view contends that only a central planning committee can rapidly and rationally coordinate and administer the process of industrialization, which, of course, must emphasize the accumulation of the capital goods sector. In the absence of an effective bourgeoisie, political administrators must act as economic planners and investors in lieu of this class. Moreover, only a highly disciplined and organized revolutionary elite can dispel or take power from reactionary and conservative elements in the population and put the plan of modernization into action, action made extremely urgent by crises in population and food. In this view, a centralized political elite must play the role of substitute capitalists in the stage

---

[54] See E.L. Wheelwright and Bruce McFarlane, *The Chinese Road To Socialism* (New York: Monthly Review Press, 1970).

[55] Dennis Wrong and Robert Heilbroner, "Economic Development and Democracy," *Dissent* 14 (November–December 1967), pp. 723–41.

of capital accumulation, for there is no bourgeoisie to do the job and there is not time to wait and see if a bourgeoisie can be cultivated or will arise. Not only must economic changes be made, but social, attitudinal, intellectual, and even religious alterations are required for modernization; these changes, together with the economic changes, will require that the state promote a new ideological creed to win the citizens away from old practices. Dissent and differences are luxuries a developing nation cannot afford. Finally, the elitist argument runs, democratic traditions are lacking; the masses are unschooled and incompetent to decide. Empirical data from the West Indies suggests that on the latter score the white and older political elite tends to feel the people are politically incompetent, whereas the younger, black leaders tend to feel the opposite.[56] The democrats are economic radicals and are aligned ideologically with the socialist states, whereas the authoritarians are economic conservatives and are aligned with the West.

In opposition to the authoritarian solution, the proponents of greater decentralization in decision making argue that an omnipotent elite may more likely make irreversible, one-sided, and foolish decisions that have catastrophic results. Inept spending of government revenues on unproductive or frivolous ventures cannot be checked such as on expensive embassies, huge public buildings, and costly aircraft.[57] Successful development requires continual feedback, debate, and criticism from within the population, for elites become increasingly isolated and walled off from the sentiments, needs, and aspirations of the people and hence make wasteful and unrealistic decisions. As for the ability of the people to participate in political life and express themselves on economic and political issues, peasants and workers are not dull clods requiring direction from above but take initiative, given the opportunity, and have considerable experience in informal decision making at the local level. Indeed, to make decisions arbitrarily through a centralized elite is to destroy the creative initiative and democratic desires of the people. And to militantly impose new ideologies and ways of life on a society may precipitate a process of cultural disintegration that undermines the possibility of ever achieving stability in a new order. The break with the past should be gradual and incorporate as much tradition into the new order as possible. Finally, authoritarian methods are no assurance of internal unity; rather they may fragment rather than integrate, alienate rather than convince, and weaken rather than strengthen national unity.

Coversely, the democratic decentralized approach is often equated with the United States. While early U.S. economic development was decentralized, industrialization rapidly brought an end to economic democracy. Workers' control is an essential component of decentralized production. Light industry with close and innovative guidance by the

---

[56] Wendell Bell, ed., *The Democratic Revolution in the West Indies* (Cambridge, Mass.: Schenkman Publishing Company, 1967), especially pp. 70–77; 93.

[57] John Hatch, "African Austerity," *The Nation*, 207 (November 4, 1968), pp. 458–61.

workers is the backbone of the economy, integrated regionally and with agricultural production. The same scheme applies for areas of social production as in education, medicine, and administration. The model here is contemporary China, whose development has set equality above gross national product, generalized experience and knowledge above specialized expertise, and workers' control above professional hierarchies. The evident progress made toward these goals portends the increasing influence of China among Third World revolutionary movements. A society may be orderly and of a central purpose without the artificial imposition of rules from above.

Still, the decision-making reality of most of the Third World countries is that of centralization *without* development, and increasingly military dictatorship, the form of government that most pleases foreign investors.

Agriculture and development

Perhaps owing to the fact that agriculture tends to be associated or linked with the very kind of society that urban elites want to move away from—i.e., agrarian or rural—agriculture has been neglected. As Myrdal points out, "The immediate cause of poverty, and thus of underdevelopment, in these countries, is the extremely low productivity of labor in agriculture."[58] It is an illusion, argues Myrdal, to believe that economic development can take place without radically raising the productivity of agricultural labor.

As noted previously, the large landholders and plantation owners are not seriously interested in efficient land use, but only in profit—a priority that usually leads to inefficient land use in the underdeveloped world. The most efficient producers are the small farmers, despite the handicaps of marginal land, lack of credit for fertilizer and implements, and labor intensive techniques. The goal of the landed aristocracy and plantation owners, foreign or native, is to perpetuate a weak, dependent, and poor rural populace easy to exploit and control. To raise agricultural productivity is tantamount to achieving a social revolution in land ownership and use. The redistribution of land to individual farmers would and has raised productivity, but this requires political overturn of the landholding system.

Small plot farming is itself inefficient compared to joint financing and ownership of agricultural production—i.e., collective and cooperative production. In China, the poor peasantry entered into a great deal of cooperative farming, and government action soon launched a national collective and communal organization of agriculture. Prosperous peasants and peasants in many areas are typically opposed to collectivization and support revolution only to remove foreign interests and the landed aristocracy.[59] They seek a return to the past or a system of individual

---

[58] Gunnar Myrdal, Economic Development in Backward Countries," *Dissent,* 14 (March–April 1967), p. 183.

[59] See Ian Clegg, *Workers' Self-Management in Algeria* (New York: Monthly Review Press, 1971), pp. 95–101.

land ownership. In revolutionary periods, it has been the wage laborers on estates and plantations (the rural proletariat) together with the landless and poor peasant who have most openly supported change.

Among the important ties between the development of agriculture and industrialization is the provision of food for urban industrial workers, fibers and raw materials for domestic industry (two thirds of all existing employment in manufacturing in the Third World depends on agricultural raw materials of textile, leather, rubber, paper, tobacco, etc.), and agricultural products for foreign exchange to buy machinery to build the industrial core and further raise the agricultural product.[60] Often overlooked is the fact that the mechanization of agriculture releases acreage previously used to sustain and feed draft animals, a fact that meant an increase of some 70 million acres to U.S. agriculture between 1920 and 1953. But mechanization also means the displacement of agricultural workers, and without industry to absorb them, they add to the urban unemployed or remain to pull down worker productivity on farms. The release of agricultural labor in the West has been an important and essential source of manpower for industrialization.

The development of agriculture must meet with a variety of obstacles.[61] First, agriculture is an area of low prestige and does not attract bourgeois educated elements in a population; they are attracted to the urban professions, government, or wherever the greatest payoff in income, power, and prestige might be. For example, of 10,541 students in Central American universities in 1962, a mere 187 were studying agriculture.[62] And of the over 100,000 Latin American students that studied in the United States from 1956 to 1965, only five percent were in agriculture. Law, economics, and medicine are far more popular.

Secondly, unlike most science and engineering knowledge, the problems and technical solutions in agriculture cannot be so easily transferred from one area of the world to another. Soil variations and diverse growing conditions render corn hybrids from Nebraska useless in Guatemala; and the equipment used for planting, weeding, and harvesting designed for United States fields and crops prove unusable in the Philippines. Nor will blue-ribbon Iowa cattle or swine thrive in Ghana. Research and development must be largely original to the native land, and agricultural experimentation is by definition slow and often discouraging. The efficacy of such a relatively simple measure of agricultural development as the application of fertilizer may be illustrated by the fact that the United States has added, through the use of fertilizers, every decade since the turn of the century the equivalent of another Iowa in agricultural land. Yet, whereas Japan uses 306 kilograms of fertilizer per hectare, Latin America uses only one; Asia, six; and Africa, four.

[60] Max F. Millikan and David Hapgood, *No Easy Harvest* (Boston: Little, Brown and Company, 1967), Chapter 1.

[61] Solon L. Barraclough, "Agricultural Policy and Strategies of Land Reform," *Studies in Comparative International Development*, Vol. IV, No. 8 (1968–69), pp. 167–97.

[62] William and Paul Paddock, *Famine—1975* (Boston: Little, Brown and Company, 1967), p. 75.

Thirdly, the peasant may be suspicious of new techniques and not readily amenable to experimentation, for his land and living conditions are too marginal to take risks. However, peasants are economic men and will respond to improved techniques if their efficiency has been demonstrated. Thus, a development program cannot stop at stockpiling fertilizers in a rural community; agents must work in the fields to demonstrate their efficacy.

Finally, the Third World as a whole is less favorably situated with regard to the proper combination of soil, temperature, and rainfall. However, technological advance and land development could overcome such deficits where they exist. Barren hillsides are capable of being turned into blooming terraces. Moreover, prime plantation land could be put into essential food production immediately.

Standing as an agricultural model to the Third World is once underdeveloped and hungry China. Macciocchi writes that

> Nothing makes you dizzy in China as much as the spectacle of this peasant population (as many people as there are in all Europe) in continual movement in the fields. The constant thing is this population, in motion like a hive. It does not stop picking, sewing, watering, cultivating. You can see that here we are at the apothesis of mass action, of a frenetic tenacity which recognizes no obstacles, and we also have here the key to why there is so much food in China, so much fruit, vegetables, meat, and fish for the cities.[63]

The U.S. Department of Agriculture has set 1985 as the point at which Third World population will have so far outrun food reserves that definite famines will occur. Malnutrition, a form of starvation, is already a fact of daily life throughout much of the Third World. Malnutrition and severely inadequate diets are daily facts of American life, too, but the problem in the United States is not one of potential or even supply but of existing maldistribution. By contrast, Third World starvation is today a matter of supply, not distribution. Even with the advanced nations included, food *shortages* as such threaten famine. Billions of dollars worth of surplus U.S. food have been sent to hungry nations under P.L. 480 or "Food for Peace," and wider starvation has thus been averted in countries such as India, Pakistan, and Turkey. The United States sent large amounts of wheat to India, yet the Paddocks contended that it was like throwing sand in the ocean. Massive famines, they argue, cannot be averted in India even if all-out emergency programs of agricultural development and aid were launched.

Most observers and nearly every indicator of the population-food situation in the underdeveloped countries agree that the past 20 years have seen no real gain in agricultural production relative to population growth. In many areas, Latin America in particular, nutrition levels have worsened. In a survey of 19 Latin American countries, an overall per capita agricultural production decline was revealed for the years 1961–68; there was a slight overall gain in per capita food production,

---

[63] Maria Antonietta Macciocchi, *Daily Life in Revolutionary China* (New York: Monthly Review Press, 1972), pp. 238–39.

but one-half of the countries realized a loss.[64] Agricultural imports were increased by 40 percent. Given the extensive deficiencies to begin with, the food problem is easily recognized as serious. But despite the bloated bellies and twisted bones, middle-class Latin American economists may deny they have a population-food problem.[65] Protein deficiencies have long been endemic in most of the Third World, and average caloric intake is below that needed for full strength and good health. With populations doubling in 25 years or so, food production must also be doubled just to maintain current levels of nutrition. To date, most of the small annual increments in food yields are the result of more intensive peasant cultivation of marginal land rather than regular acreage. Thus, with efficient use of land reform and improved agricultural techniques, most cultivated land in the Third World could be many times more productive than it has been.

THE PROBLEM OF NATIONAL UNITY

At the top of the list of internal political problems in most Third World countries is that of building a nationally integrated political system. A modicum of national unity is essential both to the implementation of programs instituted by government and to the expression and involvement of the interests and needs of the people in politics. In many instances, Third World countries constitute relatively new political states, but there are also many old established ones. In the older nations, a culture coextensive with political boundaries is often the case, but in the large majority of new nations political boundaries imposed by colonialists encompass diverse if not hostile cultural and linguistic tribes and societies. Black Africa (for example, Nigeria) epitomizes this state of internal strife, but marked dissension and internecine conflict are common throughout the underdeveloped world. Rose points out that "India is not yet a nation in a sociological or psychological sense. It is still a collection of mutually suspicious and mutually hostile extended families."[66]

In taking over the government from colonial powers, nationals typically found themselves in short supply of administrative experience. The tendency has been for the anticolonialist leader or party to become the government, without the stability and support offered by a developed civil service and party system.[67] The coup d'etat has been a regular event

---

[64] James Petras, *Politics and Social Structure in Latin America* (New York: Monthly Review Press, 1970), pp. 267–69.

[65] An economics graduate student the author once heard talk on "Revolution in Bolivia" in a Free University lecture didn't mention the food problem once, and upon questioning, denied that one existed—much to the surprise of his North American listeners.

[66] Arnold M. Rose, "Sociological Factors Affecting Economic Development in India," *Studies in Comparative International Development,* Volume III, No. 9 (1967–68), p. 171.

[67] Abdul A. Said, *The African Phenomenon* (Boston: Allyn & Bacon, Inc., 1968).

throughout the Third World, both in newly independent and more traditional nations. Increasingly, military coups and regimes have turned out or aborted constitutionally elected governments, often as not with the approval or even support of the status-quo-seeking United States. Some are bitterly opposed by the oppressed segment of the population, as in Chile, where thousands of civilians were killed by the military in 1973.

In addition to the power vacuum left by departing colonial administrations, modernizing regimes also often deal with populations who have rightly never envisaged rulers or governments, elected or otherwise, as representatives or responsible to social welfare. In parts of Southeast Asia, for example, government has traditionally been linked with religious authority in king or sultan. Traditional China viewed government with suspicion and as a totally external force that took food, money, sons, and land. In Mexico, as compared with the United States, people are less likely to feel that government has any impact on their lives, that government can improve things, that all citizens have a responsibility to participate in political life, or that citizens should expect equal treatment by a government bureau.[68] A genuinely revolutionary government, however, can win the trust and support of the people.

Several forces for national integration have been noted, such as universal education in a common language, military conscription, a national bureaucracy, political parties, a common enemy or threat, and, especially, nationalistic ideology.[69] Nationalism has been credited with the capacity to transcend religion, ethnicity, language, and culture, though the latter two would seem to be important ingredients of a highly developed and widely accepted nationalistic ideology. Nationalism, Miller argues, may be displayed by any government if it has an attachment to the country and its people, attempts to advance their welfare, and has a determination to prevent others from interfering with its policy.[70] Nationalism of the variety found in African "socialism" attempts to emphasize tribal cultures, past traditions, and the unity of African ethnic groups; but rather than emphasizing the revolutionary consciousness of the people against oppression, this philosophy of many African elites and intellectuals serves mainly to divert attention away from their own power and privilege.

Though nationalism may be an effective stimulus to national integration, it has also proven to be a threat to peace and international cooperation. Arnold Toynbee observes that nationalism is a recrudescence of worship of collective human power from which the higher religions have been seeking to liberate mankind.[71] But nationalism in the sense of a

---

[68] Gabriel A. Almond and Sidney Verba, *The Civic Culture* (Boston: Little, Brown and Company, 1965), pp. 46–54; 127.

[69] See Howard Wriggins, "National Integration," in Myron Weiner, ed., *Modernization* (New York: Basic Books, Inc., 1966), pp. 181–91.

[70] J.D.B. Miller, *The Politics of the Third World* (New York: Oxford University Press, 1966), pp. 106–7.

[71] Arnold Toynbee, *Change and Habit: Challenge of Our Time* (New York: Oxford University Press, 1966), p. 111.

commitment to an ideology of progressive change need not interfere with international cooperation or stimulate international conflict. However, conflict has been made a necessary ingredient of economic and political development, for foreign powers have militarily resisted drives for complete liberation. Nationalism has the capacity to unite internally opposing classes (e.g., rich and poor peasants, petty bourgeoisie, and manual workers) against imperialism. It did so in China, Algeria, Vietnam and Cuba. Hence, national liberation fronts are the unifying forces of the underdeveloped countries.

Nationalist revolutions and movements find especially fertile soil in a social and economic system dominated by agrarian bureaucracies that inhibit development and an urban bourgeoisie in league with foreign capital.[72] Many Latin American and Asian countries, with their landed aristocratic elites, Western-oriented urban elites, and large masses of peasants and impoverished urban dwellers, are thus prime candidates for revolution. Where landed aristocracies and established urban classes form a coalition of the status quo, as they do in Latin America and Southeast Asia, or the new black middle class of Africa appears too satisfied with neocolonialist policies,[73] otherwise conservative peasants may themselves spontaneously revolt under new stresses impinging upon them.[74] Class consciousness may solidify only after a violent outburst of frustration and discontent by peasants or urban masses rather than being an antecedent to revolt.

Research in poverty districts of Lima, Peru, and Santiago, Chile, suggests that, while the large majority of respondents affirmed that the most important national problem was economic, they did not constitute a strongly politically sensitive or aware class.[75] Yet, half of them discussed politics with friends and neighbors, and a substantial minority were very concerned about what the government was doing, had attended a political meeting or demonstration, believed in the efficacy of popular political action, and condoned violence as a way to solve political problems. Although the lower class of Santiago was more politically active and aware, the Peruvians were more receptive of revolt and violence (one-half). In both cities, the rich were thought to be of no help to the poor at all, whereas students and priests were considered to be sympathetic and helpful.

That low-income and economically insecure people often tend to be supportive of revolution is suggested by Zeitlin's findings that nearly all Cuban workers who had experienced prerevolutionary under- and unem-

[72] See Barrington Moore, Jr., *Social Origins of Dictatorship and Democracy* (Boston: Beacon Press, 1966), Chapter 9.

[73] See Frantz Fanon, *The Wretched of the Earth* (New York: Grove Press, Inc., 1968).

[74] See James Petras and Maurice Zeitlin, "Miners and Agrarian Radicalism," *American Sociological Review*, 32 (August 1967), pp. 578–86.

[75] Daniel Goldrich, Raymond B. Pratt, and C.R. Schuller, "The Political Integration of Lower-Class Urban Settlements in Chile and Peru," *Studies in Comparative International Development*, Vol. III, No. 1 (1967–68).

ployment supported the revolution.[76] Black workers, who in the prerevolutionary period had racially defined their problems, were found to be even more supportive of the revolution than prerevolutionary unemployed whites. The revolution had succeeded in transforming racially defined problems into *class* consciousness. The extent of dissatisfaction and revolutionary potential among Latin American workers is suggested by Zeitlin's findings that even two thirds of the prerevolutionary higher income and regularly employed workers were supportive of the revolution. (The Chilean working class, for example, has evinced pronounced radical political views and solidarity. It fought hard against the military takeover in September 1973.) The redistribution of wealth, the provision of jobs, free and evenly distributed medical care, the construction of rural clinics and hospitals, the elimination of malaria and polio, the sharp reduction of illiteracy, the enrollment of three-fourths of the population in free classrooms, the 40,000 students studying agronomy and fishing, the multiplication by several times of the number of students in industrial schools, the doubling of university enrollment, the provision of shoes for all, and the distribution of milk and meat to the rural population have been among the revolution's accomplishments which have earned the extent of support documented by Zeitlin (even though Zeitlin's data were gathered back in 1962).[77]

The revolution in Cuba,[78] accomplished by members of all classes, has further enhanced the appeal of socialist ideologies in the Third World, especially in Latin America.[79] As Mills has pointed out, in addition to being a moment of economic truth, the Cuban revolution was a moment of military truth: "That truth is that guerrilla bands, led by determined men, with peasants alongside them, and a mountain nearby, can defeat organized battalions of the tyrants equipped with everything up to the atom bomb."[80] (Demonstrated even more persuasively by the Vietnamese.) Third World success models are hard to come by, especially when being worked out in the face of U.S. opposition. Success is used in a relative sense, as the goals of a socialist revolution require permanent revolution, the continued politicization of the population and its active participation in all spheres of social production. In Cuba, Capouya believes that "the successes of the Cuban Revolution are the successes of a partially liberated people. Its achievements would be greater in proportion as the people came to enjoy the social initiative

---

[76] Maurice Zeitlin, *Revolutionary Politics and the Cuban Working Class* (Princeton, N.J.: Princeton University Press, 1967), pp. 65–87.

[77] See Joseph A. Kahl, "The Moral Economy of a Revolutionary Society," *Trans-action,* 6 (April 1969), pp. 30–37; and Huberman and Sweezy, *Socialism in Cuba,* pp. 86–109.

[78] See Rolando E. Bonachea and Nelson P. Valdés, eds., *Cuba in Revolution* (New York: Doubleday & Company, 1972).

[79] See James Petras and Maurice Zeitlin, eds., *Latin America, Reform or Revolution?* (Greenwich, Conn.: Fawcett Books, 1968); and Irving Louis Horowitz, Josue de Castro, and John Gerassi, *Latin American Radicalism* (New York: Random House, Inc., 1969).

[80] Mills, *Listen, Yankee,* p. 114.

now monopolized by the ruling oligarchy." He continues, "But the efficacy of Fidel Castro's intervention has been such that the Cuban people are now at a stage where they can think beyond the next meal, and they must be allowed to do so. Otherwise their leader may find that he has set the stage for another revolution, one that excludes his participation."[81]

The military

As popular sentiment grows increasingly radical, in terms of both voting and political feelings, conservative and reactionary elites have relied more heavily on military repression and coups to forestall economic and political reforms. For example, in the successful military takeovers in Latin America over the past 35 years the trend has been distinctly toward the overthrow of proreform constitutional governments. With U.S. help, the military has crushed reformist governments in Brazil, Bolivia, Guatemala, and the Dominican Republic. The U.S. feeds arms to Chile while imposing an economic blockade in a successful effort toward encouraging a right-wing military coup. The military frequently intervenes in elections or in a reformist regime, and then returns power to conservatives.[82] Where the established military brass comes from well-to-do classes, the armed forces tend to be aligned with the interests of the status quo. On the other hand, leading officers from white-collar origins may be more likely to favor change, a situation more typical of Africa than elsewhere in the Third World, but applicable also to Peru.

That an established military is not necessarily wedded to the complete status quo was documented by the Peruvian military coup of 1968, which nationalized certain primary industry and took over the most important agro-industrial firms that held 80 percent of cultivated land.[83] This development poses a reversal of customary U.S. assumptions regarding the role of military dictators such as Jimenez, Trujillo, and Chiang Kai-shek in maintaining domestic stability. However, the Peruvian junta is clearly not leading a full nationalist revolution. Rather, their strategy is to encourage foreign investments in Peruvian industry, draw the landed aristocracy into urban finance and industry, and establish themselves in control of certain core industries (though at present they have nationalized but only a small portion of oil production).[84] They have instituted a neo- or sub-imperialism within which an attempt is

---

[81] Emile Capouya, "Devolution of a Revolution," *The Nation,* October 20, 1969, pp. 416–17.

[82] Irving Louis Horowitz, "The Military Elites," in Seymour M. Lipset and Aldo Solari, *Elites in Latin America* (New York: Oxford University Press, 1967), pp. 151–65.

[83] Edmundo Flores, "Land Reform in Peru," *The Nation,* February 16, 1970, pp. 174–77.

[84] Anibal Quijano, *Nationalism and Capitalism in Peru* (New York: Monthly Review Press, 1971).

being made to transfer a larger share of power and wealth to national elites, while maintaining the working class and peasantry in submission.

The Peruvian example raises the question of the suitability of the professional military for carrying out the task of economic development. The balance of scholarly opinion in the United States tends to take a pessimistic view of the possibilities of successful modernization under professional military. Indonesia, Argentina, Burma, Thailand, Egypt, and Pakistan have been cited as cases where the military has either helped destroy a nation's economic base or perpetuate stagnation, whereas development in China and Cuba has not been dominated by military rule. While the professional military has within it the power to push forward reforms, crush opposition, and expropriate property they are infinitely less likely to do such things than is a people's liberation army. Further, the sheer cost of a military establishment (as the United States knows) acts as a huge drain on productive resources. Also a rigid bureaucratic style and mentality make the military poorly equipped to fashion a new society. Whatever their class backgrounds, the self-preservation of the military establishment itself, at whatever cost, supersedes imperatives of national economic development. The point to make is that national liberation requires military force, but economic development must be achieved through the ideological commitment and participation of the entire population. Militarism as an organizing principle cannot achieve the positive goals of social development and equality.

SOCIAL AND CULTURAL CHANGE

In examining the routes and prerequisites to economic development, we might also consider the cultural position of underdeveloped countries. Thus far we have been focusing on the political and economic aspects of development. We may also view development from the ideational perspective, investigating the role of values and ideas in change processes. For example, the psychologist David McClelland has empirically argued that a psychological element such as a desire to prove one's group as superior or a need to promote the common good is an essential prerequisite or stimulus to economic development.[85] Favorable economic conditions and opportunities are not enough, in McClelland's view, to accelerate the developmental process; in addition, there must first be an ethos of change or a need for achievement, something on the order of the historic Protestant ethic. McClelland notes that reformist religious groups, such as the Parsis and Jains in India, Indians in East Africa, and Jews, represent such desires for group improvement and need for achievement. Communists, too, McClelland believes, have managed to create the psychological conditions for economic development. McClelland's thesis would seem to closely approximate the pervasive Third World view that a nationalistic ideology is an essential weapon in the arsenal of economic development.

---

[85] David McClelland, *The Achieving Society* (New York: The Free Press, 1967).

Southeast Asian scholars consistently note the group solidarity, asceticism, and achievement orientation of the Chinese living in that part of the world.[86] The immigrant Chinese, who came as illiterate peasants, and their descendants have been successful merchants and retailers, and they are making notable progress in the professions. Their economic activity and mobility have contributed to marked discrimination against them and given rise to considerable interethnic tensions, especially in Malaya. A similar phenomenon has occurred with immigrant Indians to East Africa. Concerning the Chinese, and the Japanese as well, we might note that they have traditionally had a strong emphasis on achievement and other-directedness in securing the personalized approval of the group, as Weber noted characterized the ascetic Protestant sects.

At the opposite pole, students of Arabic, Latin, and Hindu cultures have stressed their fatalistic, passive, and rigid hierarchical world view.[87] In India, for example, any need for achievement or group success has tended to be channeled into "sanskritization" or mobility by way of emulating Brahman standards, such as avoidance of manual labor. Loomis reports that at least half of an Indian sample he studied believed that evil spirits cause disease and would go to a religious leader or temple for treatment of smallpox; yet three-fourths reported that they or members of their families had been vaccinated for smallpox.[88] The use of technology does not always mean that the users have accepted a rational or scientific world view. In Colombia, a majority of Bogota respondents felt that they would be in a better economic situation in 10 years, though there were still distinct tendencies toward traditionalism and pessimism.[89]

The psychological and cultural obstacles to change are closely tied to the dominant classes and institutions of the Third World. As noted in connection with rural Latin America, the aristocracy and large land holders are interested in preserving passivity, fatalism, and hierarchy. These are the cultural components of the status quo, they are the ideas of the ruling class intended to perpetuate a stagnant world view among the oppressed. The same is true in Arabic, African, Indian, and East Asian cultures. Religious elites may also be important instruments of mental passivity, though they may advocate change as well. In general,

---

[86] Paul Thomas Welty, *The Asians: Their Heritage and Their Destiny* (Philadelphia: J.B. Lippincott Co., 1966).

[87] Edward C. Banfield, *The Moral Basis of a Backward Society* (New York: The Free Press, 1958); Daniel Lerner, *The Passing of Traditional Society* (New York: The Free Press, 1958); S.C. Dube, *Indian Village* (New York: Harper and Row, Publishers, 1967); and M.N. Srinivas, *Social Change in Modern India* (Berkeley: University of California Press); and David G. Mandelbaum, "Status-Seeking in Indian Villages," *Trans-action*, 5 April 1968), pp. 48–52.

[88] Charles P. Loomis, "In Praise of Conflict and Its Resolution," *American Sociological Review*, 32 (December 1967), p. 884.

[89] Robert C. Williamson, "Social Class and Orientation to Change," *Social Forces*, 46 (March 1968), pp. 317–28.

however, the weight of religious philosophies has been an opiate of passivity, encouraging the subservience of the masses to the elites.

What is required for development is an ideology of change and national liberation. The underdeveloped world may not be highly educated, but its people are not ignorant and naive. Its peoples are gaining increasing insight into the sources of their condition, and the psychology of revolutionary change is either present or developing to some degree almost everywhere.

The city

In the West, urbanization has been accompanied by both a relative and an absolute decline in the numbers of people living in rural areas. Urbanization has also taken place in the Third World on a massive scale.[90] Towns with only several thousand population have mushroomed into cities of several hundred thousand, and cities with several hundred thousand population have exploded into overflowing areas of millions of persons. Unlike the West, Third World urbanization has not been the result of the push of the mechanization of agriculture and the pull of urban industrialization. Rather Third World urbanization has been the result of overall population growth; rural to urban migration has been large scale (for example, about one-fifth of Colombia's rural population migrated to urban areas in the decade of the fifties), but rural population has *also* increased.

Urbanization should be distinguished from urbanism. Urbanization refers to the sheer number of people living in localities of over 2,500, 5,000, 20,000, 100,000, or whatever number of people one chooses as a measure.[91] Although urbanization finds a general correlation with industrialization (as measured by the percent of the labor force in non-agricultural occupations), urbanization in the Third World is not particularly a reliable guide to the extent of urbanism—i.e., a set of attitudes and life styles that have largely secular justifications and underpinnings. Thus, the rapid accumulation of people in shanty-towns, favelas, and slums may involve slight traces of secularism and much transfer or importation of traditional rural value systems, or the disintegration of rural values without replacement. By the same token, the modern Western farmer may be steeped in urban manners as a result of constant contact with urbanism through the mass media.

Third World problems of sanitation, housing, food, medicine, schooling, and employment are often exacerbated and enlarged in the congested squalor of urban slums. Added to these customary difficulties are other personally and socially destructive forms of survival and escape

---

[90] Gerald Breese, *Urbanization in Newly Developing Countries* (Englewood Cliffs, N.J.: Prentice-Hall, Inc., 1966).

[91] On world urbanization, see Kingsley Davis and Hilda Hertz Golden, "The World Distribution of Urbanization," *Bulletin of the International Statistical Institute,* 33 (1954), pp. 227–43.

available to or pushed upon the desperate slum dweller, such as the pros-
titution of girls and young women, alcohol, narcotics, petty thievery, and
gambling. *Pre*-revolutionary Shanghai and Havana, and contemporary
Saigon, are characteristic.

Among the strategies of self-help and survival found in many Third
World cities, African in particular, are tribally or ethnically based benefit societies similar in function to those formed by the European immigrant groups to the United States. Help in housing, employment, finances,
funerals, or simply in times of loneliness are among the kinds of services
urban ethnic associations might provide to members.[92] The ethnic association acts as an extended family surrogate and as a mechanism for adjustment to city life. Such associations may also develop into foci for the
expression of political interests and conflicts. In Indian cities, subcastes
are performing similar functions.

Nowhere is the image of urban chaos and squalor more vividly im-
printed in Western minds than in India, Calcutta, and Bombay in particular. But the condition exists throughout the imperialized world from
the West Indies to the Philippines. Human life is cheap and getting
cheaper; Taipei, Taiwan sinks into the earth in an environment of uncontrolled filth in air and water, while U.S. corporations take huge profits
out of operations which pay young girls $1.80 a day. Congestion and
slums sprawl wherever they may. The slums of Mexico City teem with
wretched poverty, while the gleaming automobiles and hotels of the rich
stand nearby.

Contrasted to this is the concern in Peking, Hanoi, and Havana for
basic human needs and the persistent struggle for adequate housing, education, and diet. The rural population has been given maximum possible
support in medicine, education, and agricultural development to allow
people to remain in the countryside. The Chinese have undertaken an
articulated strategy of rural industrialization combined with agriculture
and the distribution of specialized urban services into the countryside so
that the urban flow may be partially stopped. There has even been a considerable movement of educated persons into the rural areas to take up
residence there and work among the people in such programs as medicine, education, and engineering. Such are the kinds of steps which are
required to attain population balance and an evenly developed society.

Education

Educational problems in the Third World begin at the most rudimentary level: illiteracy. Adult illiteracy has virtually been eliminated in the
West (about one percent illiterate), but about four-fifths of African
adults are illiterate, three-fourths of Indian adults, two-thirds of other
Asian adults, and two-fifths of Latin American adults. There are, how-

[92] See, for example, Immanual Wallerstein, "Ethnicity and National Integration in West Africa," in Pierre L. van den Berghe, ed., *Africa: Social Problems of Change and Conflict* (San Francisco: Chandler Publishing Company,
1965), pp. 472–82; and Kenneth Little, "The Study of 'Social Change' in
British West Africa," in van den Berghe, *Africa*, pp. 89–102.

ever, marked variations, ranging from under 10 percent in Argentina and Uruguay to over 90 percent in Haiti and Ethiopia. Reflecting educational privileges, males have lower rates of illiteracy than females, and urban residents lower than rural. Although large increases in school enrollments have occurred in most regions, most underdeveloped countries spend a lesser portion of their national income on education than the advanced nations, there is a serious shortage of both facilities and staff, and students' educational survival rates tend to be low. Parents and children alike often have difficulty in seeing the relevance of education to life in a poor rural village or peasant community. As a corollary of poverty, high illiteracy, and low levels of educational attainment, most Third World nations (again with exceptions such as Argentina) have extremely limited to almost nonexistent mass media availability and circulation, such as newspapers, radios, cinemas, and, of course, television.[93] The mass media could serve as a powerful conduit of public education.

Although literacy and education are essential for modernization, there is no strict formula as to how much education a person requires to participate in urban industrial society (the average educational level of the Russian worker in 1959 was only four years) or any strict relationship between levels of literacy and industrialization in Third World countries. As Golden has observed, countries such as Thailand and Panama are more literate than industrial, while Malaya and Egypt are more industrial than literate.[94] But that literacy and education are among the most critical factors in economic development, few would deny.

Oddly enough, many Third World countries are having to deal with a *surplus* of *over*educated persons, college graduates in liberal arts unable to be absorbed by a stagnating economy. Although in the early years of independence or entry into the modern world, Third World countries had a severe shortage of college graduates to fill civil service posts, today there is a growing surfeit of aspiring government bureaucrats from Indonesia to Africa who find themselves in intense competition for positions in already top-heavy state bureaucracies. They are not competing for jobs in the private economy or an industrial component of the public economy simply because there are few such jobs and few are being created. Foreigners dominate foreign business and industry and there is limited national corporate development.

The thrust of education and educational values in the Third World tends to stress such things as character building, life styles, and status rather than preparation for a productive occupation, the development of reasoning powers, and technical skills. Higher education in the Third World is seriously hampered by an elitist attitude toward business, agriculture, industrial work, and the masses. While China has over half of its advanced students in engineering, physical science, and agricultural science (and a large portion of the rest in education), the majority of

---

[93] See Ithiel de Sola Pool, "Communications and Development," in Weiner, ed., *Modernization*, pp. 98–109.

[94] Hilda Hertz Golden, "Literacy and Social Change in Underdeveloped Countries," *Rural Sociology*, 20 (March 1955), pp. 1–6.

Indian college students are enrolled in humanities, fine arts, and law.[95] Asia, Africa, and Latin America all have but a relatively small minority of college students in physical and agricultural science, engineering, or business. Of the directly applicable developmental skills, which traditionalist education defines as prestigious, medicine stands as an exception, but medical practice is oriented toward the affluent or with intentions of emigration to the U.S. or other advanced countries. The flood of doctors to the U.S. from Cuba after the Revolution attests to the typical motivations of the majority. Medical education in Cuba today, of which there is a large amount,[96] has a popular mission to serve.

In view of the history of neglect of education and literacy throughout the underdeveloped world, a revolutionary society must direct learning endeavors to people of all ages and in conjunction with regular work. This is what, in fact, has been undertaken on a massive scale in China, and to some extent in Cuba as well. Gurley has remarked that "China may be said to be just one great big school."[97] The Chinese and Cubans have both stressed the importance of integrating work with education, and endeavor at all points to tie the university and the student into the industrial and agricultural sector in an ongoing fashion. This draws a striking contrast with the elitist and remote educational systems of, say, India and Brazil.

CLASS AND REVOLUTION

The class structure of Third World nations is highlighted by the sharp and growing cleavage between a small, prosperous, and Western educated or oriented urban elite and the impoverished and uneducated masses. Elite status is based primarily on land ownership or inheritance, subimperialist roles, and ranking government military posts. Power and privilege have tended to stem originally from large land ownership in Latin America, while in Africa the source is in the control of government bureaucracies, though business, government, and military hierarchies today figure prominently in Latin American elites as well. By the same token, Latin America has a hereditary aristocracy, whereas Africa's native elites are first generational and have originated largely from average economic backgrounds. However, as is customary in social class systems, especially in an unchanging economy, the next generation of African elite will probably stem predominantly from first-generation families. Indications are already present that African elites are forming the rudiments of a self-perpetuating social class, based largely on their monopo-

[95] Ruth Adams, *Contemporary China* (New York: Random House, Inc., 1966), p. 296; and Neil J. Smelser and S.M. Lipset, *Social Structure and Mobility in Economic Development* (Chicago: Aldine Publishing Company, 1966).

[96] See Samuel Bowles, "Cuban Education and the Revolutionary Ideology," in Martin Carney, ed., *Schooling in a Corporate Society* (New York: David McKay, Inc., 1972), pp. 272–303.

[97] John Gurley, "Capitalist and Maoist Economic Development," *Monthly Review*, 22 (February 1971), p. 728.

lization of Western education, a virtual prerequisite to elite status.[98] Evidence from Thailand corroborates the tendency toward occupational inheritance within the elite and the consolidation of a closed upper class subculture, again owing importantly to a monopolization of the means to foreign academic degrees.[99] Asia has a combination of landed, state, and subimperialist elites similar to Latin America. However much Third World elites might stress international stratification, it is impossible to divert the attention of the people from marked internal inequality, often in blatant contradiction of an official equalitarian "socialist" ideology.

One of the frequent consequences of the formation of self-perpetuating elites, whether they be based on landed wealth or administrative control, is an increasing cleavage of the powerful from the masses and a growing interest and commitment to the status quo.

The fact that development cannot take place within the framework of capitalism is becoming increasingly evident. Quite apart from the role of foreign capital, the national bourgeoisie has deep stakes in the status quo. In the words of Carlos Romeo, "The national bourgeoisie is the national guardian and main beneficiary of the existing social structure."[100] Frank states the problem at greater length with regard to Brazil: "Thus the Brazilian 'national bourgeoisie,' if it can be said to exist at all, thrives only on its exploitation of the Brazilian people. It persists only through its dependence on the imperialist metropolis in the world capitalist structure."[101] Franz Fanon, who wrote on the African situation, states that "The national bourgeoisie of underdeveloped countries is not engaged in production, nor in invention, nor building, nor labor; it is completely canalized into activities of the intermediary type. Its innermost vocation seems to be to keep in the running and to be part of the racket."[102] There is something of an underdeveloped "power elite" to be found dominating the major institutional sectors of the society and taking shape into a ruling class. As Stavenhagen writes, ". . . the agricultural, financial, and industrial interests are often found in the same economic groups, in the same companies, and even in the same families."[103] Their interests are in conspicuous consumption, class and aristocratic prestige and power, and financial accumulation. "Why *should* they want to change?" asks Mills.[104]

---

[98] See Pierre L. van den Berghe, "Africa's Language Problems—Too Many, Too Late," *Trans-action*, 6 (November 1968), pp. 48–54.

[99] Hans-Dieter Evers, "The Formation of a Social Class Structure: Urbanization, Bureaucratization and Social Mobility in Thailand," *American Sociological Review*, 31 (August 1966), pp. 480–88.

[100] "Revolutionary Practice and Theory in Latin America," in Horowitz et al., *Latin American Radicalism*, p. 598.

[101] *Capitalism and Underdevelopment in Latin America*, p. 214.

[102] *The Wretched of the Earth* (New York: Grove Press, 1968), pp. 149–50.

[103] Rodolfo Stavenhagen, "Seven Erroneous Theses About Latin America," in Horowitz et al., *Latin American Radicalism*, p. 110.

[104] *Power, Politics, and People* (New York: Oxford University Press, 1963), p. 154.

With their typical monopoly on prestige and the opportunity structure, the national bourgeoisie tends to have little interest in economic growth, social modernization, expanded opportunities for talent, democracy, and equality—particularly that element most closely tied to landed wealth and aristocratic tradition.[105] A study by Delbert Miller of executives and influentials in Cordoba, Argentina, disclosed unanimous agreement that foreign capitalists should expand in their city.[106] What change is sought is for a greater cut of power and profits for the national bourgeoisie relative to foreign investors.

If the national bourgeoisie are the chief opponents of structural change, who are the radical forces? Underdevelopment has by definition precluded the development of an industrial working class of any substantial size. Even in Latin America, the most industrial of underdeveloped continents, artisans, self-employed workers, and workers in small shops are more numerous than factory workers. Such a situation cultivates a petit bourgeois and paternalistic attitude among urban workers and poses an obstacle to the development of collective working class solidarity. Thus, as James Petras has observed, "One of the more striking features that emerge from an examination of Latin American politics is the lack of social solidarity that exists in most countries among broad sectors of the urban working class."[107] Petras contends, however, that wherever economic development has encouraged concentration of workers within larger industrial operations the result has usually been mass radical political organization; Chile and Cuba serve as prime examples, in both mining and urban industrial sectors. Irving L. Horowitz emphasizes the reform orientation of urban working classes, and as being a part of the liberal center integrated into unions, the party system, and cross-cutting allegiances which dilute revolutionary activity.[108] The reform and liberalizing influence of the city upon the industrial working class, contends Horowitz, may be only tentative should change through these strategies fail; then the cities may become proving grounds for change based upon social revolution.

Fanon took an opposing view regarding the urban working class in that he considered it as close to the old system of privilege, relatively comfortable in relation to the masses, and incapable of materializing into a revolutionary force in the absence of an independent national bourgeoisie.[109] Fanon looks to the peasantry and the lumpenproletariat for a revolutionary force, strata which Marxist theory contends is incapable of

---

[105] See S.M. Lipset, *Revolution and Counterrevolution* (New York: Basic Books, Inc., 1968), Chapter 3.

[106] *International Community Power Structures* (Bloomington: Indiana University Press, 1970), p. 137.

[107] James F. Petras, "Class Structure and Its Effects on Political Development," in J. David Colfax and Jack L. Roach, eds., *Radical Sociology* (New York: Basic Books, 1971), pp. 307–8.

[108] I.L. Horowitz, "Electoral Politics, Urbanization, and Social Development in Latin America," in Horowitz et al., *Latin American Radicalism*, pp. 140–76.

[109] *The Wretched of the Earth*, pp. 108–9.

carrying out sustained revolution by themselves.[110] As Mandel argues, the peasantry cannot lead a revolution, nor can it create the means or basis for a socialist society. In Zhukov's words, "The peasantry may be said to be an army that can win only if it is under a competent command, which is generally provided by a different social milieu."[111] Russia, China, Cuba, and Vietnam support this contention.

As for the lumpenproletariat, so often rural migrants to the city, there is the same absence of class discipline and organization. Even more than small shop artisans, the lumpenproletariat is often a backward-looking stratum imbued with conservative, personal, and commercial values.[112] Their marginal and subsistence level of living leaves them with no margin or energy for organized dissent. Nevertheless, the political beliefs and conduct of the urban poor in such places as Peru, Chile, and Cuba suggest that poverty and destitution is no final barrier to class consciousness and revolutionary ideology. Portes has made the point that, even where there is no evidence of radicalism in the urban slums and disinheritance is blamed on factors such as fate, bad luck, and little education, there is enormous revolutionary potential present should the frustration be worked out in radical solutions.[113] Owing to the absence of significant industrialization in most cities, and the highly isolated nature of that which does exist, the slum population outstrips all other strata in size. There is no denying its potential revolutionary force.[114]

The political position of the petit bourgeoisie and white-collar workers, of which there are so many within government bureaucracies, is also debatable. The petit bourgeoisie may be open to nationalistic sentiments against imperialism and the collaboration of the big bourgeoisie with foreigners. As for white-collar workers, their powerlessness, economic insecurity, and dependence upon modernization for expanded opportunities may create an inclination toward radical politics in the same manner as in the factory work force. Petras has drawn our attention to the fact that white-collar workers in Chile and Uruguay have been among the best organized and most militant groups in the city.[115]

However, sharp opponents to views of "middle class" radicalism are plentiful. Their argument is particularly convincing when the old middle class of businessmen and professionals, upper-white collar workers, and

---

[110] Regis Debray, *Revolution in the Revolution?* (New York: Grove Press, 1967).

[111] Y. Zhukov et al., *The Third World* (Moscow: Progress Publishers, 1970), p. 39.

[112] Petras, "Class Structure and Its Effects on Political Development," p. 311.

[113] Alejandro Portes, "Urbanization and Politics in Latin America," *Social Science Quarterly*, 52 (December 1971), pp. 697–720.

[114] See Gary MacEoin, *Revolution Next Door: Latin America in the 1970s* (New York: Holt, Rinehart, and Winston, 1971); for a critical assessment of Latin American revolutionary activity, see Alan Riding, "What's Holding *La Revolucion?*" *The Progressive*, May 1973, pp. 41–45.

[115] Petras, "Class Structure and Its Effects on Political Development," p. 309.

administrative functionaries are in question. In Stavenhagen's words, this loose middle-class aggregate is not progressive at all; "Instead, they are economically and socially dependent upon the upper strata; they are tied politically to the ruling class; they are conservative in their tastes and opinions, defenders of the status quo; and they search only for individual privileges."[116] Stavenhagen sees the middle occupational group as a buffer for the ruling class against the masses. In the bourgeois strike in 1972 in Chile, the petty bourgeoisie of professionals and business people supported the strike, whereas students and intellectuals actively assisted the workers in running things. At the time of the military coup in 1973, the middle class openly celebrated the death of democratic socialism.

Any attempt to generalize regarding the role of various classes in the Third World is bound to run into difficulty. There are too many different societies and histories to spell out any consistent theory of class and revolution within the Third World. Maoism and Castroism, like Leninism, stress the revolutionary roles of the disinherited peasantry and workers, though all seek either to neutralize or gain allies from within other strata. The full support of the industrial labor force, small though it may be in the beginning, is essential to economic liberation. The only safe conclusion that can be made regarding classes and revolution is that the broader the popular support and democratic quality of leadership, the better are the chances of overcoming the certain forces of counterrevolution. Supporters of revolution and of counterrevolution may and do come from all levels of the social structure. The success of either depends upon the breadth and depth of support from among the masses of people. Military force administered by a minority can only postpone the ultimate decision.

---

[116] Stavenhagen, "Seven Erroneous Theses About Latin America," p. 112.

15

Toward a new sociology

C. Wright Mills has posed for the sociologist three major questions, the answers to which might be the goal of sociological theory and research.[1] The first has to do with how a society is organized or structured as a whole, its essential components and their relations, its similarities and differences with other societies, and the significance of its components for continuance or change. The second asks where this society stands in human history, how it is changing, what its meaning is for other societies, and what the essential features of the historical period in which it finds itself are. Finally, the third question asks what varieties of people dominate or prevail in the society, what varieties are coming to prevail, how they are selected and affected by their experiences, and what kinds of human nature we find and how each feature of society relate to that nature.

Mills has thus raised three great questions of structure, history, and personality. To answer them requires the use of a sociological imagination able to see wholes when only pieces appear, the meaning of little acts for big events and processes, and the force of social structure upon the individual. It requires a sociology that fully avails itself of history and the comparative method, and a psychology that sees people as social and historical actors. Mills poses these questions not only to full-time sociologists, but to every interested person. The sociological imagination is not some esoteric or secret weapon to be used only by properly initiated members of a profession. With determination and a persistent style of work, student or laymen can address themselves to these questions, and in the

---

[1] C. Wright Mills, *The Sociological Imagination* (New York: Oxford University Press, 1959), pp. 6–7.

process develop the sociological imagination. Sociologists may assist in both answering the questions and in nurturing the required imagination in others. If the sociologist performs his work successfully, he is, of course, no longer a sociologist but a person among others.

Large questions require careful and extensively documented answers. The aim of this book has been to assist its reader in searching for some of the answers to Mills's questions. Summary statements or answers to the questions of structure, history, and personality may do less to clarify than to oversimplify. Indeed, the entire book in itself is, of course, far from the scope and detail needed for convincing answers to even partial aspects of these large orienting questions, and it is doubtful that any book or set of books, no matter how long or large, could provide definitive answers. Perhaps Mills never intended that sociology could answer them satisfactorily, but only that such major questions should be the goal and orientation of the sociological enterprise.

Nevertheless, if for nothing more than a need for closure and perhaps polemics, we shall attempt some summary answers concerning the United States here. First, regarding the question of structure, the U.S. is a technologically advanced, highly stratified industrial society organized mainly around the institutions of corporate capitalism. It has become highly urbanized, specialized in membership, and bureaucratized in organization. The essential components of the society are the corporation and the state, the state serving more as an instrument to the attainment of corporate ends than an institution protecting and responding to popular needs and interests. To continue in its support of the status quo, the state has been more and more forced into the position of having to expose the ultimate source of its rule and domination, its means of violence and coercion as found in the military, the police, and secret agencies. Included within the network of components that must be considered as essential to the corporation and the state is the university and the scientific institutes it mans and runs. As an organization, the university embodies the hierarchy, specialization, and bureaucracy that have increasingly characterized the society as a whole. Although potential centers of opposition, labor unions have largely been integrated into the corporate capitalist structure in action and ideology.

These organizations or components, then—the corporation, the state, the military and police, the university, and the union—respectively stand as the main social structures, the corporation setting the prevailing themes and tendencies which the others must respond to. The family, the schools, the press, the media, and the church all exercise crucial socializing and information functions, but with some exceptions they lack autonomy and are shaped by and adapt to corporate needs. As within the state, the military, the university, and the union, all of these second-line institutions contain elements of opposition and dissent but only occasionally pose major threats to established power. The Congress, as an aspect of the state, has performed admirably on behalf of corporate interests, though here as in the media, university, and labor there exists an active opposition.

Thus, just as these second-line institutions have within them the capacity to support the status quo, so do they contain levers of change, particularly the political parties and Congress—the formal means of change available to organized publics. Although not a mass society in a *social* sense (there exist myriad primary groups and voluntary associations), the United States is a mass society in a *political* sense. There has been a notable dearth of political organization and participation in the ranks of the middle, working, and lower classes of the society. Yet a considerable amount of social and economic discontent is present, which, if channeled into political organization and activity, could foment important change. Evidences of such activity were visible in the political campaigns of 1972.

The United States is the center of international capitalism and has a far-flung military force to preserve the political status quo and protect its economic interests. Structurally the United States is similar to other Western societies, although its size, diversity, and wealth tend to mark it off from the rest. It has the least justification for the presence of poverty but contains within its borders some of the most impoverished and neglected people in all of the Western world. It shares with the Soviet Union the social inequalities and classes stemming from the industrial division of labor, a technological world view, extreme bureaucratization, and administration of power over property by delimited circles of decision makers. The United States differs from the U.S.S.R. in that the American ruling group is a class-conscious, surplus accumulating, and hereditary upper social class. A further major difference between the United States and the U.S.S.R. is that the U.S. economy depends upon imperialism and military production to maintain itself, to maintain corporate profit in the face of overproduction.

Secondly, with regard to history, the United States stands at the monopoly stage of production for private profit with automation having the potential to set the conditions for radical restructuring of economy and society. Increasingly, technological advance and bureaucratic rationality will divide the population into groups of people who are variously dispensable and indispensable to the operation of corporate capitalism, people who can contribute to its profit and growth and people who constitute a drag on its resources and threaten its stability. In this context, there exists slight hope for the black masses in the ghetto under the present corporate-dominated system of economic relations. Whether the next period of history before us will witness people gaining control of technology and directing it toward social production and freeing them from the cycle of production for class profit and corporate growth, or from personal dissipation outside the realm of corporate and government security, is possible but not easily achieved. If this does *not* occur, we should expect a no less radical restructuring of society in the area of personal freedoms and responsibilities, a deterioration of relations between the races, and an increasing utilization of official and unofficial violence.

If the corporate goals of profit and growth are not changed at home, or excluded by those abroad, there is no possibility that any marked improvement in the material condition of Third World nations will occur, and the prospects are great that militarism will continue to drain the resources and energies of the American people. Monopoly, capitalism's own internal logic, will then assure its demise. The essential social feature of the period is the revolt of the world's oppressed peoples against their oppressors. This feature is paralleled by revolts *within* industrialized society against the ruling classes and alienating institutions. The essential technological feature of the period is the atom, promising both increased freedom from material necessity and world holocaust.

Thirdly, as regards personality, the dominant type is that of the bureaucrat, selected through a stringent process of educational and administrative socialization in which emulation of superiors and conformity to established codes of behavior and value weigh more heavily than social responsibility. A human nature with strong inclinations toward external interest, group cooperation, and responsibility tends to be frustrated and blunted by demands of narrow routine, private accumulation, and monetary definitions of success. However, strong undercurrents of dissent are producing people with quite different standards and aspirations from those of the ideal bureaucrat. These persons may be found both inside and outside the established institutions of society, working toward the attainment of what they hope to be the emancipation of labor and unalienated personality. Their fate is inextricably bound up with the continuities and changes that occur in structure and history.

Between the bureaucrat and the antibureaucrat lie the vast majority of people, undesirous of being the former and more often than not threatened by the latter. Privitized and not outwardly militant, this average man is shaped in work by the imperatives of efficiency and repetition and in leisure by the contents of mass culture. As Mills observed, "And in all this bureaucratic usurpation of freedom and of rationality, the whitecollar people are the interchangeable parts of the big chains of authority that bind the society together."[2]

The crucial point in the answer to the continuity or change issue as it pertains to structure, history, and personality is whether the new middle or new working class with its formidable education, organizational abilities, and numbers are willing to continue as nothing more than "interchangeable parts of the big chains of authority." The blue-collar proletariat must be actively supportive as well.

The answers to Mills's questions must be searched out in the study of elites, the use of mass media, technology, and economic organization; the origins and development of class interests; radical movements of right and left; the dynamics of poverty and inequality; the role of consumption; political mechanisms; the nature of work; the roots of military production; racism; the supports of underdevelopment; and a structurally based social psychology. That a book such as this could be written with the assistance of materials gleaned from the literature of social science attests to the fact that a large and growing number of people are addressing themselves to such crucial topics.

---

[2] C. Wright Mills, *White Collar* (New York: Oxford University Press, 1953), p. xvii.

ETHICS IN SOCIOLOGY

Any variety of study that produces knowledge that may enhance power must bear a large portion of the responsibility concerning how such knowledge is used. Much sociology contains little of any conceivable use to persons or groups who are seeking means of strengthening their power and influence. Yet, any discipline that specializes in gathering social information is inevitably going to be of considerable interest to those seeking greater control in society. Whether such information is of scientific stature is not of decisive importance, though its utility is, of course, heightened in accordance with its explanatory power. Thus, the fact that sociology lacks the substance of a developed science[3] in no way diminishes the problems of ethics in social research and theory.

To the extent that social science has proven itself politically useful, the balance of the impact and utility has in all likelihood fallen to the already powerful. This is not to overlook the extensive amount of critical thought, which the study of society has generated among students and the general public. Knowledge can cut two ways. Nevertheless, the powerful have the resources to finance the kind of research they may specifically make use of to their own advantage, and have done so with increasing volume and frequency.

Thus, a difficult question with which sociology must concern itself is that of the uses of sociological materials.[4] Since many kinds of sociological information may be of conceivable value to someone in their efforts at controlling others, how can sociology avoid the role of subverting freedom and equality in human relations? While this dilemma of ethics in social research and publication can never be fully escaped, there are some points which should always be considered when facing the dilemma.

First, who, if anyone, is paying for the study or the information produced by the study? If it is, as it frequently is, a government agency, a major foundation, a corporation, or any institution with a direct or indirect tie to entrenched power and privilege, there is immediate reason for concern. The prospects that studies done under such auspices may enhance the position of the powerful over the powerless may be quite good, while their humanistic impact is likely to be negligible or almost so. Usually the best one can hope for is that the data or knowledge thereby produced is politically irrelevant. Frequently this is the case. (If so, the sociologist still must face the ethical question as to whether or not the resources he consumed might not have been more usefully applied elsewhere in society.)

A second precautionary question the sociologist might ask himself before he goes to work on a study is who and what are involved. Who are

---

[3] See Peter Park, *Sociology, Tomorrow: An Evaluation of Sociological Theories in Terms of Science* (New York: Pegasus, 1969).

[4] See Gideon Sjoberg, ed., *Ethics, Politics, and Social Research* (Cambridge, Mass.: Schenkman Publishing Company, 1968); Richard O'Toole, ed., *The Organization, Management and Tactics of Social Research* (Cambridge, Mass.: Schenkman Publishing Company, 1970); and J. David Colfax, "Knowledge for Whom? Relevance and Responsibility in Sociological Research," *Sociological Inquiry*, 40 (Winter 1970), pp. 77–83.

the subjects and what do I want to find out about them? Is the study one of the distribution of power and how those with power exercise their prerogatives over those without power? Or is it a study of the poor, what they are thinking and doing and planning, how they respond to certain external events, and how much more pressure they can take? The first study alternative is clearly an alternative for the new sociology. The second would seem to promise as much and very probably more to those interested in sustaining hierarchy as to those concerned with equality. An understanding of the roots of poverty is among the tasks of a new sociology, but it now seems extremely unlikely that such an understanding, and hence guides to a solution of poverty, will ever come from further study of the poor themselves. A critical analysis of existing economic institutions promises greater insight. Combining precaution one with two, if an agency of the political and economic establishment is paying for the study of the poor or any marginal group, ethical sociologist beware.[5] Such studies need not enhance control to present an ethical problem; they may be *diversionary* in intent and consequence.

Thirdly, and in conjunction with the first two questions, preliminary questions can be raised regarding *who might* be able to utilize the materials of the study and *for what* ends. These are ultimately unanswerable questions, for ostensibly sociologists do not know what they are going to find when they begin their study (though some are pretty sure). Moreover, it is humanly impossible to anticipate the full range of conceivable uses of a study in cementing power or exercising greater control. Nevertheless, one is usually able to do more than randomly conjecture on the matter.

Fourthly, should a person be satisfied that his efforts are not likely to feed the arsenals of control and manipulation, or at least that serious consideration has been given to these precautionary questions, it is mandatory that the results be presented in a fashion directly or indirectly available to all interested or implicated parties. In the case of sophisticated psychology, economics, or sociology, this means that the writer somewhere translates into laymen's language and spells out the real significance of what he is saying for the lives and life chances of the people concerned, including other social scientists.[6] Beyond that, the writer should make an effort to follow the career of the materials, condemning any possible abuse in application.

Through all of this discussion not only studies of a statistical nature are of concern, but qualitative investigations as well. To these must be added the "theories" of society that explicitly or implicitly idealize or legitimize the status quo of power and inequality. Whether the materials of sociology be "abstract empiricism," "grand theory," or something in between, the student of society encounters similar professional dilemmas.

---

[5] See Alvin W. Gouldner, "The Sociologist as Partisan: Sociology and the Welfare State," *The American Sociologist*, 3 (May 1968), pp. 103–16. As an international case, see Irving Louis Horowitz, *The Rise and Fall of Project Camelot* (Cambridge, Mass.: M.I.T. Press, 1967).

[6] Among notable efforts at such translation and spelling out has been the magazine *Society (Trans-action)* edited by Irving Louis Horowitz, and *Social Policy* edited by Frank Riessman.

To exercise caution in the ethical implications of sociological study is, as already alluded to, not to abandon the study of society as hopelessly conservative and supportive of the status quo. For those concerned with rationality in society to abandon its scholarly and empirical study would be to leave the social arena more open to hired research and control-oriented behaviorists. The latter activities themselves require sociological critique. We have already drawn attention to a number of questions and topics that demand sociological analysis and have extensively utilized related materials. Nor does the exercise of ethical responsibility in sociology require that one dispense with sociological concepts. These concepts may be used in the analysis and vocabulary of change as well as in the legitimization of the status quo. Only when the use of concepts becomes an end in itself, or the concepts are taken as objective representations of some "real" social world outside of human purpose, does conceptual sociology become an obstruction to understanding and a buttress of the status quo.[7]

The use of concepts draws the sociologist into the realm of values; for to create and apply a concept is to intervene in the meanings and definitions of social life. In addition to the use of concepts that affect the way people think about the world, sociologists find values playing a part in determining what they study, how they conduct their study, and what interpretations they place upon their completed materials. Thus, it is the responsibility of sociologists to make explicit their own assumptions and values as they pertain to their work and to leave open for all to see the steps taken in arriving at results and conclusions.

We mentioned above that sociological workers must endeavor to translate and communicate their products to the broadest possible public and follow as closely as possible their utilization. To this we might add the further measure of talking and discussing personally and directly with people not likely to be reached by even popular literature. Sociologists may be well advised to stop interviewing the American rank and file, minorities, and marginals and begin working and conversing with them. The new sociologist will want to make a democratic effort to educate with concrete illustration (if necessary) in the ways of power; the means of manipulation and control; the roots of poverty; the basis of educational, medical, and income inequality; the uses of racism; the nature of militarism and its economic role; nationalism; and cultural intolerance—in brief, to raise the level of general social awareness and common concern.

Combined with a commitment to the *understanding* of man in society and an *exposition* of the mechanics of oppressive and unjust social institutions, there is in the new sociology a driving commitment to see also the *elimination* of oppression and injustice and the expansion of a creative humanism. In view of men such as Marx, Veblen, Mead, and Mills, the new sociology is surely not a new style of work. What is new is the numbers of people now working toward the attainment of its ideals.

---

[7] John Horton, "The Fetishism of Concepts," et al., 2 (Fall 1969), pp. 9–11; and Albert Szymanski, "Toward a Radical Sociology," *Sociological Inquiry*, 40 (Winter 1970), pp. 3–13. The latter issue of *Sociological Inquiry* contains several articles germane to the discussion of politics and sociology.

Name index

Subject index

371

This book has been set in 9 and 8 point Primer,
leaded 2 points. Chapter numbers and titles
are in 24 and 18 point Primer italic. The size
of the type page is 27 x 46½ picas.